From Aldersgate to Azusa Street

From Aldersgate to Azusa Street

*Wesleyan, Holiness, and Pentecostal Visions
of the New Creation*

Edited by

HENRY H. KNIGHT III

PICKWICK *Publications* · Eugene, Oregon

Pickwick Publications
An Imprint of Wipf and Stock Publishers
199 W. 8th Ave., Suite 3
Eugene, OR 97401

www. wipfandstock.com

ISBN 13: 978-1-60608-988-0

Cataloging-in-Publication data:

From Aldersgate to Azusa street : Wesleyan, Holiness, and Pentecostal visions of the new creation / edited by Henry H. Knight III.

x + 372 p. ; cm. 23 — Includes bibliographical references.

ISBN 13: 978-1-60608-988-0

1. Methodism—History. 2. Pentecostal churches—United States. 2. Pentecostalism—History. I. Knight, Henry H., 1948–. II. Title.

BX8331.3 F55 2010

Manufactured in the U.S.A.

Contents

Acknowledgments

GRATITUDE BEGINS WITH MY colleagues in the Wesleyan/Pentecostal Consultation, whose scholarship, insight and enthusiasm has made our annual meetings so enormously fruitful. Almost all the chapters in this book were presented and discussed at a Consultation, and most of those who participated are contributors to this volume.

Much of that participation was made possible by two generous grants from the Louisville Institute, which also provided very helpful advice as we began this journey together. My own desire for a project like this was the result of over a decade ongoing conversations with Steve Land, and the specific plan for the Consultation emerged from discussions with Steve Rankin in the Spring of 2002. It was David Bundy who proposed we call ourselves the "Wesleyan/Pentecostal Consultation." We have now held five consultations, but none of those meetings would have been as inviting, productive, and enjoyable without the diligence and organizational skill of Laura Guy, who has also been my partner in planning the meetings.

I am also grateful for help in editing the chapters in this volume. The hard work and wise counsel of Stephen W. Rankin, William Kostlevy, John H. Wigger, Kimberly Ervin Alexander, and most especially D. William Faupel have considerably strengthened the book. Finally, we are indebted to our editor, K. C. Hanson, for his able advice and assistance, and to Wipf and Stock for enabling our work to reach a wider public.

Some of the chapters in this volume first appeared in an earlier form in various journals and books. We gratefully acknowledge permission to reprint them here:

Portions of the chapter by John H. Wigger, "Where Have All the Asburys Gone?" appeared in his book, *American Saint: Francis Asbury and the Methodists* (Oxford: Oxford University Press, 2009) and are used with the permission of Oxford University Press.

Dennis C. Dickerson, "Richard Allen and the Making of Early American Methodism" was first published in *The A. M. E. Church Review* (January–March, 2005) 35–39.

Dennis C. Dickerson, "Bishop Daniel A. Payne and the A. M. E. Mission to the 'Ransomed'" was first published in a longer form in *The A. M. E. Church Review* (October–December, 2005) 24–31.

Barry L. Callen, "Daniel S. Warner: Joining Holiness and All Truth" was first published in a longer form in the *Wesleyan Theological Journal* 30.1 (1995) 92–110.

The Wesleyan, Holiness, and Pentecostal Family

HENRY H. KNIGHT III

HISTORIANS HAVE FOR SOME time examined the connections between the Wesleyan Methodist movement that began in the eighteenth century, the emergence of African-American Methodist traditions and an interdenominational Holiness movement in the nineteenth century, and the birth of Pentecostalism in the twentieth century.[1] While precise relationships between these movements are a matter of scholarly debate, their historical linkage is beyond dispute.

This volume builds on that earlier work. The heart of our argument is this: each of these movements, at their inception, bears a resemblance to the others. They share common assumptions, expectations, and vision to such an extent that they constitute a distinct theological family. There are important differences within and between each one, and they emerge in different socio-cultural contexts. Yet this makes their commonalities all the more significant.

The commonalities have not gone unnoticed, especially between Wesleyanism and Pentecostalism. Several decades ago, theologian Fredrick Dale Bruner said "Pentecostalism is primitive Methodism's extended incarnation,"[2] (he did not mean this as a complement). Much

---

1. See the ground-breaking works by Vinson Synan, *The Holiness–Pentecostal Tradition* (Grand Rapids: Eerdmans, 1997); Donald W. Dayton *The Theological Roots of Pentecostalism* (Grand Rapids: Zondervan, 1987); and Walter J. Hollenweger, *Pentecostalism: Origins and Developments Worldwide* (Peabody, MA: Hendrickson, 1997).

2. Fredrick Dale Bruner, *A Theology of the Holy Spirit* (Grand Rapids: Eerdmans, 1973) 37.

more recently, in his global survey entitled *Pentecostalism: The World Their Parish*, sociologist David Martin concludes that

> We have in Pentecostalism . . . the religious mobilization of the culturally despised, above all in the non-western world, outside any sponsorship whatever, whether of their own local intelligentsias, or of the clerical and secular intelligentsias of the West. John Wesley and his associates started it, out of materials provided by Pietism. The Evangelical Revival then set off further mobilizations which in the course of experimentation cross-bred the religion of poor whites with the religion of poor blacks to create a potent and ambiguous mix capable of combustion on a global scale. Wesley had, after all, declared that his message was to *all*, not just the Elect.[3]

Though Methodism "is embarrassed to acknowledge what it fathered," says Martin, "most of the features of Pentecostalism tell tales of Methodist paternity."[4] Historian David Hempton makes a similar observation. "As it turned out," he writes, "it was not Methodism that was poised to sweep the world but its Holiness offspring, Pentecostalism." Like early Methodism, Pentecostalism was a "movement giving voice to ordinary people, thriving on mobility, depending on women, privileging personal transformation over public reform, and vigorously organizing dislocated people into noisy cells of perfectionist excitement."[5] These comments are suggestive, and call for a more sustained analysis. Our argument here, we hope, is the beginning of a conversation about what makes this theological family distinct.

Our goal in developing this argument is threefold: First, we want to show what this common vision is, without obscuring the diversity that also marks these movements. Second, insofar as this theological vision is weakened or lost in later generations, we hope to show why. Third, we want to suggest the contributions this common vision can make to the revitalization of theology and practice in the contemporary church.

This book is the result of the first four years of a six year Wesleyan/Pentecostal Consultation that has been meeting annually at Nazarene Theological Seminary in Kansas City, Missouri. Partially funded by a

3. David Martin, *Pentecostalism: The World Their Parish* (Oxford: Blackwell, 2002) 167.

4. Ibid.

5. David Hempton, *Empire of the Spirit* (New Haven: Yale, 2005) 208–9.

grant from the Louisville Institute administered by Saint Paul School of Theology, the Consultation brings together scholars who have studied various portions of these movements as well as pastors who currently participate in them. The resulting conversations have decisively impacted the chapters that follow.

We chose to examine these movements by studying a diverse array of key figures. We deliberately chose persons who represent a range of roles—denominational leaders and mavericks, institutional loyalists and come-outers, clergy and laity—and who embodied these movements in a wide variety of cultural contexts. We show them as persons in their own time and place, both shaped by their culture as well as shaping their culture, or as modeling an alternative to the dominant culture.

We hope these figures will serve to illumine the theological vision and practices that the movements have in common. What they believed about God's nature and promises has much to do with their central commitments and sense of mission in the world. We could have easily chosen many other figures who have an equal claim to recognition (and we will note some of these along the way), but we believe the ones here will amply exemplify the common vision that makes these movements a theological family.

We approach this task in two parts. This volume will focus on presenting the common vision, largely through an examination of a highly diverse set of participants in these movements. Through their lives we will be able to identify patterns of belief and ministry, as well as the issues with which they struggled. This in turn will enable us in subsequent work to develop in greater depth the implications of this for the contemporary church.

Here we can anticipate some of those common themes. The first thing to say about these movements is, at least in their beginnings, they are evangelical, emerging as they did in a series of evangelical awakenings. While a precise definition of "evangelical" is likely to be too controversial to be helpful, we can use the four qualities proposed by David Bebbington as a guide. If evangelicals are indeed characterized by "*conversionism*, the belief that lives need to be changed; *activism*, the expression of the gospel in effort; *biblicism*, a particular regard for the Bible; and what may be called *crucicentrism*, a stress on the sacrifice of Christ on the cross,"[6] then each of these movements are unquestionably

6. David Bebbington, *Evangelicalism in Modern Britain: A History from the 1730s to the 1980s* (Grand Rapids: Baker, 1989) 2–3.

evangelical at their origin. But what kind of evangelicalism? As we shall see, these movements develop each of these four terms in ways which they share, but which distinguish them from other evangelicals. They were, for example, quite different in their theology and practice from the Calvinist scholasticism of the nineteenth-century Princeton theologians (a point the Princeton theologians would gladly endorse).

We will return to Bebbington's four qualities. But first, we should note some overarching themes that influence the particular ways these four qualities are developed by these movements. The most important is their sense of the immanence of the divine in their lives and world, what more precisely might be described as the presence of transcendence.

One way to put this is that, especially in their early decades, participants in these movements experienced themselves living in a world permeated by God's activity. For many this included divine guidance or calling through dreams, visions, prayer, devotional reading of scripture, and even through seemingly ordinary circumstances or coincidences. They expected to meet God in the everyday activities of life as well as in times of corporate worship and personal or small group devotions. While this put them in tension with the prevailing intellectual consensus coming out of the Enlightenment (they were often branded "enthusiasts"), it was much more in accord with African assumptions about divine activity prevalent among African-American Christians.

In addition to divine communication, participants in these movements had a strong belief in the present power of God to transform lives. Most believed God would heal sickness through prayer. Virtually all experienced divine empowerment for ministry (identified by later holiness and Pentecostal movements by the term "power") and the transformation of the heart by God (sanctification, or "holiness"). There was wide divergence on how "instantaneous" and "gradual" elements of these transformations were related, or whether expected "blessings" are received at the moment when conditions (such as faith) are met or come at God's own timing. But there was complete consensus that such transformative activity was part of a normal Christian life. Indeed, many extended their expectation of divine transformation to the renewal of both the church and the social order itself. They had a holy discontent with the way things are, and a deep yearning for the entire creation to reflect God's holy love. This is so characteristic of these movements that we have designated them "Transformational Evangelicals."

God was therefore understood and experienced as an active agent, involved in the world and human lives in distinctive ways. What God did in the Bible God continues to do; what Jesus did in his life and ministry continues to be done through the Holy Spirit. This is not the divine immanence of liberal theology, which emphasizes continuity between God and the world and sees God at work only in the natural processes of nature, history, and human nature. Instead, it has the character of an inbreaking of God, discontinuous with or distinctive from the world, more than the sum of natural processes and influences. While not at all denying a general sense of God's providential activity, they were more impressed by the particularity of what God has done in the incarnation, cross, and resurrection of Jesus Christ. The God who has done all this for our salvation continues to work in distinctive ways through the power of the Holy Spirit and a Spirit-empowered people.

Corresponding to this divine activity is an expectant faith on our part. While holding strongly to divine initiative, these traditions understand grace as relational, that is, entailing a human response. But it is more than relational; it also expects God to act, often in response to our seeking, but frequently in surprising or unanticipated ways as well. God may answer prayer, but God may also initiate actions that then elicit our response of praise, trust, or obedience. It is this relational understanding of grace that distinguishes this family of Transformational Evangelicals from others that might be fairly termed transformational, such as the Moravian and Calvinist segments of the eighteenth-century awakening.

With this framework of divine presence and power, coupled with our expectant faith, we can return to Bebbington's four qualities of evangelicalism to see the distinctive form they took for these movements. First, they certainly had a strong emphasis on the cross of Christ as the locus of salvation. But they joined other Arminians[7] to insist, against Calvinists of a strong predestinarian inclination, that the effect of the cross is to offer salvation to all people, not just a predetermined

---

7. The term "Arminian" comes from Jacobus Arminius, who opposed the common Calvinist teachings on predestination, irresistible grace, and limited atonement. His followers were condemned by the Synod of Dort in 1618. By the eighteenth century "Arminianism" was used rather loosely to refer to views ranging from natural free will to John Wesley's "evangelical Arminianism" of universal prevenient grace. A recent study of this tradition is Roger Olson's *Arminian Theology: Myths and Realities* (Downers Grove, IL: InterVarsity, 2006).

elect. Even those whose roots were more Presbyterian or Baptist than Methodist would agree that salvation is available to everyone.

In addition, these movements add to an emphasis on the cross a focus on Pentecost. Salvation is not only accomplished on the cross but ongoing through the Holy Spirit. Rather than seeing the cross as the completion of God's salvific activity they see it as the irreversible foundation for the continuing work of God in the world, to be finally completed in the eschaton.

This leads, secondly, to conversionism. Participants in these movements resisted reducing salvation to simply receiving forgiveness of sins so that we will go to heaven when we die. Salvation was transformative. One could not know one's sins had been forgiven through the cross of Jesus Christ and continue living as if nothing had changed.

The point of salvation was not forgiveness but new life. Hence salvation was concerned not only with justification but sanctification, and not only with the world to come but the present age. Conversion is not the goal of salvation but its beginning, the doorway into a heart and life transformed by God. Participants in these movements would both proclaim and testify that there is "more" to the Christian life than forgiveness, that God seeks to sanctify our hearts and empower us for ministry. Thus they encouraged persons to expect to receive further growth or subsequent blessings from God.

Third, all these movements were highly Biblicist in that they considered the Bible the inspired and authoritative word of God. Though most preferred a literal interpretation, the strict inerrancy and rationalism so central to the Princeton theologians and fundamentalism was not at the heart of their hermeneutics. While it is hard to generalize, these movements tended to see scripture as more dynamic than static, and to have a much more central role for the Holy Spirit as the divine interpreter. Thus they not only read and thought about scripture, they also prayed and sought for God to speak through it.

Within this are some distinctive hermeneutical inclinations. From pietism they inherit the practice of expecting events in the history of Israel or Christ and the early church to also be patterns to be replicated today. This is especially true of Pentecost, which for many was not seen only as a one-time event in the life of the church, but an event to be repeated again in larger-scale awakenings and/or in each Christian life. Another is the Wesleyan tendency to understand a command by God as also a promise that God will, by grace, enable us to obey the command. Thus if God commands us to love God and our neighbor with all our hearts, God will certainly enable us to do it by transforming our hearts.

Fourth, these Transformational Evangelicals were highly activist. Indeed, they were a whirlwind of activity, engaging in evangelism, often mobilizing to effect social reform, establishing societies and benevolent institutions, and developing practices of Christian formation. What is distinctive is the purposes that govern so much of their activism. Two were pre-eminent: (1) the renewal of the church or, failing that, the establishment of a new church, and (2) missional outreach, at home and abroad.

The passion to revitalize existing churches in holiness and/or power, or in living out their implications more faithfully, is a dominant characteristic of all these movements. There was a pervasive dissatisfaction with existing denominations, seeing them as settling for a formal or "respectable" Christianity instead of embracing the new life God gives and the faithful discipleship to which God calls us. Societies, classes, bands, camp meetings, Tuesday Meetings for the Promotion of Holiness, and the like were all structures designed to renew lives and ultimately renew denominations. When persistent resistance was met to renewal, and persons either left or were thrust out, new denominations were formed. Prime reasons for conflict were the controversial nature of Wesleyan, Holiness and Pentecostal teaching; their opposition to racism, materialism, or class privilege; and desire for a more open or egalitarian polity. A secondary stream in these movements is discontent with denominationalism itself, coupled with a desire to recover the primitive church so there will be one "church of God." That these attempts inevitably led to new denominations rather than an end to denominationalism should not discount their vision of Christian unity.

Transformational Evangelicals sought to embody this new life and faithful discipleship. They were in many ways countercultural communities, experiencing and witnessing to something like an eschatological inbreaking in their midst. They were often noticeably more egalitarian than the surrounding culture, providing leadership roles for women, ethnic minorities, and persons in lower socio-economic classes. They objected to a "genteel" evangelicalism that preached conversion while leaving unjust or unholy social practices unchanged. It was often when existing denominations became more accommodated to the prevailing racial or class practices that new denominations were formed.

None of this is to say that these movements are pure models of the Kingdom of God, only that they were drawn to it and to an extent approximated it in ways that set them apart from the surrounding culture. Their counterculturalism could be moderate or radical: it is, for example, a long way from a Midwestern holiness camp meeting to the parlor in the Palmer home in New York City, and differences of that sort could produce tensions within these movements. Nor were they against education, as some have alleged, though many had no formal education due to lack of opportunity because of race, class, or gender—or slavery. They were in fact founders of a multitude of colleges, seminaries, and bible colleges.

This does mean that participants in these movements often acquired a renewed sense of self that was at odds with prevailing cultural attitudes. If God is love then they were loved, if Christ died for them then they had a God-given worth and dignity that the world could not take from them. If they were sanctified and empowered by the Holy Spirit, then God has moved them from whatever passive roles society has assigned to Spirit-filled activity. As participants in God's work in the world, they could be agents, even leaders.

Theirs was a this-worldly missional activism. Whether they were post or premillinneal, they had an optimism and excitement about what God was doing in the world, and a passionate desire to participate in it. Evangelism—the sharing of the good news of Jesus Christ with others—was at the heart of their activism. Also central was proclaiming and testifying to Christians that there is more to the Christian life than forgiveness, that sin can be defeated, love can reign, and lives can be empowered. But in addition to these was an astounding range of social outreach: soup kitchens, literacy classes, benevolent societies, abolitionism, women's rights, inner city ministries, and temperance. They also made the practice of divine healing central in a way it had not been for centuries, and never before in Protestantism. Not everyone took the same approach to social action—most were involved in compassionate ministries, some in political action for social reform, and many in healing ministries. But it is clear that participants in these movements could not envision missional outreach without both evangelism and social concern.

The figures we examine do not embody all of these themes equally. They were persons of their time or culture, just as we are of ours. They could combine far-seeing vision with disappointing limitations. Sometimes we wonder, even accounting for context, why they could not see their prejudices more clearly. Yet at the same time we can find ourselves inspired by their vision, challenged by their incisive social critique, and encouraged by their hope.

We have been speaking throughout of these movements at their beginnings. It is clear that over time most began to de-emphasize or abandon much of this early heritage. Some of this was due to their eventual accommodation to culture, and with it their loss of a sense of divine presence and power. We are convinced that such a loss was neither inevitable nor desirable. But even more we believe that this distinctive form of evangelical Christianity has much to teach the contemporary church. We hope our examination of this history will enable the church today to recover practices that lead to greater faithfulness and new life.

The Eighteenth Century:
The Birth of Methodism

PART ONE

Introduction

METHODISM WAS BORN IN a culture that was radically different from today. England in the eighteenth century was largely rural and agricultural, and closer in many ways to the medieval than to the emerging modern world. Most of the towns were quite small, and only a handful of cities had populations in the 10–20,000 range. London, with half a million residents, was the great exception. As the century progressed, population began to gradually shift to a few of the larger cities, but even by 1800 England retained its predominantly rural character, with political and economic power in the hands of the large landowners.

One of the economic forces driving people to cities was the enclosure of land. Removed from what had been common land, persons were now forced to leave and find work elsewhere, in the textile mills or coal mines. In some cases, such as in the small textile mills of that day, the wages were often good, enabling some workers to even make enough to move into a different social class. When this happened to Methodists, they often began to then conform to the values and lifestyle of others in that class, a matter of deep concern to John Wesley who wrote numerous warnings against abandoning holiness for material wealth.

Whether or not their wages were good, workers led a precarious existence. They were usually just one economic disruption (such as a rise in corn prices) away from either losing their job or facing hunger or homelessness. Working conditions were often unsafe and unhealthy, and women and children as well as men often worked 12–15 hour days, six days a week, just to make a subsistence wage. Living conditions were no better, and many lives were marked by poverty, alcoholism, disease, and illiteracy. John Wesley and his Methodists would engage in a wide range of ministries to these workers, including literacy classes, health care, and providing such basic necessities as food, clothing, and shelter.

This was a very hierarchical society, though not in the economic class sense that is commonly assumed today. Considerable income disparities did exist (though they would be worse in the next century), but class distinctions in the eighteenth century were based on "rank" or "order," and rooted in one's family heritage or occupation. Society was ordered with aristocrats and gentlemen of property at the top, common wage earners at the bottom, and in between a middling class of tenant farmers, tradesmen, and skilled craftsmen. It was from this latter group that the majority of the Methodists came.

With this structure came an assumption of how the social order should work. The different ranks in society were interrelated by a set of rights and obligations, in which all were to benefit. Those in the higher ranks were due deference by those beneath them, but at the same time had a responsibility to purchase products from or provide work for the middling and lower ranks. Widespread belief that they had failed to meet their obligations could lead to social unrest.

Life in eighteenth-century England was precarious, and it could also be cruel. There was a high infant mortality rate. Susanna Wesley, John's mother, raised ten children, but nine more died at birth. The average life expectancy was the mid-30s. The conditions of hospitals, orphanages and prisons were primitive at best, and being imprisoned for debt was common, as Wesley's father Samuel unhappily experienced. Hangings were well-attended public events.

METHODISM AND THE EIGHTEENTH-CENTURY AWAKENING

In many ways Methodism was a challenge to this social order. Because Wesley's Methodists in particular utilized lay preachers and leaders, women as well as men, it enabled them to fill roles that were considered improper for persons of their rank, gender and education. Wesley sought to bring education to the people by producing inexpensive tracts and books, often abridgements of larger volumes. He also encouraged lay preachers and leaders to write spiritual journals and letters, some of which he published.[1] All of this tended to give persons a dignity and status in conflict with that assigned to them by the prevailing social order.

---

1. See for example Vicki Tolar Burton, *Spiritual Literacy in John Wesley's Methodism: Reading, Writing & Speaking to Believe* (Waco, TX: Baylor University Press, 2008).

Wesley's movement was part of a much larger trans-Atlantic religious awakening, often called the "Great Awakening" in America.[2] This awakening was the result of the confluence of three seventeenth-century spiritualities. High Church Anglicanism, of which the Wesleys were a part, emphasized sacramental piety (especially the Lord's Supper) and the recovery of the spirituality of the primitive Christianity of the first few centuries of the church. A second influence was Puritanism, which was originally a Calvinist movement to purify Anglicanism of Roman Catholic practices, but after the Elizabethan Settlement had separated from the established church to form Dissenting denominations. It had developed a vibrant spirituality focused on conversion and Christian growth. John Wesley's parents, though High Church, had both been raised in the ethos of Puritan Dissent. The third influence was Pietism, a movement in Lutheran and Reformed churches on the continent that emphasized the new birth, a changed heart and life, lay-led small groups, and an irenic spirit. Anthony Horneck (1641–1697) helped merge continental Pietism and High Church spirituality in the Church of England, and began a movement to establish religious societies that ultimately involved John Wesley's father Samuel.[3]

Although there had been earlier sporadic revivals, the beginning of the eighteenth-century awakening could be dated in 1734, when the Northampton, Massachusetts parish of Jonathan Edwards (1703–1758) experienced a dramatic revival. Edwards' 1737 account of this remarkable event, in *A Faithful Narrative of the Surprising Work of God,* had a huge impact on those Protestants in the English speaking world who would come to be called "evangelicals." A year after the Northampton revival Howell Harris (1714–1770), a layman, and Daniel Rowland (1713–1790) an Anglican priest, were leading similar revivals in Wales.

---

2. For an excellent account of the eighteenth century awakening in the English-speaking world, see Mark A. Noll, *The Rise of Evangelicalism: The Age of Edwards, Whitefield and the Wesleys* (Downers Grove, IL: InterVarsity, 2003). Accounts that place the awakening in conjunction with events on the continent include W. R. Ward, *The Protestant Evangelical Awakening* (Cambridge: Cambridge University Press, 2002) and Ted A. Campbell, *The Religion of the Heart* (Columbia: University of South Carolina Press, 1991).

3 On Horneck's influence see Scott Thomas Kisker, *Foundation for Revival: Anthony Horneck, the Religious Societies, and the Construction of an Anglican Pietism* (Lanham, MD: Scarecrow, 2008).

But it would be George Whitefield (1714–1770)[4], Anglican priest and itinerant evangelist, who would unite the English, Welch, Scottish, and American revivals into a single, interrelated awakening.

Whitefield, Edwards, Harris, and Rowland were all Calvinists. Indeed it would be Calvinists who would dominate the awakening, later including the Countess of Huntingdon (1707–1791) in England. The German-based Moravian Brethren, led by Count Ludwig von Zinzendorf (1700–1760), was highly influential in both England and America, and brought a variant of Lutheran Pietism into the awakening. John and Charles Wesley, and later their ally John Fletcher, were a third strand of the awakening, Arminian in theology and committed to a form of holiness called Christian Perfection.

While at the beginning Calvinists and Wesleyans who itinerated and formed religious societies were all termed "Methodists," it would be Wesley's branch of the awakening, with its distinctive theology and practices, which would ultimately be designated as "the people called Methodists." More than the others, it would continue to grow in England, and then abundantly flourish in the fertile soil of America.

---

4. See Harry S. Stout, *The Divine Dramatist: George Whitefield and the Rise of Modern Evangelicalism* (Grand Rapids: Eerdmans, 1991); and Frank Lambert, *"Peddlar in Divinity": George Whitefield and the Transatlantic Revivals* (Princeton: Princeton University Press, 1994).

2

John Wesley and the Quest for Holiness

Henry H. Knight III

JOHN WESLEY (1703–1791) WAS a central figure in the eighteenth century awakening. His distinctive theology and pattern of spiritual practices that marked his "connection" set him apart from the awakening's mainstream and the Church of England's dominant ethos. Nevertheless, his movement had the greatest impact, especially in America.

Wesley was an unlikely person to lead the awakening. His parents, both children of nonconformist clergy, became zealous adherents of the established church as young adults.[1] Samuel became a priest at Epworth. Susanna, widely read with a sharp theological mind, gave her children a strict but richly devotional environment. Although without financial means, the Wesleys managed to send their sons to Oxford.

THE VISION OF HOLINESS

The youngest two, John and Charles (1707–1788), became discontented with nominal Christianity at Oxford. Reading spiritual writers like Thomas á Kempis, Jeremy Taylor and (later) William Law, John, by 1725, understood true Christianity as holiness of heart and life. He concluded that inward holiness consists of Christian perfection, or perfect love, which is manifested outwardly through holy living. Attaining holiness, he believed, would give him an assurance of God's acceptance.

1. Samuel and Susanna's parents refused to accept the Elizabethan Settlement that retained some Roman Catholic practices in the church, and were removed from their positions as priests. They became part of the Dissenting churches. Despite John Wesley's Anglican sympathies, he objected to the intolerance shown to his grandfathers.

From 1725 to 1738 Wesley experimented with several means to attain this goal. He ultimately rejected mystical quietistic approaches. Instead, he embraced a range of spiritual disciplines, including an intense devotional life, sacramental piety, and ministering to the poor and imprisoned. These disciplines marked the life of their little Oxford group, derisively called the "Holy Club" or "Methodists."

Later, as a missionary, John met resistance while trying to impose strict discipline in the undomesticated colony of Georgia. There Wesley was both a rigid traditionalist and religious innovator. On one hand he sought to enforce triune immersion of infants (a rule the Church of England had long neglected) and only accepted baptisms by clergy who were in apostolic succession. On the other, he encouraged hymn singing instead of lining the psalms, a new practice considered blasphemous by many.

When Wesley barred a young lady from communion for failing to publish banns prior to her wedding—a woman Wesley had courted but who married another—it ignited a flame of growing resentment. Indicted by a grand jury, Wesley returned to London under a cloud to plead his case with the colony's trustees. He was exonerated but not reassigned. Despairing, he wrote, "I, who came . . . to convert the Indians, was never myself converted to God?"[2]

The answer to his dilemma was close at hand. Charles and John had sailed to Georgia with a group of German-speaking Christians called Moravian Brethren.[3] When a violent storm threatened the ship, the Germans exhibited an assurance that deeply impressed the Wesleys. Now with both brothers back in London—Charles had had his own difficulties in Georgia—they resumed their contact with the Moravians. The leader, Peter Böhler, convinced John that saving faith comes instantaneously as God's gracious gift, and is accompanied by an assurance of God's acceptance. Convert's testimonies reinforced Böhler's argument from scripture. As John began to preach the doctrine he was barred from many pulpits.

---

2 W. Reginald Ward and Richard P. Heitzenrater, eds., *Journals and Diaries I* (Nashville: Abingdon, 1988) Jan. 29, 1738, 214 [Vol. 18 of *The Works of John Wesley*].

3. The Moravian Brethren were led by Count Nicolas Von Zinzendorf (1700–1760), and began as a union of Christians from various traditions finding sanctuary from religious persecution. While denying the necessity of a struggle with sin prior to conversion, the Moravians, like all pietists, emphasized a religion of the heart.

On May 21, 1738, Charles experienced a conversion that gave him faith and assurance. It marked the beginning of the most prolific hymn writing career in history. Three days later John

> went very unwillingly to a society in Aldersgate Street, where one was reading Luther's Preface to the Epistle to the Romans. About a quarter before nine, while he was describing the change which God works in the heart through faith in Christ, I felt my heart strangely warmed. I felt I did trust in Christ, Christ alone for salvation, and assurance was given me that he had taken away *my* sins, even *mine*, and saved *me* from the law of sin and death.[4]

The full theological implications of this experience would not become clear for over a decade. Wesley came to understand that: justification, or forgiveness, was the doorway into sanctification (growing in love and other fruit of the Spirit); regeneration (new birth) that accompanies justification is the beginning of sanctification; and holiness (perfection in love) is the goal. The assurance Wesley sought came as a gracious gift received by faith, based solely on Christ's work on the cross. The motive for seeking holiness of heart and life shifted from a desire to gain an assurance to a grateful, loving response for what one had received.

THE EVANGELICAL AWAKENING

While the import of this for Wesley's ministry was not immediately evident, within a year its basic direction was clear. Revival sparks were already occurring in England and Wales. George Whitefield (1714–1770) was the key figure setting those sparks ablaze. Whitefield, a younger contemporary and friend of the Wesleys, was once an aspiring actor. His dramatic sermons had enormous impact on Great Britain and America. After a successful stint in Georgia, his preaching in Bristol drew thousands. Committed to move to Wales and then back to America, Whitefield asked John to continue the work in Bristol.

Wesley was at first repelled by the irregularity of Whitefield's open air preaching. He wrote that he was "so tenacious of every point relating to decency and order that I should have thought the saving of souls almost a sin if it had not been done in a church."[5] But in April, citing

4 *Journals and Diaries I*, May 24, 1738, 249–50.

5. Word and Heitzenrater, eds., *Journals and Diaries II* (Nashville: Abingdon, 1990) March 29, 1739, 46 [Vol. 19 of *Works*].

the Sermon on the Mount as precedent, John began to preach outside Bristol. People were deeply affected by his sermons. He continued this itinerant ministry for the remainder of his life. In May, Charles began field preaching as well.

Initially, the term "Methodist" was applied to preachers who itinerated without regard to parish boundaries or the parish priest's approval; and to their followers. Whitefield was initially the most prominent "Methodist," but over time the term came increasingly to designate the Wesleyans.

The awakening's message was justification and new birth through faith in the atonement of Jesus Christ. By the mid-1740s, however, it became clear the leadership was not of one theological mind, and distinctive connections emerged. Most were Calvinists, such as George Whitefield and the Countess of Huntingdon in England and Howell Harris's "Calvinistic Methodists" in Wales. The Moravians continued to promote their brand of Lutheran pietism. Wesley and his connection was the Arminian[6] alternative.

THE PROMISE OF HOLINESS

Wesley's disagreement with Calvinists[7] went to the gospel's heart. His insistence that love is God's "reigning attribute, . . . that sheds an amiable glory on all his other perfections,"[8] was in sharp contrast with the Calvinist portrayal of God who sovereignly decrees some to salvation and others to damnation. Wesley concurred that our hearts are totally corrupted and we are unable to turn to God apart from grace. However, he insisted prevenient grace is universally available to *all* persons. Thus, he denied the Calvinist claim that grace is irresistible. Grace, he reminded Methodists, does not "take away your liberty, your power of choosing

6. Arminianism originated with the Dutch Calvinist Jacobus Arminius (1560–1609) who rejected double predestination, limited atonement, and irresistible grace. His followers were condemned as heretics by the Synod of Dort (1619). Wesley's Arminianism most likely came indirectly, through Anglican sources than directly form Arminius. But it was a term he embraced, founding *The Arminian Magazine* in 1777. See Herbert Boyd McGonigle, *Sufficient Saving Grace* (Carlisle, UK: Paternoster, 2001).

7. While Wesley disagreed with and sometimes found himself in controversy with strict Calvinists, he often drew upon more moderate Calvinists in his theology and practice.

8. John Wesley, *Explanatory Notes Upon the New Testament* (London: Epworth, 1950) 1 John 4:8, p. 914.

good or evil;" God "did not *force* you; but being *assisted* by his grace you, like Mary, *chose* the better part."[9] Grace is relational, an encounter with the transforming presence of God's love, eliciting our response.

Salvation for Wesley is the transformation of hearts and lives. Created in God's loving image, humanity fell from righteousness. Salvation is God restoring persons to that image. Indeed, it is more. While our first parents knew God's love, they did not know its full depth as revealed in the cross of Jesus Christ, where "Th' immortal God hath died for me."[10] Because of Christ, humanity can attain a higher degree of holiness, and a fuller image of the loving God.[11]

Salvation, then, has to do both with what God has done *for* us in Christ and what God does *in* us through the Spirit. While salvation encompasses "the entire work of God, from the first dawning of grace in the soul till it is consummated in glory," [12] its focus is justification and sanctification. In justification a person experiences forgiveness and God's acceptance which changes the relationship with God from dutiful and fearful obedience to that of beloved child. In sanctification we are born anew, and grow in love. Critical of those who reduced salvation to a happy afterlife, Wesley insisted salvation "is not something at a distance: it is a present thing . . . ye are now in possession of."[13]

The experiential nature of salvation is evident in two ways. First, faith is not only trusting in Christ but also enables us to know God. Through faith we not only experience God's presence, but those things that are past (the cross) or future (the eschaton) as present realities that transform us.

Second, Wesley understood sanctification in terms of "affections" or "holy tempers" (love, faith, hope, peace, gratitude, joy). These are not passing feelings but abiding dispositions: the point is not to have loving feelings but to *be* a loving person. Since these are holy dispositions, they lead to holy lives. They are lenses through which we see the world as

---

9. "The General Spread of the Gospel," 11, in Albert C. Outler, ed., *Sermons II* (Nashville: Abingdon, 1985) 489 [vol. 2 of *Works*].

10. "Hymn 27" in *A Collection of Hymns for the Use of the People Called Methodists*, Franz Hilderbrandt and Oliver A. Beckerlegge, eds. (Oxford: Clarendon, 1983) 114 [vol. 7 of *Works*].

11. See "God's Love to Fallen Man" in *Sermons II*, 422–35.

12. "The Scripture Way of Salvation" 1.1 in *Sermons* (Nashville: Abingdon, 1984) 156.

13. Ibid.

God sees it. "Affections" are relational: we have these holy tempers as we remain in relationship with God.[14]

Christian perfection comes when the holy tempers of love for God and neighbor fill our hearts and govern our lives. While we never entirely do God's will ("involuntary transgressions" remain), we can be freed from intentional sin and motivated by love. Wesley believed Christian perfection was a promise of God that could be attained before death, followed by continued growth.

Wesley understood salvation as gradual and instantaneous. Awakened sinners enter a conscious relationship with God, coming to recognize the power of sin and their need for grace. Then, at a moment of God's timing, they experience conversion (justification and new birth). They gradually grow in sanctification, until in a second instantaneous work of transformation, they are filled with love and begin growing in perfection. Thus instantaneous works are preceded and followed by gradual transformation, through an ongoing relationship with God.

THE PURSUIT OF HOLINESS

This process of salvation was enabled by participation in weekly small groups where members were held accountable for the practice of spiritual disciplines. The most important of these groups were "classes" and "bands".[15] Classes consisted of 10–12 members accountable to a threefold discipline: do no harm, do good to others, and attend God's ordinances. Led by laity, members reported how faithfully they had kept the discipline during the week; the leader would then offer advice and encouragement. Every Methodist belonged to a class, and membership was open to any awakened sinners who desired salvation.

The bands were for those who had experienced justification and new birth, and were growing in sanctification. They were more confessional, focusing on sin that remained. Also lay led, they were smaller than classes and membership was voluntary.

---

14. Wesley shares this understanding of Christianity consisting of affections or holy tempers with Jonathan Edwards. See Gregory S. Clapper, *John Wesley on Religious Affections* (Metuchen, NJ: Scarecrow, 1989); and Richard B. Steele, *"Gracious Affections" and "True Virtue" according to Jonathan Edwards and John Wesley* (Metuchen, NJ: Scarecrow, 1994).

15. See David Lowes Watson, *The Early Methodist Class Meeting* (Nashville: Discipleship Resources, 1985).

This discipline required participation in means of grace.[16] These means included works of piety (scripture reading, prayer, communion, fasting, Christian conferencing) and works of mercy (to the neighbor). Practicing these disciplines was the central way Methodists maintained relationship to God and neighbor, and experienced the Spirit's transforming power.

The regular practice of means of grace and the weekly meetings aided Methodists in avoiding the Christian life's dangers. One danger, formalism, was the common misunderstanding that going to church made one a good Christian. The discipline helped avoid the formalism by keeping the focus on transforming relationships with God and neighbor. A second danger, enthusiasm, was the tendency to seek intense religious experiences, confusing degree of intensity with depth of spirituality. The means of grace enabled one to test feelings to determine if they were from God, and kept the focus on knowing God.

This is not to say Wesley discouraged phenomena associated with the awakening, such as falling to the ground under the Spirit's power. Emotional and physical manifestations commonly accompanied conversion, and the palpable experience of God's presence was often a feature of worship. Wesley believed deliberate emulation of manifestations was enthusiasm; genuine works of God resulted in fruit produced in hearts and lives.[17]

THE WITNESS TO HOLINESS

These phenomena were not, however, the heart of the revival. "At the first breaking out of" a work of God, Wesley observed, "there may be a shower, a torrent of grace" that could continue "for several weeks or months." But it gradually subsides, and "the work of God" is "carried on by gentle degrees." The "kingdom of God ... will silently increase, wherever it is set up, and spread from heart to heart, from house to house, from town to town, from one kingdom to another."[18] In Wesley's vision the ultimate goal is the renewal of the church—Protestant, Catholic, and Orthodox—in holiness, such that the non-Christian will be drawn to the gospel. This was the lens, through which he understood "God's design

16. See Henry H. Knight III, *The Presence of God in the Christian Life: John Wesley and the Means of Grace* (Metuchen, NJ: Scarecrow Press, 1992).

17. See Ann Taves, *Fits, Trances, and Visions* (Princeton: Princeton University Press, 1999) Part One.

18. "The General Spread of the Gospel" 15, 17, in *Sermons II*, 493.

in raising up the Preachers called Methodist," who would "reform the nation, particularly the church, and . . . spread scriptural holiness over the land."[19]

This witness included lifestyle and social concern. Wesley warned against the danger of riches. In contrast to the Puritan claim that honest wealth is a sign of divine favor, Wesley saw affluence (which he defined as possessing more than is sufficient for food, clothing, and lodging) as a threat to love for God and care for neighbor. Those who have more than enough should give all they can to those who do not have enough.[20]

Like the pietists, Wesley engaged a wide range of social ministries. In an age when lands were enclosed, and people displaced to work in factories and coal mines; the evils of poverty, illiteracy, alcoholism, and disease were rife. Feeding the hungry, visiting the sick, tending the prisoner, and showing strangers hospitality were common features of Methodism. Wesley provided lodging for widows, schooling for children, and short term loans for small businesses.

Wesley also cared about health. Many persons lacked medical care, so he opened clinics, diagnosed illnesses, and prescribed cures. In 1747 he published *Primitive Physick*, suggesting remedies for over 200 illnesses. Drawing on current medical literature, Wesley's bias was for simple, traditional cures that ordinary people could obtain. In addition, he frequently turned to prayer for miraculous healing, whether the cause of the illness was natural or demonic. Finally, he advocated good health practices: temperate diet, exercise, and proper sanitation.[21]

With few exceptions, the leadership of his evangelistic, formational, and social ministries was primarily lay. Most of his preachers were not ordained.[22] Laity led the classes, oversaw the chapels and directed social

19. "Minutes of Several Conversations," Q.3, in *The Works of John Wesley*, 3rd ed. (London: Wesleyan Methodist Book Room, 1872) vol. 8, 299.

20. His many sermons on this include "Upon Our Lord's Sermon on the Mount, VIII" (1748), "The Use of Money" (1760), "The Good Steward" (1768), "The Danger of Riches" (1781), "On Riches" (1781), and "The Danger of Increasing Riches" (1791). In "Causes of the Inefficacy of Christianity" (1789) Wesley argues the accumulation of riches due to the failure to practice of self-denial is the central cause undermining the spread of scriptural holiness.

21. See E. Brooks Holifield, *Health and Medicine in the Methodist Tradition* (New York: Crossroad, 1985) chapter 2; and Deborah Madden, *A Cheap, Safe and Natural Medicine: Religion, Medicine and Culture in John Wesley's Primitive Physic* (New York: Rodopi, 2007).

22. Most notable among the ordained clergy, in addition to Charles Wesley,

ministries. Wesley's connectional system provided leadership opportunities not available through church or society.

More striking was women's leadership. Many served as class leaders and directed social ministries. Eventually, some became lay preachers. The evolution toward preaching was gradual, beginning with public prayer and testimony, moving to exhortation, followed by preaching the sermon itself. Rather than assigning women preachers to circuits, Wesley gave them letters of endorsement thus enabling them to preach under Methodist auspices throughout England.[23]

Finally, we should take note of Charles Wesley's contribution. Though the two brothers sometimes had disagreements, they shared a vision of a church renewed in holiness. While Charles preached and helped oversee the growing movement, it was his hymns that had the greatest impact. Covering an enormous range of theological and liturgical ground, they enabled doctrine to touch the heart as well as the mind. They became a means of grace, through which worshippers sought the God's promises and experienced the reality of what God has done in Jesus Christ.[24]

HOLINESS AS HEAVEN BELOW

In speaking of justification and new birth, Charles Wesley gives these words to Christ:

> With me, your chief, ye then shall know
>   Shall feel your sins forgiven;
> Anticipate your heaven below,
>   And own that love is heaven.[25]

---

were John Fletcher and William Grimshaw. On Grimshaw see Frank Baker, *William Grimshaw 1708–63* (London: Epworth, 1963).

23. For the role of women in Wesley's movement see Earl Kent Brown, *Women of Mr. Wesley's Methodism* (Lewiston, NY: Mellon, 1983); Paul W. Chilcote, *John Wesley and the Women Preachers of Early Methodism* (Metuchen, NJ: Scarecrow, 1991); and Chilcote, *She Offered Them Christ* (Nashville, Abingdon, 1993).

24. Charles Wesley wrote approximately 6500 hymns. For more on his life and ministry, see John R. Tyson, *Assist Me to Proclaim: The Life and Hymns of Charles Wesley* (Grand Rapids: Eerdmans, 2008); Gary Best, *Charles Wesley: A Biography* (London: Epworth, 2006); and Kenneth G. C. Newport and Ted A. Campbell, eds., *Charles Wesley: Life, Literature & Legacy* (London: Epworth, 2007).

25. "Hymn 1" in Hilderbrand and Beckerlegge, eds., *A Collection of Hymns for the Use of the People Called Methodist*, 81.

The new birth, which begins sanctification, is "heaven below." It is a theme Charles would repeat, and a promise John would (in other language) proclaim.

What is striking in this phrase is God's movement and the resultant reality. The movement is from God to us: "Love divine, all loves excelling, joy of heaven to earth come down."[26] Whereas Calvin typically understood the Lord's Supper to take the worshipper to heaven, the Wesleys saw God's presence coming to us.[27] They had a strong emphasis on divine presence, and therefore on the Holy Spirit, not only in the Lord's Supper but in field preaching and all the means of grace.

The reality produced was eschatological—the life of the kingdom of God, the life of God in the human heart. The transforming power of the Holy Spirit brings this life, perfecting persons in love. It was this hope for holiness that governed Wesley's vision and encouraged Methodists to have an expectant faith in God's power.

BIBLIOGRAPHY

Collins, Kenneth J. *John Wesley: A Theological Pilgrimage*. Nashville: Abingdon, 2003.
Heitzenrater, Richard P. *Wesley and the People Called Methodists*. Nashville: Abingdon, 1995.
Rack, Henry D. *Reasonable Enthusiast: John Wesley and the Rise of Methodism*, 3rd rev. ed. London: Epworth, 2002.

On Wesley's Theology

Collins, Kenneth J. *The Theology of John Wesley: Holy Love and the Shape of Grace.* Nashville: Abingdon, 2007.
Maddox, Randy L. *Responsible Grace: John Wesley's Practical Theology*. Nashville: Abingdon, 1994.
Runyon, Theodore. *The New Creation: John Wesley's Theology Today*. Nashville: Abingdon, 1998.

26. Ibid., "Hymn 374," 545.

27. See Lorna Khoo's discussion in *Wesleyan Eucharistic Spirituality* (Adelaide, Australia: ATF, 2005) 135.

3

John Fletcher's Trinitarian Theology of Grace

MATTHEW K. THOMPSON

B Y ALL ACCOUNTS, JOHN Fletcher was a saint. Contemporaries described an almost "superhuman holiness" in characterizing Fletcher's Christian devotion.[1] His life was spent cultivating the holiness preached by his mentor, John Wesley, and the Methodist movement he embraced shortly after arriving in England from his native Switzerland. A man of immense intellectual gifts accompanying his spiritual fervor, Fletcher stands as a seminal figure across all streams of tradition addressed in this work, Wesleyan, Holiness and Pentecostal.

Fletcher, arguably Wesley's earliest and most trusted theological interpreter,[2] produced a theological corpus that provided all three streams of the Wesleyan trajectory with a paradigmatic understanding of the triune God's work in the world. One of his primary theological occupations was in defending Arminianism against Calvinism, which he developed and expanded into a systematic expression of God's work in the world in salvation history. Fletcher's remarkable life and thought qualify him as a crucial early figure in this vital trajectory of the Christian church.

1. Patrick Streiff, *Reluctant Saint? A Theological Biography of Fletcher of Madeley*, trans. By G. W. S. Knowles (Peterborough, UK: Epworth, 2001).

2. This is Laurence W. Wood's contention in his *The Meaning of Pentecost inn Early Methodism: Rediscovering John Fletcher as John Wesley's Vindicator and Designated Successor* (Lanham, MD: Scarecrow, 2002).

FLETCHER'S LIFE

Jean Guillaume de la Flechere was born in Nyon, Switzerland, on Lake Geneva, probably on September 11, 1729, the youngest of five girls and three boys.[3] Deeply committed to the Christian faith in which he was reared, Fletcher sought to live a virtuous life of piety in his student days at the University of Geneva,[4] where he studied under Jacob Vernet,[5] who published a ten-volume work on the truth of the Christian religion.[6] Despite this, Fletcher did not pursue theology as his primary course of study.[7] Rather, he planned for a military career, but an injury, disillusionment with military life and the lack of an appointment to a military post convinced him to abandon this path.[8]

Fletcher traveled to England in the summer of 1750, and began work as a private tutor for the Hills, a wealthy Shropshire family, in the autumn of 1751.[9] Throughout all this, he was known for his serious devotion and determination to live a holy life. This ardent desire for holiness prompted Mrs. Hill to jest that Fletcher sounded like a Methodist, a jape which piqued Fletcher's interest in the people called Methodists. Much to the initial chagrin of Mrs. Hill, Fletcher sought the Methodists out and became closely acquainted with the movement while in her employ.[10]

Up to this time, Fletcher's ardent efforts at Christian living had been a reaction against his native Reformed Christianity with its emphasis on unconditional election. Consequently, however, he struggled with a legalistic, works-oriented path to salvation comprised of serious self-appraisal and ethical striving for justification.[11] These early encounters with the Methodists redressed this soteriological misstep:

> [Methodist] preaching tore his piety to shreds. Among the Methodists, . . . righteousness by works, even in its noblest form, was condemned; the sinfulness of every human being before God was stressed; Christ was proclaimed as the redeemer and

3. Streiff, *Reluctant Saint?* 3.

4. Ibid., 13.

5. Ibid., 15

6. Ibid., 12.

7. Ibid., 306.

8. Ibid., 16–17.

9. Ibid., 21.

10. Ibid., 25–26.

11. Ibid., 31ff.

> the renewer of life; the Holy Spirit was promised, bringing assurance of salvation and power for holiness; all the emphasis was laid on the renewal of a person's whole life, and the believer was promised deliverance from servitude to sin.[12]

No longer could Fletcher believe that righteousness was accessible through his own moral efforts, but he was still convinced of the need of a transformed life. What the Methodists did was show him that the transformation he sought comes as a gift of God.

> Now, as at an earlier stage, Fletcher believed that in order to be received into communion with God one required renewal, that is to say, victory over servitude to sin. The decisive difference . . . was the question as to how this renewal could be achieved. Earlier, Fletcher had tried to fight against sin with his own resources. Now, however, the realization that the power must come from God, and that he needed to turn to Christ, seemed to force itself upon him.[13]

This realization, accompanied by an intense awareness of God's gracious mercy to him in Christ, led Fletcher to enter into a formal covenant with God, which delineated all he was surrendering to God and all he was asking of God to enable him to walk in his newly transformed life.[14]

By this time, Fletcher had made the decision to pursue holy orders. He was ordained a deacon in the Church of England on March 6, 1757; he was ordained a priest on March 13 and installed as the curate of Madeley on March 14; he became vicar of Madeley in 1760.[15] Fletcher's acceptance of his charge at Madeley greatly chagrined his mentor, John Wesley, who had envisioned, and indeed offered, Fletcher to succeed him as the leader of the Methodist movement.[16] Fletcher remained at Madeley until his death in 1785, but he did not restrict his ministry solely to the parish. He also served as the first President of Lady Huntingdon's theological college at Trevecca in 1768,[17] though the mounting tensions

---

12. Ibid., 31–32.
13. Ibid., 32.
14. Ibid., 34–40.
15. Ibid., 49.
16. Ibid., 133–34.
17. Ibid., 143.

between Wesleyan and Calvinistic Methodists on campus eventually prompted his resignation.[18]

Fletcher proved unable to fulfill Wesley's vision of succeeding him as the leader of the Methodist revival due to his premature death in ill health. Indeed, Wesley survived him by six years. Nevertheless, Fletcher's theological contribution to the Methodist movement is arguably second only to Wesley's own. Like his mentor, Fletcher's theology featured a robust soteriology as its central motif. Even more so than Wesley, however, he emphasized the distinctive role of the Holy Spirit in soteriology. This allowed him to develop a systematic expression of the Wesleyan faith that explicitly connected personal and cosmic salvation, grace and freedom and creation and eschaton in a Trinitarian dispensational framework deeply imbued with a rich pneumatology.

FLETCHER'S TRINITARIAN DISPENSATIONALISM

Fletcher described God's grace as manifested in God's self-revelation throughout salvation history. In making God's self known as a loving Trinity of Persons through a triadic dispensational salvation history, God renovates both the individual human and, indeed, the entire cosmos.

Though often compared with the dispensational system of the mystical Calabrian Abbot Joachim of Fiore, Fletcher's dispensationalism, shares far more similarity with a much older schema, that of the great Cappadocian Father Gregory of Nazianzus.[19] Like Gregory, Fletcher understands the Age of the Father as stretching from creation to John the Baptist, at which point the Age of the Son commences and continues until Pentecost, when the Age of the Spirit begins, which in turn carries us to the eschaton. And as with Gregory, Fletcher sees this progressive

---

18. Ibid., 148. Lady Huntingdon was a staunch defender of the Calvinist variety of Methodism, while Fletcher, of course, remained a Wesleyan. Though Fletcher sought to reconcile the two factions throughout his career (214), he became the most articulate and theologically sophisticated advocate of the Wesleyan party. He felt that Calvinism "in its highest form led to antinomianism, Manichaeism and fatalism on the one hand, and to ungodliness, arrogance and despair on the other" (165).

19. I have argued this at length elsewhere. See my *Kingdom Come: Revisioning Pentecostal Eschatology*, forthcoming, esp. ch. 4 and 5, and my "Into All Truth: Divine Pedagogy as Soteriology in the Trinitology of Gregory Nazianzen and John Fletcher," unpublished paper presented at the Upper Midwest Regional Meeting of the American Academy of Religion, Luther Seminary, April 13, 2007.

divine self-revelation in developmental stages as salvific. God becomes known through God's Trinitarian acts in history for our salvation.

> In these dispensations God acts in a sustaining, a redemptive, or a convicting and sanctifying way. What at a lower level remains hidden to knowledge becomes plain at a higher level. Both sets of distinctions can be applied to history as a whole and to an individual person. Thus, on the one hand, historically, the dispensation of the Father is given to everyone. The dispensation of the Son was promised to God's people in the Old Testament, and found fulfillment in the life, death and resurrection of Jesus Christ. The dispensation of the Spirit was promised to the disciples of Jesus, and found fulfillment after Pentecost. On the other hand, in relation to individuals and their growth in faith, the Father can draw people who believe in him as Creator to the Son as their redeemer. Christ can fill those who believe in him as redeemer with the fullness of the Holy Spirit.[20]

Humanity's sinfulness had effectively severed relationship with the triune God, but God's overtures of grace in subsequent salvation history progressively restored that relationship, culminating in the glorification of Jesus the Christ and the sending forth of the Holy Spirit. "Fletcher referred to this development of grace in salvation history as a progressive shining forth of God's being like different rays of light until the fullness of his Triune grace was made known. When the fullness of the divine rays was revealed, then the fullness of salvation took effect. And that did not happen until Jesus was glorified and the Spirit was given to the Church."[21]

Like Wesley, Fletcher conceived of salvation as a process, a *via salutis* that was punctuated by crisis moments such as justification, entire sanctification, etc.[22] These stages in individual salvation mirror the broader dispensational framework of salvation history:[23] the work of the Son is appropriated in justification, understood as forgiveness of sins, and the work of the Spirit is manifested in sanctification, understood as the eradication of the sinful nature. However, though the entire Trinity is

---

20. Streiff, *Reluctant Saint?*, 202.

21. Wood, *Meaning of Pentecost*, 126.

22. This, of course, provided a fertile theological seedbed for the later Pentecostal doctrine of subsequence in soteriology.

23. Donald W. Dayton, *Theological Roots of Pentecostalism* (1987; reprint, Peabody, MA: Hendrickson, 2000) 150.

involved in the salvation of the individual and the world, it is the special work of the Spirit in facilitating this entire process, from first to last, which, in its entirety, Fletcher called the New Birth.

> Several times Fletcher described the new birth as the two great works of the Holy Spirit in the repentant soul: justification and sanctification. In every case justification precedes sanctification. Fletcher's distinctive contribution was to treat the new birth as the inclusive term embracing both justification and sanctification. Sanctification begins as a work of the Spirit in the forgiveness of sins. The body of sin is not thereby destroyed, but its power is curtailed. Sanctification is a long-term progressive work. When Fletcher included sanctification within the concept of the new birth, he did it with the thought that the renewal of human beings in the image of God—in perfect love for God and neighbour—could only be attained as the goal of sanctification. In other words, new birth in its fullness corresponded essentially to Wesley's understanding of Christian perfection.[24]

Entire sanctification, for Fletcher, is a "baptism of the Holy Spirit." Thus, while it is true that Wesley emphasized the role of the Spirit in salvation to a higher degree than most Western thinkers of his day, Fletcher's pneumatological emphasis was even greater. The Spirit was an active power working constantly to renew each individual,[25] as indeed the Spirit had worked in the broader history according to this same salvific pattern. Israel's exodus from bondage in Egypt and the crossing of the Red Sea are a type for justification and water baptism, while the crossing of the Jordan River and conquest of Canaan are a type for the baptism of the Holy Spirit (entire sanctification). The first stage delivers from slavery,

---

24. Streiff, *Reluctant Saint?*, 53–54. One should note here two at least apparent departures from Wesley: 1) Fletcher construes the New Birth, which Wesley views as an early crisis point in the process of salvation, as essentially a synonym for salvation in its entirety; and 2) Fletcher refers to entire sanctification as a "baptism in the Holy Spirit," a personal Pentecost event that represents the fullness and maturity of Christian life in the present world. Though Dayton and Wood have a long-standing disagreement on the degree of acceptance Wesley granted to this systematic reconfiguration of his theology (with Dayton expressing strong reservations), it seems clear that Fletcher, at any rate, felt his construction was faithful to the thought of his spiritual father, as did later adherents to both the Holiness and Pentecostal traditions.

25. Ibid., 304–5.

while the second, as a fulfillment of the promise of the first, provides entrance into the Promised Land.[26]

The same twofold pattern can be seen in the twin missions of the Son and Spirit. Christ's death defeats sin, while his resurrection conquers death. The Spirit then applies the work of the Son to us, canceling our servitude to death and finitude, so that we can in turn, through the power of the Spirit, defeat sin.[27] The process can be demonstrated by the following chiastic pattern:

A: Jesus assumes sin (2 Cor 5:21) and kills it on the cross.
　　B: The Father raises Jesus by the Spirit, defeating death,
　　　sin's consequence.
　　B': Justifying faith is faith in the risen Christ (Rom 10:9), who
　　　has defeated death, destroying its power to enslave us to sin in
　　　an attempt to circumvent our finitude.
A: Sanctification/Spirit baptism empowers us to walk in newness of
　　life, conquering sin (Rom 6:22), since we have been freed from it.

This two-step process is necessary for living the full-fledged Christian life. "Fletcher believed that participating in Jesus' resurrected life (a personalized Easter moment) and the outpouring of his Spirit (a personalized Pentecost moment) are required before one is duly considered a full citizen of the Kingdom of God. To be sure, Fletcher did not divorce Easter and Pentecost, but, rather, he saw them as existing in a continuum of grace."[28]

A THEOLOGY OF GRACE AND FREEDOM

Fletcher's defense and systematization of Wesley arose from his understanding of this continuum of grace and how it operated vis-à-vis free will. As noted above, Fletcher was an ardent defender of the Arminian wing of the Methodist movement, and thus a stalwart opponent of individual predestination to salvation or reprobation. However, much like his mentor, he had no Pelagian (nor semi-Pelagian, for that matter) delusions with regard to the role of the human will in salvation. Like Wesley

---

26. See Wood, *Meaning of Pentecost*, 114ff.

27. This view of sin, consequence and salvation is strongly reminiscent of Eastern Christian formulations. See John S. Romanides, *Ancestral Sin*, trans. by George S. Gabriel (Ridgewood, NJ: Zephyr, 1998; reprint, 2008).

28. Wood, *Meaning of Pentecost*, 117.

and his other Protestant forebears, he saw that the will was corrupted in the fall into sin. However, also like Wesley, he understood God's grace as *empowering* rather than *overpowering* the will of fallen humanity, restoring individuals to the capacity for devout Christian living.

> Fletcher was postulating a free will which, following the Fall, was naturally only capable of evil, but which, thanks to the grace of God given to all people, was now capable of good. Free will was no longer indebted, as for Adam, to the creative grace of God, but now, for all people, to God's redeeming grace. The freedom of the will does not detract from free grace, since free will has its basis in free grace. Neither does human freedom of action deprive God of the honour due to him. There is no place for self-glory or pharisaical pride, since all that is good and well-pleasing to God is the outcome of God's grace. The human will can be convinced but not compelled, otherwise it ceases to be free will.[29]

Grace is indeed free (not earned), but it in turn makes the recipient free. The freedom given in grace is that which empowers the believer to be transformed into the likeness of Christ. Sanctification is the goal of the Christian life, and grace does not declare anyone righteous without making them so, and the forgiveness of sin in justification frees us to live in victory over sin.[30] Final victory over sin is possible only through the infilling of the Holy Spirit, which Fletcher hoped for and sought following his conversion experience.[31]

It is through this understanding of grace and freedom, couched in the Trinitarian dispensational framework of salvation history, that Fletcher recasts the doctrine of election,[32] contra his Reformed roots and Calvinist contemporaries. Everyone is elected for grace in Christ, but not everyone is granted the same measure of revelation. People are judged by their response to the measure of revelation they are granted.[33] Thus, election is not specifically or necessarily for salvation, but for revelation, and this in the service of God's broader redemptive plan for humanity.[34]

29. Streiff, *Reluctant Saint?*, 200.

30. Ibid., 304–5.

31. Ibid., 305.

32. Ibid., 307.

33. Ibid.

34. Ibid., 204.

All of this is in accord with Fletcher's two fundamental soteriological axioms: "all our salvation is due to the grace of God through Christ Jesus, and our damnation is our own doing by removing ourselves from that grace."[35] He includes a robust doctrine of grace and election within a broad Trinitarian dispensational pattern manifested in salvation history, facilitated by a rich pneumatology that would go on to impact not only his own Methodist movement, but its children and grandchildren as well.

CONCLUSION

John Fletcher of Madeley's all too brief life nonetheless provided him with enough time to make momentous and lasting contributions to not only his own Anglican and Methodist traditions, but also to the church universal. His zeal for the gospel of Jesus Christ and his pursuit of personal holiness stood as sterling examples for his own time and ours, and his theoretical articulation and lived experience of a fully orbed salvation have inspired Methodist, Holiness and Pentecostal Christians as they have arisen to work for the Kingdom in the present day.

BIBLIOGRAPHY

Dayton, Donald W. *Theological Roots of Pentecostalism.* 1987; reprint, Peabody, MA: Hendrickson, 2000.

Streiff, Patrick. *Reluctant Saint? A Theological Biography of Fletcher of Madeley* Translated by G. W. S. Knowles. Peterborough, UK: Epworth, 2001.

Wood, Lawrence W. *The Meaning of Pentecost in Early Methodism: Rediscovering John Fletcher as John Wesley's Vindicator and Designated Successor.* Lanham, MD: Scarecrow, 2002.

---

35. Ibid., 196–97.

4

The People Called Methodists

Stephen W. Rankin

There is a prevalent bias in the church today that downplays and even tries to avoid doctrine. "Doctrine divides," the saying goes, so we are better off not talking about it and getting people all riled up to no good end. Many think conflict over it is unnecessary because they believe doctrine has nothing to do with real life. It is the stuff of the academy: endless abstractions that only the technically-trained can understand. A bumper sticker says, "My karma ran over my dogma," which is a trendy way to say that life's experiences are much more powerful and relevant than fixed doctrines.

A similar, though more sophisticated, attitude can be found among scholars heavily influenced by certain ideas from Immanuel Kant. Kant was deeply engaged in the Enlightenment project to find a sure foundation for knowledge. Kant proposed two kinds of knowledge. The first was knowledge of the objective world, such as that pursued by scientific inquiry. Here Kant argued that, as beings limited by space and time, we could not know things as they are, but only as they appear to us. The second kind of knowledge was subjective, and included a universal moral imperative. It was this subjective knowledge that provides the foundation for both God and ethics.

After Kant, the tendency has been to understand doctrine not as an "objective" or factual statement about God's nature and activity but as an expression of our subjectivity or experience. Doctrine has been reduced in authority and impact. The tendency has been to shift away from the authority of specific doctrines to religious experience, which purports to give people a larger degree of latitude in understanding their faith. It has resulted in a general sense of "liberation from" doctrine.

For people in the Wesleyan tradition this move to experience has had a particular appeal. John Kent, a British Methodist theologian, provides a good example in his recent work, *Wesley and the Wesleyans*.[1] Kent, in Kantian fashion, distinguishes "primary religion" from "secondary theological explanation." "Primary religion" has to do with experience. It is, in short, the language of religious feelings. It is raw and unsophisticated, but heartfelt and, in that sense "real." "Secondary theological explanation" is the language of formalized doctrine. It originally flows from experience, but in the hands of technically-trained religious leaders, it becomes artificial, abstract and imposed "top-down." "Secondary theological explanation," according to this view can be dangerous to authentic faith or experience.

We therefore live in a context that, for these and other reasons, downplays doctrine. To be sure, anyone who has studied church history knows of the numerous divisions and hostilities within the church. We pray for unity. A spirit of generosity and pragmatism calls for us to minimize doctrinal differences. People in the Wesleyan family, however, should beware of carrying this prejudice too far. We cannot so easily divorce doctrine from life. Ironically, downplaying doctrine has impoverished the life of the Wesleyan family.

In the following essay we will summarize very briefly the core aspects of Wesley's doctrine of the Christian life that was both the most controversial and, according to Wesley, the reason God called Methodists into existence. Wesley understood the scriptures to teach that the Christian life has a goal—a trajectory—that produces maturing disciples who love God without reserve and who love neighbors and enemies in practical, sacrificial, Christ-like ways. Doctrine logically connects with life at this level. The quality of life early Methodists experienced often mirrored this doctrine[2] that Wesley championed throughout his ministry.

---

1. John Kent, *Wesley and the Wesleyans* (Cambridge: Cambridge University Press, 2002).

2. It is easy, in our day, to identify doctrine with what Wesley calls "religious opinions" and then dismiss doctrine with facile references to Wesley's sermon "Catholic Spirit." This is a mistake.

METHODISM'S DOCTRINAL "GRAND DEPOSITUM"

John Wesley spent virtually his entire ministry advocating for and defending the doctrine of Christian perfection,[3] that "grand depositum," he wrote, "for which Methodists were chiefly raised up."[4] The term is still a controversial one, because of the implication of flawlessness (which Wesley did not hold), but the doctrine Wesley advanced is deeply rooted in scripture and powerfully useful for envisioning the goal of the Christian life. The fastest way into the topic, therefore, is to focus on two or three of Wesley's sermons, in which the promise and goal of Christian maturity (perfection) are clearly explicated. We will watch for the link Wesley makes between the change that the Holy Spirit works in the hearts of believers and the love they demonstrate in practical ways toward their neighbors. That change takes place in the "affections"[5] or "habitual dispositions of the soul," as Wesley termed them. According to Wesley's trajectory of Christian maturity, the fruit of the Spirit in people's lives demonstrates a transformation in what they desire, feel and think. These changes produce a related change in the way people act toward their neighbors and even their enemies. Christians perfected in love so identify with Christ and his kingdom that they find themselves loving people as Jesus loves them and doing the things that Jesus did (does).

In Wesley's sermon, "On Perfection," he states, "This is the sum of Christian perfection: it is all comprised in that one word, love."[6] That love always includes both God and neighbor. It thus reflects the very mind of Christ. The person who shares the mind of Christ is changed through and through by the gracious action of the Holy Spirit. As Wesley put it, this change "includes the whole disposition of his mind, all his af-

---

3. There are several terms that Wesley variably used: "being made perfect in love," "sanctification," "full salvation," "holiness." For simplicity's sake, I will stick with "Christian perfection."

4. John Telford, ed., *The Letters of John Wesley*, 8 volumes (London: Epworth, 1931) 8:237–38.

5. "Affections" is a term much used in Wesley. Affections have emotional qualities but are not identified with emotions, since emotions are transitory feeling states. Affections are more dispositional and, over time, are shaped by the Holy Spirit (through Christian practices) to come in line with the character of Christ. For a detailed explanation of John Wesley's view of religious affections, see Gregory S. Clapper, *John Wesley on Religious Affections: His Views on Experience and Emotion and Their Role in the Christian Life and Theology*, Pietist and Wesleyan Studies 1 (Metuchen, NJ: Scarecrow, 1989).

6. *The Works of John Wesley*, Bicentennial Edition, (Nashville: Abingdon, 1986) 3:74.

fections, all his tempers, both toward God and man." These qualities are made visible in the believer through the fruit of the Spirit. Wesley argued that, though Galatians 5:22–23 uses a number of terms to describe the fruit of the Spirit, it is, in truth, all of one reality: the "one undivided fruit of the Spirit" is love, so that the "glorious constellation of graces"[7] (i.e. joy, peace, long-suffering, gentleness, etc.) are all subsumed in love. This gracious affection necessarily produces a compassionate and loving response toward other people. Acts of sacrificial love for others is the logical (though supernatural) result of the work of God in the believer's heart. The doctrine of Christian perfection, for Wesley, is simply a naming and explanation of what he believed God ultimately intended to produce in Christians.

One of Wesley's favorite Bible verses was Romans 14:17, "For the kingdom of God is not meat and drink; but righteousness, and peace, and joy in the Holy Ghost." In his sermon, "The Way to the Kingdom," though Wesley uses Mark 1:15 ("The kingdom of God is at hand: repent ye, and believe the gospel") as the theme verse, he structures the sermon around Romans 14:17. The kingdom of God is found, not in outward things, but in the heart. As with the fruit of the Spirit, since righteousness, peace and joy are all matters of the heart, we are talking about what might be loosely termed in modern language, psychological traits. Romans 14:17 plays an important role in Wesley's thinking precisely because it locates the work of the kingdom of God in the affections. Because the Spirit is at work, one's heart's desire becomes God and God's will rather than self. Furthermore, because God becomes the heart's primary (and eventually, according to the doctrine of Christian perfection, sole) desire, the believer takes on more and more of the qualities that reflect the kingdom of God: "humbleness of mind, gentleness, meekness, long-suffering," as well as the banishment "of doubt, fear and painful uncertainty." In the place of doubt and fear the believer finds true joy. "Wherever [the peace of God] is fixed in the soul, there is also 'joy in the Holy Ghost.'"[8]

From these Spirit-infused dispositions comes the desire to love and serve the neighbor. This desire—in the logic of the divine economy—is a necessary (and utterly inevitable) concomitant to the desire for and love of God. Wesley states: "the second great branch of Christian righ-

---

7. Ibid., 75.

8. *The Works of John Wesley,* Bicentennial Edition, (Nashville: Abingdon, 1986) 3:222–24.

teousness is closely and inseparably connected therewith, even 'Thou shalt love thy neighbor as thyself.' 'Thou shalt love'—thou shalt embrace with the most tender goodwill, the most earnest and cordial affection, the most inflamed desires of preventing or removing all evil and of procuring for him every possible good—'thy neighbor . . .'"[9] This link between love for God and love for neighbor has been easily lost in the controversies surrounding the doctrine of Christian perfection, much to the detriment of Wesleyan and Wesley-related movements. Nonetheless, there are examples from the history of the Wesleyan movement to show the power of this trajectory.

We thus find in this brief survey the inherent link in Wesley's thought between doctrine and life. Wesley believed God had promised Christian perfection to all believers. While the recipient of Christian perfection can literally feel love for God and neighbor, it was not "mere feeing" that God was trying to instill. The empirical evidence of the reality of God's love in the believers' heart was the practical and tangible expression of love for the neighbor (and even the enemy). This is precisely why doctrine does not divide but unites. If we take Wesley at his word, this doctrine both promises and describes the life of God in the human soul.

With these considerations in mind, it is very difficult, if not impossible; to understand the impact of the Wesleyan tradition without considering how the people called Methodists interacted with Wesleyan doctrine. Doctrine and experience are inextricably, dialectically intertwined. I am tempted to lift the word "perichoresis" from its usual usage in describing the mutual indwelling of persons of the Trinity and employ it to describe the intimate connection in the Wesleyan movement between doctrine and life. We are attempting to gaze on a mystery: the interplay between thoughts, feelings and actions. Each shapes and is shaped by the other. Let us look briefly at an example from early Methodist history that shows the aim Wesley had in mind in promoting Christian perfection.

THOMAS FILDES AND THE STRANGERS' FRIENDS SOCIETY

Thomas Fildes was a grocer in Manchester, England in the late 1700s, and a member of the Methodist society there. He was one of the founding members of a new movement known as the Strangers' Friends Society, formed in Manchester in 1791. The purpose of this organization was

9. Ibid., 221.

to find and tend to the poorest of the poor in Manchester's burgeoning industrial tenement slums. The city had grown steadily throughout the eighteenth century, from a small market town of roughly two thousand to more than one hundred thousand by century's end. People came there to work in the growing cotton industry and wound up living in hastily-built dwellings. The unfortunates living in the basement "apartments" found themselves below the level of the street, with raw sewage running in the ditches outside a solitary window opening with no way to close it. The conditions were appalling as the tenements were hopelessly infested with vermin and all kinds of diseases. The Strangers' Friends Society raised money to provide clean bedding, food, medicine and sometimes larger items like furniture for people suffering these afflictions. They also shared the Gospel with the people they visited, combining attempts to tend to both material and spiritual needs.[10]

Thomas Fildes kept a diary of his experiences as a visitor for the Strangers' Friends Society.[11] He once found a family of thirteen, for example, living in one room. Nine of them had fevers. He was able to provide them medicine and reported later to his diary that all had recovered. The outcome was not always so happy. On another occasion, he found a woman and her three children living in a basement apartment, imprisoned there with her husband's corpse. He had been ill for half a year and had finally succumbed to the disease. The woman had no way of removing his body from the apartment, so the family simply had been co-existing with it when Fildes found them. He helped to provide a proper burial.

Visitors with the Strangers' Friends Society delved into spiritual matters with their wards as well. Fildes' diary recounts his interaction with a woman named Meriam Heywood. When he first met her she had been ill already three months. He did all he could to care for her medical needs, but went beyond them to the spiritual, counseling with her about the condition of her soul. She seemed to think that her physical affliction would atone for her sins. After explaining God's love and her fallen state, Fildes recorded that she began to cry out for mercy, struggling might-

10. Members of Methodist societies were not eligible to receive help through the Strangers' Friends Society. The societies "took care of their own" through other means. The ministrations of SFS were strictly for people outside Methodism.

11. All references to Thomas Fildes and his experience in the Strangers' Friends Society come from his manuscript diary, housed in the Manchester Central (Public) Library, Misc. 777/1.

ily to "catch one drop of that healing stream and he who never lets any strive in vain washed all her sins away."

From the Fall of 1791 until the end of 1803, the Strangers' Friends Society distributed more than six thousand four hundred pounds in aid to approximately sixty thousand people. In today's figures, it would amount to roughly fourteen thousand dollars. When we take into account that a person could live reasonably well on thirty or forty pounds a year in those days, we can see that it was a healthy sum of money raised by Methodists—for total strangers.[12]

Thomas Fildes was likewise instrumental in the formation of the first Sunday School in Manchester. Space does not permit, but we could tell a similar story about Methodist leadership in the Sunday School movement, which was growing at the same time as the Strangers' Friends Society was operating.[13] Within a few years there were thousands of children enrolled in Sunday Schools in Manchester. These were the days before child labor laws and Manchester was becoming an industrial city. These children would be condemned to a life of grinding poverty if someone did not care for them. Many of them literally lived on the streets, abandoned by parents who could not feed them. In the Sunday Schools, they learned to read (and eventually to write), but they also learned cleanliness and "social graces" and other skills that would help them improve their lives.

DOCTRINE AND LIFE IN THE PEOPLE CALLED METHODISTS

These efforts of Methodists to serve other people are notable, inspiring and challenging.[14] When one asks about the impetus for such displays of practical love, one must consider the role that Methodism's "grand depositum" played. The difficulty in making this claim—linking doctrine and practice in particular ways—however, is a monumental historiographical challenge. How does one show that a particular teaching

12. The existence of the Strangers' Friends Society in Manchester prompted other similar relief efforts. The Manchester Poor Committee was a parallel effort which some members of the SFS helped to initiate as well.

13. The SFS had groups in other large cities, as well, including London. However, as a sub-group within Methodism, it was never a large society. For example, in Manchester, the society never had more than thirty members at any given time.

14. Thomas Fildes died of typhoid fever, which he contracted while visiting the sick in Manchester. He literally gave his life for the sake of others.

caused the behavior exemplified by people like Thomas Fildes? It would thrill a researcher's heart to find a "paper trail," a statement in Fildes' own hand, for example, saying something like, "I experienced Christian perfection and because of it I felt moved to give my life away in service to others." In Fildes' case, all we have available to us is the scrap of diary to which we have referred. Many of the testimonies to Christian perfection are recorded in published sources such as the *Arminian Magazine*, but they serve an apologetic purpose, which was to defend and uphold the doctrine both to Methodists and to their detractors.[15] They are therefore not as helpful as we might wish.

Still, there are tantalizing glimpses. In Manchester Methodism's history there is chronological proximity between revivals in which a significant number of people gave testimony to having experienced Christian perfection and the organization of efforts to serve the poor. In that sense, the history "matches" what John Wesley envisioned the doctrine of Christian perfection to produce. In the 1780s, for example, Manchester Methodists experienced renewal and the preachers appointed to that station mentioned a significant number of testimonies to Christian perfection. At the same time, Methodists became active in promoting Sunday Schools and joined societies calling for the abolition of slavery.[16] In 1791 they formed the Strangers' Friends Society. There is no way to show direct causation between the revival and the demonstrable, tangible "loving one's neighbor as oneself" exemplified in these activities, yet the logic of Christian perfection and the manner in which John Wesley described it suggest that the practices did follow from the doctrine. It is worth considering or perhaps re-considering, therefore, the power of this "grand depositum" for people in the Wesleyan and related families.

15. The doctrine of Christian perfection brought dissension within the ranks of Methodism as well as outside. Much of the problem lay with the word itself, but there were deeper theological differences that separated Wesleyans from Reformed thinkers.

16. In the American context, a similar case could be made for the connection between Christian perfection and service to others. Douglas Strong has demonstrated a direct link between efforts to abolish slavery in the United States and the doctrine of holiness. See Douglas M. Strong, *Perfectionist Politics: Abolitionism and the Religious Tensions*, Religion and Politics Series (New York: Syracuse University Press, 1999).

BIBLIOGRAPHY

Clapper, Gregory S. *As If the Heart Mattered: A Wesleyan Spirituality*, Pathways in Spiritual Growth. Nashville: Upper Room, 1997.

Hatch, Nathan O., and John H. Wigger, editors, *Methodism and the Shaping of American Culture*. Nashville: Kingswood, 2001.

Knight, Henry H., III. *Eight Life-Enriching Practices of United Methodists*. Nashville: Abingdon, 2001.

PART ONE

Pastoral Response

RODNEY McNEALL

D R. RANKIN ASSERTS THAT John Wesley considered the "grand depositum" of the Methodist movement to be the doctrine of Christian Perfection and provides illustrations of how that was exemplified in eighteenth-century British Methodism. Dr. Knight articulates how John and Charles Wesley made the pursuit of Christian Perfection not only a personal quest but an emphasis that would drive the entire movement in the larger context of the eighteenth-century awakenings. And Dr. Thompson shows how John Fletcher's influence and theological innovations would shape not only the Methodism of his day but provide fertile resources for Holiness and Pentecostal spirituality. Given John Wesley's assertion of Christian Perfection and its emphasis in early British Methodism as the "grand depositum" to the wider church and world, I wonder though, if somehow the structured, global denominations of today have somehow overdrawn on this original deposit. This is not to make light of either the contribution that Methodism has made to the church as a whole or John Wesley's assertion, but is more of a statement regarding how the denominations that retain the Methodist name have accounted for this inheritance over time.

As a pastor of the United Methodist church, the language of Christian perfection, entire sanctification, or even the "way of salvation" is mostly foreign to the congregations I have served. Yet it's not the lack of theological language that is troubling as much as a lack of clarity of purpose that this doctrine could and would provide for the church as inheritors of this grand deposit. Thus, what is at stake is more than recovering a language and theological terminology for today's church. Rather, I suggest that to recover an emphasis on "the means of grace" that gave shape and vitality to a Methodist movement, might restore the same shape and vitality to the immediate inheritors of that legacy.

Churches build new buildings and employ new technologies in ministry. We appropriately discuss and incorporate the finer points of family systems theory in clergy boundaries and healthy church initiatives. We attend committee meetings, invoke consultants, build mission and vision statements, attend leadership training seminars and read volumes of books all with different methodologies, theological underpinnings, and implications. In itself this is a healthy process, as each innovation in the area of theology, social sciences, business practice, and technology may very well provide fertile ground for the church to bear fruit for God's kingdom. However, as we appropriate from these divergent areas of expertise, are we doing so with a critical eye toward the assumptions that lie beneath?

Unlike the Wesleys, Fletcher, and early Methodism, it is hard to detect an overarching theology at work in today's Methodism (at least United Methodism) that provides coherence in appropriating these resources for the purposes of knowing God and knowing God's purposes for us. Perhaps this is the fruit that results from doctrine being seen as divisive, as discussed by Dr. Rankin. The danger is in allowing these innovations to subtly alter the ends for which the church exists, especially if these methodologies seem helpful in maintaining the church as an institution. To continue the banking metaphor, it may be that today's United Methodism is not bankrupt as much as other deposits have been made along the way such that the original seems less significant, especially in light of a contemporary aversion to matters of doctrine.

As this opening section clearly indicates, Christian Perfection was not merely an abstract concept to be articulated and debated among the intelligentsia of the day. Rather, the Wesleys, Fletcher, and the People called Methodists pursued Christian Perfection as an attainable, practical goal for all Christians. It was what defined who they were as Christians. Striving toward Christian perfection was (and is) a life giving, life-transforming relationship with the Trinitarian God that not only provided the assurance they sought as forgiven people in Jesus Christ, but the means by which to grow in that faith and love, and to express it towards others. It provided the coherent theo-logic by which other voices could be heard, evaluated and filtered. Yet the raw materials, so to speak, of Christian perfection lay in the means of God's grace. As Dr. Knight clearly points out, the means of grace as acts of piety and mercy were not what justified the Methodist before God (this was by grace through faith alone). Rather prayer and fasting, searching the Scriptures, participating in Holy Communion, engaging in Christian conversations, as well as works of service and justice are the ways in which God has provided for Christians to keep their "focus on knowing God" through faith. For early British Methodism, the means of grace were central to loving God and loving neighbor, and therefore central to the "way of salvation."

This is significantly more than a utilitarian approach to Christian piety and ministry. This is significantly more than statistics, technology, capital campaigns and committees. However, it is what could give them all Godly purpose and meaning. It moves our acts of piety from sanctifying decisions already made through church political processes towards practicing the presence of God in order to hear God amidst all other voices that demand to be heard. Practicing the means of grace creates the opportunity for Christians to experience God's love and life transforming presence so that love may become the reigning "temper" of their heart. Perhaps the question is not whether we should be engaged in all the other activities the church may engage, but are those activities moving us toward Christian perfection, experiencing God's love, and helping us to love our neighbor? Maybe it is not doctrine that divides us as much as other forces working to influence the church.

The dangers that the means of grace countered in early Methodism were formalism and enthusiasm. Is that so different than what the church faces today cloaked differently?

The Early Nineteenth Century: Spreading Scriptural Holiness

Introduction

METHODIST BEGINNINGS[1]

METHODISM BEGAN IN AMERICA at the initiative of laity who had immigrated to the colonies from Ireland. First were Robert Strawbridge (c. 1732–1781) and his wife, Elizabeth, who settled in Maryland in the early 1760s. Fueled by Robert's powerful preaching, they organized the first Methodist class meeting in America, and brought many others into the movement as lay preachers and class leaders, including Jacob Toogood, the first African American Methodist preacher. Methodist societies and preaching stations were established throughout Maryland, Delaware, and parts of Virginia and Pennsylvania. Though not ordained, Strawbridge nonetheless began offering the sacraments, and would later ignore attempts by official Methodism to get him to stop. He was the first of a long line of Methodist mavericks.

In 1766 in New York, Barbara Heck (1734–1804) challenged her cousin Philip Embury (1728–1773) for his spiritual laxity—she threw the deck of playing cards he and his friends were using into the fire—and urged him to take on his role of preacher and class leader as he had done in Ireland. Embury did so, and his growing society was joined two years later by another lay preacher, Capt. Thomas Webb (1724–1796), formerly of the British army. A fiery preacher who wore a green eye patch, Webb in turn spread the work further, including forming a society in Philadelphia, then the largest city in America. These new Methodist societies were interracial from their inception.

It was when these Methodists sought assistance from John Wesley that he became aware of the work in America. He responded by send-

---

1. Standard accounts of the history of Methodism include Frederick A. Norwood, *The Story of Methodism in America* (Nashville: Abingdon, 1974). Frank Baker, *From Wesley to Asbury* (Chapel Hill: Duke University Press, 1976) is an especially helpful resource on the beginnings of Methodism in America.

ing pairs of lay preachers as missionaries, some eight in all, starting 1769. With the coming of the American Revolution, however, most of the missionaries returned to England. Of the eight, only Francis Asbury remained a Methodist preacher in America.

After the Revolution the Methodist movement was in disarray. No longer able to rely on ordained Anglican clergy for the sacraments, Methodist lay preachers in the South decided to ordain one another. It was Asbury who convinced them instead to wait and seek a solution from John Wesley.

Because he was unable to obtain ordinations through the regular episcopal channels, Wesley took a more radical step. Believing that God had made him responsible for the people called Methodists, and that the position of bishop was not a separate category of ordination but rather an office given to some ordained elders who were set apart for it, Wesley decided to exercise episcopal authority himself. To the dismay of many Anglicans, including his brother Charles, John Wesley ordained two of his lay preachers, and ordained as well an Anglican priest, Thomas Coke (1747–1814) to serve as Superintendent in America—in effect, as Bishop. They were instructed to go to America, ordain Asbury, and make him a Superintendent as well.

So at the Christmas Conference in 1784, in Baltimore, Maryland, a new denomination was formed: the Methodist Episcopal Church. Although it retained much of the characteristics of a renewal movement, the new denomination drew as well upon the polity and doctrine of its Anglican parent. But it did so in a radically new context, symbolized by the fact that the American lay preachers had to come together in conference to *vote* whether or not to approve Wesley's instructions.

The new denomination shared the Methodistic mission with two German-speaking movements.[2] The first was the United Brethren in Christ, co-founded by Philip William Otterbein (1726–1813) and Martin Boehm (1725–1812). Otterbein was a formally educated ordained minister in the German Reformed Church. Deeply grounded in pietism, he came to America in 1752 to serve the growing German-speaking people

---

2. The standard account on the history of the German movements is Bruce J. Behney and Paul H. Eller, *The History of the Evangelical United Brethren Church,* ed. by Kenneth W. Krueger (Nashville: Abingdon, 1979). The Church of the United Brethren and the Evangelical Association merged in 1948 to form the Evangelical United Brethren Church; in 1968 the EUB Church merged with the Methodist Church to form the United Methodist Church.

in the middle colonies. He was friends with Asbury and participated in Asbury's ordination at the Christmas Conference. By 1774 he led an association of pastors promoting holiness and revival, and was organizing laity into class meetings.

Martin Boehm was a Mennonite farmer and lay preacher who in 1767 experienced a conversion while plowing his field. Later that year, Boehm was preaching at a "Great Meeting" in Isaac Long's barn in Pennsylvania. Otterbein attended, and at the end of the sermon embraced Boehm with the words "Wir sind Bruder" ("we are bretheren"). Eventually their friendship led to a collaborative relationship. They began to license other preachers, and formally organized the Church of the United Brethren as a new denomination in 1800. Both were elected bishops.

The other German-speaking movement was begun by a Lutheran brick-maker, Jacob Albright (1759–1808). After his conversion in 1790 he joined the Methodist Episcopal Church and later was given a license to preach. But he believed God was calling him to focus on German-speaking Americans. He began forming class meetings and authorizing others to preach. He held his first preachers conference in 1803, and in 1807 the group formally organized as "The Newly Formed Methodist Conference," with Albright as bishop. In 1816, the name was changed to the Evangelical Association.

THE SPREAD OF METHODISM[3]

Methodism thrived in post-revolutionary America. The hierarchical culture of rank and deference that had dominated colonial American society came under populist assault, as more and more everyday people saw themselves as just as worthy of respect as their social betters. Methodist and Baptist preachers challenged the clerical monopoly of formally educated elites, asserting the right of common people to heed the call of God to preach. They found support for their views in scripture, from

3. The story of Methodists, Baptists, and others in post-revolutionary America is told in the influential book by Nathan Hatch, *The Democratization of American Christianity* (New Haven: Yale University Press, 1989). Important studies of early Methodism include John H. Wigger, *Taking Heaven By Storm: Methodism and the Rise of Popular Christianity* (New York: Oxford University Press, 1998); Dee E. Andrew, *The Methodists and Revolutionary America, 1960–1800* (Princeton: Princeton University Press, 2000); and A. Gregory Schneider, *The Way of the Cross Leads Home* (Bloomington: Indiana University Press, 1993).

Jesus' own beginning as a carpenter's son to the common origins of most of the disciples. They were, in short, more egalitarian, democratic, and individualistic.

While traditional society emphasized property, wealth, and family name, the Methodists honored the circuit rider who had no property and often no family. Moreover, the preaching of the circuit rider challenged each individual to make his or her own commitment to Jesus Christ. This called upon women to take initiative, and often to publically respond and testify, in contradiction of cultural expectations of female passivity and silence in public.

Methodism was both well-organized and highly experiential. Preachers were annually appointed to their circuits by Bishop Asbury at conference. The Methodist Episcopal Church was organized by annual conferences, quarterly meetings, local churches, and class meetings. As a missional movement, it spread by preachers organizing classes, who would then come together as new local churches. As America moved west, Methodism with its itinerating preachers and lay-led classes was ideally suited to move with it. This missional polity and the spiritual discipline linked to the weekly class meetings was central to early Methodist identity.

The experiential side was seen not only in much of the preaching, but in the significance of dreams and visions for personal spirituality. The quarterly meetings in particular combined fervent preaching and exhortation with the intense mourning of those under conviction of sin, as well as shouting and falling down under the power of the Spirit. Because ordained clergy were present, the meeting concluded with the Lord's Supper, which was itself often an occasion for the experience of God's presence.[4] In short, early Methodism was permeated by a radical supernaturalism in which the presence and power of God was experienced with transformative effect.

Quarterly meetings were among the precursors of the camp meetings.[5] Originally an interdenominational gathering, camp meetings were

4. See Lester Ruth, *A Little Heaven Below: Worship at Early Methodist Quarterly Meetings* (Nashville: Abingdon, 2000).

5. On camp meetings see John B. Boles, *The Great Revival* (Lexington: University of Kentucky Press, 1972); and Charles A. Johnson, *The Frontier Camp Meeting* (Dallas: SMU Press, 1955). Baptist revivalism, the "Great Meetings" of the German-Americans, and especially the "Holy Fairs" of Scottish Presbyterians were other precursers to camp meetings. On the latter, see Leigh Eric Schmidt, *Holy Fairs: Scottish Communion and*

embraced by Bishop Asbury and became virtually a Methodist practice. The earlier ones were every bit as exuberant as the quarterly meetings, and later ones still retained the experiential impact of powerful preaching.

It was Francis Asbury that supervised and directed this increasingly complex missionary enterprise. Though episcopal leadership was contrary to the democratic tendencies of early America, Asbury was no ordinary bishop. He received the same pay as his preachers, and traveled greater distances. Still, Methodism could also produce persons like Lorenzo Dow, who operated largely outside the official organization but were highly influential as passionate preachers of the Wesleyan message.

DIVERSIFICATION AND SCHISM

While many Americans, including Methodists, prospered in the east, others began to seek opportunity by moving west. By 1860 American territory stretched from the Atlantic to the Pacific, and westward migration had brought large numbers of settlers past the Mississippi River. Canals, steamships, and railroads knit the widely spread population centers more closely together. And, while many early Methodists had opposed slavery and believed it was dying out, the invention of the cotton gin had made slavery profitable. Slavery spread across the South to the Mississippi and beyond and became deeply imbedded in southern culture; northern dependence on southern cotton brought increased acceptable there as well.

Early Methodism proved quite adept at adopting practices and forms of popular culture for missional purposes. Yet at the same time, it found it more difficult to discern how culture could also shape and even compromise mission.

As Methodism gained larger numbers of adherents, and became increasingly middle class in its composition, it faced inevitable pressure to abandon its countercultural features and accommodate to cultural norms. This led to conflict within the Methodist Episcopal Church, as many resisted what they saw as the abandonment of Methodist essen-

---

American Revivals in the Early Modern Period (Princeton: Princeton University Press, 1989).

tials. There were four overlapping areas of conflict, each leading to factionalism and schism.

The first was racism and discrimination. While assumptions of white superiority were certainly made in reference to Native Americans, Mexicans, and others, the focus in Methodism was on relations between whites and African Americans. A sizable proportion of Methodists consisted of African Americans, both slave and free, and in the early days there was at least more relative equality within Methodist gatherings than in the larger culture. But that began to change as whites resisted African Americans moving into leadership positions and began to segregate the seating in churches, placing African Americans in the rear or the balcony.

It was just such discrimination by whites that led to the founding of the first African American Methodist denominations, the African Union Church by Peter Spencer (1782–1843) in Delaware in 1813, and the African Methodist Episcopal Church by Richard Allen in 1816. Allen, a former slave, was a licensed Methodist preacher at an interracial church in Philadelphia when in 1792 white trustees tried to forcibly move African Americans from a section of the church. Led by Allen, many African Americans left and decided to build their own church, which was dedicated by Bishop Asbury in 1794. It was persistent attempts to hinder or control the new church that led Allen to leave the MEC in 1796, and later join with others who had similar stories of discrimination to form the new AME denomination.

More would follow. Around 1824 James Varick (1750–1827) and others formed the African Methodist Episcopal Zion Church in New York, a denomination that would include antislavery activists Frederick Douglas, Harriet Tubman, and Sojourner Truth. After the Civil War, the Colored Methodist Episcopal Church (now Christian Methodist Episcopal Church) would be formed by African Americans leaving the Methodist Episcopal Church, South. It should be noted that large numbers of African Americans remained within the Methodist Episcopal Church as well, many seeking to challenge racism from within.[6]

6. The standard account of African American Methodism is H. V. Richardson, *Dark Salvation: The Story of Methodism as it Developed Among Blacks in America* (Nashville: Abingdon Press, 1976). Recent studies focusing on the antebellum period include Sylvia R. Frey and Betty Wood, *Come Shouting to Zion* (Chapel Hill: University of North Carolina Press, 1998); and J. Gordon Melton, *A Will to Choose: The Origins of African American Methodism* (Lanham, MD: Rowman & Littlefield, 2007).

Racism—the assumption of white racial superiority—was characteristic of white culture in both the north and the south. Yet it was ob-
jectionable to some Methodists not only because it contradicted stated
American commitments to liberty and equality, but even more because
it was inconsistent with Wesleyan claims of God's universal love for all
and the moral imperatives of holiness of heart and life.

American democratic ideals fueled a second area of conflict around
denominational polity. Democratically inclined Methodists raised such
issues as whether the denomination should have bishops, appointments
of the itinerating preachers should be made by bishops or by the conferences, and laity should be represented in conference as well as the
preachers. The first schism over democratizing Methodism occurred in
1792, when James O'Kelly (1735–1826), not wanting to leave the area in
Virginia where he had a large following, challenged the practice of episcopal assignment of the preachers. Accusing Asbury of having British
rather than American sensibilities, O'Kelly argued for appointment by
vote of conference, and led a group of preachers out of the Methodist
Episcopal Church to form the Republican Methodist Church.[7] A
much more serious schism was in 1830, leading to the founding of the
Methodist Protestant Church, which abolished the episcopacy and gave
laity representation in its conferences.

The third and most momentous issue faced by the Methodist
Episcopal Church, as well as the nation as a whole, was slavery. The MEC
originally had taken a firm antislavery stance, and some slave owners,
like the preacher Freeborn Garretson (1752–1827) freed their slaves
when they were converted. But southern pressure led the denomination
to modify and then abandon that position, even ultimately refusing to
call slavery an evil. While some southern Methodists sought to encourage
more humane treatment of slaves (and others ignored even that admo-
nition), in the south there was no significant opposition to slavery itself.
Northern and western church leaders like Nathan Bangs (1778–1862)
and Peter Cartwright[8] (1785–1872), while personally opposed to slavery,
sought to maintain unity by marginalizing the more radical calls for un-

7. The Republican Methodist Church soon became known as the Christian Church
or Christian Connection. It merged with the Congregational Church in 1931, and
through further mergers eventually formed part of the United Church of Christ.

8. On Cartwright see Robert Bray *Peter Cartwright, Legendary Frontier Preacher*
(Champaign: University of Illinois Press, 2005).

compromising opposition to slavery. Church leaders feared that to state their opposition to slavery would simply lead to their being barred from reaching out to the slaves with the gospel. In the end the denomination split over slavery, with the Methodist Episcopal Church, South forming 1845. It was a precursor to what would happen to the nation as a whole in 1860.

One of the leading abolitionists was New England Methodist preacher Orange Scott (1800–1847). Scott, who had risen to the position of Presiding Elder, had a crisis of conscience over slavery in 1833. Arguing that slavery was sin, and thus incompatible with a Wesleyan commitment to holiness, he persuaded the majority of the New England preachers to oppose slavery. Defeated in 1836 in his attempt to get the General Conference to take a stand against slavery, he was branded an anarchist and removed as presiding elder. After continuing the struggle for several more years, he finally left in 1842 to form the Wesleyan Methodist Church.[9]

THE HOLINESS MOVEMENT[10]

The Wesleyan Methodists were part of the Holiness movement that had emerged in the 1830s. This was the fourth issue faced by Methodism, though major conflict would not occur until the latter half of the nineteenth century. The Holiness movement emphasized Wesley's teaching of Christian perfection or entire sanctification as a second transformative experience following conversion, and immediately available to all Christians through consecration of one's life to God and faith in God's promise of sanctification in scripture.

Wesleyan Methodists sought to live out the full implications of holiness teaching, and no more so than in upstate New York. There they were at the center of widespread, radical commitment to holiness that involved churches from many denominations. They believed as persons became entirely sanctified it would be reflected in their politics, leading to the abolition of slavery and other evils. They also sought to establish pure, egalitarian holiness churches, devoid of all hierarchies of privilege, whether due to race, class, gender, or ecclesiastical authority. Much of

9. See chapter 7 of Donald W. Dayton, *Discovering an Evangelical Heritage* (New York: Harper & Row, 1976).

10. The standard history of the Holiness movement is Melvin E. Dieter, *The Holiness Revival of the Nineteenth Century*, 2nd ed. (Lanham, MD: Scarecrow, 1996).

the energy behind the early movement for women's rights came from this region.[11]

The leading theologian of the Holiness movement was Phoebe Palmer in New York City. Her sister, Sarah Lankford (1806–1896), had experienced entire sanctification in 1835. She then moved two ladies prayer meetings from their respective Methodist Episcopal churches to her home, and renamed the combined group the Tuesday Meeting for the Promotion of Holiness. In 1837 Phoebe Palmer experienced entire sanctification, and began presiding over the Tuesday Meeting in 1840, now open to men and held in the parlor of her home. Under Palmer's leadership the movement spread through periodicals, books, revivals, and the proliferation of Tuesday meetings in cities across the country and around the world. Her "altar theology" of consecration, faith, and testimony became the dominant teaching of the Holiness movement.

Although Palmer avoided political issues at the Tuesday meetings, she was a tireless evangelist and actively sought to provide clothes, food, and medical care for the poor. She was also a strong advocate for women's ministry, arguing both men and women were equally baptized with the Holy Spirit and equally called to proclaim the gospel. By the late 1850s she was also equating entire sanctification with the baptism of the Holy Spirit, recovering and mainstreaming the way the terms were used by John Fletcher and many early Methodists on both sides of the Atlantic.

Wesleyan ideas of holiness also took root in denominations outside Methodism. One influential strand of holiness teaching was the Oberlin Perfectionism of Charles G. Finney (1782–1875) and Asa Mahon (1799–1889). Finney[12] was of Presbyterian background. He began a ministry in upstate New York that led to his becoming the leading mass evangelist in America. Finney's controversial "new measures," including a colloquial style of preaching, altar calls, the use of a mourners' bench, and a call for a decision on the part of the hearer, would become standard practices in revivalism. Notably he also strongly encouraged women as well as men to pray and speak in public.

Finney's commitment to holiness as a second work of grace began while he was teaching at Oberlin College. Like Palmer, Finney took em-

---

11. See Douglas M. Strong, *Perfectionist Politics* (Syracuse: Syracuse University Press, 2000).

12. On Finney see Charles E. Hambrick-Stowe, *Charles G. Finney and the Spirit of American Evangelicalism* (Grand Rapids: Eerdmans, 1996).

phases common in frontier camp meetings and recast them for a more middle-class, urban audience. But he was more radical than Palmer on many social issues. He actually called for the abolition of slavery, established or supported churches that did not segregate seating by class, gender, or even race, and was a sharp critic of common business practices that contradicted Christian love. Many of his followers were even more radical on these issues than he was.

While Oberlin Perfectionism had a huge impact on antebellum Christianity in the north, it was the Higher Life movement that had a more enduring influence. Key figures were Presbyterian William Boardman (1810–1826) and a husband and wife team from the Quaker tradition, Robert Pearsall Smith (1827–1899) and Hannah Whitall Smith (1822–1911). Boardman's *The Christian Higher Life* was widely read and reprinted throughout the nineteenth century and was probably the single most important influence in making Wesleyan views on sanctification acceptable to non-Methodist audiences. Hannah Whitall Smith's *The Christian Secret of a Happy Life* became and remains a classic of holiness spirituality. While Phoebe Palmer and her husband Walter spoke to Methodist audiences in England, Boardman, the Smiths, Asa Mahon, and others brought the holiness message to non-Methodists. The Keswick Conventions were held to promote an English version of higher life theology, and later in the century the Keswick movement would in turn cross back over the Atlantic and spread through North America.

In the last decade before the Civil War tensions between holiness advocates and a more genteel form of Methodism were increasingly visible. This was nowhere more evident than in the upstate New York region that had once produced radical holiness churches and Finneyite revivals. B. T. Roberts was deeply concerned that the Methodist Episcopal Church there had turned away from a tradition of camp meetings, class meetings, scriptural holiness, and forthright opposition to slavery, and accommodated instead to fashionable lifestyles, secret societies, and other trappings of middle class propriety. In particular, he objected to the prevailing practice of renting pews, which gave wealthy members prominence and relegated the poor to the back of the church. His unwavering commitment to evangelism, holiness, and the poor resulted in his expulsion from the MEC, and the founding of the Free Methodist Church.

Roberts, like Phoebe Palmer, was a strong advocate of women preaching (though the Free Methodists would not heed his advice to ordain women until after his death). Yet some have argued that, in general, Palmer made the Holiness movement acceptable to increasingly middle-class Methodists while Roberts proclaimed a more radical version of holiness that challenged middle class assumptions. While there is some truth to this observation, it should not obscure the way Palmer and Roberts, like many others, all felt a radical claim of holiness on their lives, and all sought to work out its implications, leading them all in various ways to challenge many of the cultural assumptions of their day.

AMERICAN METHODISM

METHODIST EPISCOPAL CHURCH (1784)
Thomas Coke
Francis Asbury

Republican Methodist
Church (1792)
James O'Kelly

UNITED BRETHREN
IN CHRIST (1800)
Philip W. Otterbein
Martin Boehm

AFRICAN UNION CHURCH (1813)
Peter Spencer

EVANGELICAL
ASSOCIATION (1807)
Jacob Albright

AFRICAN METHODIST EPISCOPAL
CHURCH (1816)
Richard Allen

AFRICAN METHODIST EPISCOPAL
ZION CHURCH (1821)
James Varick

METHODIST PROTESTANT
CHURCH (1830)

First Colored Methodist
Protestant Church (1850)

WESLEYAN METHODIST
CHURCH (1843)
Orange Scott
Luther Lee

METHODIST
EPISCOPAL
CHURCH,
SOUTH (1844)

METHODIST
EPISCOPAL
CHURCH

UNION AMERICAN
METHODIST
EPISCOPAL
CHURCH (1865)

FREE METHODIST
CHURCH (1860)
B. T. Roberts

AFRICAN UNION FIRST
COLORED METHODIST
PROTESTANT CHURCH
(1866)

CHURCH OF THE
NAZARENE (1895-1908)
Phineas Bresee

COLORED METHODIST
EPISCOPAL CHURCH (1870)
William Henry Miles

PILGRIM HOLINESS
CHURCH (1897)
Seth Cook Rees

METHODIST CHURCH (1939)

EVANGELICAL
BRETHREN
CHURCH (1946)

CHRISTIAN METHODIST
EPISCOPAL CHURCH (1956)

WESLEYAN CHURCH
(1968)

UNITED METHODIST CHURCH (1968)

Hal Knight, 2008

62

5

Where Have All the Asburys Gone?

Francis Asbury and Leadership in the Wesleyan, Holiness, and Pentecostal Traditions

JOHN H. WIGGER

O N A PERFECT FALL day in October 1924, "with not a fleck of cloud in the sky," a vast crowd of Washington dignitaries converged at the corner of Sixteenth and Mount Pleasant Streets. They had come to dedicate a larger than life bronze statue of Francis Asbury on horseback. Amid cries of "Hear! Hear!" and vigorous applause, President Calvin Coolidge declared that Asbury had laid "the foundation of a religious civilization," by which "our country has enjoyed greater blessings of liberty and prosperity than were ever before the lot of man." For the monument builders, Asbury symbolized not only Methodism, but American Protestantism writ large. They hoped that his image would stand as a symbol of the church's continuing role in American society. In the late nineteenth century most Protestants had taken it for granted that America was a Christian nation and that the advance of the nation was closely tied to that of the church. Bishop Hamline echoed this sentiment at the monument dedication, declaring, "Asbury must be called great, because he laid the foundation of the great Christian empire, of the increase of whose ministry and peace there shall be no end."[1]

---

1. H. K. Carroll, ed., *The Francis Asbury Monument in the National Capital* (New York: Methodist Book Concern, 1925) 31, 33. Portions of this chapter appear in *American Saint: Francis Asbury and the Methodists* (2009) and are used with Oxford University Press's permission.

Yet by the 1920s Hamline's confidence was not universally shared even within the church. By that time many American Protestants found themselves increasingly caught between new "scientific" ways of thinking on the one hand and emerging Fundamentalism on the other. The Scopes monkey trial took place in Dayton, Tennessee, the summer after the Asbury monument dedication. This perhaps explains why Methodist leaders and scholars of the early and mid-twentieth century tried so hard to depict Asbury as thoroughly rational and patriotic, the kind of person who would have felt perfectly at home in modern America. Even William Warren Sweet, the University of Chicago professor who did more than anyone to bring to light Methodist sources in the first half of the twentieth century, tended to depict Asbury as the patron saint of dispassionate rationalism and decorum. The end result was to obscure much of what made Asbury such an effective and important leader.[2]

FROM METALWORKING TO MINISTRY

Francis Asbury was born in August 1745 and grew up on the outskirts of Birmingham, England, the metalworking center of England's early industrial revolution. Asbury's father, Joseph, was a farm laborer and gardener, employed by two local wealthy families. Despite limited resources, Asbury's parents were determined that their son would receive a good education. They sent him to the only school in the area, a charity school at Sneal's Green, about a quarter mile from the family's cottage. But the schoolmaster's severity filled Asbury "with such horrible dread, that with me anything was preferable to going to school." At about age thirteen Asbury left school and soon entered an apprenticeship to a local metalworker. He continued in his apprenticeship until about age twenty-one, when he left to become a full-time Methodist preacher. As a metalworker's apprentice and the son of a gardener, Asbury understood the lives of working people. This later enabled him to establish a close bond with American Methodists, the vast majority of whom came from the lower and middle ranks of society. The bond was particularly strong between Asbury and the American Methodist preachers, almost all of

2. George Marsden, *Fundamentalism and American Culture*, 2nd ed. (New York: Oxford University Press, 2006) 11–21; David C. Lindberg and Ronald L. Numbers, eds., *When Science and Christianity Meet* (Chicago: University of Chicago Press, 2003). For an example of Sweet depicting Asbury as devoted to order, see William Warren Sweet, *Methodism in American History* (New York: Methodist Book Concern, 1933) 159.

whom had been farmers and artisans before turning to preaching, and almost none of whom attended college or came from families of more than moderate wealth. The formal education of most was limited to a few years of common school. They accepted Asbury so thoroughly because he was one of them.[3]

The death of Asbury's sister Sarah in May 1749 at the age of six was a severe blow to his mother, Elizabeth. According to Asbury, his mother sank "into a deep distress at the loss of a darling child, from which she was not relieved for many years." The tragedy of Sarah's death drove Elizabeth to search for deeper spiritual meaning in life. Asbury's religious convictions seem to have grown along with his mother's. As his spiritual curiosity increased, Elizabeth directed him to a Methodist meeting at Wednesbury, a nearby village. Asbury was impressed by the zeal of the preachers and their listeners, and after an intense search for the assurance of salvation he experienced conversion at about age fifteen. In its basic outline, his conversion was typically evangelical. It would have been thoroughly recognizable to all early Methodists, who had themselves passed through a similar set of experiences. This provided a crucial bond between Asbury and other early Methodists, both in England and America. Asbury began circuit preaching in England at about age twenty-one, and came to America to preach in 1771 at age twenty-six. In 1784 he was elected a bishop of the Methodist Episcopal Church, a position he held until his death in 1816.[4]

---

3. Francis Asbury, *The Journal and Letters of Francis Asbury*, ed. Elmer T. Clark, J. Manning Potts and Jacob S. Payton, 3 vols. (London: Epworth Press; Nashville: Abingdon, 1958) 1:721 (Hereafter *JLFA*). On the early itinerant preachers in America, see John Wigger, *Taking Heaven by Storm: Methodism and the Rise of Popular Christianity in America* (New York: Oxford University Press, 1998; paperback, University of Illinois Press, 2001) 48–79. Previous biographies of Asbury include: Darius L. Salter, *America's Bishop: The Life of Francis Asbury* (Nappanee, IN: Evangel, 2003); L. C. Rudolph, *Francis Asbury* (Nashville: Abingdon, 1966); Ezra Squier Tipple, *Francis Asbury: The Prophet of the Long Road* (New York: Methodist Book Concern, 1916); Frederick W. Briggs, *Bishop Asbury: A Biographical Study For Christian Workers* (London: Wesleyan Conference Office, 1874). On the Asbury family, see David J. A. Hallam, *Eliza Asbury: Her Cottage and Her Son* (Studley, Warwickshire: Brewin, 2003). On the school at Sneal's Green, see George Griffith, *The Free Schools and Endowments of Staffordshire* (London: Whittaker, 1860) 429–31.

4. *JLFA*, 1:720

A DIFFERENT KIND OF LEADER

During Asbury's forty-five year career in America he and the Methodists largely succeeded in filling the religious void created by the American Revolution. The leading churches of colonial America, the Congregationalists in New England and the Anglicans in the South, largely failed to keep up with American expansion after the Revolution. Across rural America it was the Methodists, and to a lesser extent the Baptists and Presbyterians, who took religion to the people. In the process America became a more religious place than it had been before the war.

Yet Asbury did not build the foundation for this success in ways that we might expect. He was not a great communicator or an intellectual. He never wrote a book and his journals are not exactly a riveting read. His sermons were often disjointed and hard to follow and he rarely dominated the floor at annual and general conferences. Nathan Bangs first heard Asbury preach in June 1804. "His preaching was quite discursive, if not disconnected, a fact attributed to his many cares and unintermitted travels, which admitted of little or no study . . . He slid from one subject to another without system."[5] This is more or less what everyone said about Asbury's preaching. In short, he was not the sort of intellectual or colorful public figure that we are often drawn to.

All the same, Asbury deeply influenced the development of American Methodism, and by extension the Wesleyan, Holiness, and Pentecostal traditions, and indeed much of America's evangelical religious culture. He did this through his piety, transparency, cultural sensitivity, and ability to organize.

Asbury's piety ran deep, changing little during his forty-five years in America. He usually rose at 4:00 or 5:00 a.m. to pray for an hour in the stillness before dawn. As an act of voluntary poverty he rode unimpressive horses (though he named them and treated them well) and used cheap saddles and riding gear. His clothes were generally neat, but also inexpensive and plain. Asbury gave away nearly all of the money that came his way, often to widows and others in distress that he met on the road. Once, according to Henry Boehm who traveled some 25,000 miles with Asbury from 1808 to 1813, he came across a widow in Ohio whose only cow was about to be sold to pay her debts. Determining that

5. Abel Stevens, *Life and Times of Nathan Bangs, D.D.* (New York: Carlton & Porter, 1863) 128.

"It must not be," Asbury gave what he had and collected enough from bystanders to satisfy the woman's obligations. This kind of charity won him a great deal of respect from nearly everyone who knew him.[6]

Voluntary poverty is nothing new in the history of the church, but Asbury maintained his commitment to a simple life even as Methodists became generally more prosperous.[7] During his career, membership in America increased from a few hundred to 200,000. By 1876 all branches of Methodism in the United States could count more than 38,000 itinerant and local preachers, more than 2.9 million members, and more than 2.2 million children enrolled in Sunday Schools. Growth in numbers brought new wealth. By 1860 American Methodists owned nearly twenty thousand buildings, almost 38 percent of all churches in the United States. Following Asbury's death, Methodists launched a sustained campaign to found colleges and universities, opening more than two hundred schools and colleges between 1830 and 1860. Methodists were also leaders in popular publishing. All of this brought political clout, particularly in new western states like Ohio, and a comfortable sense of middle-class respectability.[8]

6. Henry Boehm, *Reminiscences, Historical and Biographical, of Sixty-Four Years in the Ministry* (New York: Carlton & Porter, 1866) 448.

7. On voluntary poverty and the church in medieval Europe, see Lester K. Little, *Religious Poverty and the Profit Economy in Medieval Europe* (Ithaca, NY: Cornell University Press, 1978).

8. Wigger, *Taking Heaven*, 175–80; Matthew Simpson, *Cyclopedia of American Methodism* (Philadelphia: Louis H. Everts, 1880) 586–607; John Wigger, "Methodismus/ Methodisten: II. Kirchengeschichtlich, 3. Nordamerika," in *Religion in Geschichte und Gegenwart*, 4th ed., edited by Hans Dieter Betz et al., vol. 5, (Tübingen: Mohr/Siebeck, 2001); John Wigger, "Ohio Gospel: Methodism in Early Ohio," in *The Center of a Great Empire: The Ohio Country in the Early Republic*, ed. Andrew R. L. Cayton and Stuart Hobbs (Athens: Ohio University Press, 2005) 62–80. On the rise of Methodism in the larger context of antebellum American history, see Dee E. Andrews, *The Methodists and Revolutionary America, 1760–1800: The Shaping of an Evangelical Culture* (Princeton: Princeton University Press, 2000); Catherine Brekus, *Strangers and Pilgrims: Female Preaching in America, 1740–1845* (Chapel Hill: University of North Carolina Press, 1998); Roger Finke and Rodney Stark, *The Churching of America, 1776–1990: Winners and Losers in Our Religious Economy* (New Brunswick, NJ: Rutgers University Press, 1992); Nathan O. Hatch, *The Democratization of American Christianity* (New Haven: Yale University Press, 1989); David Hempton, *Methodism: Empire of the Spirit* (New Haven: Yale University Press, 2005); Christine Leigh Heyrman, *Southern Cross: The Beginnings of the Bible Belt* (Chapel Hill: University of North Carolina Press, 1997); Cynthia Lynn Lyerly, *Methodism and the Southern Mind, 1770–1810* (New York: Oxford University Press, 1998); Mark A. Noll, *America's God: From Jonathan Edwards*

Asbury welcomed the salvation of so many lost souls, but spent much of his declining years worrying about the perils of prosperity. "Repectable! Ah! there is death in that word," he wrote in May 1809. "We are losing the spirit of missionaries and martyrs, we are slothful, we can only tell how fields were won, but by our brethren and sisters, not by us," he added in a letter to Lewis Myers, a presiding elder in the South Carolina Conference, in August 1810.[9]

Asbury's piety was influential, at least in part, because it was so evident to those around him. He lived one of the most transparent lives imaginable. For more than four decades Asbury essentially lived as a houseguest in thousands of homes across the land. This manner of life "exposed him, continually, to public or private observation and inspection, and subjected him to a constant and critical review; and that from day to day and from year to year," wrote Ezekiel Cooper, who knew Asbury for more than 30 years. He had no private life beyond the confines of his mind. He would not have retained the respect of the tens of thousands who saw him up close in intimate settings for long if his spiritual devotion had been halfhearted. In fact, the closer people got to Asbury the more they tended to respect him in this regard. This was the foundation on which all of his accomplishments were built. His spiritual devotion produced a "confidence in the uprightness of his intentions and wisdom of his plans, which gave him such a control over both preachers and people as enabled him to discharge the high trusts confided in him," observed Ezekiel Cooper.[10]

This transparency does much to explain Asbury's ability to draw others to him. It is remarkable how many people became life-long friends after a single evening spent in his company. He knew the hopes,

---

to *Abraham Lincoln* (New York: Oxford University Press, 2002); Russell E. Richey, *Early American Methodism* (Bloomington: Indiana University Press, 1991); Beth Barton Schweiger, *The Gospel Working Up: Progress and the Pulpit in Nineteenth-Century Virginia* (New York: Oxford University Press, 2000); William Sutton, *Journeymen for Jesus: Evangelical Artisans Confront Capitalism in Jacksonian Baltimore* (University Park: Pennsylvania State University Press, 1998). For a useful collection of essays on early American Methodism, see Nathan O. Hatch and John H. Wigger, eds., *Methodism and the Shaping of American Culture* (Nashville: Kingswood, 2001).

    9. *JLFA*, 2:602, 3:433.

    10. Ezekiel Cooper, *The Substance of a Funeral Discourse, Delivered at the Request of the Annual Conference, on Tuesday, the 23d of April, 1816, in St. George's Church, Philadelphia: on the Death of the Rev. Francis Asbury, Superintendent, or Senior Bishop, of the Methodist Episcopal Church* (Philadelphia: Pounder, 1819) 21, 25–26.

fears, and desires of his people as they confronted a profoundly changing world because he spent so much time in their company. People found him approachable and willing to listen to their concerns more than they found him full of inspiring ideas. "He was charitable, almost to excess, of the experience of others," remembered Nicholas Snethen.[11]

The third element of Asbury's leadership model was his cultural sensitivity. John Wesley and Asbury were alike in their ability to understand and adapt to popular culture. In his biography of Wesley, Henry Rack argues persuasively that Wesley was a "cultural middleman" between Methodists on the one hand and clergyman and educated gentlemen in England on the other.[12] In the same manner Asbury mediated between Wesley and ordinary Americans. Wesley and Asbury were both aware that the church was losing touch with great numbers of ordinary people, including industrial workers in England's expanding cities and rural migrants on America's growing geographical peripheries. This led Asbury to do things in America that he would not have done in England. He accepted the emotionalism of southern worship in the 1770s, promoted camp meetings in the early 1800s, and reluctantly acquiesced to southern Methodists holding slaves. This mediating impulse, transmitted from Wesley through Asbury, became a trademark of American Methodism.[13]

Nonetheless, Asbury did not accept American culture wholesale or without reservation. Shortly after his first trip to the South in the 1770s, he came to realize that slavery was a great moral evil, though he could see no workable solution to its presence in the church. The reality of Methodists holding slaves haunted Asbury for the last thirty years of his life. Furthermore, cultural adaptation is never a static thing, since both the church and the broader culture are always changing. Initially most Methodists agreed with Asbury that wealth was a snare. But as Methodists became generally more prosperous they lost their fear of

11. Nicholas Snethen, *A Discourse on the Death of the Rev. Francis Asbury, Late Bishop of the Methodist Episcopal Church in the United States* (Baltimore: Harrod, 1816) 4. The literature on the early industrial revolution in England is, of course, immense. On the forges and mills near Asbury's home, see D. Dilworth, *The Tame Mills of Staffordshire* (London: Pillimore, 1976) 40–52.

12. Henry Rack, *Reasonable Enthusiast: John Wesley and the Rise of Methodism* (London: Epworth, 1989) 352.

13. On American Methodism and slavery, see Donald G. Mathews's path breaking, *Slavery and Methodism: A Chapter in American Morality, 1780–1845* (Princeton: Princeton University Press, 1965).

creeping affluence. Taking note of the end of Thomas Jefferson's un-popular embargo on trade with Europe in April 1809, Asbury could not help but "fear much that these expected *good times* will injure us:—the prosperity of fools will destroy; therefore affliction may be best, and God may send it, for this is a favoured land: Lord save us from ruin as a peo-ple!" Unfortunately for Asbury, by this time fewer and fewer Methodists were sure that they wanted to be saved in this way.[14]

The fourth way that Asbury communicated his message was through his organization of the Methodist church. Asbury was a brilliant administrator who knew rural, commonplace America as well as anyone of his generation. He rode more than 130,000 miles on horseback and crossed the Appalachian Mountains some sixty times during his career in America. The endless conversations he had with preachers, members, and people he met on the road gave him a good feel for the church and the nation. The give and take of these exchanges provided him a broad perspective and allowed him to cultivate consensuses across the church. By the time the preachers met in conference he often needed to say little. "He knew . . . the art of governing, and seldom trusted to the naked force of authority. Indeed, the majesty of command, was almost wholly concealed, or suspended by the wonderful faculty, which belongs to this class of human geniuses, and which enables them to inspire their own disposition for action, into the breasts of others," wrote Nicholas Snethen. This assessment is all the more remarkable considering that Snethen, who observed Asbury at many conferences from 1794 to 1814, left the Methodist Episcopal Church for the Methodist Protestant Church be-cause he did not think the former was democratic enough. Asbury could be stubborn once his mind was made up, but his decisions were usually not capricious.[15]

While Methodists themselves are declining in membership in the United States today, other groups that derive from the Wesleyan heri-tage, including much of the Holiness movement and Pentecostalism, are thriving, as is evangelical culture in general, which Methodism did much to create. Pentecostalism remains one of the fastest growing religious traditions worldwide. Asbury did much to create the religious and cul-tural patterns behind this growth through his piety, transparency, cultur-al sensitivity, and ability to organize. While other religious leaders have

14. *JLFA*, 2:600.
15. Snethen, *Discourse on Asbury*, 6.

embodied some of these characteristics, few have combined them all to the extent that Asbury did. Why is this so? Anyone interested in vitality and renewal in the church would do well to ponder Asbury's legacy.

BIBLIOGRAPHY

Hatch, Nathan O. *The Democratization of American Christianity.* New Haven: Yale University Press, 1989.

Hempton, David. *Methodism: Empire of the Spirit.* New Haven: Yale University Press, 2005.

Wigger, John. *American Saint: Francis Asbury and the Methodists.* New York: Oxford University Press, 2009.

6

Richard Allen and the Making
of Early American Methodism

DENNIS C. DICKERSON

RICHARD ALLEN, THE FOUNDER and first elected and consecrated bishop of the African Methodist Episcopal Church, experienced Methodism in three stages during his long life between 1760 and 1831. Writing in his autobiography, an aging Allen proclaimed his allegiance to the Wesleyan way. "I could not be anything else but a Methodist," he declared, "as I was born and awakened under them."[1] As a convert in 1777 Allen matured as a Methodist in a period of evangelistic expansion. Moreover, he preached as an itinerant exhorter in the Middle Atlantic mostly to white audiences and became acquainted with Wesleyanism as a religious movement largely without structure or pretension. Settling in Philadelphia in 1786, almost two years after the crucial "Christmas" Conference in Baltimore, Allen encountered Methodism as different from what he knew at the time of his conversion in Delaware and during his travels as a circuit rider in New Jersey, Maryland, and Pennsylvania. He regretted that the Baltimore gathering marked "the beginning of the Episcopal Church amongst the Methodists." Clergy were elevated to the episcopacy and "were said to be entitled to the gown." These trappings of denominational development signaled to Allen that religion commenced a decline among Methodists starting with the "Christmas" Conference. The ugly result of this spiritual declension was the raw racism that he confronted at St. George Church in Philadelphia where he

1. Richard Allen, *The Life Experience and Gospel Labors of the Rt. Rev. Richard Allen* (Nashville: A.M.E. Sunday School Union/Legacy Publishing, 1990) 28.

and other African Americans, either in 1787 or in the early 1790s, were manhandled and forced to retreat into their already established Free African Society.

Hence, Allen moved into another phase of his Wesleyan experience. In dedicating a new edifice to house an African Methodist Episcopal congregation in 1794 and in launching a separate denomination bearing the same name in 1816 Allen raised another religious body that recaptured what he thought that Methodism had lost. As a result, "African Methodists in the United States became the preeminent American heirs to the Wesleyan movement. While majority white Methodists allowed invidious social distinctions to compromise their evangelical thrust and intrude upon their ecclesiastical practices, African Methodists maintained commitments to preach and practice religious and social equality, irrespective of societal pressures."[2] Therefore, Allen, ever the quintessential Methodist, developed within African Methodism what he remembered as essential to the religion that he drew from circuit riders on Delaware frontier. "The Methodists were the first people," he said, "that brought glad tidings to the colored people." They also were the same people with whom he toiled as itinerant preacher who seemingly transcended color and class as they testified to his homiletical proficiencies.[3] Seeking salvation and living piously was primary to these persons until their preachers and bishops took to the "gown."

CONVERSION AND MINISTRY

Born a slave in Philadelphia and sold with his parents and siblings into Delaware, Allen, as an adolescent, received the "glad tidings" of Methodist preachers and underwent a stirring spiritual conversion. Though seeming saved, several "old, experienced Christians" doubted the depth or authenticity of his salvation. Hence, Allen sought "the Lord afresh" through marathon prayers and devotions. Then, "all of a sudden my dungeon shook, my chains flew off, and glory to God, I cried. My soul was filled. I cried enough for me-the Saviour died." God had heard his prayers and now Allen was saved and his sins were "pardoned." This pentecostal process had antecedents in other Wesleyan conversions. One historian

2. Dennis C. Dickerson, *Religion, Race, and Region: Research Notes on A.M.E. Church History* (Nashville: A.M.E. Sunday School Union/Legacy Publishing, 1995) 13.

3. Allen, *Life Experience*, 19, 28.

noted, for example, that an English soldier, in recounting his conversion over three decades before Allen's religious awakening declared that "my chains fell off and my heart was free." This language from Charles Wesley's hymn "And Can It Be That I Should Gain" became standard terminology for Methodist converts. Allen's use of the phraseology showed that he indeed had become a Christian and a Methodist. Drawing his slave master, Stokeley Sturgis into the Methodist fold enabled Allen to purchase his freedom in 1783 to become an itinerant preacher.[4]

Allen traveled throughout the Middle Atlantic and interacted with countless Christians who acknowledged him as a fellow Methodist. He recalled that he met in New Jersey Benjamin Abbott, "that great and good apostle." Allen described him as "one of the greatest men that ever I was acquainted with. He seldom preached but what there were souls added to his labor. He was a man of as great faith as any that I ever saw." Allen added that Abbott "was a friend and father to me." He also preached near Radnor, Pennsylvania where whites insisted that he extend his stay so as to preach additional sermons. Allen observed that "many souls were awakened and cried unto the Lord to have mercy upon them." These easy interactions with Wesleyan whites, many of whom endorsed Methodist opposition to slavery, showed a religious body without distinctions of color and class and one devoted exclusively to salvation, spirituality, and piety.[5]

These behavioral norms seemed alien to white members at St. George, Philadelphia. Like their counterparts at the Baltimore General Conference, according to Allen, Methodist ministers and members increasingly recognized rank and hierarchal authority within an evolving denominational structure. With unusual suddenness the egalitarian status of blacks within Wesleyan circles changed to correlate with their degraded position in secular society. These racial realities invaded Methodism in the 1780s and 1790s and displaced the spiritual zeal of preachers in the 1770s who drew Allen into the Wesleyan movement. The religiosity that Allen remembered among the "old, experienced Christians" in

---

4. D. Bruce Hindmarsh, "'my chains fell off, my heart was free': Early Methodist Conversion Narrative in England," *Church History* 68 (1999) 910; See "And Can It Be That I Should Gain," *The African Methodist Episcopal Church Hymnal* (Nashville: A.M.E. Sunday School Union, 1984; 2000) 459. Allen, *Life Experience*, 15–17.

5. Allen, *Life Experience*, 17–19.

Delaware no longer defined contemporary American Methodism. To recapture what was lost Allen established African Methodism.

THE BEGINNING OF AFRICAN METHODISM

Although Bishop Francis Asbury dedicated and named Allen's church and affirmed it as a constituent part of the Philadelphia Methodist Conference, Allen's insistence upon Bethel's independence and autonomy precipitated several conflicts between him and successive pastors at St. George. After he secured in 1801 from the state supreme court an African Supplement to Bethel's charter and called a convention in 1816 to form the African Methodist Episcopal connection, Allen succeeded in launching an independent Wesleyan body. It was marked by strict adherence to the Methodist discipline, singing from Allen's own compilation of Wesleyan hymns, and openness to all in need of salvation. Allen recited in his memoir:

> Ye ministers that are called to preaching,
> Teachers and exhorters too,
> Awake! Behold your harvest wasting,
> Arise! There is no rest for you.

> To think upon that strict commandment
> That God has on his teachers laid
> The sinners' blood, who die unwarned,
> Shall fall upon their shepherd's head.[6]

Hence, African Methodism, in Allen's lifetime, spreading northward to New York, westward beyond the Alleghenies, southward to South Carolina, and daringly into Haiti, embodied what Asbury said of white and Methodists in 1796. He noted "the superficial state of religion among the white people who are called Methodists," but he declared, "if we had entered here to preach only to the Africans, we should probably have done better." Allen seemed to validate Asbury's observation.[7]

ALLEN'S WESLEYANISM

Allen, according to his understanding of the Methodist movement, emphasized to his followers three attributes that marked them as Wesleyan

6. Ibid., 76.

7. Quoted in Dickerson, *Religion, Race, and Region*, 13.

adherents. First, Allen drew a sharp line of demarcation between church and culture. He was deeply disillusioned with American Methodists because "they conform more to the world and the fashions thereof." He added that "the discipline is altered considerably from what it was. We would ask for the good old way, and desire to walk therein." He regretted "people who are heartily in love with this world; who can see no greater happiness than wealth or power upon earth." He observed that "the love of this world is a heavy weight upon the soul, which chains her down and prevents her flight towards heaven." Greater attention to charity, for example, "would loosen" ties to the world and help such persons in their "struggle to disengage" from the world. Such worldly sentiments, Allen believed, had damaged American Methodism. He intended for African Methodism to avoid these pitfalls.[8]

Second, Allen contended that the fruit of faith was charity. Whenever Christians shared their "substance or the produce of our labors towards the relief and support of the poor and needy" then "we improve our talents to the glory of God and the welfare of our immortal souls." Just as John Wesley's stand against slavery was a fruit of his faith, African Methodists and their benevolent white friends "have wrought a deliverance for many from more than Egyptian bondage." These Christians have helped toward the salvation of souls. They were like Jesus Christ, who while teaching and preaching, "never omitted one opportunity of doing good" and healing those "laboring under sickness and disorders."[9]

Third, Allen held that preaching a simple gospel validated through experiential religion was key to pleasing and knowing God. When his "dungeon shook" and his "chains flew off," Allen seemed sanctified through a second search for salvation. So strong was his spiritual transformation that he "was constrained to go from house to house, exhorting my old companions, and telling to all around what a dear Saviour I had found." Preaching a simple gospel, Allen contended, helped to produce these religious results. "I feel thankful that ever I heard a Methodist preach," said Allen. "We are beholden," he noted, "to the Methodists, under God, for the light of the Gospel we enjoy; for all other denominations preached so high flown that we were not able to comprehend their

---

8. Allen, *Life Experience*, 28, 82–83

9. Ibid., 75–77.

doctrine. Sure am I that reading sermons will never prove so beneficial to the colored people as spiritual or extempore preaching."[10]

I noted in another essay that "Allen was a quintessential Wesleyan. He was among the first generation of Americans, both black and white, whom Methodist circuit riders converted to Christianity. He imbibed their zeal for the gospel, their burden to save the lost, and their ubiquitous presence in various venues where they preached in churches, camp meetings, and the countryside to rich and poor, black and white, and free and slave. Methodist evangelism and egalitarianism both depended upon deep religiosity and spirituality. These Methodist characteristics became a standard by which Allen would judge future Wesleyan practices and assess their adherence to the Christian faith." Hence, Allen, in developing his own understanding of the Wesleyan movement, tried to preserve in African Methodism the timeless tenets of Christianity. He emphasized a suspicion of worldly entanglements, the fruits of faith pursued in charity and mercy toward the disadvantaged, and the primacy of experiential religion. Despite a slave background and the lack of formal education, Allen's Wesleyan vision seemed faithful to what Methodist founders envisaged for this "religion of the warm heart."[11]

---

10. Ibid., 13–14, 28.

11. Dennis C. Dickerson, *A Liberated Past: Explorations In A.M.E. Church History* (Nashville: A.M.E. Sunday School Union, 2003) 18–19.

7

The Eccentric Cosmopolite

Lorenzo Dow and Early Nineteenth-Century Methodism

DOUGLAS M. STRONG

ON AN AUGUST DAY in 1823, a young minister named David Marks sat on the platform behind the famous preacher, Lorenzo Dow (1777-1834). Dow spoke that day—as he often did—about the free will that God has given to every person to choose or reject righteousness and the dangers of believing in Calvinist predestination. As was his custom, Dow used humor throughout the sermon, which "excited considerable laughter in the assembly." The most hilarious moment occurred at the very climax of the discourse. "We are not to suppose," Dow exclaimed, "that God Almighty will bring men in by *irresistible* power, as I pull this man." At that instant, Dow seized the collar of Marks' coat, drawing him right up out of his seat. An uproarious howl burst forth from the congregation.

After the meeting, a rather disconcerted Marks came up to Dow and asked him "what his motive was in being thus eccentric." Marks thought that "the ministration of the word of God ought to be with much solemnity"; such frivolous actions, he believed, could arouse "a trifling spirit" in the hearers. Dow's response to the youthful preacher was straightforward:

> There is so much fatality [fatalism] in these little villages, that many sinners will not repent; and still they will cast the blame on God, saying they cannot do otherwise; therefore they must be convinced of their false doctrine which is leading them to

destruction. My object is to impress truth on their minds, in such a manner, and by such circumstances as are innocent, and yet will not permit them to forget it. And as to their laughter, I have nothing to do with it.

For two weeks that summer, Marks, a holiness-preaching Freewill Baptist itinerant, accompanied Dow as he traveled throughout central New York State. Dow often partnered with regionally-known revivalists such as Marks on his evangelistic tours. Marks' account of Dow's ministry provides us with insights into aspects of early nineteenth century Methodism that had important implications for the future direction of the Wesleyan movement in America.[1]

RATIONALISTIC SENTIMENTALIST

Dow's preaching took place during a time of transition in the understanding of how the human self acquires knowledge. More specifically, the form and content of his message indicate a reliance on both rationalistic and sentimental conceptions of perceiving religious truth. On the one hand, Dow's comments demonstrate an unacknowledged dependence on Lockean epistemology—couched, of course, in extremely simplified and colloquial language. In the nineteenth century, Enlightenment ideas were often popularly represented by a body of thought known as Common Sense Realism, a philosophy that, in its American form, was rather crudely adapted from its original Scottish expression.[2] According to this empiricist logic, information obtained by the senses produced a kind of mark or impression stamped on the self. Influenced by this line of thinking, Dow explained that his strange tactics were an intentional strategy "to impress truth on [the] minds" of his listeners "in such a manner" that they would never forget it. Dow created a mechanism in which sensory images were linked with rational discourse in order to teach

1. Marilla Marks, ed., *Memoirs of the Life of David Marks, Minister of the Gospel* (Dover, NH: Free-Will Baptist Publishing Establishment, 1846) 110–12.

2. On the pervasiveness of common sense thought in antebellum religious discourse, see Sydney Ahlstrom, "The Scottish Philosophy and American Theology," *Church History* 24 (1955) 257–72; George Marsden, *The Evangelical Mind and the New School Presbyterian Experience* (New Haven: Yale University Press, 1970); Theodore Dwight Bozeman, *Protestants in an Age of Science: The Baconian Ideal and Antebellum American Religious Thought* (Chapel Hill: University of North Carolina Press, 1977); Mark Noll, "Common Sense Traditions and American Evangelical Thought," *American Quarterly* 37 (1985) 216–38.

a moral lesson—in this case, that salvation was only obtainable when people actively exercised their free will.[3]

On the other hand, Dow's preaching style and personal behavior also indicated a reliance on nonrational means of understanding and communicating religious truth. He often confided in dreams and visions,[4] encouraged dramatic displays of emotional religious ecstasy, and was noted for his uncanny ability to predict the future.[5] Marks related a typical incident regarding Dow's apparent clairvoyance. One morning, Marks arrived unannounced at Dow's lodging. To Marks' great surprise, the innkeeper had been told by Dow to prepare breakfast for him and to set a place for him at the table, even though Marks "had not intimated to any one the slightest intention of coming to the place at th[at] hour."[6] On one level, such conduct can be viewed simply as a carryover of pre-critical, pre-scientific supernaturalism; Dow was unapologetic about his implicit trust in the "unscrutible will of Providence."[7] But on a deeper level, Dow's attention to the ego and his deliberate cultivation of intuitive experiences can be viewed as intimations of an emerging Romantic sentimentality. Dow would have agreed with Nathaniel Hawthorne that "deep meaning" is often communicated to a person's "sensibilities," while "evading the analysis of the mind."[8]

Dow combined the rational with the nonrational, the temporal with the eternal. Using one of his typically empirical statements, for example, he was convinced of an idea because his "mind was impressed"; but the impression that he received was stamped on his mind during a supernatural visitation—"a dream of the night." In another instance of seemingly conflicted images, he often declared that the "power of God was

3. Marks, ed., *Memoirs*, 111n; Dow regularly spoke about thoughts that were "impressed" or "imprinted on the mind." See Lorenzo Dow, *History of Cosmopolite: or the Writings of Rev. Lorenzo Dow: Containing His Experiences and Travels, in Europe and America, up to near His Fiftieth Year. Also, His Polemic Writings. To Which is Added, The "Journey of Life,"* by Peggy Dow, Revised and Corrected with Notes, 6th ed. (Philadelphia: Rulison, 1855) 9, 10, 19, 21, 23, 36, 44–45, 47, 64, 84, 90, 91, 93, 104, 105, 106, 109, 129, 232. The first edition of Dow's published journal appeared in 1804.

4. Dow, *History of Cosmopolite*, 9, 10, 15, 18, 23, 24, 25, 27–28, 40, 55, 75, 79, 80, 98–99, 157, 205, 208, 247, 314; Charles Coleman Sellers, *Lorenzo Dow: The Bearer of the Word* (New York: Minton, Balch, 1928) 55–56, 223–24.

5. Dow, *History of Cosmopolite*, 16, 45, 50, 52, 103, 111, 126, 153, 170, 306, 313.

6. Marks, ed., *Memoirs*, 111.

7. Dow, *History of Cosmopolite*, 117, 121, 126, 136, 145, 183.

8. Ibid., 126.

sensibly present."[9] Dow's pattern of uniting the logical with the mysterious was characteristic of other revivalists during the antebellum period. Charles Finney's preaching was known for its lawyerly reasoning, yet he encouraged sinners to model their spiritual lives after his own rather sentimental conversion experience during which he felt "the impression" of the Holy Spirit, "like a wave of electricity."[10] Likewise, Phoebe Palmer developed a propositional, almost contractual understanding of holiness while at the same time fostering the perception that intense, God-given emotions often accompanied the attainment of entire sanctification.[11]

ECCENTRIC DEMOCRATIZER

Dow's unusual appearance, unconventional methods, and the amazing geographic breadth of his itinerancy assured him a wide notoriety. Marks summarized, in an understated way, that Dow's "manner of preaching was very peculiar [and] its character is generally known."[12] Indeed, the one commonly known trait of Lorenzo Dow—both in the early nineteenth century and in the early twenty-first century—is that his "preaching was very peculiar." Although dubbed "Crazy Dow" both then and now, historians also know that Dow was a herald of Christian democratization.[13]

The characterization of Dow as an idiosyncratic religious democratizer was a perception that he consciously cultivated. He proudly identified himself, for instance, with a rather unique label: "the eccentric cosmopolite." This represents Dow's two-fold sense of vocation. He saw himself both as an eccentric—an independent anti-establishmentarian, and as a religious cosmopolitan—a messenger called by God to extend the universal imperative of the gospel.[14] These dual aspects of Dow's self-conception were also characteristic of many American Methodists,

9. Ibid., 89, 96, 104, 106.

10. Charles G. Finney, *Memoirs of Rev. Charles G. Finney. Written by Himself* (New York: Barnes, 1876) 20.

11. Harold E. Raser, *Phoebe Palmer: Her Life and Thought* (Lewiston, NY: Edwin Mellen, 1987) 159, 266.

12. Marks, *Memoirs*, 110.

13. Dow, *History of Cosmopolite*, 44, 46, 50, 60, 86, 117, 119, 259; Nathan O. Hatch, *The Democratization of American Christianity* (New Haven: Yale University Press, 1989) 36–40, 130–33.

14. Dow, *History of Cosmopolite*, 304, 314.

including later Holiness evangelists, and are a useful way to comprehend the Wesleyan/Holiness movement in the nineteenth century.

The concept of "eccentricity" literally refers to something that is off-center, someone who deviates from the established pattern of accepted conduct. An accusation of being "eccentric" was considered a badge of honor among those people in the early republic who saw themselves as challengers of existing structures, and as a way of distinguishing oneself from the undemocratic elites that exercised power in both church and state. The eccentric self-understanding was also related to the means by which religious knowledge was communicated. When Marks asked Dow "what his motive was in being . . . eccentric," Dow replied that he was simply using an effective way to impart the gospel. Dow promoted the public portrayal of himself as a "crazy" preacher because such a depiction "brought many out to the different meetings."[15]

People on the frontier relished the designation of being "eccentric." Compared to the "staid" services of the Presbyterians and Congregationalists, for example, the early revivals and camp meetings of the Methodists were noted for their "eccentricities" and their "vehemence of manners." Cary Allen, the Methodist-converted leader of the Hampden-Sydney College revival, the event that is often cited as the beginning of the second Great Awakening, was said to have exhibited a "sanctified eccentricity." Numerous other preachers—some well-known, such as Peter Cartwright, and many others who had only local reputations—were renowned for their idiosyncrasies.[16] Likewise, an account of wilderness exploits that was to become nationally famous was titled the *Sketches and Eccentricities of Col. David Crockett*.[17] In such company, Lorenzo Dow can rightfully be interpreted as a type of Davy Crockett, a religious counterpart to the frontier myth of a larger-than-life "common man."

15. Marks, *Memoirs*, 111; Dow, 60.

16. George Peck, *Early Methodism within the Bounds of the Old Genesee Conference from 1788 to 1828; or, The First Forty Years of Wesleyan Evangelism in Northern Pennsylvania, Central and Western New York, and Canada* (New York: Carlton & Porter, 1860) 180, 185, 265, 276, 279, 394, 420, 443, 462; William Henry Foote, *Sketches of Virginia, Historical and Biographical, Second Series* (Philadelphia: Lippincott, 1855) 223–40; Sellers, *Lorenzo Dow*, 90; Philemon H. Fowler, *Historical Sketch of Presbyterianism within the Bounds of the Synod of Central New York* (Utica, NY: Curtiss and Childs, 1877).

17. [Matthew St. Clair Clarke], *Sketches and Eccentricities of Col. David Crockett, of West Tennessee* (New York: J. & J. Harper, 1833).

These eccentrics were deliberately contrasting themselves to the polished mores of genteel culture—values that represented the privileges available only to a powerful upper class. They believed that liberty could exist only among citizens who lived in relative equality, unfettered by arbitrary authority either in the church or the state. Institutional hierarchies, deference expected to certain positions due to prescribed status, and the securing of one's livelihood through financial speculation or the labor of someone else, all produced unfair advantage of one person over another. These things interjected someone or something between individuals and their natural right to personal liberty. What was demanded instead was equal opportunity for all.

Dow and his fellow eccentrics were attempting to apply democratic principles to ecclesiastical and civil structures that were perceived as undemocratic. Predestinarian doctrine, unrestrained denominational hierarchies, antirepublican government, and slavery were all seen as evidences of the imposition of arbitrary human authority upon the freedom of the individual's conscience.[18] Ideally, Dow believed, the Christian religion ought to be a model of liberty—an ally of American democracy, for both affirmed the natural rights of all persons, both asserted the benefits of free choice, and both desired the construction of a godly, democratic society. Only a corruption from its original ideals had made Christianity undemocratic.[19]

As the nineteenth century progressed, some Americans came to believe that an unrestricted entrepreneurial climate would provide the best setting for democratic equal opportunity. Dow, however, was worried that middle class consumerism could lead to a reliance on materialism and even to a new social stratification.[20] Indeed, at the same time that Dow

18. Herbert F. May, *The Enlightenment in America* (New York: Oxford University Press, 1976) 322–24, views enthusiastic evangelical religion as the opponent of Enlightenment rationalism. Hatch, throughout his *The Democratization of American Christianity*, makes the stronger case that the emphases of enthusiastic evangelicalism demonstrated a democratic popularization of Enlightenment principles.

19. Dow, *History of Cosmopolite*, 243, 262, 329, 437ff.; Sellers, *Lorenzo Dow*, 75, 108, 142, 222. See *The Union Herald* 6 (11 August 1841) 64; William Goodell, *The Democracy of Christianity; or An Analysis of the Bible and Its Doctrines, in Their Relation to the Principle of Democracy*, 2 vols. (New York: Cady and Burgess, 1852); Gerrit Smith, *Abstract of the Argument, on the Public Discussion of the Question, "Are the Christians of a Given Community the Church of Such Community?"* (Albany, NY: Green, 1847) 10; *The Friend of Man* 1 (23 June 1836) 1.

20. Dow, *History of Cosmopolite*, 100, 116, 303, 332.

was promoting democratic principles by uplifting plain folk eccentricity, institutional Methodism was attempting to become more "respectable." Methodist enthusiasm was so subdued by the late 1820s, for instance, that revival meetings were regularly described as "perfectly orderly."[21] As a sure sign of their acceptance, even Presbyterians began to cooperate with Methodists—first informally and then officially—receiving them by the 1840s as brethren who were equally "decent and in order."[22]

Dow reacted to these evidences of Methodist consolidation and *embourgeoisement* with disregard for denominational rulings and continuing nonconformity in his personal behavior. When Conference authorities denied him a license to preach, he preached anyway. As Methodists became more affluent and their manner of dress more refined, he kept wearing long hair, a long beard, and shabby clothes. Marks was convinced that Dow's odd appearance was not the result of careless slovenliness but, rather, "exhibited studied convenience . . . independent from the changeable fashions of this age of superfluities." As the Church became more middle class—accepting as valid the general society's status distinctions between lay and clergy, rich and poor, slave and free, male and female—Dow refused to submit to narrowly defined definitions of a person's appropriate sphere. Accordingly, he parted his hair in the middle—like a woman. He also urged women to preach, encouraged lay control of church government, denounced slavery, and affirmed the equality of all persons.[23] Many of these eccentricities became commonplace among Holiness folk a generation later.

One can see why Dow was so attracted to those Methodists in Britain who were interested in returning to "primitive" practices. In both Britain and in America, Dow represented an older vision of Methodism as an anti-establishment church devoted to the needs of the margin-

---

21. See James H. Hotchkin, *A History of the Purchase and Settlement of Western New York, and of the Rise, Progress, and Present State of the Presbyterian Church in That Section* (New York: Dodd, 1848) 322, 477, 545; Peck, 459, 466.

22. Presbyterians in New York State, for example, did not officially recognize Methodists until 1849, when the New York synods began exchanging fraternal delegates with the upstate Methodist conferences (Robert Hastings Nichols, *Presbyterianism in New York State* [Philadelphia: Westminster, 1963] 144), but informal relations occurred much earlier, especially on the local level. See Hotchkin, *History of the Purchase and Settlement*, 435; Peck, 364, 435.

23. Dow, *History of Cosmopolite*, 45, 101, 102, 124, 127, 264, 315, 343; Sellers, *Lorenzo Dow*, 56, 95.

alized.[24] It is in this way that he was most determinedly eccentric (or off-center), particularly in relation to a Methodism that was becoming economically and institutionally established. Bourgeois Methodism was uncomfortable with this visibly ragged symbol of its own ragged past.

COSMOPOLITAN EVANGELIST

Lorenzo was not only an "eccentric," however; he also considered himself (somewhat paradoxically) to be a "cosmopolite." The superficial meaning of the term is plain: Dow was a constant itinerant. Similar to his erstwhile nemesis, Francis Asbury, Dow journeyed from New England to Mississippi, up and down the East Coast and across the Appalachians, often several times a year. He also traveled to Britain on three occasions. In Marks' description of a typical two week period, Dow preached at least twelve times that are recorded, and on each occasion he spoke to congregations numbering between 1,500 and 6,000 people.[25]

Beyond the obvious referent, however, Dow's desire to be known as a cosmopolite suggests a set of values that were becoming common in post-Revolutionary American society. These values included openness to new ideas, a diffusion of information, a perspective that stressed the worldwide implications of actions rather than being parochial in scope, and the ideal of a universally enlightened populace. According to such thinking, the key to a truly egalitarian society was the wide dissemination of knowledge.[26]

As originally formulated, this Enlightenment ideology assumed that the higher levels of society would become cosmopolitan first. Traditionally, those in the upper class were the people who had access to education and the means to be exposed to new places and new ideas. Thus the gentry were the ones who were best equipped to encourage a broad-minded worldview and to share that understanding with those below them—a kind of enlightened *noblesse oblige*. In the early American

24. Richard Carwardine, *Transatlantic Revivalism: Popular Evangelicalism in Britain and America, 1760–1865* (Westport, CT: Greenwood, 1978) 106–7, 125; Sellers, *Lorenzo Dow*, 109, 114; Julia Stewart Werner, *The Primitive Methodist Connexion: Its Background and Early History* (Madison: University of Wisconsin Press, 1984) 45–47.

25. Dow, *History of Cosmopolite*, 25, 50, 83, 201; Marks, *Memoirs*, 110–12; Carwardine, *Transatlantic Revivalism*, 106–7.

26. Dow, *History of Cosmopolite*, 282; Richard D. Brown, *Knowledge is Power: The Diffusion of Information in Early America, 1700–1865* (New York: Oxford University Press, 1989) 224ff.

republic, however, this top-down strategy for the dissemination of truth was being challenged by the forces of democratization. Enlightenment ideals were being transposed into the popular idiom of the common people—a democratizing of the cosmopolitan vision. Several trends during this time—which would soon lead to what has been termed a communications and transportation revolution—provided a leveling effect regarding the accessibility of knowledge. Greater efficiency in modes of transportation allowed for greater mobility, public education created a more literate population, and cheaper printing and other inexpensive ways of obtaining information were becoming available. While earlier popular culture had been primarily oral, it was now evolving in written forms as well, by making effective use of the new technologies of the day. Even common preachers could publicize their ideas—and promote their careers. Dow was one of the very first of the frontier plain folk to be widely published.[27]

Along with Dow's challenge to hierarchical structures, it is interesting to note a rather startling fact: Dow was a Mason.[28] Despite all of his democratic eccentricity, Dow still found that it was expedient for him to connect with the influential social network of Freemasonry. That is because, by the early nineteenth century, affiliation with the fraternity had ceased to confer an elite economic status on its members; rather, it offered the promise of access to higher levels of education and the dissemination of knowledge.[29]

As a democratic eccentric, Dow decried any ascription of worth that was dependent on financial status. And, although involved in several money-making schemes himself, he preached on the dangers of material consumption—"the cursed love of money."[30] Dow's ambivalence

27. Sellers, *Lorenzo Dow*, 72, 74; Brown, *Knowledge is Power*, 224ff.; Hatch, *Democratization of American Christianity*, 128–33.

28. Edward Thompson Schultz, *History of Freemasonry in Maryland*, 4 vols. (Baltimore: Medairy, 1884–1887), 2: 238; Richard P. Jackson, *The Chronicles of Georgetown, D.C. from 1751 to 1878* (Washington, DC: Polkinhorn, 1878) 288–89; Sellers, *Lorenzo Dow*, 224–25, citing Lorenzo Dow, *Omnifarious Law Exemplified.* Dow preached at Masonic temples, and when he died in 1834, he was given a Masonic burial rite.

29. Steven C. Bullock, "A Pure and Sublime System: The Appeal of Post-Revolutionary Freemasonry," *Journal of the Early Republic* 9 (1989) 359–73; Sellers, *Lorenzo Dow*, 226.

30. Dow, *History of Cosmopolite*, 100, 116, 303, 307–8, 332; Sellers, *Lorenzo Dow*, 76–77, 97, 200, 241.

regarding economic upward mobility was compatible with the Masonic message, for Freemasonry in the early republic taught that not every important value was material. More important to them was the ideal of cosmopolitanism, which taught that enlightened truth was to be universally diffused. When this concept was applied to Christianity, it became evident to Dow that the claims of the gospel should be widely disseminated. Calvinist determinism seemed to represent a narrow view of human accessibility to the truth of the gospel, while Arminianism provided an all-embracing offer of the gospel, and hence a larger vision of the society. Being a cosmopolite for Dow meant a compulsion to share the gospel with all those who, in his understanding, did not have it. Dow's idea of going to Ireland, and later to England, was an attempt to fulfill the cosmopolitan concern to disseminate truth as broadly as possible. As a Wesleyan cosmopolite, Dow was convinced of the need for each person to experience a soteriological upward mobility—a chance for every person to know the justifying and sanctifying grace of God. In this way, Dow expressed a theological rendering of the cosmopolitan ideal. His message was eccentric—a democratized theology—but the goal was cosmopolitan, because the message was to be proclaimed universally.[31]

Within a few years, most evangelicals denounced Freemasonry; the fraternal order became for them a symbol of all that was antidemocratic in nineteenth century America. The Holiness movement, in particular, rejected secret societies, perceiving them as blasphemous institutions. Nonetheless, the Holiness folk retained the cosmopolitan concept of a universal diffusion of knowledge as championed by the Masons and other Enlightenment-influenced Americans. Among Holiness evangelists, the knowledge that was to be diffused throughout the world was the knowledge of a holy God empirically experienced through Christian conversion and sanctification. Thus, at the same time that Holiness people rejected many of the bourgeois values of their nineteenth century environment, they also retained significant aspects of the early national period culture.

31. Dow, *History of Cosmopolite*, 74, 84, 117, 121, 145, 175, 248, 250, 254, 274, 284, 448ff.; Werner, *The Primitive Methodist Connexion*, 45.

HOLINESS PROTOTYPE

The two emphases in Lorenzo Dow's vocational conception had implications for those who would come after him. Dow's eccentricity challenged the hierarchical power structures of his day, especially the institutionalism of Methodism.[32] In this Dow was a prototype for the general trend toward independence and anti-institutionalism among many nineteenth century Methodists, including those within the Holiness movement. Dow was similar to Hugh Bourne, B.T. Roberts, William Taylor, William and Catherine Booth, Phineas Bresee and others who (at least at first) did not have an antipathy toward institutional Methodism, but neither did they revere it. Rather than depending on denominational organizations for promotion, they were self-promoters who relied on populist-oriented *ad hoc* structures.[33]

The later Holiness people were also like Dow in regard to his cosmopolitanism. Holiness preachers, similar to Dow, were somewhat ambivalent about the Methodist system but never ambivalent about the Church's evangelistic commitment. On the one hand, the Methodist itinerancy provided them with an initial model of a cosmopolitan strategy for ministry; on the other, they often felt hemmed in by the accountability of a connection that seemed unfriendly or unresponsive to their concerns. For Dow and many nineteenth century Methodists, then, the Methodist system both motivated and constrained their missionary zeal.[34]

Dow remained loosely within that system and simply carried on as an eccentric. A generation later, many Holiness folk were not so fortunate. Their eccentricities ran up against a less flexible structure; thus, they established their own mechanisms for evangelism. In each case, however, the overriding vision was a cosmopolitan one—the universal dissemination of gospel truth and the encouragement of deeper experiences with God.

---

32. Dow, *History of Cosmopolite*, 325, 543ff.

33. Werner, *The Primitive Methodist Connexion*, 26–28, 64–74.

34. Dow, *History of Cosmopolite*, 117, 122, 146, 149, 152, 256, 272, 290, 321; Leonard I. Sweet, *The Minister's Wife: Her Role in Nineteenth-Century American Evangelicalism* (Philadelphia: Temple University Press, 1983) 46–47.

BIBLIOGRAPHY

Hatch, Nathan. *The Democratization of American Christianity.* New Haven: Yale University Press, 1989.

Carwardine, Richard. *Transatlantic Revivalism: Popular Evangelicalism in Britain and America, 1760–1865.* Westport, CT: Greenwood Press, 1978.

8

Phoebe Palmer

Spreading "Accessible" Holiness

DIANE K. LECLERC

FOR SEVERAL DECADES NOW, the initial comment made by various historiographers about Phoebe Palmer is one of amazement: How could such an influential figure be completely neglected for over eighty some years after her death? It is true. Having been one of the most famous women in her time, her name virtually disappears relatively soon after her death in 1874. The silence about her lasted until works by John Peters in 1956,[1] and Timothy Smith in 1957[2] resurrected and advocated for more scholarly interest in Palmer. In answer to the call put forth by Peters and Smith, more such scholarship has in fact emerged, if slowly. It was thirty years later when full-length treatises of Palmer's life, work and influence first appeared. Numerous articles have also been published, as well as more recent dissertations.

Details of her life and thought unquestionably position her as a figure within—indeed, at the very heart of—the nineteenth-century American Holiness movement. Yet her influence reaches beyond this movement into the Protestantism of her day more generally, as well as the borders of America. She was a woman with international recognition.

Thomas Oden stands as an enthusiastic voice for her theological and spiritual vision. "Phoebe Palmer's spirituality, as shown especially

---

1. John L. Peters, *Christian Perfection and American Methodism* (Nashville: Pierce and Washabaugh, 1956).

2. Timothy L. Smith, *Revivalism and Social Reform* (Nashville: Abingdon, 1957).

through her autobiographical writings and her spiritual-counsel essays, is deeply grounded in classical Christianity, not on the fanatic, idiosyncratic fringe of centerless enthusiasm. She deserves to be counted among the most penetrating spiritual writers of the American tradition."[3] But Oden's assessment is hardly uniform. There are many interpretations of Palmer—not all favorable.

At the very least, Palmer is recognized now for her advancement of the cause for women. Palmer has been cited as a key contributor to the nineteenth-century debate concerning the role of women in the church. Donald Dayton writes, "It was . . . the denominations produced by the mid-nineteenth century 'holiness revival' that most consistently raised feminism to a central principle of church life. This movement largely emerged from the work of Phoebe Palmer."[4]

Palmer did write a book on women in ministry generally, and as preachers specifically. But I would argue that Palmer's convictions regarding the meaning of holiness and their underlying theological assumptions clearly come *before* her "feminism" and only *consequentially* lead to it. It is not just an isolated belief that radicalized Palmer's holiness movement regarding gender roles. Her whole theological vision takes the movement to the implications of empowerment for all. In other words, egalitarianism is not a side issue in the Holiness movement that can easily be excised from its theology. As Palmer exemplifies, it permeates throughout. In light of its effect on American religious culture and beyond, her theology deserves to be explored further. We will turn to a more in depth rendering of her theological vision, after a short biographical review.

PALMER'S BIOGRAPHY: FEMININE REVOLUTIONARY

Phoebe Worrall was born December 18, 1807. Her father, Henry met another young Methodist, Dorothea Wade and married her. Phoebe was the fourth of the eight who survived to adulthood. The home of the Worrall's is described as a place of intense religious devotion. Besides the home, Phoebe's spiritual development was directly influenced by the family's involvement in their Methodist church. A significant figure for

3. Thomas Oden, "Introduction," in *Phoebe Palmer, Selecting Writings*, ed. Thomas Oden (New York: Paulist, 1988), see 2–3, 8.

4. Donald W. Dayton, *Discovering an Evangelical Heritage* (New York: Harper & Row, 1976).

the rest of her life was Nathan Bangs, who taught Phoebe her catechism in 1817. By all accounts, her spirituality developed at a very early age, and showed unusual maturity in her comprehension of theology and in piety of life. Later her writings will evidence intricate insights into Scripture and holiness theology, despite only an eighth grade education.

In 1826, Phoebe met Walter Clarke Palmer, who according to Charles White, embarked on three projects as a young man: "establishing a medical practice, superintending the Sunday school at the Allen Street Methodist Episcopal Church, and wooing Phoebe Worrall."[5] Walter and Phoebe married on September 28, 1827. While it has been said that the Palmers were well suited both in interest and personality, and that they maintained a quite blissful marriage, their lives were not without difficulty, even great tragedy.

It was on their first wedding anniversary that Phoebe gave birth to a son, Alexander. Thus began a spiritual struggle that deeply shaped her developing theology. By her own admission, she put off having him baptized, because she could not admit publicly that she was giving him to God without reservation. This brought intense guilt when the baby died eleven months later. "I felt that he was *taken* away—not *given* up—*torn* from my embrace—not a *free-will offering*."[6] She did not question God, but acknowledged her own "idolatry." A few months later, the Palmers had a second son, Samuel. One can speculate that this time she saw herself as "Hannah," willing giving up *her* Samuel to God. Unfortunately, he lived only seven weeks. Her understanding of this experience as another deep failure of "idolatry" compelled her to vow to not make this mistake again. Her theodicy here is horrific, but not unusual for her day. God took the children as punishment for her sin. And yet, this experience, and those to come did in fact shape a crucial element of her theology of consecration in her famous "formula" of sanctification.

Her spiritual struggles continued, despite a new resolve to press on. She had inherited an Americanized version of Wesley's call to Christian perfection. And yet, Palmer found such a quest elusive until another tragedy hit. A second daughter was born in 1835. Unfortunately, unimaginable suffering struck again. A maid was careless with an oil lamp and set Eliza's crib on fire. This paved the way for seeking entire sanc-

---

5. Charles White, *The Beauty of Holiness* (Grand Rapids: Francis Asbury, 1986) 4.

6. Phoebe Palmer, *The Way of Holiness, With Notes by the Way* (New York: W. C. Palmer, [1843], 1867) 254–55.

tification more deeply. Palmer finally reached that "day of days" on July 26, 1837. Palmer attributed sanctification's delay to a lack of realization of the "depth" and gravity of truly surrendering her "idols." This day, founded upon her interpretation of incredible tragedy, was indisputably a turning point in Phoebe Palmer's life and vocation, and for the American Holiness movement. Out of it she developed the famous "Altar Covenant" that aided persons seeking entire sanctification. It consisted of three steps: consecration, faith, and testimony.

It was after this experience that Palmer's life began to change and expand in significant, even incredible ways. The Palmers had moved into a house on the lower East side of New York City[7] and began living with Phoebe's sister Sarah and her husband Thomas Lankford. After Sarah's sanctification experience, she combined two women's meetings into one that met on Tuesday mornings in their home. It was a period of time when their local Methodist church was experiencing great revival. At the first meeting, Sarah was astonished to see many, even notable Methodist women find radical victory in prayer. Those Tuesday meetings have sometimes been credited for the holiness revival that sprang forth and expanded for decades to come. It is certainly true that when Phoebe assumed leadership and the meetings began to include men, some of the most prominent Methodist leaders of the 19th century were influenced by what happened in that parlor, many attending themselves. The meetings also influenced many major religious leaders who were not Methodists.

Palmer's acclaim quickly expanded. For the next thirty plus years, her ministry was widespread—theologically rigorous, dynamically revivalistic, and socially relevant. Besides traveling extensively throughout the United States—preaching at revivals, and later camp meetings—she also spent several years abroad in the same vocation. She is thought to be a revivalist of the caliber and popularity of Charles Finney himself. She also wrote dozens of books and tracts as well as editing the most influential holiness magazine of the century.[8] She started the famous Five Points inner city mission and is said to have produced a theological imperative

7. I visited 54 Rivington Street on what would have been Palmer's 189th birthday (Dec. 18, 1996). There is nothing there to indicate the significance of the location. Coincidently, however, across the street at 61 Rivington stands the Chinese Church of the Nazarene.

8. The *Guide to Holiness* was under Palmer's editorship from 1864–1874. During that time circulation reached 40,000.

that subsequently made women's charity work common-place.[9] She was influential in Methodist higher education. And she never considered herself anything but staunchly faithful to the Methodist tradition, and to Wesley himself.

PALMER'S THEOLOGY: THE MEANS TO THE MASSES

The character of Palmer's holiness theology has been a matter of much interest and debate. It is beyond the scope of this study to delve extensively into the intricacies of her expansive theology and the odd variety of estimations of it. And yet, Palmer's theological streams that flow directly into the oceanic ethos of the later American Holiness movement's social emphases. The following issues will receive attention: her "Pragmatism"; her (miscalled)-"Pelagianism"; and her "Pentecostalism" as they reinterpret Wesley for a new context and as they reveal an explicit theological vision with historic social implications.

Pragmatism. Palmer was initially hesitant to embrace the sentimentalized American appropriation of Wesley's doctrine of assurance as applied to entire sanctification. Palmer disposed of this type of passively received, almost mysteriously acquired assurance as a great hindrance to many seeking heart purity. In its place she prescribed a faith independent of a specific emotional response and initiated what critics call a new rationalism that chilled the "warmth" of Methodism. This prescription was given because of her own difficulty in attaining an assurance (or "witness of the Spirit") that precisely fit the emotionally charged exhortations of early nineteenth-century American Methodist preaching. Palmer has been called a "creative detour" to this tendency in Methodism. [10]

Palmer did struggle for several years to match her own experience with a dictated experience of assurance of entire sanctification. In retrospect, Palmer attributed much of her struggle *both* to the obtuse sophistication of more "professional" Methodist theology and to a sentimentalized ethos found among the Methodist grassroots. In an attempt to sort through her own spiritual struggle, she dismissed the theologians and the expectations of a sentimental experience and turned to the

---

9. See Smith, *Revivalism,* 169–71.

10. Al Truesdale, "Reification of the Experience of Entire Sanctification in the American Holiness Movement," *Wesleyan Theological Journal* 31 (1996) 116–17.

Scriptures directly.[11] What she was rejecting was the technical theology of her day, not theology in general. And what she was rejecting was *prescribed* emotionalism, not religious emotion in general. Hers was in fact not a cold rationalism, but a somewhat novel and yet clear pathway to the holy life. Pragmatically worked out, her "way" opened the door to entire sanctification for thousands.

It is important to note that Palmer was not rejecting Wesley's doctrine of assurance altogether. And yet, in her own theological formation, Palmer greatly modifies the meaning of assurance and its means of attainment. Melvin Dieter has commented that "the newness then, essentially was a change in emphasis resulting from a simple, literal Biblical faith and the prevailing mood of revivalism combined with an impatient, American pragmatism that always seeks to make a reality at the moment whatever is considered at all possible in the future."[12] There is no doubt that this pragmatism is at work in Palmer's theology, a kind of "holy pragmatism."[13] It cannot help but affect how sanctification is preached as we encounter mid-to-late nineteenth-century expressions of holiness.

11. For this, she has been characterized as "anti-theological" and anti-Wesleyan. Paul Bassett critiques Palmer's shift away from Wesley's more balanced understanding of the theological sources, i.e., the "quadrilateral" (although Bassett resists this term), toward a shallow bibliocentrism and mournfully attributes the unfortunate course of mid-to-late nineteenth-century holiness thought to Palmer's naivete. See Paul Merritt Bassett, "The Theological Identity of the North American Holiness Movement," in *The Variety of American Evangelicalism*, eds. Donald W. Dayton and Robert K. Johnson (Downers Grove, IL: InterVarsity, 1991) 72–108. While evidence does show that Palmer considered herself a "woman of one book," she, like Wesley, respected and utilized other sources for her own thought. Besides evidence that shows she read extensively in Wesley and Fletcher's works and even in the patristic sources themselves, by her own admission she always read the Scriptures with commentaries at her side. See Phoebe Palmer, *Israel's Speedy Restoration and Conversion Contemplated; or Signs of the Times in Familiar Letters By Mrs. Phoebe Palmer* (New York: Gray, 1854) 3.

12. Melvin E. Dieter, *The Holiness Revival of the Nineteenth Century,* Studies in Evangelicalism (Metuchen, NJ: Scarecrow, 1980) 31.

13. Harold Raser also recognizes a pragmatism in Palmer's theology: "Her's is a very practical theology which eschews strictly theoretical considerations in favor of those *things* which have a direct payoff in terms of bringing about the desired religious experience. One might even say that Palmer's thought constitutes in its essence a 'theology of means' pertaining to holiness, so preoccupied is she with actually getting persons to the place where they are made 'holy' and live lives of 'perfect love'. . . a kind of holy pragmatism." Harold Raser, *Phoebe Palmer: Her Life and Thought,* Studies in Women and Religion (Lewiston, NY: Mellen, 1987) 150.

Miscalled-Pelagianism. Palmer has been misinterpreted on the point of Pelagianism. Palmer's call for active faith is no less grace-based than Wesley's more passive stance. When critiques of Pelagianism are made, it is *The Way of Holiness* that is most often quoted. But in Palmer's more personal works, it is more transparent that she is *not* resting on *her own efforts* in the process of reaching the crisis of entire sanctification, nor is she separating faith from devotion. While *The Way of Holiness* does portray faith as believing the promises of God as represented in his written Word, Palmer's expression of faith in her diaries and letters is deeply personal; she incisively perceives the *relational* and devotional aspect of faith. Abraham is often used as a model of faith in her letters and diaries;[14] she represents him as believing "the promise" of God, but also as representing a deep trust in the person of God. Palmer affirms that one's ability to turn from idols, consecrate everything, and "believe the promise" is not accomplished through human ability, but rather through one's reception of God's prevenient grace. She resists and rejects her own efforts as utterly fruitless. Her assertion of faith is filled with language of God's prior, prevenient action, specifically through His Spirit. And yet, an aspect of her optimism and emphasis on human activity (synergism?) in the act of faith does have an important consequence. One's spirituality need not be mediated by another person (i.e., clergy), thus there is a type of spiritual independence that gives rise to a revivalistic fervor not bound to specific ecclesiastical structures.

Pentecostalism. John Fletcher was the first to link entire sanctification with "the baptism of the Holy Spirit." Asa Mahan, Phoebe Palmer's contemporary, wrote a book by that title that gave biblical and theological justification for linking the Pentecostal image with the individual's experience of entire sanctification. After some correspondence with Mahan over the issue, Palmer took the image and popularized it. What occurred in Acts 2 occurred to the disciples, to those who already believed in Christ for salvation. Their Pentecostal baptism was thus interpreted by Palmer as an instantaneous event and a "second work" of the Spirit, different from anything they had experienced previously. Palmer readily adopted the Pentecostal experience as a transferable experience

14. E.g., Palmer's diary entry for September 11, 1837, in Richard Wheatley, *The Life and Letters of Mrs. Phoebe Palmer*, The Higher Christian Life (New York: Garland, 1984) 46–48. According to Oden, "The testing of Abraham in the command to sacrifice his only son would henceforth become for her a principal metaphor of her own experience," Oden, "Introductory note to September 11, 1837," in Palmer, *Selected Writings*, 132.

for all believers and preached its imperative necessity in her revivals and camp meetings, and in her written works. This would greatly affect the way the doctrine of entire sanctification was expressed in the Holiness movement; and "her popularization of Pentecostal language . . . laid a firm foundation for later Pentecostal developments."[15] Certainly *not* limited to them, this theology was particularly significant for women's religious experience.

Women began to see their own potential for ministry and usefulness in church and society and started to challenge structures that would limit them. Nancy Hardesty elaborates: "[Palmer] affirmed that Christians were not only justified before God but were also regenerate, reborn, made new, capable of being restored to the Edenic state. For women it made possible the sweeping away of centuries of patriarchal, misogynist culture in the instant. . . . The argument that 'this is the way we've always done it,' holds no power for someone for whom 'all things have been made new.'"[16]

Palmer's Pragmatism, miscalled-Pelagianism and "Pentecostalism", then, contain a strong call for women to live out their new spiritual potential. Since her theology contained an idealism that made all things seem possible, limitations were determined only by one's own disobedience; as a result of this theological premise, women began to strive toward the realization of the "new life" they claimed. These women believed they had equal access to the "Pentecostal power" available through the Holy Spirit; they were equally capable and *responsible* to be "Pentecostal witnesses" to what God can do in a life that is entirely devoted. To be empowered through sanctifying grace compelled women to enter the sphere of society and effect change. It often meant ministering to the physical needs of others, especially to those of a lower social position, as evidenced by Palmer's strong emphasis on "mission" work.

But it was perhaps the last step in Palmer's three step formula that affected women most directly. Her emphasis on public testimony usually took the form of varying degrees of insistence that testimony was not only essential to the promulgation of Christian holiness, but even more essential to the personal retention of that grace. One had to give public testimony in order to be "clear in his experience." Palmer describes her

15. White, *Beauty of Holiness*, 158.

16. Nancy Hardesty, *Women Called to Witness: Evangelical Feminism in the Nineteenth Century* (Nashville: Abingdon, 1984) 83.

own experience: "The Spirit then suggested: If it is a gift from God, you will be required to declare it as his gift, through our Lord Jesus Christ, ready for the acceptance of all; and this, if you would retain the blessing, will not be left to your own choice. You will be called on to profess this blessing before thousands!"[17] Because of the requisitional nature of Palmer's injunction to speak, women across the United States, in Canada, and in Great Britain began, like her, to testify in public, standing in mixed assemblies to proclaim God's sanctifying power despite the fact that it was considered "undignified" for a woman to speak in public at all. Therefore, if a woman professed entire devotion to God and counted herself free from idols and an absorption in domestic cares, she must be willing to do what God next asked of her, even if it went against social norms or protocol, even if it meant God called her to preach.

Questions regarding her fidelity to Wesley and the dangers of her formulaic offer of entire sanctification will no doubt continue. But it is important for us to recognize that her theology of holiness had wider consequences. Interwoven in the fiber of Palmer's view of holiness is an inextricable message of human equality, which, quite frankly, changed the world for the disempowered of the nineteenth century. As the Holiness movement (rightly) looks for a re-articulation of holiness theology for the twenty first, it must retain in its expression enough pragmatism and enough "Pentecostal" empowerment to keep a robust, yet precious egalitarianism close to its heart.

BIBLIOGRAPHY

Heath, Elaine A. *Naked Faith: The Mystical Theology of Phoebe Palmer*, Princeton Theological Monograph Series 108. Eugene, OR: Pickwick, 2009.

Leclerc, Diane. *Singleness of Heart: Gender, Sin, and Holiness in Historical Perspective*. Lanham, MD: Scarecrow, 2001.

Raser, Harold. *Phoebe Palmer: Her Life and Thought*. Lewiston, NY: Mellen, 1987.

White, Charles E. *The Beauty of Holiness*. Grand Rapids: Zondervan, 1986.

17. Palmer, *The Way*, 39–40.

9

Gospel Simplicity

Benjamin Titus Roberts and the Formation of the Free Methodist Church

DOUGLAS R. CULLUM

IN 1825, AS BENJAMIN Titus Roberts entered his toddler years, significant events were taking place in Western New York that would significantly impact the unfolding of his life. The first generation of settlers
came to an end, the completion of the Erie Canal ushered in a period
of a relatively stable agrarian economy, and "twelve crowded years" of
revivalistic passion began that would shape the religious mentality of the
region for years to come.[1] The formation of the Free Methodist Church,
thirty-five years later in 1860, was one manifestation of the various social
and religious currents that converged in the mid-nineteenth century. The
revival fires of Charles Finney and other evangelists had seared a nearly
indelible brand on the religious beliefs and practices of many people
in the now infamous "burned-over district" of Western New York.[2] The

1. Whitney R. Cross, *The Burned-Over District: The Social and Intellectual History of
Enthusiastic Religion in Western New York* (Ithaca: Cornell University Press, 1950) 55.

2. The older, standard analysis of the burned-over district is Cross, *The Burned-Over
District*. For more recent treatments, see Judith Wellman, "The Burned-Over District
Revisited: Benevolent Reform and Abolitionism in Mexico, Paris, and Ithaca, New York,
1825–1842" (PhD diss., University of Virginia, 1974); Paul E. Johnson, *A Shopkeeper's
Millennium: Society and Revivals in Rochester, New York, 1815–1837* (New York: Hill &
Wang, 1978); Linda Pritchard, "The Burned-Over District Reconsidered," *Social Science
History* 8 (Summer 1984) 243–65; Curtis D. Johnson, *Islands of Holiness: Revival Religion
in Upstate New York, 1790–1860* (Ithaca: Cornell University Press, 1989); Douglas
Mark Strong, "Organized Liberty Evangelical Perfectionism, Political Abolitionism and

conscience of the nation was in turmoil over the issue of slavery. And the once rural, humble Methodists were beginning to climb the middle-class ladder in the new urban centers of America.

B. T. ROBERTS AND THE ORIGIN
OF THE FREE METHODIST CHURCH

The young B. T. Roberts could not have envisioned the catalytic influence he would one day wield toward the organization of a new branch of the Methodist tradition. From childhood, Roberts was impacted by mainline Methodist culture. Born on July 23, 1823, in the hill country of Cattaraugus County, New York, his contact with the Methodists began at least as early as 1834, when his father, Titus Roberts, was converted. The elder Roberts soon felt a call to preach, and in 1839, joined the Genesee Conference of the Methodist Episcopal Church (MEC) as a probationary member. Thus a Methodist ethos was part of B. T. Roberts' life from the time he was ten or eleven years old. But his own experience of gospel transformation would not occur for another decade. In May 1844, while preparing for a career in law, Roberts encountered the gospel in a way that resulted in a dramatic change in his sense of vocational calling. Within months of his conversion Roberts began an educational journey in the Methodist tradition at Genesee Wesleyan Seminary (Lima, New York) and Wesleyan University (Middletown, Connecticut). Four years later, in 1848, Roberts joined the Genesee Conference as a probationary member and was appointed to Caryville, New York, his first pastoral appointment in the MEC.[3]

Roberts' ministry in the Genesee Conference began with great promise but ended in disillusionment. Albert Outler observed that one of the unique charisms of the American Methodist movement from its earliest days was its "distinctive mingling of primitivism and

---

Ecclesiastical Reform in the Burned-Over District" (PhD diss., Princeton Theological Seminary, 1990); and James A. Revell, "The Nazirites: Burned-Over District Methodism and the Buffalo Middle Class" (PhD diss., State University of New York at Buffalo, 1994).

3. For these and additional details of Roberts' early life, see Howard A. Snyder, *Populist Saints: B. T. and Ellen Roberts and the First Free Methodists* (Grand Rapids: Eerdmans, 2006) 3–40; Clarence Howard Zahniser, *Earnest Christian: Life and Works of Benjamin Titus Roberts* (Published by the author, 1957) 11–15; and Benson Howard Roberts, *Benjamin Titus Roberts: A Biography* (North Chili, NY: The Earnest Christian Office, 1900) 1–8.

churchliness."[4] Most often this combination among Methodists was a happy one. But occasionally it became the catalyst for explosive disagreement and change. In the case of the early Free Methodists and their parent body, the MEC, the tension between primitivism and churchliness came to be fought on the battle ground of which of these two accents most adequately represented the essentials of genuine Methodism. The irony, of course, given Outler's thesis, is that both of these emphases were authentically representative of the American Methodist psyche. While early Free Methodists drank deeply from both streams of their religious inheritance, it was the strength of the primitivist impulse—their longing for the authenticity of an older, more pristine era of Methodism—that produced the most distinctive features of early Free Methodist piety.

This impulse was most evident in Roberts' 1857 article "New School Methodism."[5] Supported by the strength of a large segment of the lay membership of the Genesee Conference, Roberts argued that a new breed of progressive Methodism threatened to undermine the purity of original Methodist doctrine, discipline, and practice.[6] Specifically, Roberts insisted that historic Methodist teaching on the distinctive nature of God's justifying and sanctifying grace was being blurred by certain principal leaders in the Conference, those Roberts named "New School Methodists." Moreover, Roberts maintained that the Genesee Conference had begun to accommodate itself to prevailing cultural trends, and that the true gospel, and therefore "the glory" of Methodism, was beginning to depart. More than any other single publication, Roberts' thought in "New School Methodism" laid the theological foundation for the particular constellation of emphases that would ultimately result in

---

4. Albert C. Outler, "'Biblical Primitivism' in Early American Methodism," in *The Wesleyan Theological Heritage: Essays of Albert C. Outler*, eds. Thomas C. Oden and Leicester R. Longden (Grand Rapids: Zondervan, 1991) 153; see also Revell, "The Nazirites," 21–22.

5. Benjamin Titus Roberts, "New School Methodism," *The Northern Independent*, 20 and 27 August 1857, 6; for a readily accessible copy of "New School Methodism," see Appendix A in Leslie R. Marston, *From Age to Age a Living Witness: A Historical Interpretation of Free Methodism's First Century* (Winona Lake, IN: Light and Life, 1960) 573–78.

6. For an excellent discussion of the significance of "New School Methodism," see Snyder, *Populist Saints*, 382–98. For a description of the lay movement and strength of a democratic impulse in the origin of the FMC, see Douglas R. Cullum, "Gospel Simplicity: Rhythms of Faith and Life Among Free Methodists in Victorian America" (PhD diss., Drew University, 2002) 163–208.

the formation of the Free Methodist Church: On the positive side, early Free Methodists argued *for* a rigorous adherence to the doctrines and practices of primitive Methodism, and the equal representation of clergy and laity in the policy-making bodies of the Church; negatively, they stood equally firm *against* the slavery of human beings, membership in secret or oath-bound organizations, and the pew rental system.

The latter of these issues—the pew rental system—may serve as a window through which to view key features of nineteenth-century Free Methodism: its emphasis on the universality of God's grace and its mission to the poor. The term "free" Methodist, which ultimately would become the name of the new denomination, was originally coined to refer to congregations that did not employ the pew rental system of church support. B. T. Roberts was relentless in his advocacy of the need for free churches. Theologically, he insisted that God's universal offer of salvation was not compatible with the human partiality engendered by the pew system. Pragmatically, Roberts believed that this demanded special effort toward proclaiming the gospel to the poor, those least likely to be reached by churches that catered to the wealthy who could afford the luxury of paid pews. He argued that the church was to be the place where the rich and poor knelt down together and where everyone would "be made to realize that the Lord is the maker of them all."[7] This, of course was not possible as long as the pew system prevailed.

> If the gospel is to be preached to the poor, then it follows, as a necessary consequence, that all the arrangements for preaching the gospel, should be so made as to secure this object. There must not be a mere incidental provision for having the poor hear the gospel; this is the main thing to be looked after. . . . Hence houses of worship should be, not like the first class car on a European railway, for the exclusive, but like the streets we walk, free for all. Their portals should be opened as wide for the common laborer, or the indigent widow, as for the assuming, or the wealthy.[8]

From Roberts' perspective, the upwardly-mobile, progressive "New School Methodism" of his day had forsaken Methodism's original mis-

---

7. Benjamin Titus Roberts, "Free Churches," *Earnest Christian* 1.2 (February 1860) 38. See also Benjamin Titus Roberts, "Free Churches," editorial, *Earnest Christian* 1.1 (January 1860) 9, where Roberts contended that "there must not be a mere incidental provision for having the poor hear the gospel; this is the main thing to be looked after."

8. Roberts, "Free Churches," 9.

sion of spreading "scriptural holiness over these lands." The publication of this article was the single most decisive factor that led to Roberts' expulsion from the Methodist Episcopal Church in 1858.

CONTOURS OF EARLY FREE METHODIST PIETY: GOSPEL SIMPLICITY

Free Methodism's core beliefs and practices were largely a direct inheritance from the Methodist Episcopal Church. Yet this inheritance was filtered through a passionate commitment to an earlier era of Methodist faith and practice. The presence of such an internal tension was not unique to Free Methodist origins and has often been observed in studies of similar religious groups.[9] But what was it among early Free Methodists that served to hold together these seemingly disparate tendencies? The following analysis argues that the motif of "gospel simplicity" may serve as the central hub around which early Free Methodism's beliefs and practices were organized.[10] "Simplicity," for this branch of nineteenth-century Methodism, meant "sincerity, singleness of character, probity, frankness, freedom from all guile, and from all artifice and dissimulation."[11] This motif in the writings of early Free Methodists offers insight into the biblical and theological commitments that lay behind their choices as they negotiated the churchliness—primitivism tension. *Gospel simplicity* as early Free Methodism's basic orienting perspective may be seen by use of the time-honored Methodist rubrics of *doctrine, discipline,* and *practice.*

9. See, for example, the following helpful discussions: Richard T. Hughes, "Recovering First Times: The Logic of Primitivism in American Life," in *Religion and the Life of the Nation: American Recoveries,* ed. Rowland A. Sherrill (Urbana: University of Illinois Press, 1990) 193–218; Melvin E. Dieter, "Primitivism in the American Holiness Tradition," *Wesleyan Theological Journal* 30 (Spring 1995) 78–91; and the essays by Richard Hughes, George Marsden, Franklin Littell, Susie Stanley, and Grant Wacker, in Richard T. Hughes, ed., *The Primitive Church in the Modern World* (Urbana: University of Illinois Press, 1995).

10. For an explanation of the function of such an orienting concern, as well as the discernment of a "basic orienting perspective" in the theology of John Wesley, see Randy Maddox, *Responsible Grace: John Wesley's Practical Theology* (Nashville: Abingdon, 1994) 17–19.

11. Benjamin Titus Roberts, "Simplicity," *Earnest Christian* 28.2 (1874) 37.

DOCTRINAL SIMPLICITY: AN EXPERIENTIAL PIETY

The primitivist impulse that figured prominently among the leaders of the early Free Methodist movement was sounded in the very first issue of B. T. Roberts' *Earnest Christian* magazine [1860]. Its opening salvo was a clarion call to all who concurred with Roberts that churches of all branches had suffered a general decline of substantive Christian experience. In reaction to this decline, Roberts believed that there were "many sincere and earnest persons throughout the land, anxiously inquiring 'for the old paths.'"[12] What was needed was an earnest re-appropriation of the soteriological heart of biblical religion. Such doctrinal simplicity was at the center of Roberts' vocational self-understanding. He made it clear that his writing and editorial endeavors would attempt to stand in the gap: "It is for this increasing class of persons that we write—for those who are in earnest to gain Heaven, and anxious to know the conditions upon which eternal happiness can be secured."[13]

With the doctrine of salvation at the heart of early Free Methodist theology, it was the personal experience of God's transforming grace that lay center stage in their presentation of the gospel. Roberts promoted an "experimental religion" which he understood to be the "foundation and life of practical piety, as well as the indispensable condition of final salvation."[14] The experience of conversion, or the embrace of personal faith in Christ, was the pivotal point in a person's movement from spiritual darkness to light. But this experience was interpreted neither as the originating moment nor the penultimate goal of the work of God's grace in human life. Rather, the experiential piety of early Free Methodists was inclusive of all the stages along the way of

12. Benjamin Titus Roberts, "Object and Scope of This Magazine," *Earnest Christian* 1.1 (1860) 5.

13. Roberts, "Object and Scope of This Magazine," 5. For other examples of early Free Methodism's declensionist interpretation of church history, see David F. Newton, "Satan's Devices," *Earnest Christian* 3.5 (1862) 160; Benjamin Titus Roberts, "The Old Paths," *Earnest Christian* 11.1 (1866) 8–10; A. J. Day, "Decline of Power in the Methodist Episcopal Church," *Earnest Christian* 15.1 (1868) 9–10; [Cecil], "Declension in Religion," *Earnest Christian* 28.3 (1874) 79–80; and J. J. Gridley, "The Old Paths," *Earnest Christian* 53.1 (1887) 10. Note also that the masthead of the denomination's weekly paper, *The Free Methodist*, displayed the biblical quote that came to hold semi-official status as a denominational motto: "Remove not the ancient landmark which thy fathers have set" (Proverbs 22:28).

14. Roberts, "Object and Scope of This Magazine," 5.

salvation: "from the first awakening of the sinner to his conversion, his deliverance from sin, his crucifixion to the world, and his baptism with the Holy Ghost, til he is filled with all the fulness of God."[15] Moreover, the doctrine of Christian holiness was given special attention, not as a department of theology distinct from the doctrine of salvation, but as the biblical vision of Christian existence and the essential source of spiritual power for a life of practical piety.

Free Methodism's soteriologically-focused doctrinal simplicity demanded that nothing should be permitted to divert the focus of one's life away from the gospel call to "a deep and genuine religious experience." Nineteenth-century Free Methodists felt called to do all they could "to secure a return to Gospel simplicity and purity wherever there has been a departure from them."[16] Individual Christians were exhorted to become *specialists* in the kingdom of God: "If you would attain to perfection in the Christian character," Roberts exhorted, "you must give to this your study and your time. There must be a simplicity of intention manifest to all, and which enters into all the transactions of life. You must seek *first*— that is, chiefly—the kingdom of God and his righteousness."[17] They were convinced that doctrinal or experiential simplicity must precede practical simplicity, that an internal conversion is necessary for any genuine external change of life. Thus, early Free Methodist doctrinal simplicity demanded that unflagging attention be given to the crucial matter of coming into and remaining in a right relationship with God.

DISCIPLINARY SIMPLICITY: AN EGALITARIAN PIETY

Free Methodism's emphasis on the singular importance of a personal experience of saving grace had a marked impact on the expectations it had for the conduct of its members. Gospel simplicity was expected to be the touchstone by which the appropriateness or inappropriateness of any possible behavior would be evaluated. "This simplicity of purpose," wrote Roberts, "begets simplicity of life."

> This is manifested not in one way merely, but in every way. There is no double dealing in business. There is no praying for the salvation of souls, and then, for the sake of making money, helping them down to hell in the ordinary avocations of life. No business

---

15. Ibid.

16. "Vital Godliness," editorial, *Earnest Christian* 9.5 (1865) 162.

17. Roberts, "Simplicity," 38.

is engaged in, no matter how profitable, that is naturally demoralizing in its tendency. God never compels his servants to work for the devil. The business selected is not only proper in itself, but is carried on upon Christian principles. Crooks and turns, artifices and misrepresentations are avoided. Everything is done in a straight-forward manner. No cunning devices are employed. All is conducted upon principles of the strictest integrity . . . The inward disposition manifests itself in the outward conduct.[18]

A central feature of the early Free Methodist disciplined life was the insistence that the offer of gospel transformation was for all persons without regard for status or race. Anything that ran counter to the universality of God's saving intention was anathema. It was this doctrinal and disciplinary focus that lay behind the social positions taken by the denomination in its formative struggle. The slavery of human beings, the holding of membership in oath-bound secret societies, and the practice of the pew rental system—each of these was perceived to compromise the simplicity of a gospel message which was intended to be for all people alike. Early Free Methodists sought earnestly to shape their churchly policies by the egalitarian mandate of the gospel. In their requirement of free pews, their patterns of fiscal stewardship, their focus on ministry to the poor, and their sharing of governance and leadership with lay women and men, Free Methodists disciplined their faith around an uncompromising insistence that the gospel must be freely available for all persons. Thus, it was an egalitarian piety that assisted nineteenth-century Free Methodists in demarcating the distinctive contours of the denomination's societal involvement.

PRACTICAL SIMPLICITY: AN ESCHATOLOGICAL PIETY

The ordinary rhythms of early Free Methodist life were regulated by another aspect of their soteriological focus: the expectation of future and final salvation. Both domestic and corporate practices were made to serve the one great hope of their earthly existence. This single-minded focus was at the heart of their practical piety.[19] They believed that ev-

18. Ibid., 37–38.

19. For an observation of a similar piety among Pentecostals, see Grant Wacker, "Searching for Eden with a Satellite Dish: Primitivism, Pragmatism, and the Pentecostal Character," in *The Primitive Church in the Modern World*, ed. Richard T. Hughes (Urbana: University of Illinois Press, 1995) 143–47.

ery facet of earthy life was invested with eternal significance. In their private devotional practices, family relationships, as well as in their various corporate gatherings in Christian community, Free Methodists saw themselves as sojourners in a land that was not their true home. They maintained intentional religious practices in order to prepare themselves for the day when faith would become sight, and they were finally in the intimate presence of God. This was to be the all-consuming passion of their personal lives. Those who truly embraced the call of gospel simplicity would allow nothing "to divert their attention from the work to which they have consecrated their lives."[20] Thus, it was an eschatological piety that gave shape to early Free Methodist methods and practices of spiritual growth and Christian nurture. But it must be noted that their eschatological focus was no end-times escapism as was sometimes the case with the later rise of dispensational theology. For nineteenth-century Free Methodists, the prospect of an eternity with Jesus prodded them to work faithfully for righteousness and justice in the lives of people and social structures of the world for which Christ came.

Thus Free Methodists of the nineteenth century were a rigorously single-minded people. At the very center of their religious piety was a soteriology. They sought to shape their lives around no other hub than the *gospel message*. Their soteriological commitments nurtured a distinctive way of looking at and living in the world. It was a piety of gospel simplicity that they hoped would shape every aspect of their lives, individually and corporately. As an all-pervasive theological self-consciousness, gospel simplicity became the defining feature of the Free Methodist way of life. It was this theological core that they sought to keep at the very center of their expression of the Christian faith. They looked back to an earlier era and found what they believed were the pristine days of Methodism when "fleeing from the wrath to come" and "spreading scriptural holiness" was the essence of every facet of the Christian life.

---

20. Roberts, "Simplicity," 37.

BIBLIOGRAPHY

Cullum, Douglas R. "Gospel Simplicity: Rhythms of Faith and Life Among Free Methodists in Victorian America." PhD diss., Drew University, 2002.

Snyder, Howard A. *Populist Saints: B. T. and Ellen Roberts and the First Free Methodists.* Grand Rapids: Eerdmans, 2006.

———. "'To Preach the Gospel to the Poor': Missional Self-Understanding in Early Free Methodism (1860–90)." *Wesleyan Theological Journal* 31 (1996) 7–39.

PART TWO

Pastoral Response

CORKY ALEXANDER

WE ARE BLESSED AS ministers to have had a number of pioneers that have opened doors for us. We know that no one gets to where they are alone. Even the very fabric of the way we do church is a product of godly souls who have paved the way for us, in thought, word and deed.

As we walk through our church sanctuaries, we see objects that serve as reminders of those who have gone before us. It is not the objects themselves, and in the end not even the individuals who have been associated with them that hold our attention, but the thousands who have been able to participate with and around these objects due to their influence. I would like to mention a few of these objects and pioneers.

THE CHURCH DOORS HAVE BEEN OPENED

The itinerant bishop in Wesleyan and Pentecostal traditions, as a leader, is a different animal than any other leader in society. An itinerant bishop such as Francis Asbury is more effective if he/she has been bi-vocational (the longer, the better), not too successful as a pastor (or else would still be there as Emeritus), not too nice, but very down to earth. The churches that will need the bishop's encouragement the most will have as their pastors the most common of ministers. When Asbury tried to reproduce Wesley's connectionalism on the sprawling acreage of the American Frontier, it must have stretched him. It clearly stretched the office and by the rugged texture of the continent made the office extremely coarse and increasingly more pragmatic, even more pragmatic than even John Wesley could have imagined. The church doors must be opened. Asbury, like those that would follow in his footsteps as bishops, travel not just because they have to, but because they delight in a big world with wonderful diversity, where they long to open hearts and doors.

THE PEW DOORS HAVE BEEN OPENED

Pews of an earlier time, unlike ours, had doors on them that separated those with standing and those without. The ministerial practices of John and Charles Wesley, which attract us so much, was often a seeming contradictory blend of Churchmanship and fearless association with common and often dangerous people. While my churches never would have rented a pew to an affluent family, the class distinctions run much more subtly, merely posting in a plate on the end of the pew, highlighting the donor that demands your respect and who is paying for the utilities and facility in which you are allowed to have a conversion of the approved type.

B. T. Roberts' critique of slavery and his denunciation of an upwardly mobile Methodism was a statement against accommodation of prominent culture and a message that God loves even those who don't have access to a pew. Anytime our churches have tended in the direction of prominent culture, the doctrine of Sanctification and its accompanying doctrine of "Social Holiness" have been its first losses. One would think that a message of Christian Perfection would be unreachable to the masses, but through its social holiness, it is reaching out to those who could neither have thought of or have opportunity to occupy a pew. The pew has not only been opened in the sanctuary, it is open throughout the whole fallen world.

THE ALTAR HAS BEEN OPENED

Securing access to a pew is not the end, but only the beginning. The "Altar Theology" of Phoebe Palmer has aided us in being able to get up out of our pews and come to the altar of prayer, for this altar is where the blessings of God will be received. This altar, and the way to it, like the altars of the Old Testament tabernacle and temples, is a spiritual journey. The Apostle Paul says, "The person without the Spirit does not accept the things that come from the Spirit of God but considers them foolishness, and cannot understand them because they are discerned only through the Spirit." (1 Cor 2:14, TNIV). Consequently, there have been of necessity spiritual guides who have helped us to learn how to make this journey and how to help other seekers pray through to the blessings that Christ died to bring. Thankfully, due to the efforts of Palmer, and those like her, the altar has remained open.

THE PULPIT HAS BEEN OPENED

Most of our preachers can be heard in various places of their sermons, about the vital experience of their Gospel salvation. Oh, there are some that became ministers because their father was a minister, or his father before him. Sadly, due to the professional development of the Christian ministry, there are even a few that have that have never experienced the glad benefits of justification. For the most part, Wesleyan and Pentecostal preachers are former residents of the shaken dungeon. Forgive me for breaking a major homiletical rule in speaking of myself, but I must give my testimony. "My dungeon shook, my chains fell off." I don't want to argue with you about music styles. I am not interested in defending my theological stance. I want to talk about my chains falling off. The openness of our pulpits, thanks to courageous pioneers like Richard Allen, has resulted in living testimonies who stand and preach living messages. This has been at the same time fearful and wonderful.

My prayer today is that all these stations of holiness and Pentecost that these pioneers have opened for us remain wide open for generations to come.

The Later Nineteenth Century: Chastened Hope and Expectant Yearning

PART THREE

Introduction

A CHANGING AMERICA

IN THE DECADES BEFORE the Civil War America was marked by a restless optimism. At least for white Americans the horizons seemed limitless: plenty of land out west for upwardly mobile people to acquire, and growing prosperity in the east. Americans thought of themselves as free of the dead hand of European traditions—free to start things afresh, think new thoughts, and invent a new society. It was a congenial environment for Wesleyanism, which emphasized the graced moral freedom of each individual and held a vision of perfection in love, not only for each human heart but for all of human society.

Yet Francis Asbury noted early on that young people seeking to make their fortunes out west were not the most promising hearers for a gospel calling for self-giving love. Materialism was as much at the heart of American culture as the vision of a renewed society. Cultural conflict was inevitable, and at the center of that conflict was the most prominent example of economic self-interest, that of slavery.

Slavery was not only wrapped up in profit, it was thoroughly tainted by racism. Even many white abolitionists assumed the superiority of the white race. This made slavery the one intractable issue that neither religion nor politics could budge. It took a Civil War with massive casualties to finally bring slavery to an end. And with the end of slavery also came the end to much of that early optimism that had marked the evangelical awakenings and the Holiness movement.

Many holiness people had tended to oppose both slavery and war. But they were confronted with a choice: wage war to preserve the union and end slavery, or abstain from war and let slavery continue. Most chose war, but with that choice came a loss of innocence. After the Civil War, in the wake of its devastation, there was a change of mood. Though still committed to evangelism and holiness, hope for Christian transformation of the social order was more cautious. Transforming the lives of persons seemed much more straightforward than the transformation of society.

The later nineteenth century was marked by massive social change. Waves of immigrants, largely Roman Catholic, began settling in the Northeast and Midwest. The industrial capitalism that had emerged before the Civil War now became the dominant economic force. Wealth was concentrated in relatively few hands, and monopolistic practices put severe pressure on both farmers and consumers. By 1920 more Americans lived in cities than in rural areas. Racism continued to shape society nationwide, and with the end of reconstruction, Jim Crow laws began to institutionalize segregation in the South.

Industrial capitalism was radically changing American culture. In rural and small town society, people tended to know one another, and do business with their neighbors. Persons from varied occupations or social classes freely mingled. In contrast, industrialization separated consumers from producers, and stratified labor and management. Workers lived in vastly different neighborhoods from owners. Wages were low, working and living conditions were poor, and practices like child labor were common. Protestant reactions to conditions in urban America tended to divide what had been the Finneyite union of evangelism, personal piety, and social reform. The new social gospel movement challenged the systemic causes of poverty, and argued that the economic system itself needed changing. Revivalism emphasized personal conversion, and many Christians argued poverty was due to personal vices and poor work habits. There were, however, some Christians who resisted a dichotomy of personal salvation and social reform, holding instead a more holistic vision.[1]

Immigration was also changing American society, even as the new immigrants were at the same time becoming Americanized. Protestants, who by now largely assumed an evangelical understanding of conversion and had adopted the revival practices of Finney, were faced with a large

---

1. The story of eight of these Christians, from both the nineteenth and twentieth centuries, is told in Douglas M. Strong, *They Walked in the Spirit* (Louisville: Westminster John Knox, 1997).

body of mostly working poor from a very different religious tradition. In general, their response to the immigrants was to seek to bring them to an evangelical conversion as well as inculcate what they believed were moral practices and good work habits.

TEMPERANCE, THE ROLE OF WOMEN, AND RACE

The heavy involvement of Protestants in the temperance movement put them strongly at odds with Catholic immigrants who had more European assumptions about socializing in taverns or beer gardens. But the prevalence of alcohol was a severe social problem in America, and not just among immigrants. Alcohol destroyed families and harmed entire communities. The temperance movement was seen at the time as a socially progressive cause that united a broad array of Protestants.

One of the leaders in the temperance movement was Frances Willard (1839-1898), founder of the Women's Christian Temperance Union. Both of her parents enrolled in Finney's Oberlin College, and later left the Congregational Church to join the Methodist Episcopal Church. Following a teaching career, during which she became the first woman college president in America, and service as an evangelist with Dwight L. Moody, Willard formed the WCTU. The WCTU not only sought to ban alcohol but empower women; in 1883 it endorsed women's suffrage. Willard supported the ordination of women in her book *Woman in the Pulpit*, and in 1888 was among the first women elected to General Conference, though they were denied the right to be seated.

The Methodist Episcopal Church had become increasingly hostile to women preachers. Holiness evangelist Maggie Newton Van Cott (1830–1914) had received her call to preach through both the encouragement of a pastor and a dream involving John Wesley. After preaching a six week revival, she received an exhorter's license in 1868 and her preacher's license in 1869. By 1880 she had traveled over 140,000 miles and held over 10,000 revival meetings. But that same year the Methodist Episcopal Church revoked all the preaching licenses issued to women. Anna Howard Shaw, another preacher, left the MEC to be ordained by the Methodist Protestants.

The predominantly African American Methodist denominations were no more welcoming of women as preachers or as ordained clergy. Holiness evangelist Julia Foote, of the African Methodist Episcopal Zion Church, preached for more than fifty years before being ordained shortly before her death. Women of all races found the Holiness movement to be much more open to their ministry than the traditional Methodist denominations.

Indeed by the 1880s Methodism began increasingly to reflect the values of the middle class, and to distance itself from its rural past. For the predominantly white denominations this also meant accepting the racial attitudes and disparities of the prevailing culture, although there were those like MEC Bishop Gilbert Haven (1821–1880) who challenged those assumptions. In the predominantly African-American denominations there was a general consensus on the need for strong educational institutions, but some disagreement over whether or not to retain practices from the past. AME Bishop Daniel A. Payne was strongly opposed when he sought to abandon the patterns of worship rooted in the camp meetings. African-American Methodists all sought to remain faithful to Wesleyanism, but unlike their white counterparts found they could not teach or proclaim those Wesleyan doctrines without addressing questions of race and human equality.[2]

THE HOLINESS MOVEMENT[3]

In the later nineteenth century the holiness movement flourished and diversified. While the largest contingent was found in the traditional Methodist denominations, especially the Methodist Episcopal Church, it also produced a wide array of new denominations.

One of the most important leaders of the Holiness movement was John Inskip (1816–1884), an MEC minister. Originally an opponent of the movement, he had twice professed entire sanctification only to lose it, and was a strong critic of the uncharitable judgmentalism he found among some of its advocates. But in 1864, after his wife claimed entire sanctification through consecration and faith, he led his congregation to the altar and made his own consecration to God.

Inskip was one of the founders and first President of the National Camp Meeting Association for the Promotion of Holiness, formed after

2. See C. Jarrett Gray, "Soteriological Themes in African-American Methodist Preaching, 1876–1914" (PhD dissertation, Drew University, 1993)

3 The best history of the holiness movement during this period is Melvin E. Dieter, *The Holiness Revival of the Nineteenth Century*, 2nd ed. (Latham, MD: Scarecrow, 1996). For more on the theological developments see Donald W. Dayton, *The Theological Roots of Pentecostalism* (Metuchen, NJ: Scarecrow, 1992).

the success of a holiness camp meeting he organized in Vineland, New Jersey, in 1867. Devoted fully to preaching sanctification, the camp meeting movement was seen by its supporters as means to renew Methodism. Inskip and his allies were critics of Methodism's easy accommodation with wealth and respectability, its neglect of class meetings and a devotional life, and its tolerance of dancing, drinking, gambling, circuses, and other vices. Others of course disagreed, seeing the Holiness movement as extremist and out of the mainstream. By the 1880s these tensions would lead to open conflict in much of traditional Methodism. Some would leave to form new denominations, though many others would remain.

One who stayed was Amanda Berry Smith, a lifelong member of the African Methodist Episcopal Church. Experiencing entire sanctification through the preaching of John Inskip in 1868, Smith began her own preaching ministry in 1870. She became an internationally known holiness evangelist, preaching in three different countries from 1878–90. This was a remarkable ministry for an African-American woman in the late nineteenth century.

One who did leave his denomination was Phineas Bresee. A Methodist Episcopal Church minister first in Iowa and then in California he served as pastor of all the major MEC churches in Los Angeles. He experienced entire sanctification in 1867 and became involved in the holiness movement, and in 1894 felt a calling to minister to the poor. Opposed by his bishop, Bresee left to organize a new congregation in the inner city called the Church of the Nazarene. By 1908, his church merged with others across the country to form the denomination of that same name, with Bresee as its first President. It should be noted that at its founding, one fourth of the Church of the Nazarene's ordained ministers were women.

By the late 1890s more radical visions of holiness were emerging. In England, Catherine Booth (1829–1890), the daughter of a Methodist lay preacher, married Methodist evangelist William Booth (1829–1912) in 1855. Influenced by holiness writings and preachers, including Walter and Phoebe Palmer in 1859, Catherine began preaching and William sought to be a holiness evangelist. When the Methodist New Connection refused, they left in 1861 to become itinerant evangelists. They founded the East London Christian Mission in 1865 to minister to the very poor, which in 1878 became The Salvation Army. By 1880, the Army began its work in America.[4]

In Cincinnati, Ohio, Martin Wells Knapp started God's Bible School and published *The Revivalist*, a periodical that would have a national circulation. In contrast to both denominational loyalists and those who reject denominations, he partnered with Seth Cook Rees (1854–1932) to form an association called the Holiness Union, which sought to bring together persons regardless of denomination. He was also a stalwart supporter of women's ministry, interracial gatherings, divine healing, and premillennialism.[5]

The pre-eminent opponent of denominational sectarianism was Daniel S. Warner. Originally a minister with the Winebrenner Church of God, Warner left that body when they objected to his holiness preaching. Warner argued that after Constantine, what had been a pure Church of God had become a creedal church. In this Age of the Spirit God was calling for Christians to leave their sectarian denominations and form one holy, nondenominational "Church of God." Called the Evening Light Saints, Warner's movement was interracial, had women as well as men as ministers, and proclaimed the promise of divine healing and sanctification. After Warner's death the movement became a non-creedal denomination, the Church of God (Anderson, Indiana), and has remained faithful to Warner's vision of egalitarian holiness.

The highly diverse Keswick wing of the holiness movement was also continuing to grow in many non-Methodist traditions. The Christian and Missionary Alliance, was formed in 1887 from Baptist and Presbyterian roots[6], and led by A. B. Simpson (1843–1919). In addition to his strong emphasis on missions, Simpson taught a four-fold gospel of Christ as Savior, Sanctifier, Healer, and Coming King. While Simpson is best described as a significant exponent of one strand of Keswick theol-

---

4. On the Booths, see Roger J. Green, *Catherine Booth* (Grand Rapids: Baker, 1996); and Roger J. Green, *The Life and Ministry of William Booth* (Nashville: Abingdon, 2006).

5. The Holiness Union would in 1922 later merge with the Pilgrim Church to form the Pilgrim Holiness Church, under the leadership of Rees. That denomination would then merge with the Wesleyan Methodist Church to form the Wesleyan Church in 1968.

6. Begun in 1887 as two parachurch organizations, the Christian Alliance (committed to holiness) and the Evangelical Missionary Alliance were united in 1897 as the Christian and Missionary Alliance. It became officially a denomination in 1947.

ogy, his understanding of the atonement and the indwelling of Christ as bringing humanity to a higher condition than was possessed before the Fall into sin, a new creation patterned after the Divine nature, echoes the theology of John Wesley.[7]

HEALING, EQUALITY, AND THE SECOND COMING

In this brief survey of diverse expressions of the Holiness movement several emphases have occurred repeatedly: healing, the second coming of Christ, interracial congregations and leadership, and the equality of women in the church. All of these would characterize the Holiness movement by the end of the nineteenth century.

John Wesley had taught that God heals both miraculously through prayer and also through medicine and doctors. A new healing movement began in the nineteenth century that was opposed by many in traditional Methodism but embraced by the Holiness movement.[8] Methodist Ethan O. Allen (1813–1902) began a healing ministry after experiencing healing from consumption in 1846 through the prayer of his class leader. Then Sara Mix, of the African Methodist Episcopal Church, experienced healing in 1877 through Allen's ministry, and became the first African-American healing evangelist in America. But the central figure in the healing movement was an Episcopalian and doctor, Charles Cullis (1833–1892), who read of Dorothea Trudel's healing ministry in Europe and in 1870 prayed for Lucy Drake, who was healed of a brain tumor. He began to hold annual healing conventions in Old Orchard, Maine, and other cities, and convinced other holiness leaders of his healing theology, including John Inskip, William Boardman, A. B. Simpson, and Carrie Judd Montgomery. Montgomery (1848–1946) was an Episcopalian who helped found the Christian and Missionary

---

7. On A. B. Simpson's theology see Bernie A. Van De Walle, *The Heart of the Gospel: A. B. Simpson, the Fourfold Gospel, and Late Nineteenth Century Evangelical Theology,* Princeton Theological Monograph Series 106 (Eugene, OR: Pickwick, 2009); and Charles Nienkirchen, *A. B. Simpson and the Pentecostal Movement: A Study in Continuity, Crisis, and Change* (Peabody, MA: Hendrickson, 1992).

8. On the healing movement see Nancy A. Hardesty, *Faith Cure* (Peabody, MA: Hendrickson, 2003); Donald W. Dayton, *The Theological Roots of Pentecostalism* (Metuchen, NJ: Scarecrow, 1992) and Heather D. Curtis, *Faith in the Great Physician* (Baltimore: Johns Hopkins University Press, 2007). An account of the healing movement in the Church of God (Anderson, Indiana) is found in Michael S. Stephens, *Who Healeth All Thy Diseases* (Lanham, MD: Scarecrow, 2008).

Alliance, and later was a minister in the Assemblies of God. Her theology of first believing on the basis of scripture that God has healed you, and then acting on that belief, became widespread in the healing movement, though others would question whether healing occurs as automatically or as certainly as that theology suggests.

With their concern for the poor, upholding equality of women, and the interracial nature of much of their ministry, the Holiness movement faced its strongest test in the American south. Southern culture had sharply delineated racial and gender roles, and Methodism there was so resistant to the Holiness movement that discussion of sanctification in any form had largely been discontinued. But by the 1880s, holiness advocates were bringing their message to white and black audiences in the South, aided by the explosion of new holiness periodicals and books. Their meetings, especially when interracial, were attacked verbally and physically. The Methodist Episcopal Church, South acted to discipline and expel clergy with holiness sympathies. The holiness preachers claimed their authority to preach was from the Holy Spirit, not a denomination, and that persecution could be expected in the latter days just prior to the return of Jesus.[9]

This points toward the increased eschatological urgency that marked the late nineteenth century Holiness movement. In general, the postmillennial optimism of the first half of the century was replaced by premillennial expectation of the immanent return of Christ.[10] While often seen as otherworldly escapism, this assessment does not do justice to the continued holiness commitment to the present work of the Holy Spirit in sanctification, healing, and alleviating social conditions.

One reason premillennialism was so attractive to so many in the Holiness movement lies in the economic depression of the 1890s and the political defeat of populism as a reform movement. As holiness people saw farms go under and hardworking people reduced to poverty, and financial elites grow in wealth and political power, they sought theological answers to their suffering. Holiness leaders like L. L. Pickett proclaimed

9. See Randall J. Stephens, *The Fire Spreads: Holiness and Pentecostalism in the American South* (Cambridge: Harvard University Press, 2008).

10. While this premillennialism often included the adoption of elements of John Nelson Darby's dispensationalism such as the rapture, it was nonetheless much more open to the present work of the Spirit. Many Wesleyans in the holiness movement resisted this new eschatology due to its Calvinistic orientation. D. S. Warner was an amillennialist.

that when Christ returned, those with excessive wealth would have their property confiscated by Jesus and given to those who had unjustly lost their own. Some holiness radicals went further, predicting the end of private property itself.[11]

This was a period of yearning for better things—lives freed from sin and sickness, communities freed of inequality and poverty, for the present work of the Spirit and the soon return of Christ. The language of Pentecost and baptism of the Spirit was prevalent, and the hope was that the church of the Book of Acts would be restored in the last days.

While the Holiness movement within both traditional denominations and the newer denominations and movements was characterized by Pentecostal expectancy, there were certain figures who radicalized that sense of eschatological urgency. Frank. W. Sandford (1862–1948) founded the Shiloh Community, a Bible School in Maine. Emphasizing world evangelization, Sandford believed God had called him to the role of Elijah as the forerunner to the second coming of Christ, Even more influential was John Alexander Dowie, whose Christian Catholic Apostolic Church and healing ministry in Zion City, Illinois, became a seedbed for Pentecostalism. He also ultimately saw himself as the Elijah preceding the second coming.

More theologically orthodox was evangelist Maria B. Woodworth-Etter, whose meetings were marked by healings and the experience of trances and falling under the power of the Spirit, reminiscent of early Methodism and frontier camp meetings. She was in fact a forerunner, and later a participant, in the Pentecostal revival that was soon to break forth in the new century.

11. See William Kostlevy, "Neither Silver Nor Gold: The Burning Bush Movement and the Communitarian Holiness Vision" (PhD dissertation, University of Notre Dame, 1996).

THE HOLINESS MOVEMENT

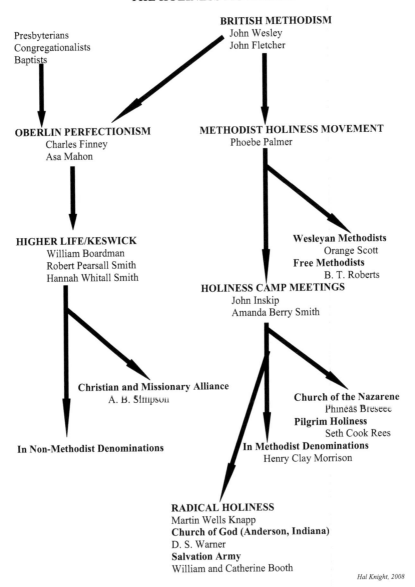

BRITISH METHODISM
John Wesley
John Fletcher

Presbyterians
Congregationalists
Baptists

OBERLIN PERFECTIONISM
Charles Finney
Asa Mahon

METHODIST HOLINESS MOVEMENT
Phoebe Palmer

HIGHER LIFE/KESWICK
William Boardman
Robert Pearsall Smith
Hannah Whitall Smith

Wesleyan Methodists
Orange Scott
Free Methodists
B. T. Roberts

HOLINESS CAMP MEETINGS
John Inskip
Amanda Berry Smith

Christian and Missionary Alliance
A. B. Simpson

Church of the Nazarene
Phineas Breseee
Pilgrim Holiness
Seth Cook Rees

In Non-Methodist Denominations

In Methodist Denominations
Henry Clay Morrison

RADICAL HOLINESS
Martin Wells Knapp
Church of God (Anderson, Indiana)
D. S. Warner
Salvation Army
William and Catherine Booth

Hal Knight, 2008

10

Bishop Daniel A. Payne and the A.M.E. Mission to the "Ransomed"

Dennis C. Dickerson

Anyone who attended the General Conference of the African Methodist Episcopal Church in 1908 in Norfolk, Virginia may have been astonished to learn the church motto was changing. Bishop Daniel A. Payne's nineteenth-century creedal statement, "God Our Father, Christ Our Redeemer, Man Our Brother," now read as "God Our Father, Christ Our Redeemer, the Holy Ghost Our Comforter, Man Our Brother!" Why this change occurred, no one seems to know. It could be argued that the Azusa Street revivals in 1906 had challenged the nation's oldest black religious body to acknowledge the present reality of the Holy Ghost and to remind African Methodists that sanctifying power from the third person in the Godhead stirred the same religious enthusiasm that marked their Wesleyan origins.

Payne believed fully and thoroughly in the Holy Ghost, and credited this power for his religious awakening and conversion. Concerning his Methodist class meetings in Charleston, South Carolina, he said, "I have felt the Spirit of God moving my childish heart." Moreover, when he fully confessed Christianity Payne recalled the revival in which God "poured out his awakening and converting power upon his waiting children, and many souls were converted and sanctified by it." He proudly declared "of this number I was one."[1] Yet, Payne's determination to instill order and discipline in the worship of unlettered, unlearned, and formerly en-

---

1. Daniel A. Payne, *Recollections of Seventy Years*, (New York, Arno Press and the New York Times, Reprint 1969) 16–17.

slaved African Americans made him wary of their potential response to the Holy Ghost. It seemed sufficient for them to know that their worth as human beings was anchored in the fatherhood of God and the finished redemptive work of Jesus Christ. These divine gifts cemented the brotherhood and sisterhood of all humankind. At the same time, Payne refused to encourage rituals and practices that might blaspheme the same Holy Ghost whose sanctifying power completed the work of salvation. To solve this dilemma Payne simply deleted any mention of the Holy Ghost in the denominational motto.

Though he seriously embraced the Holy Ghost in his sermons and theological works, Payne saw the denominational motto as a popularized presentation of A.M.E. Church doctrine. Payne felt free to signal his fear of lifting up the Holy Ghost in the motto lest some African Americans view it as license and a cover for blasphemous beliefs and unorthodox practices. While he served as pastor of one A.M.E. congregation in Baltimore in the 1840s, for example, Payne, in altering the order of service, tried "to correct some bad customs of worship, and especially to moderate the singing and praying bands, which then existed in the most extravagant form." At another church he took exception to the singing of "spiritual songs" or "Corn-field Ditties."[2]

After Payne was elected to the bishopric in 1852, he observed during his many years of travel other excesses in African American worship. Following his sermon at a "bush meeting" at yet another church, the congregation "formed a ring, and with coats off sung, clapped their hands and stamped their feet in a most ridiculous and heathenish way." The pastor heeded Payne's request that the people stop this demonstration, but they persisted in "singing and rocking their bodies to and fro . . . for about fifteen minutes." Payne then approached the "ring" leader and told him "it was a heathenish way to worship and disgraceful to themselves, the race, and the Christian name." Although the group disbanded, the "ring" leader, after Payne's afternoon sermon, rebuked the bishop for his negative views. "Sinners," he said, "won't get converted unless there is a ring." When Payne said that only "the Spirit of God and the word of God can convert sinners," the leader answered by saying "the Spirit of God works upon people in different ways. At camp-meetings there must be a ring here, a ring there, a ring over yonder, or sinners will not get convert-

2. Ibid., 81; 93–94.

ed." Payne observed that these notions and behavior were widespread and "regarded as the essence of religion."[3]

Payne objected to songs with such lyrics as:

> Ashes to ashes, dust to dust;
> If God won't have us, the devil must.
> It was way over there where the coffin fell;
> I heard that sinner as he screamed in hell.

"Prayer," Payne also noted, "was only a secondary thing, and this was rude and extravagant to the last degree." He was repelled because "the man who had the most powerful pair of lungs was the one who made the best prayer . . . he who could sing the loudest and longest led the 'Band,' having his loins girded and a handkerchief in hand with which he kept time while his feet resounded on the floor like the drum-sticks of a bass drum." In some places these demonstrations were described as the "Voudoo Dance." To clergy who could not ban this "incurable religious disease," Payne proposed that they "let such people go out of the Church than remain in it to perpetuate their evil practice." Their continued presence would "disgrace the Christian name and corrupt others." Payne admonished that "the time is at hand when the ministry of the A.M.E. Church must drive out this heathenish mode of worship or drive out all the intelligence, refinement, and practical Christians who may be in her bosom."[4]

Payne believed the religiously untutored should be discouraged from making mischievous and unscriptural appeals to the Holy Ghost. In the eighteenth century John Wesley already had acknowledged the issue in drawing distinctions among religious enthusiasts. Citing Wesley, Payne said some descended into "religious madness—a religious madness arising from some falsely imagined influence or inspiration from God, at least from imputing something to God which ought not to be imputed to him, or expecting something from God which ought not to be expected from him." There were still other enthusiasts "who in preaching or prayer, imagine themselves to be so influenced by the Spirit of God as indeed they are not." Though Payne was referring specifically to uneducated clergy, his condemnation of these preachers also reflected

---

3. Ibid., 253–54.
4. Ibid., 254–56.

his denunciation of worshipers who misunderstood and misused the inspiration and stirring of the Holy Ghost.[5]

Payne was a practitioner of what Wesleyan scholar Thomas A. Langford described as "practical divinity." John Wesley, according to Langford, "understood theology to be intimately related to Christian living and the proclamation of Christian faith." Wesley made "traditional theology" intelligible to his hearers and challenged them to live "in holiness of heart and life."[6] Payne adopted this view and struggled hard as a pastor, historiographer, college founder and president, bishop, and ecumenist, to bring orthodoxy to A.M.E. Church worship and belief. Examples of "extravagant" religious behavior, probably derived from the African background, and from a misreading of Christian spirituality, persuaded Payne to press African Americans in general and African Methodists in particular to live according to puritanical standards and to observe the Wesleyan regimen of prayer, scripture study, and abstemious habits.

The African Methodist Episcopal Church represented for Payne a primary vehicle for realizing Wesley's "practical divinity." Though open to members of all races, the A.M.E. Church aimed its energies and efforts toward the evangelization and uplift of African Americans. The denomination seemed divinely ordained to fight for black freedom and to offer Wesleyan discipline to the newly emancipated. Payne took seriously what A.M.E. founder Richard Allen observed about the suitability of Methodism to African Americans. Allen declared "we deemed it expedient to have a form of discipline, whereby we may guide our people in the fear of God, in the unity of the Spirit, and in the bonds of peace." Payne agreed with the A.M.E. Church founder, and sought to implement his vision.[7]

---

5. *African Methodist Episcopal Church Magazine* 1.12 (1844) 302 (courtesy of Reverend Mark Tyler, Macedonia A.M.E. Church, Camden, NJ).

6. Thomas A. Langford, "John Wesley and Theological Method" in Randy L. Maddox, ed., *Rethinking Wesley's Theology For Contemporary Methodism* (Nashville, Kingswood /Abingdon, 1998) 35, 38.

7. Richard Allen, *The Life Experience and Gospel Labors of the Rt. Rev. Richard Allen*, (Nashville: A.M.E. Sunday School Union, reprint, 1990) 33; For an assessment of Daniel A. Payne's significance in A.M.E. Church history, see Dennis C. Dickerson, *Religion, Race, And Region: Research Notes In A.M.E. Church History* (Nashville: A.M.E. Sunday School Union/Legacy Publishing, 1995) 35–48.

Payne was born free in Charleston, South Carolina on February 24, 1811. His preoccupation with pedagogy for preachers and parishioners became another means to implement Wesley's "practical divinity." When he opened a school for blacks in Charleston, he experienced the pernicious impact of "the slave-holding power." When his school was closed, he fled swiftly to New York City. He studied at Gettysburg Theological Seminary and affiliated for almost seven years with the Lutheran Church, mainly in the anti-slavery Franckean Synod.[8]

Despite a deepening commitment to the ministry Payne never abandoned his passion for teaching. He joined the A.M.E. Church in 1841 and transferred his educational energies to crusades for an educated clergy and to the establishment of Wilberforce University in 1863. What he wanted for A.M.E. ministers he also desired for A.M.E. members. When the Civil War emancipated four million African Americans, Bishop Payne led the founding of the South Carolina Annual Conference in 1865 out of which other A.M.E. jurisdictions emerged. Denominational expansion provided venues to preach to newly freed blacks about the difference between liberty and libertine living. Sobriety and restraint in social behavior also had its counterpart in the spiritual sphere. In these settings Payne, a true Wesleyan, activated his belief that clergy had obligations to preach the gospel and exhort listeners to manifest its teachings in their daily lives.

When Congress and President Abraham Lincoln agreed to abolish slavery in the District of Columbia in 1862, Bishop Payne addressed an audience of manumitted men and women about the challenges of freedom. He admonished them to pray to God and celebrate their "holy Freedom." Their liberty, however, meant they should "not lounge in sinful indolence, not to degrade yourselves by vice nor to corrupt society by licentiousness, neither to offend laws by crime, but (go) to the enjoyment of a well regulated liberty." Payne exhorted ex-slaves "to be religious" and "godly." He added "we entrust you to never be content until you are emancipated from sin, from sin without, and from sin within you." Freedom from sin, he said, "is attained only through the faith of Jesus, (and) obedience to Jesus. As the American Congress has ransomed you, so certain, yea, more certainly has Jesus redeemed you from the guilt and power of sin by his own precious blood." He told them to learn to

---

8. James Kenneth Echols, "Daniel Alexander Payne and the Lutheran Church," *A.M.E. Church Review* (October–December 2001) 113; 118.

read the Bible because its teachings "will purify your hearts and make them the abodes of the Ever Blessed Trinity." As a result, Payne declared emancipated African Americans "will be morally prepared to recognize and respond to all the relations of civilized and christianized life." Most importantly, blacks should train their offspring in proper eating, decent attire, and the avoidance of "luxuries of which we are so fond."

He hoped that this type of education should "penetrate the heart." He warned that education which forgets, or purposely omits, the culture of the heart, is better adapted to devilism than manhood. But the education which reaches the heart, moulds it and humbles it before the Cross. Payne also wanted the emancipated to adhere to "godliness and honesty." He said "the godly man, is he who fears God and keeps his commandments. Such a man will be honest in words as well as in deeds; in matters of truth as well as in matters of property. Honesty is the only policy of godliness." He admonished "colored men, write this sentiment upon your hearts, engrave it in your memory. Let all your thoughts, words, actions, be controlled by this principle, (that) it is always safe to be honest, as it is always safe to be godly."[9]

To achieve these objectives the agency of African Methodism was indispensable. He explained this view in 1868 to the Society for the Promotion of Collegiate and Theological Education at the West. The A.M.E. Church, Payne proudly asserted, "is the first organization in the United States which undertook the special care of the enslaved and self-emancipated Freedmen." In fact the church saved many from slavery "the worst form of infidelity that which denies the existence of God." When blacks fled to Canada, the denomination set up the British Methodist Episcopal Church "to lead the Freedmen into the bosom of the Church of God there to teach them the habits of industry, thrift, and virtue. Hence, the A.M.E. Church showed itself as "an Asylum from the blasphemous and degrading spirit of caste," as a venue for blacks to discover "free minds and space to rise," and where they could find "powerful motives for mental and moral culture." Additionally, the denomination established Wilberforce University "to aid in the special work of en-

---

9. Daniel Alexander Payne, "Welcome to the Ransomed" in Milton C. Sernett, *African American Religious History: A Documentary Witness*, 2nd ed. (Durham: Duke University Press, 1999) 233, 234–35, 240.

lightening and Christianizing the Freedmen." The school aimed to train teachers "to the ministry of the Freedmen."[10]

The denomination, Payne testified, exercised a three fold influence among newly emancipated blacks. First, the church's religious impact showed in the evangelization of 600,000 people "impressing them with our ideas of God and Man, in their relations to each other as Creator and creature-with our conceptions of truths evangelic, and their relations to our common humanity." The second impact lay in moral teaching. These principles which affected "the conjugal, the paternal, the filial, [and] the social" drew from "religious teachings" and they "necessarily affect the moral nature of this mass of human beings." Political influences also illustrated the A.M.E. impact among ex-slaves. These denominational partisans declared "that when a Christian approaches the poll, he is morally bound to cast his vote for no one, but an open and fearless advocate of liberty, justice, and all righteousness." Payne also surveyed several southern states and listed various public offices that A.M.E.s held during Reconstruction. In South Carolina, for example, nearly thirty A.M.E.s, several of whom were ministers, served in the state legislature. In North Carolina there was one A.M.E. in the lower house of the legislature and two were in the state senate. Hence, the denomination, according to Payne, played a crucial role in shaping how blacks behaved in both their public and private lives.[11]

Nonetheless, Payne failed in eradicating egregious violations of Christian belief and practice. In those places where the "ring "ceremony occurred Payne reported that some pastors resisted his admonitions on the matter. They told Payne they "could not succeed in restraining them, and an attempt to compel them to cease would simply drive them away from our Church." His efforts to educate clergy also appeared unsuccessful. To Booker T. Washington, Payne, as late as 1890, ruefully reported that "I say emphatically, in the presence of the great Head of the Church, that no more than one-third of the ministers, Baptist and Methodist, in the South are morally and intellectually qualified." One problem, he said, was the large number who exchanged farming for preaching "because

---

10. Daniel A. Payne, *Bishop Payne's Address Before the College Aid Society* (Xenia, OH: Torchlight, 1868) 3–4; 6–7 (found in Bridwell Library at the Perkins School of Theology, Southern Methodist University, Dallas, Texas).

11. Ibid., 5–6.

they thought it would be an easier way to get a living."[12] Since clergy were cowardly or uneducated, those who espoused and practiced unorthodox beliefs and rituals encountered either token opposition or abject acquiescence. An exasperated Payne could do no more than constantly harangue and denounce the excessive emotionalism and callisthenic gyrations of seemingly spirit-filled worshipers. Perhaps Payne believed that his creation of a denominational motto would allow him the last word on these controversial issues. He removed the temptation from the motto to appeal to the Holy Ghost to sanction questionable rituals and practices.

This may be the reason Payne doubted the value of revivals. Though he participated in them in his younger years, Josephus R. Coan said that "close observation of revival methods and results led him to the conclusion that on the whole they were more of a liability than an asset." Coan added that "Payne insisted on "intelligent worship," "the true method of serving God," (and) religious practices which were in "harmony with the religion of Jesus." Revivals as he knew them were extravagances of worship."[13]

Payne proposed the motto, "God Our Father, Christ Our Redeemer, Man Our Brother," at the 1856 General Conference. James H. Cone, the father of black theology and an A.M.E minister, though he interpreted Payne's motto as "within the social and political context of the Church's origin," made only a minimal mention of the Holy Ghost. He merely noted that A.M.E. bishops never inquired about "whether the Holy Spirit proceeded from the Father alone or (from) the Father and the Son." These prelates were generally unconcerned about these and other theological controversies. What mattered to them was the fatherhood of God to all humankind, Christ as "black people's liberator, and that "brotherhood and sisterhood are grounded in the fatherhood and motherly presence of God in black life." Payne would have endorsed Cone's characterizations, and would advise the A.M.E. Church to go no further on the issue else a

---

12. Payne, *Recollections of Seventy Years*, 255; Daniel Alexander Payne to Booker T. Washington, November 3, 1890, in Louis R. Harlan, ed., *The Booker T. Washington Papers*, vol. 3, 1889–95 (Urbana: University of Illinois Press, 1974) 97–98.

13. Josephus R. Coan, *Daniel Alexander Payne: Christian Educator* (Philadelphia: A.M.E. Book Concern, 1935) 129–30.

doctrine of the Holy Ghost might put African Methodism in doctrinal jeopardy through the excesses of ecstatic black religion.[14]

Clearly, Payne overreacted, and wrongly deleted a powerful source of empowerment and celebration for A.M.E. members. He would not have been comfortable at the Azusa Street revivals which were held in Los Angeles in a former A.M.E. Church. Most A.M.E.s did not agree with Payne. His contemporary, Bishop Henry M. Turner, for example, dissented from Payne's view and endorsed black folk religion. Disagreement also came from those who attended the 1908 General Conference which corrected Payne's motto and declared "God Our Father, Christ Our Redeemer, the Holy Ghost Our Comforter, Man Our Brother!"

14. Daniel A. Payne, *History Of The African Methodist Episcopal Church* (Nashville, Publishing House of the A.M.E. Sunday-School Union, 1891) 359; James H. Cone, "'God Our Father, Christ Our Redeemer, Man Our Brother': A Theological Interpretation of the A.M.E. Church," *AME Working Papers* (1977) II–2; II–8; II–11.

11

Julia Foote

Exemplifying the Holiness Message of Fervency, Inclusion, and Unity

DOUGLAS M. STRONG

JULIA A. J. FOOTE (1823–1900)[1] was virtually unknown to scholars of American religion until relatively recently, when she was lifted from obscurity by historians such as William Andrews.[2] Known primarily for her role as a pioneering woman evangelist of color, Foote is also important because her career so clearly demonstrates many of the central themes of late nineteenth century Holiness revivalism.

Born in Schenectady, New York, Foote was converted at age fifteen at a Methodist meeting, married the next year, and then moved with her husband to Boston, where she joined an African Methodist Episcopal Zion congregation. While there, as she encountered visions, physical healing, and religious enthusiasm, Foote received the gift of entire sanctification through the baptism of the Holy Spirit. Such an occurrence was similar to that of many women (and men) in the late 1830s, but

---

1. The date of Foote's death is listed variously as 1900 or 1901. In this article, I have chosen to use 1900 because one reputable source states that Foote died on 22 November 1900. William Jacob Walls, *The African Methodist Episcopal Zion Church: Reality of the Black Church* (Charlotte, NC: A.M.E. Zion, 1974) 112. Another source, however, indicates that Foote attended the 1901 General Holiness Assembly in Chicago. Charles Edwin Jones, *A Guide to the Study of the Holiness Movement* (Metuchen, NJ: Scarecrow, 1974) 632.

2. William L. Andrews, ed., *Sisters of the Spirit: Three Black Women's Autobiographies of the Nineteenth Century* (Bloomington: Indiana University Press, 1986).

Foote found herself moved a step further when she felt called to exhort and pray publicly about her spiritual experience. Her pastor—the Rev. Jemiel Beman—tried to repress her call, but Foote nonetheless persevered and, without recognition until the very end of her life, determined "to testify to the suffering of the blood of Jesus Christ to save from all sin." With single-minded vocational purpose, she preached this "second distinct work of the Holy Ghost" through cleansing by the baptism of the Spirit, "illumination" (spiritual wisdom) through "the Spirit of Truth," and holy living. This holy living would be demonstrated by adhering to a strict behavioral code and distancing oneself from all things that were "worldly."[3]

Many womanist historians have used Foote's life story to fortify their particular theories of black women's self-actualized drive to overcome sexism and racism: "She possessed an inordinate faith in herself" (Bettye Collier-Thomas); she participated in "religious self-recovery" (Yvonne Chireau); and she "reformulate[d] her identity through self-recovery" (Delores Williams).[4] In contrast to these characterizations of the self's quest for personal power, when we read Foote's own description of the source of her spiritual confidence, she unfailingly credited her success to the empowerment of the Holy Spirit. According to Foote's account, the cause of her authority and identity change was not internal, but an external intervention of the divine—what Susie Stanley, Cheryl Sanders, and Estrelda Alexander refer to as the "sanctified self" or a liberating ethic of empowerment.[5] Gregory Schneider has stated well that such women had a "confidence in a self that was no longer a woman's own self, but God's,

3. Julia A. J. Foote, *A Brand Plucked from the Fire: An Autobiographical Sketch* (Cleveland: Lauer & Yost, 1886) 3–4, 53, 116.

4. Bettye Collier-Thomas, *Daughters of Thunder: Black Women Preachers and Their Sermons, 1850–1979* (San Francisco: Jossey-Bass, 1998) 59; Yvonne Chireau, review of Kimberly Rae Connor, *Conversions and Visions in the Writings of African-American Women,* in *Journal of the American Academy of Religion* 64 (1996) 694–95; Delores S. Williams, "A Womanist Perspective on Sin," ed. Emilie Maureen Townes, *A Troubling in My Soul: Womanist Perspectives on Evil and Suffering* (Maryknoll, NY: Orbis, 1993) 143.

5. Susie Stanley, *Holy Boldness: Women Preachers' Autobiographies and the Sanctified Self* (Knoxville: University of Tennessee Press, 2002); Cheryl Sanders, *Empowerment Ethics for a Liberated People* (Minneapolis: Fortress, 1995); Estrelda Y. Alexander, *Limited Liberty: The Legacy of Four Pentecostal Women Pioneers* (Cleveland: Pilgrim, 2007).

and that, nevertheless, felt freer and more authentic than she had ever felt simply on her own."[6]

The apex of Foote's ministerial career was in the late 1870s and 1880s. For a number of years, she was a highly-sought evangelist: the lead preacher at the Women's Holiness Camp Meeting in Mount Tabor, New Jersey, and at multiple other camp meetings throughout the northeast and Midwest. Her reputation continued through the latter part of the nineteenth century, culminating in her becoming the first woman deacon (in 1894) and the second woman elder (in 1899) to be ordained in the AME Zion Church. These honors were not credentialing for her ministry but rather were recognition—at the end of her life—for service well done.[7]

Foote's celebrated preaching in the 1880s coincided with a crucial decade in the history of the Holiness movement, a time when Holiness advocates were alienated from upwardly mobile mainstream Methodists and increasingly viewed as "holy rollers." During these years, many Holiness folks either "came out" or were pushed out of the major Methodist denominations.[8] Through her peripatetic preaching and through the publication of her spiritual memoir (*A Brand Plucked From the Burning*, first printing, 1879), Foote helped to define and represent this new, self-consciously separate Holiness movement in three ways: (1) In light of mainline Methodist de-emphasis and even criticism of religious fervency, she re-emphasized the importance of divine immediacy and spiritual ecstasy; (2) By repudiating "prejudice" in all its forms, she articulated a direct theological connection between holiness and social inclusion—as opposed to the social stratification that came to characterize "respectable" Methodism; and (3) Her ministry became emblematic of the Holiness movement's stress on spiritual unity—based on the believers' common experience of the Holy Spirit, rather than the mainline Methodist stress on ecclesiological unity—based on denominational loyalty.

6. A. Gregory Schneider, *The Way of the Cross Leads Home: The Domestication of American Methodism* (Bloomington: Indiana University Press, 1993) 182.

7. Stanley, *Holy Boldness*, 242; Daniel S. Warner, "Journal of D. S. Warner," Archives, Anderson University, 345, 380; Walls, *The African Methodist Episcopal Zion Church*, 111–12.

8. Other holiness-oriented Methodists, however (such as Henry Clay Morrison), chose to remain within the mainline Methodist denominations, viz. the Methodist Episcopal Church and the Methodist Episcopal Church, South

Aside from her autobiography, we do not have a large amount of primary evidence regarding Foote's ministry—other than references to the effectiveness of her preaching in the writings of her co-workers. These colleagues were part of an extensive network of Holiness evangelists who traveled in tandem, on an informal circuit, to various assemblies and conferences. By looking at the careers of Foote and those with whom she ministered and circulated most closely, we find many common themes, and can therefore identify the distinctive character of the Holiness movement in its heyday.

Two of the Holiness preachers most often associated with Julia Foote were Daniel S. Warner (1842–1895) and Thomas K. Doty (1833–1913). Warner, who became the founder of the Church of God (Anderson), mentioned his joint ministry with Foote on several occasions. Regarding a three-day revival, for example, Warner wrote in his journal that "Sister Foot [sic] preached. This has been a glorious meeting. Souls [were] saved every day." At another service where Warner and Foote were speaking, Warner stated that "great power was upon us and all the sanctified said that it was the most profitable meeting they had ever attended." In the late 1870s and 1880s, Foote and Warner were both connected to loosely-associated holiness organizations (or "bands") in Ohio and were co-leaders of the 1880 Western Union Holiness Convention in Jacksonville, Illinois. [9]

Thomas Doty also interacted with Foote on a regular basis.[10] A leading Holiness evangelist, Wesleyan Methodist clergyman, and editor of the monthly *Christian Harvester* newspaper, Doty was known for the "fervor of his spirit" and was considered as one of the founding leaders of the Holiness movement. Highly eccentric in his mannerisms, "always frail in health and slight in form," Doty "with his black cap, a shawl under his arm and a bundle of *Christian Harvesters*, was a loved and familiar figure for many years" at Holiness gatherings. Doty stressed the supernatural gifts of the Spirit, especially the miraculous healing of the sick.[11]

9. Daniel S. Warner, "Journal of D. S. Warner," 345, 380; Jones, *Guide to the Study of the Holiness Movement*, 632. I am indebted to Susie Stanley and Merle Strege for pointing me to this information.

10. One example is the General Holiness Assembly in Chicago, which Jones indicates that both Foote and Doty attended. Foote was one of those who "endorsed" the Assembly. See Jones, *Guide to the Study of the Holiness Movement*, 620, 632.

11. Ira Ford McLeister, *History of the Wesleyan Methodist Church in America* (Syracuse: Wesleyan Methodist, 1934) 276–77. See Doty's *The Two-Fold Gift of the Holy*

Doty wrote the introduction for Julia Foote's autobiography, and he was the person who published the book at the offices of his *Christian Harvester* paper. He was also on the program with her for speaking engagements on numerous occasions. Along with Foote, Doty strongly defended women's preaching—because, as he said, "today is a pentecostal day." Doty expressed his admiration for Foote's evangelistic ability when he recounted that "those of us who heard her preach last year . . . where she held the almost breathless attention of five thousand people, by the eloquence of the Holy Ghost, know well where is the hiding of her power." Other themes that Foote developed in her autobiography, such as the importance of fervent faith and the evils of prejudice, are echoed in Doty's writings. It is difficult to know to what degree Foote and Doty influenced each other, for both evangelists were writing about similar ideas during the same period, but they were clearly allies with a shared vision in complementary ministries.[12]

Doty's book, *Lessons in Holiness* (1881), is a seminal text for understanding late nineteenth century Holiness emphases. In this manual for preachers, a kind of primer for the Holiness movement, Doty speaks about concepts that were essential for Julia Foote and other Holiness evangelists. First, Doty discusses the importance of the "witness of the Spirit to holiness," which he understood as "an undercurrent of sensibility in the things of God." These "thrills of the divine life" included "ecstasy" as "a high degree of emotion," "special faith" to achieve answers to prayer for healing, and shouting as "an instinctive outburst of reverence and love." "Give me both the Blesser and the blessing," Doty exuded. "All holy emotions involve a movement of the divine."[13] Julia Foote wrote in a similar vein: she describes her own fervent experiences of faith and encourages such experiences in others.[14] These manifestations of emotional, ecstatic faith became a hallmark of the Holiness movement in the 1880s, as it moved closer toward the Pentecostal ideas that would dominate at the turn of the twentieth century.

Ghost (Cleveland: Christian Harvester, 1890) 203, in which he stressed the emotional aspects of sanctification and the supernatural gifts of the Spirit, while declaring that tongues "is unknown at the present day."

12. Foote, *A Brand Plucked from the Fire*, 7, 112–16; T. F. Doty, *Lessons in Holiness* (Cleveland: Thomas Doty, 1881) 214.

13. Doty, *Lessons in Holiness*, 75, 78, 91–98.

14. Foote, *Brand Plucked from the Fire*, 115–16.

Julia Foote's stress on the problem of prejudice and the need for inclusion among Christians was a second emphasis held by some of the more radical exponents of the late nineteenth century Holiness movement. Foote wrote passionately about the bigotry that she had experienced firsthand and her belief that only God's holiness could overcome such discrimination. "O Prejudice! Thou cruel monster! Wilt thou ever cease to exist? . . . Not until all shall know the Lord, and holiness shall be written . . . upon all things in earth as well as in heaven. Those who are fully in the truth cannot possess a prejudiced spirit. They cannot reject those whom Christ has received."

Thomas Doty agreed with his friend Julia Foote. "Holiness takes the prejudice of color out of both the white and the black," Doty wrote in his introduction to Foote's autobiography. In his book, *Lessons in Holiness*, Doty insisted that "holiness destroys the line of color-prejudice. It is an equalizer; for holiness is equal everywhere, and holy fellowship is on a level." Quoting from the book of Acts, Doty insisted that God "hath made of one blood all nations of men."

Foote and Doty believed that worldly pursuits ("worldliness") led to carnal reasoning which led to faulty judgments about others, but holiness led to a "Spirit of Truth" which would lead to the acceptance of everyone.[15] Though not all were so clearheaded about the rampant racism and sexism of the day, Doty, Foote and a few other late nineteenth century Holiness advocates spoke out against the generally accepted social norms that were characteristic of affluent mainline congregations. Understanding this Holiness stress on social inclusion helps us to comprehend more clearly the early twentieth century transition to the racially integrated Pentecostal message of (Holiness-influenced) William Seymour.

A third theme articulated by Julia Foote, Thomas Doty, D. S. Warner, and other late nineteenth-century Holiness leaders was their loathing of ecclesiastical power and denominational distinctions—especially as manifested in the Methodist church. These humanmade divisions, they concluded, must be overthrown by the Holy Spirit's power. True holiness would destroy church institutions. Though Doty and Warner would later disagree over whether one's separation from a denomination or one's acceptance of holiness teaching was most essential,[16] in the 1880s they

---

15. Ibid., 3, 7, 48, 65, 96; Doty, *Lessons in Holiness*, 139, 144.

16. Melvin E. Dieter, *The Holiness Revival of the Nineteenth Century* (Lanham, MD: Scarecrow, 1996) 211–12, 216–17.

joined forces to attack "the evil of sectarianism." As Doty expressed in the *Christian Harvester*, "The possessor of perfect love . . . overleaps denominations in spirit, and so regards all the sanctified as his brethren." Warner conveyed his admiration for the "frankness with which . . . the editor of the Harvester . . . a holy man of God . . . acknowledges that 'denominations are directly or indirectly the result of sin.'"[17]

Foote cooperated with people and congregations from many denominations—Methodist Episcopal, African Methodist Episcopal Zion, Wesleyan Methodist, Free Methodist, Mennonite, Church of God, and Presbyterian. Similar to her publisher, Thomas Doty, she could not understand those who supported only one church institution. Like Doty and Warner, she held that they who "hold fellowship with Christ . . . cannot reject those whom he has received, nor receive those whom he rejects, but all are brought into a blessed harmony with God and each other." Going beyond the theological arguments of Doty and Warner, however, Foote asserted that "those who are fully in the truth cannot possess a prejudiced or sectarian spirit." Foote directly connected her anti-denominationalism with her understanding of prejudice, since any form of separation or exclusion reflected a sinful disposition. For Julia Foote, then, a person's fervent holiness experience of spiritual devotion would necessarily result in "a blessed harmony with God and each other"—a breaking down of the barriers of race, sex, and sect.[18]

BIBLIOGRAPHY

Andrews, William L., editor. *Sisters of the Spirit: Three Black Women's Autobiographies of the Nineteenth Century.* Bloomington: Indiana University Press, 1986.

17. Andrew L. Byers, *Birth of a Reformation, or The Life and Labors of Daniel S. Warner* (Anderson, IN: Gospel Trumpet, 1922) 214–16, 218–21.

18. Foote, *Brand Plucked from the Fire*, 3–4.

12

Daniel Sydney Warner

Joining Holiness and All Truth[1]

BARRY L. CALLEN

IN ITS EARLIEST DECADES the Holiness Movement in America sought to be a reforming force *within* existing church structures. Eventually many movement adherents, often reluctantly, became separatists, judging themselves forced out of the churches because of their commitment to holiness. Daniel Warner (1842–1895) and the Church of God movement (Anderson, Ind.) he helped inspire came especially early in this "separatist" process. Warner's come-outism was inspired by a vision of the church outside *all* denominations, enabled by the dynamic of holiness. He cared deeply about the unity of believers, saw holiness as the way to it, and judged the continuing existence of multiple and often competitive denominational structures to be an evil among God's people that God intended to end.

Warner's conversion was in a Winebrennarian revival meeting being held near Montpelier, Ohio, in 1865. Warner then received his ministerial license from the West Ohio Eldership in 1867, having decided that this body represented best the true faith and practices of the New Testament church.[2]

---

1. This chapter is based on a longer article of the same name published in the *Wesleyan Theological Journal* 30.1 (1995) 92–110.

2. For a recounting of this whole story, see Barry Callen, *It's God's Church! Life and Legacy of Daniel Warner* (Anderson, IN: Warner, 1995)

THE NEW COMMISSION

Within ten years Warner was gripped by a "new commission" that he felt God had given him. According to the March 7, 1878, entry in his personal journal: "The Lord showed me that holiness could never prosper upon sectarian soil encumbered by human creeds and party names, and he gave me a new commission to join holiness and all truth together and build up the apostolic church of the living God."

Both Warner's affinity with and his questioning of the reform-from-the-inside approach of the mainstream Holiness movement can be seen in the 1880 convention of the Western Union Holiness Association held in the Brooklyn Methodist Episcopal Church in Jacksonville, Illinois.[3] The planning committee said that this gathering, comprised of about two hundred holiness leaders from a range of denominations and states, would only be in the interests of holiness. Thus, it was to be "strictly and purely undenominational."

Daniel Warner had been asked to make a formal address, an honor in this select ecumenical crowd. The topic of Warner's address to the convention was "The Kind of Power Needed to Carry the Holiness Work." The main point he made was that "it is the power of God Himself that is needed for this work." He warned that "the devil is set against this work. . . . We need God's power to the fullest degree promised to meet this adversary." "God is looking around to find someone he can trust," announced Warner. God "generally finds them among the holy ones."

Some of the statements by other speakers heard by Warner at this convention stirred the evolving struggle within him. For instance, Thomas Doty from Cleveland, Ohio, editor of the *Christian Harvester,* said that "if you belong to a church, it is your duty to promote holiness right in it: in the Presbyterian church, as a Presbyterian; in the Baptist church, as a Baptist, etc." Doty admitted that he disliked the whole denominational idea, but said God "permits it, and so must we."

As Warner heard such men speak in these ways, "the conviction was being cemented in his heart and mind that there was no room for him and for the burning message he felt in a situation where denominationalism was being exalted and continued membership in a denomination

---

3. See the published *Proceedings* (1881) now housed in the archives of Anderson University. Also see John Leland Peters, *Christian Perfection and American Methodism* (Nashville: Abingdon, 1956) 136; and Charles Edwin Jones, *Perfectionist Persuasion: The Holiness Movement and American Methodism* (Lanham, MD: Scarecrow, 1974) 55.

was being made a requirement of continued fellowship and acceptance."[4] The message beginning to burn inside Warner tended to question the easy, status-quo assumption that God passively permits rampant division of Christ's body, the church.

Warner believed deeply in the church and refused to accept the claim that genuine reliance on the Holy Spirit to establish and guide the church inevitably is the way of anarchy. Since holiness cannot prosper on sectarian soil, Warner judged, his new commission to "join holiness and all truth together" impelled him to take definitive action.

I'M COMING OUT!

His vigorous come-out view was rooted in a pivotal event in April, 1881. While conducting a revival meeting in Hardinsburg, Indiana, Warner reported that he "saw the church." No longer would he be patient with church bodies that organized their lives on the basis of sect recognition and requirements. What he now "saw" was God's intended alternative, a Spirit-inspired, Spirit-enabled, Spirit-governed, and Spirit-unified gathering of all God's people. Holiness also is to extend to *the church,* not only to the inward experience of individual believers. Visible unity is a key aspect of the church's intended holiness.

Instead of passive acceptance of the usual compromises, Warner determined to be faithful to a fresh vision, a new way of conceiving how things might be for the church of the Spirit. God always has been in the business of regathering the faithful. God intends a church that is *visible* in this world, not one that is *invisible.* Warner now chose to walk the ancient prophetic path that announced God's higher intention. As Merle Strege puts it, Warner rejected "the American religious *status quo,* the business-as-usual way of denominational religion."[5] Since the church really is God's, surely there is a better way of showing it to the world than settling for a network of quarreling and divisive denominations.

This prophetic position brought an immediate crisis in Warner's relationship with the National Holiness Association.[6] "The Spirit showed

4. Harold Phillips, editorial in *Vital Christianity* (October 20, 1974) 8

5. Merle Strege,. *Tell Me Another Tale: Further Reflections on the Church of God.* (Anderson, IN: Warner, 1993) 96.

6. Warner's specific involvement focused primarily in the Indiana Holiness Association, which at one point named him as a vice-president (Dieter, 255). He also had significant contact with the larger holiness movement in both Ohio and Illinois

me," he wrote, "the inconsistency of repudiating sects and yet belonging to an association that is based on sect recognition."[7] He went to a meeting of the Indiana Holiness Association in Terre Haute, Indiana, and tried to get changed the "sect endorsing clause" of the association so that its membership would be open "to all true Christians everywhere." The effort failed. So Warner reported in the *Gospel Trumpet* (June 1, 1881): "We wish to co-operate with all Christians, as such, in saving souls—but forever withdraw from all organisms that uphold and endorse sects and denominations in the body of Christ."

The stance of the Holiness Movement at first did not generate for itself the dilemma faced by Warner. Its purpose was to be a transdenominational renewal force. Its primary concern was not the evil of denominationalism but rather the evil of nominal Christianity. By the 1880s, however, frustrated by attempts to renew existing churches, many holiness converts had begun considering the possibility of one or more distinctively holiness denominations. Warner was a pioneer of this "come out" trend, although he opposed the very idea of denominations, *even new ones organized under a holiness banner.*[8] It lead to an inevitable clash. Henry Wickersham reported in 1900: "Before this he [Warner] was in good standing with many editors and sectarian holiness workers, but because of his decided stand for the truth, he was denounced in their papers, set at naught by the ministry, and rejected by his former friends."[9]

The significance of Warner is clear. In this earliest phase of the life of the Church of God movement, "it was Warner who was prophet, teacher, evangelizer, poet, advisor, theologian—the *voice* of the reformation. Since the *Gospel Trumpet* was the only formal organizational entity, it was Warner's dominant personality and the *Trumpet* that kept

7. *Gospel Trumpet* (June 1, 1881).

8. In 1993 Barry Callen, a contemporary leader of the Church of God movement, became editor of the *Wesleyan Theological Journal,* current publication of the holiness body from which Warner withdrew more than a century earlier. A sect-endorsing clause no longer is required by this holiness body. Warner's vision is admired in principle by today's Christian Holiness Association, but it is not actively pursued as such. The primary agenda remains more the Christianizing of Christianity by in-depth renewal through the holiness experience and the holy life.

9. Henry Wickersham, *A History of the Church.* (Moundsville, WV: Gospel Trumpet, 1900) 300.

the movement from disintegrating into a thousand isolated and disconnected parts."[10]

Having ruptured his formal tie to the holiness movement, Warner
wasted no time in questioning his future with the Northern Indiana
Eldership of the Churches of God by which he was licensed as a minister. In October, 1881, he attended a meeting of the Eldership in Beaver
Dam, Indiana. There he tried and again failed to have accepted the
radical implications of his holiness-unity vision. He proposed that this
body "conform more perfectly to the Bible standard with reference to
government" by ending the practice of granting ministerial licenses and
eliminating formal church membership procedures so that all who bore
the fruit of true regeneration would belong automatically by the action
of God. When this body said a firm "no," five people walked out of the
meeting with Warner, declaring that they were "coming out" of all sec-
tism. Thus was constituted in Beaver Dam the first congregation of the
Church of God movement.

This walk-out was repeated later in the same month in Carson City,
Michigan. Joseph and Allie Fisher, staunch *Trumpet* supporters, had
asked Warner to come to Michigan to speak to a special holiness meeting
being held prior to the annual camp meeting of the Northern Michigan
Eldership, also a breakaway from the General Eldership of the Churches
of God (Winebrennerian). The local congregation objected to the holiness meeting, so the Fishers and twenty others left the Eldership.

The "Carson City Resolutions" that they agreed to include this: "That
we adhere to no body or organization but the church of God, bought by
the blood of Christ, organized by the Holy Spirit, and governed by the
Bible . . . That we recognize and fellowship, as members with us in the
one body of Christ, all truly regenerated and sincere saints who worship
God in all the light they possess, and that we urge all the dear children of
God to forsake the snares and yokes of human parties and stand alone
in the 'one fold' of Christ upon the Bible, and in the unity of the Spirit"[11]
Here were elements of the rationale for a new movement, one intending
to be truly trans-denominational in the sanctifying and unifying power
of the Spirit. Joined were the passion for Christian holiness, the dream of
Christian unity, and the belief that the first enables the second, but only

---

10. Robert Reardon, *The Early Morning Light* (Anderson, IN: Warner, 1979) 24.

11. Barry Callen, *The First Century*, 2 vols. (Anderson, IN: Warner, 1979) 1:295–96.

when free of the artificial restrictions of human attempts to organize and "run" the church.

With the Beaver Dam and Carson City walk-out events, a new "movement" was gaining momentum and definition. The *Gospel Trumpet* was the movement's primary medium of conveyance, with Warner its tireless visionary and mouthpiece. This cause drew considerable sympathy from many Christians longing for more vision and power, more holiness and unity than they had found to date.

NEW MOVEMENT OF THE CHURCH OF GOD

Warner would devote the remaining fourteen years of his life to restoring the unity of God's people through the sanctifying work of the Holy Spirit. He and many others "saw the church" as a vision of the seamless, undivided body of Christ.[12]

The "perfect love" of sanctification, he argued, enables Christians to live above sin, including the sin of rending the body of Christ. Human lines of denomination, race, sex, and social status are to be discounted, even ignored in the face of the transforming grace of God in Christ. The emphasis should be on *seeing*, not arrogantly claiming to *be* the whole, pure, undivided church. His vision called for refusing either to erect or recognize human controls on Christian fellowship. It's God's church! The church exists for mission, and disunity is hurtful to the church's attempt to bear a credible witness in the world.

Warner finally had found a church home with *the whole body of Christ*. He sensed God moving to complete the sixteenth-century Protestant reformation and the eighteenth-century Wesleyan revival in a "last reformation."[13] Historian John Smith summarizes Warner's "enlightenment" experience this way:

12. For examples, see Charles E. Brown, *The Church Beyond Division* (Anderson, IN: Gospel Trumpet, 1939); Charles E. Brown, *When the Trumpet Sounded* (Anderson, IN: Gospel Trumpet, 1951); and Barry Callen, *First Century*, 1:123–240.

13. Late in Daniel Warner's ministry he increasingly couched his view of the evolving new movement of the Church of God in terms rooted in a church historical interpretation of the Bible's apocalyptic literature (especially the books of Daniel and Revelation). See *The Cleansing of the Sanctuary* (Warner and Herbert Riggle, 1903); Frederick Smith's *What the Bible Teaches* (1913), and *The Last Reformation* (1919); and John Stanley, "Unity Amid Diversity: Interpreting the Book of Revelation in the Church of God (Anderson)," *Wesleyan Theological Journal* 25 (1990) 74–98.

He had found the freedom in Christ for which he had so long sought. A new ingredient entered his life. It was as if he had been released from a great load and for the first time was able to stand erect. He felt as though he had stepped from the condemnatory shadow of his own and all other sectarian walls and now stood in the full light of truth—the "evening" light of which the prophet Zechariah had spoken. There was indeed cause for rejoicing. God had begun a new work in the church.[14]

BIBLIOGRAPHY

Callen, Barry. *It's God's Church! Life and Legacy of Daniel Warner.* Anderson, IN: Warner, 1995.

Fudge, Thomas A. *Daniel Warner and the Paradox of Religious Democracy in Nineteenth-Century America.* Lewiston, NY: Mellen, 1998.

14. John Smith, in *Vital Christianity* (July 25, 1965), 8. See also John Smith's unpublished doctoral dissertation, "The Approach of the Church of God (Anderson, IN) and Comparable Groups to the Problem of Christian Unity" (University of Southern California Graduate School of Religion, 1954).

13

God's Trustee

Martin Wells Knapp and Radical Holiness

WALLACE THORNTON JR.

MARTIN WELLS KNAPP WAS a central figure in the radical holiness movement that developed during the last two decades of the nineteenth century that spawned hundreds of Holiness and Pentecostal denominations, publications, camp meetings, schools and other institutions.[1] He illustrates the empowerment of the egalitarian, primitivist, and radical faith impulses that pervaded the Holiness revival. His ministry fueled forces which touched innumerable lives through the enterprises he spearheaded, including the International Holiness Union and Prayer League (1897), pre-curser of the Pilgrim Holiness Church, and God's Bible School and Missionary Training Home (1900).

His biographer, A. M. Hills, called Knapp one of "God's Surprises."[2] Hills noted that he possessed practically no natural advantages. From the time of his birth in 1853 in a log cabin in Calhoun County, Michigan, through an unremarkable career at Albion College, which spanned six years and found him still two years short of graduation at age twenty-three, to several pastorates in the Michigan Conference of the Methodist Episcopal Church, his life was unremarkable. He also lacked the "physical advantages" beneficial to successful leadership: "He was only about five

---

1. On this growth, see Vinson Synan. *The Holiness-Pentecostal Tradition: Charismatic Movements in the Twentieth Century* (Grand Rapids: Eerdmans, 1997) 31–32, 43.

2. A. M. Hills, *A Hero of Faith and Prayer; or, Life of Rev. Martin Wells Knapp* (1902; reprint, Noblesville, IN: Newby Book Room, 1973) 15.

feet four or five inches high, and weighed about one hundred and twenty pounds. The proportions of his body were not fine: the various parts and members of his body, in their general effect, seemed as if they had been thrown together or had chanced to come together by some laughable accident of nature. The first impression he made upon a strange audience was always unfavorable."[3]

Despite this, Knapp gained widespread recognition as an effective leader after his experience of entire sanctification. Revivalist W. B. Godbey noting his blending of personal piety and spiritual magnetism, suggested, "Though Brother Knapp in his wonderful . . . sweetness in manner, reminded me of an angel instead of a man, yet he had a power over the human will which was absolutely indescribable and apparently irresistible."[4] Hills interpreted this charisma as proof of "the uplifting, ennobling, and transforming power of the Holy Ghost on a life"—exemplifying the truth of I Corinthians 1:26–29.[5]

GOD'S SURPRISES: EGALITARIANISM

One of Hills' primary objects in writing Knapp's story was to promulgate the egalitarian vision of the Holiness movement, by inspiring the "lowly born" and others with "natural limitations" to surmount "untoward circumstances and unfriendly environments" because "the Spirit of God is mightier than human deficiencies and hostile conditions."[6] Knapp's biography provides numerous illustrations of the egalitarian impulse at work.

Most notably, Knapp broke with the status quo regarding women in ministry. This was rooted in his conversion experience in which he credited the influence of two women—his mother, Octavia, and his first wife, Lucy J. Glenn.[7] Early in their marriage, Lucy assumed equal status as co-minister with Martin indicating that their entrance into ministry and marriage were two aspects of a single decision.[8] In addition to collaborating in revival campaigns, Lucy conducted many meetings alone,

3. Hills, *Hero*, 27.

4. W. B. Godbey, *Autobiography of Rev. W. B. Godbey, A. M.* (Cincinnati: God's Revivalist Office, 1909) 367.

5. Hills, *Hero*, 27, 18–19.

6. Ibid, 27.

7. Ibid, 32.

8. See M. W. Knapp, "Glorified," *The Revivalist* (October 1890) 3.

as demands for their preaching services mushroomed with the positive reception of *The Revivalist* (1888), the oldest non-sectarian holiness periodical still being published.

This promotion of women's leadership continued to characterize Knapp's ministry after Lucy's death in 1890. His second wife, Minnie Ferle, although not a preacher like Lucy, employed her gift "with the pen" expanding *The Revivalist*'s horizons with a column dedicated to world missions.[9] After her husband's death, Minnie was named one of three trustees of the ministries Knapp had launched. Two others, Bessie Queen and Mary Storey, joined Minnie in completing this administrative triumvirate. Queen, daughter of an influential Cincinnati businessman, was converted under Knapp's ministry in 1897 and quickly advanced to become Minnie's assistant in *The Revivalist* office.[10] Within months after Knapp's death, she became *de facto* editor. Storey had been one of the first local holiness advocates to throw her support behind the Knapps when they relocated to Cincinnati in 1892. Having abandoned a lucrative management career to pursue full-time evangelism, Storey blazed a trail of holy fire through areas of the mid-South traditionally hostile to women ministers, leaving many in agreement with Knapp's contention that women were "among the most effective of Pentecostal preachers."[11]

Numerous other women held prominent positions in the ministries led by Knapp, especially at God's Bible School (GBS), which was founded as a co-educational institution with the insistence that "God says, 'He will pour out His spirit upon His handmaidens, and they shall prophesy,' and they should have equal training with the 'sons.'"[12]

Such egalitarian commitment also led Knapp to cross ethnic, economic, geographic and denominational lines. The "color line" was breached both by Knapp's outreach to African-Americans in his mission work on Cincinnati's Sycamore Street and by his support of such workers as Amanda Berry Smith.[13] Worship and classes at both Revivalist Chapel

9. "Mrs. Knapp's Work to Go On," *The Revivalist* (October 1890) 3.

10. "Rev. Knapp Was Fined the Costs," *Cincinnati Post* (July 17, 1901), 6; "Salvation Testimonies," *The Revivalist* (May 24, 1900).

11. M. W. Knapp, *Lightning Bolts from Pentecostal Skies; or, Devices of the Devil Unmasked* (Cincinnati: M. W. Knapp, 1898) 231.

12. M. W. Knapp, *Pentecostal Letters, Selected from the Correspondence of M. W. Knapp* (Cincinnati: Office of God's Revivalist, 1902) 104.

13. "Sparks From Amanda Smith," *The Revivalist* (June 1893) 1.

and GBS were integrated, likely providing William J. Seymour, of Azusa Street fame, with "his first exposure to a racially mixed congregation."[14]

Knapp's efforts to empower the poor extended to both urban and rural communities. In 1894, he established "a Holiness Industrial School" at Beulah Heights, near Flat Rock, Kentucky, insisting that the needs of the mountain folk were just as urgent as those in "foreign lands."[15] This school served as a prototype for GBS, which Knapp located near inner-city Cincinnati.[16] Knapp's vision for ministry to the poor also included the establishment of a rescue home for unwed mothers and their children and an orphanage. Most remarkable was the Thanksgiving Dinner and Convention. The first dinner (1901) fed three hundred and witnessed over seventy-five conversions or sanctifications.[17] This success, viewed by Knapp as verification of the linkage between social ministry and personal salvation,[18] inspired the dinner to become an annual event which expanded to feed as many as 20,000 during the Great Depression.

Knapp's ministry transcended another barrier that still loomed at the end of the century—sectionalism. His move from Michigan to Cincinnati placed him at the strategic rail link where northern and southern evangelists would traverse the Mason-Dixon Line. Knapp quickly bridged the gap between holiness exponents from various regions by employing Southern Methodist Beverly Carradine and Northern Methodist John Thompson at the convention in 1893, with the resultant fellowship leading Knapp to exult that here "the North and South met and embraced each other."[19]

At the same convention, Knapp also invited the ministry of Baptist Edgar Levy, reflecting a commitment to interdenominational fellowship.

14. James T. Connelly, "William J. Seymour," in Charles H. Lippy, ed., *Twentieth-Century Shapers of American Popular Religion* (New York: Greenwood, 1989) 381–87. See also C. M. Robeck Jr., "William Joseph Seymour," in *The New International Dictionary of Pentecostal and Charismatic Movements*, rev. ed., Stanley M. Burgess, ed. (Grand Rapids: Zondervan, 2002) 1053–58.

15. "A Holiness Mission Industrial School," *The Revivalist* (February 1894) 3; "Bulah (sic) Heights Holiness School," *The Revivalist* (July 1895) 2.

16. M. W. Knapp, *Back to the Bible; or, Pentecostal Training* (Cincinnati: M. W. Knapp, 1900) 29.

17. "Christmas Dinner," *God's Revivalist and Bible Advocate* (December 19, 1901) 12.

18. "Thanksgiving Revivals," *God's Revivalist and Bible Advocate* (November 28, 1901) 3.

19. "Cincinnati Holiness Convention Notes," *The Revivalist* (June 1893) 1.

Several of Knapp's closest colleagues included non-Methodist holiness advocates, particularly Quakers such as Seth C. Rees, who was elected first General Superintendent of the Holiness Union that Knapp formed. The Union represented his commitment to preserve the interdenominational nature of the Holiness revival with a response to the "Church Question" that put him at odds with several other holiness leaders. He rejected both the denominational option, embodied in H. C. Morrison's attempt to keep the Holiness movement primarily within the confines of Methodism and Phineas F. Bresee's effort to create a new holiness denomination.[20] On the other hand, he found equally unappealing the "anarchistic come-outism" he perceived in the anti-denominational option pursued by the Church of God (Anderson).[21] Instead, he sought to chart a middle course of "associationism," hoping to provide in the Union fellowship for all "members of the New Testament Church, which exists in different denominations, and which probably can never be united in one denomination, however pure."[22]

GOD'S AGENDA: PENTECOSTAL PRIMITIVISM

Beyond egalitarianism, Knapp's response to the "Church Question" reflected his disillusion with mainline Protestantism. He ultimately concluded that Methodism had "ceased largely to be a New Testament Church"[23] and, just months before his death, left the MEC.[24] This odyssey began with Knapp's own experience of entire sanctification which was accompanied by a dramatic confirmation, including "a sensation something like an electric shock", healing from the results of sunstroke that occurred during his youth, and "a definite call to evangelistic work."[25] The phenomenal response to Knapp's subsequent ministry is seen through *The Revivalist* which reached 25,000 subscribers by 1901. Its ultimate

20. "Sectarian Narrowness," *God's Revivalist and Bible Advocate* (January 3, 1901) 8.

21. "Sect-fighting Sectarianism," *God's Revivalist and Bible Advocate* (February 21, 1901) 8.

22. "The Need of Holiness Unions," *The Revivalist* (February 8, 1900) 3.

23. M. W. Knapp, "Back to the Bishops," *God's Revivalist and Bible Advocate* (March 14, 1901) 8.

24. See his defense in *Pentecostal Aggressiveness; or, Why I Conducted the Meetings of the Chesapeake Holiness Union at Bowens, Maryland* (n.p.: M. W. Knapp, n. d.).

25. Martin Wells Knapp, *Out of Egypt Into Canaan* (1888; reprint, Salem, OH: Schmul, 2000) 138–44.

effect transformed an amalgamation of followers from various regions and denominational backgrounds into a cohesive movement for radical holiness.

If *The Revivalist* was the chief organ for promulgating holiness themes, then GBS became the chief laboratory for implementing them. When the school opened with seventy-two students on September 27, 1900, it was clear that, as the *Cincinnati Post* put it, this school would "be different from any other in the world."[26] Following an educational model more akin to a vocational school for training technicians with job-specific skills than to a liberal arts approach, Knapp sought to train soul-winners skilled in handling the Bible, thus avoiding the course followed in many seminaries of "cramming the coal-bins of the soul full of the sawdust of secular knowledge instead of the coal of the Word of God."[27] Indeed, the motto at GBS was "Back to the Bible."

Knapp urged every student to seek entire sanctification, an experience he equated with the apostolic experience on the Day of Pentecost. Leon Hynson has observed, the "geographical center" of this teaching was GBS,[28] where the necessity of Pentecostal experience and the centrality of Scripture were inextricably interwoven. Knapp explained, "The Word of God is the coal which feeds the fire and which keeps [the person] going. The baptism with the Holy Ghost is the fire itself. As the engine stops without coal, so the believer can accomplish little unless, like Barnabas, he is 'full of the Scriptures.'"[29] Knapp radicalized the traditional concept of double-inspiration, providing the hermeneutical nexus of "Word and Fire" that laid the foundation for a new worldview—Pentecostalism.

At the heart of this worldview was "Pentecostal primitivism", a blending of Wesleyan perfectionism with radical primitivism—seeking restoration of New Testament Christianity in three areas: ecclesiastical, ethical, and experiential. The unique formulation resulting from this blending took the axiom that the New Testament Church described in Acts 2–4 is normative, providing the ideal pattern for the Church in all age. "Back to the Bible" was narrowed to mean "Back to Pentecost."

26. "School for Bible Study," *Cincinnati Post* (August 1, 1900) 6.

27. Knapp, *Back to the Bible*, 14–15.

28. Leon O. Hynson, "They Confessed Themselves Pilgrims, 1897–1930)," in *Reformers and Revivalists: The History of The Wesleyan Church*, ed. Wayne E. Caldwell (Indianapolis: Wesley Press, 1992) 227 [217–64].

29. Knapp, *Back to the Bible*, 14.

Pentecost and the great revivals which followed it in the primitive Church are the patterns which the Holy Spirit has left for us to follow. They declare in thunder tones that if we would see Pentecostal results, there must be Pentecostal repentance, Pentecostal prayer, Pentecostal sanctification, and *conformity to Pentecostal conditions and practices.* The great spiritual principles which were magnified by the apostles are the same now as they were then, and insistence upon them will bring similar results.[30]

As William Kostlevy indicates: "The radical holiness impulse, far from a revival of the old-time religion is, in fact, best understood as a new religious movement."[31] This became apparent as Knapp and his colleagues heralded what they considered to be the Pentecostal essentials—faith in Christ as Savior, Sanctifier, Healer, and Coming King. Thus, while other practices (such as tongues-speaking) would be adopted by later Pentecostals as evidence of repeated Pentecost, a fully-developed Pentecostal ideology was already championed by Knapp by 1900.

GOD'S PROPRIETORSHIP: DIVINE IMMANENCE

Knapp adjusted the four-fold gospel to accommodate another ideal—radical faith. While the "faith principle" had been popularized earlier by such figures as George Muller, Knapp uniquely elevated faith work by identifying it as an essential element of repeated Pentecost, in effect creating a "five-fold" gospel expressed in the formula of Christ as "Savior, Sanctifier, Doctor, *Banker,* and Coming King."[32]

Predicated on confidence in divine immanence, radical faith suggested both reliance *on* God and responsibility *to* God. He broke established convention among holiness periodicals by refusing to publish secular advertisements believing such practice betrayed faith in "God by leading publishers to depend on Egypt for help instead of [God's] promises."[33] Likewise, Knapp sought "to inculcate the faith principle of support in God's Work"[34] with workers in its early days receiving no

30. "Our Revival Model," *The Revivalist* (December 6, 1900) 1.

31. William Kostlevy, *Moving Beyond Phoebe Palmer: Holiness Movement Research Challenges and Opportunities in the 21st Century* (Wilmore, KY: n.p., n. d.) n.p.

32. Beatrice M. Finney, "My Call to Africa," *God's Revivalist and Bible Advocate* (December 19, 1901) 11.

33. "Why We Do Not Insert Worldly Advertisements," *God's Revivalist and Bible Advocate* (August 1897) 5.

34. Knapp, *Back to the Bible,* 14–15.

salary—their "bank check" being dependence on the "Savior's promise" to supply their needs.[35]

As faith was rewarded, it gave justification to Knapp's name for the school campus—the "Mount of Blessings". This name indicated Knapp's goal for GBS to become, not so much an agent of political or cultural change, but a prophetic witness to society through individual transformation and by demonstrating in community the validity of Pentecostal principles, in effect becoming a "city set on a hill." The success of this effort prompted Oswald Chambers in 1906 to assert, "This is truly Holiness socialism."[36]

For Knapp, divine immanence not only obligated God to provide for the saints, it also called for the saints' submission to divine ownership. The sanctified could rely on God as Supplier only if they looked to God as Proprietor. This led Knapp to radicalize the New Testament concept of stewardship, with an insistence "that all profits above" necessities "shall be given 'in His name,' as near as can be estimated, as Christ, the Proprietor Himself, would give it were He personally present."[37] Ultimately, he inferred from Matthew 6:19 and the communal sharing described in Acts 2–4 that the "*accumulation of property for self is absolutely prohibited.*"[38]

Knapp took several steps to implement this including naming the school he started for God and renaming his periodical *God's Revivalist and Bible Advocate* (1901). He explained, "I want people to know that there is one place, one paper, one school where God is honored as the chief Head, and where the work belongs absolutely to Him."[39] Next he deeded the GBS campus to God, simply listing himself as trustee and debarring his heirs from claiming it as an inheritance after his death.[40]

Stewardship of the resources of mental ability and physical vitality coalesced in a commitment to "hygienic holiness"—maintaining the

35. "Bible-School Opening," *God's Revivalist and Bible Advocate* (August 8, 1901) 15.

36. Oswald Chambers, "A Great and Blessed Season," *God's Revivalist and Bible Advocate* (January 17, 1907) 5.

37. Knapp, *Lightning Bolts*, 89.

38. Ibid, 91 (original emphasis). See also William Kostlevy, "Nor Silver, Nor Gold: The Burning Bush Movement and the Communitarian Holiness Vision" (PhD diss., University of Notre Dame, 1996) 37–38.

39. Hills, *Hero*, 332–33. See also Knapp, *Pentecostal Letters*, 79–80.

40. "Not for Personal Profit," *God's Revivalist and Bible Advocate* (August 1, 1901) 15; and "School for Bible-Study," *Cincinnati Post* (August 1, 1901) 6.

body's optimal fitness as "the temple of the Holy Ghost" (1 Cor 6:19–20). Seth C. Rees asserted, "Those who have received their Pentecost live pure, holy lives. They never practice unclean habits . . . They do not use wine, beer, tobacco, snuff, or opium."[41] Those experiencing Pentecost would carefully monitor what entered their minds, choosing to read "holiness and reform books and papers" instead of "sensational novels and periodicals."[42]

This pervasive God-consciousness received mixed reaction. In particular, leaders of the National Holiness Association looked askance at the prominence Knapp granted to such themes as divine healing and premillennialism, accusing him of derailing his followers from the "main line" of entire sanctification onto "side-tracks."[43] Knapp responded that these elements of repeated Pentecost were like spokes supporting the holiness hub and to minimize them would "tear the hub out of the wheel and ruin it."[44]

The clash of these alternate visions came to a climax in Chicago in May 1901, when a revival sponsored by Knapp's associates overlapped with the General Holiness Assembly called by NHA supporters. The radicals' campaign elicited far more seekers, over two thousand in all, giving it the largest response of any holiness meeting since the Civil War. This swayed many of the Assembly's delegates, so that they passed a doctrinal statement "endorsing premillennialism and divine healing", in effect signaling tacit surrender to the radicals.[45] Knapp felt vindicated. He exulted, "For years we had been praying that God would send us a Pentecost . . . The prayer has been answered in a measure in different places, but, so far as we know, never so fully as in the recent revival in Chicago."[46]

In fact, the Chicago revival signaled a colossal shift—the older Methodist Holiness movement had been largely replaced by the newer

---

41. Seth Rees, *The Ideal Pentecostal Church* (Cincinnati: Revivalist, 1897) 13.

42. "Counteracting Influences," *The Revivalist* (July 1892) 3.

43. See "Among the Holiness Periodicals" *Christian Witness and Advocate of Bible Holiness* (October 18, 1900) 5.

44. "The Hub of the Gospel Wheel," *The Revivalist* (June 1897) 2.

45. Kostlevy, *Nor Silver*, 116. C. 3 (96–126) of this work recounts the Chicago revival in fascinating detail.

46. "God Answering By Fire, or the Great Chicago Revival," *God's Revivalist and Bible Advocate* (May 30, 1901) 1, 6 cited in Kostlevy, "Nor Silver," 125.

Pentecostal Holiness movement.[47] However, Knapp would remain only as an inspiring memory to those whom he had guided in the quest for repeated Pentecost. Exhausted by his heroic efforts to carry the Pentecostal banner forward against numerous foes, he succumbed to typhoid fever and died on December 7, 1901, remembered by his supporters as "a martyr to the work."[48] In many ways, his vision of pristine Christianity lives on through his heirs in the Holiness and Pentecostal traditions, who would do well to review his commitments to equality, purity, and faith.

BIBLIOGRAPHY

Hills, A. M. *A Hero of Faith and Prayer; or, Life of Rev. Martin Wells Knapp.* Cincinnati: Mrs. Martin Wells Knapp, 1902.

Kostlevy, William. "Nor Silver, Nor Gold: The Burning Bush Movement and the Communitarian Holiness Vision." PhD diss., University of Notre Dame, 1996.

Thornton, Wallace, Jr. *Back to the Bible: The Story of God's Bible School.* Cincinnati: Revivalist Press, forthcoming.

47. Kostlevy, "Nor Silver," 125.

48. Bessie [Queen], "Translated," *God's Revivalist and Bible Advocate* (Dec. 19, 1901) 1–2.

14

Amanda Berry Smith

Woman at the Intersections

ESTRELDA ALEXANDER

A MANDA BERRY SMITH, THE late nineteenth- and early twentieth-century evangelist, missionary and social reformer, was born a slave in Maryland in1837. After her father purchased the family's freedom, they resettled near York, Pennsylvania. Her parents were conductors of one of the main stations of the Underground Railroad and Amanda inherited a legacy of social involvement that would significantly influence and form her ministry. Even as a child, she considered herself religious and—in words echoing Harriet Tubman—she insisted, "I do not remember a time from my earliest childhood that I did not want to be a Christian."[1] Despite such early interest, her journey to conversion was rocky, including a point where she doubted God's existence.[2]

THE ROAD TO CONVERSION

Her first memorable religious experience came at thirteen, while attending a Methodist Episcopal Church. She joined the congregation, attending class meetings for a time, but the experience was tainted by racial constraints and seeming contradictions. In her almost entirely white

1. Amanda Berry Smith, *An Autobiography: The Story of the Lord's Dealing with Mrs. Amanda Smith, the Colored Evangelist* (1893; reprinted, Schomburg Library of Nineteenth-Century Black Women Writers; New York: Oxford University Press in 1988) 43.

2. Ibid., 29.

class meeting, Amanda was forced to stay late because she was always the last person taught. Yet her employers expected that, even if she needed to leave class early, their servant would be available on time to serve them. When these expectations conflicted, Amanda stopped attending the class meeting, and caught between its racial stratification and her white employer's expectation of a black hireling, the fruit of that initial religious experience were short-lived. [3]

In 1854, at seventeen, she married Calvin Divine. The marriage proved unhappy because although Calvin had professed religion "for his mother's sake" he was often drunk and, at least verbally, abusive. One of the couple's two children died in childhood. Calvin enlisted to fight in the Civil War and never returned. Whether he died or deserted Amanda is unknown.

When he didn't return, she presumed him dead and married James Smith, a lay preacher twenty years her senior. In 1863, he and Amanda moved to Philadelphia and joined that city's Bethel AME Church, the mother church of the denomination. When they married, Amanda looked forward to ministry with her husband, an ordained AME deacon who indicated he would pursue the pastorate. But James had a change of heart. Not only was he never ordained, he rejected the idea of Amanda pursuing ministry, became involved with secret societies, and encouraged Amanda's involvement in their women's auxiliaries. Though she acquiesced for a time, once she experienced sanctification, Amanda saw involvement in these organizations as incompatible with holiness · teachings.

Throughout their short married life, the couple often lived separately. Though this arrangement was generally because of financial necessity, they didn't get along and her resignation from the women's groups divided them more. They had three sons, all of whom died in infancy. James died in 1869 when Amanda was thirty-two. She never remarried. The only child to survive to adulthood was her daughter, Mazie, though she later adopted two African children.

During her marriage to Calvin, Amanda had a near death experience in which she saw a vision of an angel telling her to "return" and saw herself preaching. Thus began the spiritual odyssey that involved an ongoing struggle with Satan over the state of her soul. This conflict

---

3. Ibid., 27–28.

led her eventually to come to the place of assurance and she "never from that day . . . had a question in regard to conversion."[4]

SANCTIFICATION AND THE HOLINESS MOVEMENT

Yet Smith still searched for "the blessing" or sanctification. She experienced that sanctification one Sunday morning under the ministry of John Inskip, famed Methodist pastor and leader of the National Holiness Camp Meeting movement. Significant evidence of that sanctification involved acceptance of her own blackness as a gift from God.

Smith's ministry began with a women's prayer meeting in her apartment. From there, she began speaking in African American congregations throughout the New York City area. During this period, Amanda attended Phoebe Palmer's Tuesday Meetings for the Promotion of Holiness and heard Palmer expound on entire sanctification which manifest itself in personal purity. Smith applied Palmer's ideas to the racial and class divisions she experienced. She broadened Palmer's understanding of sanctification to see it as giving a sense of empowerment she called "enduring grace"—a peace that keeps us pleasant and cheerful under difficulties, that keeps us humble and truthful under trials and temptations [and] must prevail in a distressing hour—and cleanses [our] hearts of self-doubt and racism.[5]

Kelly Mendiola contends that, although many identify Palmer's holiness theology as a major source of modern Pentecostalism, they fail to demonstrate how Palmer's middle-class parlor holiness emphasizing personal perfection developed into Pentecostalism's emphasis on holiness as a means to triumph over social oppression as well. For Mendiola, Smith provides a missing piece in transforming nineteenth-century Holiness thought to American Pentecostalism.[6] Though Smith never accepted the doctrine of initial evidence, she foreshadowed early Pentecostal understandings of the link between spiritual empowerment and elimination of prejudice.

---

4. Ibid., 49.

5. *Christian Recorder* (January 2, 1873) 1.

6. Kelly Willis Mendiola, "'On Victory She Goes': Amanda Berry Smith and the Transformation of the Nineteenth-Century Holiness Movement," paper presented at the British Association for American Studies Annual Conference, University of Wales Swansea, April 6–9, 2000.

Smith first encountered white camp meetings as an observer who initially felt subjected to disparaging treatment, including being excluding from speaking and being stared at; she spoke at her first such meeting in 1870 in Oakington, Maryland when "the Lord laid it on me to give my experience of how I found the great salvation."[7] She was warmly received by the audience, for as she spoke, "He blest me greatly and the people as well."[8] Smith's emotive delivery stirred the congregation so much that they took up an offering for her.

INTERNATIONAL HOLINESS EVANGELIST

She spent the next eight years traveling and speaking, primarily along the East Coast. In 1878, she traveled to England where she developed friendships with Hannah Whitehall Smith and Mary Broadman that opened an opportunity to attend the Keswick Conference for the Promotion of Higher Life. From there, she received invitations to preach throughout the United Kingdom. Her work in Europe during this period made her the first international black woman evangelist.

In 1879, W. B. Osborne, holiness leader and organizer of the Ocean Grove New York Camp Meeting invited Smith to India. She spent two years there, holding meetings in large cities and numerous smaller towns and villages. Her ministry was uniquely curious not only because she was a woman minister within male dominated Indian culture, but also a black former slave within a highly stratified caste system.

She then traveled to Africa, spending almost eight years establishing temperance societies throughout Liberia and Sierra Leone, preaching in local churches and camp meetings, organizing prayer bands, and organizing and teaching in separate church related schools. While there, she focused on two major concerns: the status of women and children's education. Her work showed some success and there were great victories, but it was not without controversy and experiences of strong criticism and bouts of depression. Some male missionaries, especially among the Plymouth Brethren, opposed her efforts, not because of her race, but because a woman claimed authority to be in ministry and preach.

Though affiliated with the AME Church, it did not appoint Smith whose missionary efforts were largely taken on by faith. Institutional

7. Smith, *Autobiography*, 168.
8. Ibid., 167.

missions support came from the Methodist Episcopal Church, supplemented by donations from individual supporters and her work with various groups including Bishop William Taylor. The famed Methodist missionary leader once commented that she "had done more for the cause of missions and temperance in Africa than the combined efforts of all missionaries before her."

Smith remained a member of the African Methodist Episcopal Church throughout her life, though her relationship to AME congregations and leaders was often distant and generated some of her harshest criticism. Since the nineteenth-century AME church adopted standards of decorum that repressed emotive worship, Smith was criticized for teaching sanctification and promoting emotive worship. The church's rigid structure supported middle class gender norms, yet leaders chided her for not supporting the denomination's burgeoning women's effort. Since an educated clergy was a sign of its middle class stability, Smith's lack of education made her ministry less acceptable within this community than in the white holiness community. Despite their criticism and her lack of ordination, Smith involved herself in denominational politics. But interestingly, Smith never pressed to open ordination to women. Instead, she simply attempted to fulfill her God-given mandate to preach and evangelize.

Noted as much for singing as preaching, her rich contralto voice intoning Negro spirituals and Methodist hymns moved staid audiences to shouting mixed with tears, breaking down resistance of those reluctant to hear from a black woman. That voice earned her the moniker "singing pilgrim" as well as the privilege of sharing the stage of the AME annual conference with the famed Fisk Jubilee Singers. She was also noted for writing a number of hymns that have become standard within the black Holiness and Pentecostal traditions.

Outside the religious realm, racism remained a reality within the larger framework of social organizations in which Smith was involved. Temperance and abolitionist movements generally excluded black women from their ranks. Yet in 1875, she was a charter member of the Women's Christian Temperance Union, becoming one of few African American women to gain visibility there. The charisma and giftedness of those, like Smith, who were included were romanticized as larger than life, making them seem unlike other blacks. Yet Smith developed deep friendships with WCTU leaders Frances Willard, Annie Wittenmyer and Mary Coffin Johnson that proved pivotal in her later ministry, including landing her a position as National Evangelist for the organization and keeping her story on the pages of *Union Signal*, the organization's magazine, through the 1890s.

THE IMPACT OF HER LIFE AND MINISTRY IN AMERICA

In 1890, she returned to the United States, spending two years preaching throughout the East. She then settled in Harvey, Illinois, a pristine planned temperance community 20 miles south of Chicago that attracted newcomers by advertising its moral, religious and temperance character. By 1893, she had written and published her autobiography, *An Autobiography: The Story of the Lord's Dealings with Mrs. Amanda Smith, the Colored Evangelist*. Its clarity and depth reflect the sharpness of mind of this largely self-taught woman. In that same year, she began efforts to establish the Smith Orphans' Home for Colored Children, using proceeds from the publication as part of its support. Ground for this first orphanage for black children in Illinois was broken in 1895. It was complete in 1899.

The home emphasized "industrial training" for blacks: manual and farm labor for boys, domestic service for girls. Race politics limited government support for the home and jeopardized its success. It drew its major support from the women's clubs, bolstered by proceeds from a monthly newspaper entitled *Helper* that Smith published for that reason.

Smith suffered from ill health throughout her life. Her first bout with serious illness came at age fourteen, when doctors told her parents she probably would not live. While serving as a Liberian missionary, she had six bouts with malaria and also suffered respiratory problems and chronic arthritis. Illness caused her to retire from the orphanage in 1912, though she continued fundraising efforts.

Her involvement with the white religious community did not lack notice or criticism by either black or white contemporaries. Blacks attributed her involvement with whites to greed or expediency. Whites concluded that it was only logical that a black person would desire to have more contact with them than other blacks. Mendiola suggests a more pragmatic explanation for Smith's alignment with whites in that she was somewhat alienated from the AME's strategy of racial uplift through assimilation and attracted to the encouragement of women's preaching and evangelistic ministry she found in white holiness circles.[9] Mendiola contends Smith used her speaking and writing to shed light on the plight of reconstruction era blacks,[10] and gain a voice among whites and blacks at a time when black women were " . . . the least heard people in America."[11]

Smith was not always comfortable in white circles, and though her acceptance among whites was uncommon for blacks of her day, she was never oblivious to the existence of racism even among Christians. Her autobiography demonstrated acute awareness of these realities when she writes, "I think some people would understand the quintessence of sanctifying grace if they could be black about twenty-four hours."[12]

Despite patronizing attitudes of some white colleagues, Smith maintained a number of relationships with influential holiness leaders that allowed her freedom to work and minister in contexts closed to other blacks—women or men. While some were necessary associations, others such as that with John Inskip and his wife, Martha were genuine friendships that moved Smith to the forefront of the Holiness movement and introduced Smith to prominent leaders, ensuring that Smith frequent coverage in the holiness press. Inskip also benefited from the relationship because Smith continuously mentioned him in her testimony of sanctification, making repeated references to his role in introducing her to the experience. Wealthy pottery manufacturer, George Sebring, was another friend and admirer. In 1913, Sebring, a devout Christian, built the town of Sebring, Florida and reserved a cottage near the lake for Smith.

Smith also maintained close relationships with a number of blacks including Ida Wells Barnett, noted civil rights leader, anti-lynching activist and journalist who served on the orphanage board. As one of Smith's strongest supporters, she nevertheless chided her for not taking a stronger stand against lynching. She counted Mary Church Terrell, founder of the Colored Women's Clubs that served as a major element in the African American expression of the late 19th century Progressive movement as a close friend.

9. Mendiola, "The Hand of a Woman: Four Holiness-Pentecostal Evangelists and American Culture, 1840–1930" (PhD dissertation, University of Texas at Austin, 2002) 142.

10. Ibid.

11. Mendiola, "Hand of a Woman," 144.

12. *Autobiography*, 116–17.

More importantly, Smith did not distance herself from the harsh reality of what it meant to be black in a racist society. Neither was she unappreciative of her blackness and African heritage. Rather, her deep concern for the spiritual and material welfare of blacks led her to speak of those on the African continent as "my people." At the end of her life, her greatest desire was for God to raise up leaders in the cause of racial uplift. "I pray that many of my own people will be led to a more full consecration and that the Lord may come upon some of the younger women who have talent, and have better opportunities than I have ever had, and so must do better work for the Master, so that when I have fallen in battle, and can do no more, they may take up the standard and bear it on."[13]

She impacted that next generation of blacks through her autobiography, which was reprinted in at least six editions. One of the better-known works by nineteenth-century African American woman writers, it was widely received in holiness and African American circles. COGIC founder Charles Harrison Mason was so impressed by its depiction of her experience of sanctification and emphasis on holiness that he sought the experience for himself.[14]

Smith died in 1915 after a series of strokes. Throughout her life, she operated at the intersection of two spiritual realities: independent black Methodism and the white Holiness movement. She understood the Gospel's social, as well as, spiritual implications and the experiences of salvation and sanctification, and spent her life preaching that Gospel and doing social outreach across four continents. Born into slavery, she initially feared white people and disdained her own blackness. Yet throughout her life, her ministry in both called attention to the disparity between these two worlds, though never gaining her full acceptance by either.

---

13. Smith, *Autobiography*, 506.

14. Ithiel Clemmons, *Bishop C. H. Mason and the Roots of the Church of God in Christ* (Bakersfield, CA: Pneuma Life, 1996) 5.

BIBLIOGRAPHY

Hardesty, Nancy, and Adrienne Israel, "Amanda Berry Smith: A 'Downright, Outright Christian,'" in *Spirituality and Social Responsibility: Vocational Vision of Women in the United Methodist Tradition*. Nashville: Abingdon, 1993.

Israel, Adrienne. *Amanda Berry Smith: From Washerwoman to Evangelist*. Lanham, MD: Scarecrow, 1998.

Jacobs, Sylvia M. "Three Afro-American Women: Missionaries in Africa, 1882–1904," in *Women in New Worlds*. Nashville: Abingdon, 1982.

Smith, Amanda Berry. *An Autobiography: The Story of the Lord's Dealing with Mrs. Amanda Smith, the Colored Evangelist*. 1893; reprinted, Schomburg Library of Nineteenth-Century Black Women Writers; New York: Oxford University Press in 1988.

15

Phineas Franklin Bresee

Recovering the Original Spirit of Methodism

HAROLD E. RASER

D URING THE YEAR 1866 American Methodists celebrated the
Centennial of their church. Methodist historians and popular
orators alike told stirring stories of a century of spiritual vitality and
expansive growth that had made Methodism by far the largest and most
widespread Protestant movement in the U.S.

In many parts of America Methodism was still in expanding. One
such place was Iowa, literally part of the American "frontier" at this time.
Iowa's population had swelled from less than 200,000 people in 1850 to
almost 700,000 by 1860. Methodism had moved in with the first settlers,
had quickly established itself as the largest Protestant denomination in
the state, and was continuing to grow rapidly. Many Iowa Methodist
preachers lived the life of the "circuit riders" of the preceding century;
they rode on horseback or in horse drawn wagons from settlement to
settlement, and farm to farm, conducting worship and offering what
pastoral care they could during their brief, periodic visits.

Not all Methodist preachers in Iowa, however, were riding circuits
at the time of the centennial. Many Methodist preachers in Iowa were
settling into town and city pastorates where they had care of only one
congregation. Some congregations were becoming large and affluent
enough to support a full-time minister and to build and maintain permanent church buildings. In addition, Iowa Methodists were turning

their attention to future needs of the church, especially clerical and lay education.

BRESEE'S IOWA MINISTRY: FROM DISTRESS
TO EMPOWERMENT

Prominent in Iowa Methodism in 1866 was young Phineas Franklin Bresee (1838–1915).[1] Bresee had moved to Iowa with his family in 1857 when he was eighteen years old, and within months had become a Methodist preacher, assisting an older colleague on a "four week circuit" (i.e., it took four weeks to visit all the "preaching points" on the circuit, which included schoolhouses, farmhouses, and at least one log cabin). Bresee had been converted to Christianity in a Methodist "class meeting" in his hometown in Franklin County, New York just a few years before.

Phineas Bresee began his ministry as the circuit "evangelist" with special responsibility for conducting periodic "protracted meetings" or "revival campaigns" across the circuit. "Revivals" and "camp meetings" were still primary means used by Methodists to call persons to Christian faith and to devotion to the work of the church. Bresee became convinced that frequent "revivals" are necessary for the health of every congregation.

In 1858, after one year as an "assistant" preacher, Bresee was given his first "solo" circuit. After serving with notable success in this and two subsequent circuits, Bresee was appointed in 1862 (only twenty-three years old at the time) to a congregation in Des Moines that had a permanent building and a parsonage to house their pastor. Bresee's work for two years in Des Moines earned him an appointment as "Presiding Elder"—a district superintendent over a group of churches and preachers. This was a promotion for the young Bresee, but the new work once again called for almost continuous traveling by horse and buggy over

---

1. There are three major biographies of Phineas F. Bresee: E. A. Girvin, *Phineas F. Bresee: A Prince in Israel* (Kansas City, MO: Nazarene, 1916); Donald P. Brickley, *Man of the Morning: the Life and Work of Phineas F. Bresee* (Kansas City, MO: Nazarene, 1960); Carl Bangs, *Phineas F. Breseee: His Life in Methodism, the Holiness Movement, and the Church of the Nazarene* (Kansas City, MO: Beacon Hill Press of Kansas City, 1995). The oldest was written by a close personal associate of Bresee, and is based largely on conversations with and letters from Bresee stretching over a period of nearly twenty years. *Man of the Morning* is based on the author's doctoral dissertation. The most recent biography is the fruit of many years of research by a historian whose parents were among the first generation of Nazarenes in the Pacific Northwest of the U.S.

prairie expanses visiting the churches and preachers under his care. The hard travel and heavy responsibility wore on Bresee, and after two years he requested to be reassigned as a pastor. In 1866 he was appointed pastor at Chariton, Iowa.

Bresee advanced regularly to pastor a series of larger and more prestigious congregations over the next seventeen years. Thus, he packed much of the story of American Methodism's first century into his own biography. Bresee was steeped in "frontier Methodism" and revivalism. His earliest experience of Methodism involved itinerant preachers, outdoor meetings, fervent preaching, and informal, revivalistic worship. Bresee found the same familiar frontier form of Methodism, but it was moving into a building and consolidating mode. Church buildings needed to be built, Methodist schools needed to be established, and Methodist publications were required to promote the church and to rally and encourage the Methodist faithful. Phineas Bresee poured himself into *all* of this for twenty-six years (1857–1883).

Phineas Bresee's personal biography took a distinctive and fateful turn, however, in that centennial year of American Methodism. Bresee was experiencing considerable personal distress. The exact nature of this distress is not completely clear, but Bresee had struggled through several very challenging ministerial assignments in the years before going to Chariton, and the Chariton congregation, although relatively large and affluent, was apparently quite contentious. Bresee said that about a quarter of the congregation was always angry with him for something, "but not the same quarter, as they took turns."[2] Also, Bresee had used his travel time during the previous two years as Presiding Elder to read widely and had apparently encountered authors and ideas that unsettled him and challenged his Christian faith.

We can probably assume that Bresee went to Chariton more or less "burned out" in body and spirit. He was steadily climbing the ladder of ecclesiastical "success." He was working extraordinarily hard to "make things go." But at the same time he was wrestling with personal issues, including intellectual doubts, and with a sometimes combative congregation. Many years later Bresee recalled of this time in his life: "I had a big load of carnality on hand always" which "had taken the form of anger, and pride, and worldly ambition." He also remembered that,

---

2. Girvin, *Phineas F. Bresee*, 50.

"at last, however, it took the form of doubt . . . it seemed that I doubted everything."[3]

All of these things came together in the early months of Bresee's pastorate at Chariton to provoke a personal crisis in his life. This came to a head in a protracted meeting during Bresee's first winter there (winter of 1866–1867). Bresee was serving as the "evangelist" (a typical Bresee practice). It was a bleak, snowy night. The crowd was small, but Bresee preached fervently, and urged seekers to the mourner's bench. No one responded, even though Bresee moved among the congregation, personally inviting people to pray (another typical Bresee practice). Then suddenly, Bresee later declared, "in some way it seemed to me that this was *my* time, and I threw myself down across the altar and began to pray for myself." As a result, Bresee claimed that he experienced a fresh empowering of divine grace that resolved his various personal and professional struggles. Bresee in later years referred to this experience as his "baptism with the Holy Ghost" in which "the Lord gave him more grace, liberty, and blessing in every way."[4] The importance of this experience is twofold: first, it occurred at a critical point in the history of American Methodism, and second, it was the initial step for Phineas Bresee down a road that would eventually lead him out of mainstream Methodism and into the role of founder of an important new denomination.

BRESEE AND "ORGANIZED HOLINESS"

As the centennial year of American Methodism, 1866 was a time when American Methodists recalled their past, reflected on what their movement had been and what it had become, and contemplated its future shape. Not coincidentally, in the summer of 1867 the first distinctively "holiness" camp meeting was held in the mostly Methodist village of Vineland, New Jersey, organized, conducted, and attended mainly by Methodist ministers and laypeople. The special purpose of this camp meeting was to revive "the work of holiness in the Church" by helping Christian believers to "realize a Pentecostal baptism of the Holy Ghost."[5] At the close of this meeting the National Camp Meeting Association for

---

3. Ibid., 50.

4. Ibid., 52.

5. Advertising insert titled "General Camp-Meeting" in *The Guide to Holiness*, July 1867.

the Promotion of Holiness (later Christian Holiness Association) was organized.

The Vineland "holiness" camp meeting and the National Camp Meeting Association marked the crystallization of a "movement" that had been building within American Methodism since at least the 1830s. This "Holiness movement" (whose chief spokesperson up to this time had been Phoebe Palmer) had as its objective the preservation and propagation of the historic Wesleyan-Methodist doctrine of Christian Perfection. Supporters of this movement feared that this distinctive Wesleyan-Methodist doctrine and the life of earnest, simple "holiness" that it entailed were in danger of being neglected as Methodism in America grew rapidly in membership, expanded geographically, and became more affluent and "worldly." "Holiness people" dedicated themselves to keeping Christian perfection at the center of Methodism's identity.[6]

Even though Phineas Bresee's decisive religious experience occurred in the winter of 1866–1867 just as holiness partisans were organizing for a more vigorous crusade to propagate Christian perfection in the future, Bresee did not actually identify with "organized holiness" until almost twenty years later. It was not until 1885 that Bresee became an outspoken advocate of a distinct "second blessing" of "full sanctification" as defined by the Holiness movement and made this and the life of "holiness" the central theme of his ministry.

Between 1867 and 1883 Bresee continued to serve as a Methodist minister in Iowa. He apparently continued to enjoy the blessing of the "Baptism with the Holy Ghost," and continued to occupy prominent ministerial roles, but he gave no indication whatsoever of supporting the "organized holiness" work that was rapidly spreading across the U.S. during these years. In 1883, however, Bresee moved with his family from Iowa to Southern California and over the next few years was appointed pastor of a series of large, prominent Methodist congregations. It was in the first of these, Fort Street Church in Los Angeles (also called "Old First Church"), that Bresee seems to have first encountered people fervent about "organized holiness" and began to be drawn by them into the

6. The standard accounts of the development of the "Holiness movement" are Melvin E. Dieter, *The Holiness Revival of the Nineteenth Century* (Metuchen, NJ: Scarecrow, 1980); and Charles E. Jones, *Perfectionist Persuasion: The Holiness Movement and American Methodism, 1867–1936* (Metuchen, NJ: Scarecrow, 1974).

"Holiness movement." By the time Bresee moved on to his next pastoral assignment he had fully thrown in his lot with "organized holiness" and was on his way to becoming its chief spokesperson in Southern California.

Less than ten years later (1894) Bresee withdrew from the Methodism that he had served so notably for thirty-seven years to engage in full-time independent "holiness work." In 1895 he organized the first congregation of the Church of the Nazarene, a "holiness" church that one hundred years later had grown to over a million and a half members scattered literally around the globe. Bresee served the Church of the Nazarene as its first General Superintendent for the last twenty years of his life.

THE "BAPTISM OF THE HOLY GHOST"
AND THE SHAPE OF HOLINESS MINISTRY

Phineas Bresee's trajectory through nineteenth century Methodism and on into independent holiness work illuminates some of the central tensions, transitions, and challenges affecting American Methodism at the end of its first century. It also helps to illuminate the nature of the American Holiness movement.

As noted, Phineas Bresee was born on the frontier, experienced Methodism in its frontier form, and began his ministry in Iowa under largely frontier conditions. Itinerant ministers, fervent evangelization, frequent camp meetings and protracted meetings, revivalistic forms of worship, heartfelt religion, and simple piety were the chief elements of "frontier" Methodism. Bresee learned all this early, and would value these elements as essential to authentic Christianity for the rest of his life. However, in Iowa Bresee also experienced a Methodism transitioning from youthful movement to a more settled "denomination." Iowa Methodism was consolidating its gains—publishing religious literature, building permanent churches buildings, establishing colleges, and otherwise creating the necessary structures of denominational life. Bresee appears to have also embraced these aspects of a more settled "institutionalized" church, and excelled at leading congregations that largely reflected this side of nineteenth century Methodism. He also learned and practiced various "institution building" skills that served him well when he later founded and led the Church of the Nazarene.[7]

On the other hand, Phineas Bresee became increasingly disillusioned during his thirty-seven years of Methodist ministry with the growing affluence of many Methodists and with a certain spiritual "coldness" and "formality" that he sensed in some congregations. He was also troubled by some of the theological reappraisal taking place in Methodism in the second half of the nineteenth century. He feared that "Higher Criticism" and other forms of "creeping rationalism" were undermining Methodist commitment to traditional Christian orthodoxy.

Bresee's "Baptism with the Holy Ghost" may be seen as a turning point for him in dealing personally with the changing shape of Methodism. This "baptism" (which language he apparently did not use until he learned it in the 1880s from the "organized holiness movement") reinforced Bresee's sense that authentic religion is heartfelt and experientially dramatic. Whatever else a church might be, it *must* be a place where people *experience* the presence of God, and where they *freely* express their response in worship. The doctrine of the Baptism with the Holy Ghost, which Bresee championed with increasing ardor from the mid-1880s on, seems to have appealed to him (aside from the fact that he came to believe that it was scriptural and central to Wesleyan Methodism) largely because it maximized the divine *presence* in human experience. To be "baptized with the Holy Ghost," according to Bresee, means that the Holy Spirit of God is "resident in man," cleansing the human heart from sin and providing power for service to one's neighbors ("God's dynamite in the soul").[8] After Bresee's "baptism" he became increasingly impatient with and critical of tendencies in "Victorian" Methodism toward more formal styles of worship and decreasing emphasis on "revivalistic" experiential religion.

7. Bresee was notably active in leadership in Iowa Methodism. He pastored its largest congregations, served as a Presiding Elder, was a leading member of the board of trustees of Simpson College during its reorganization as a liberal arts institution (his work for Simpson earned him an honorary "Doctor of Divinity"), served as a conference "visitor" (i.e., trustee) of Garrett Biblical Institute in Evanston, IL, and was editor of the *Inland Advocate*, one of several regional Methodist papers carrying the *Advocate* name, among other things.

8. See "To Know Him," a sermon based on Philippians 3:10–11, in Phineas F. Bresee, *The Certainties of Faith: Ten Sermons by the Founder of the Church of the Nazarene* (Kansas City, MO: Nazarene, 1958), 86–87. See also "The Atmosphere of the Divine Presence," a sermon based on Isaiah 33:14 in *The Certainties of Faith*, 91–95.

Bresee's conviction that revivalistic, experiential religion is the essence of authentic Christianity also had implications for his generally negative attitude toward the theological reappraisal taking place in late nineteenth-century American Methodism. The felt presence of a supernatural God in a person's life (and in the life of a congregation) attested to the authority and truth of the Bible as traditionally interpreted. Any approach to the Bible or Christian faith that appeared to weaken their supernatural and divine character was, for Bresee, contradicted by the experience of the "abiding Spirit" alive "in human souls."

As for the growing affluence of many Methodists in the late nineteenth century, Phineas Bresee first embraced, and then rejected this. Throughout his ministry in Iowa, Bresee was quite comfortable with wealth and cultivated close relationships with his more wealthy and influential parishioners. In fact, he seems to have considered himself one of them. For nearly twenty years he dabbled in business ventures in partnership with a friend, a Methodist-preacher-turned-business speculator. However, it was a disastrously failed business deal with this friend that drove Bresee away from Iowa to Southern California in 1883. After this disaster (and personal embarrassment) Bresee pledged that he would never again dabble in business and would give himself wholly to preaching the Gospel.[9]

From this point on Bresee became increasingly critical of the new wealth in many Methodist congregations. He also began to emphasize the fact that earliest Methodism directed itself primarily to the poor and marginalized and that, in fact, the whole tenor of scripture challenges pretensions of human wealth and power and calls for special care and protection of the poor, widows, orphans, prisoners, and other marginalized and powerless people. By 1894 Bresee had become so driven by a burden for ministry to the poor that he left Methodism in order to work

9. Noting Bresee's "executive" abilities, Carl Bangs remarks that Bresee could easily have "been a corporation president"—see Bangs, *Phineas F. Bresee*, 99. The nature of the "failed" business venture in which Bresee was involved is not entirely clear. Bresee himself blamed it on bad luck and natural disasters (earthquake and resultant flooding of a silver mine) and this is the story passed along without question by E. A. Girvin, *Phineas F. Bresee*, 72–76; Donald Brickley, *Man of the Morning*, 82–84; and Timothy L. Smith, *Called Unto Holiness: The Story of the Nazarenes, the Formative Years* (Kansas City, MO: Nazarene, 1962) 94–95. However, Bangs has dug more deeply into the sources, and as a result paints a more complex, somewhat less savory picture involving fraud—although probably not on the part of Phineas Bresee himself—see Bangs, *Phineas F. Bresee*, 97–104.

full-time in a downtown holiness mission in Los Angeles that served the poor. When this arrangement did not work out as he hoped, Bresee organized the Church of the Nazarene to minister "in the neglected quarters of the cities and wherever also may be found waste places" through means of "city missions, evangelistic services, house-to-house visitation, caring for the poor, comforting the dying."[10]

Thus Phineas Bresee's personal disillusionment with pursuing wealth, his experience of the plight of the poor in an explosively expanding urban area, and his religious experience and the way in which he came to interpret it theologically combined to cause him to become increasingly dissatisfied with the growing affluence of much of late nineteenth century Methodism. This, together with his deeply held commitments to a revivalistic, experiential form of Christianity, which he believed was becoming less and less characteristic of Methodism, led him—somewhat unwillingly—out of denominational Methodism and into the role of founder of a new independent "holiness" church. His vision for the Church of the Nazarene was, "to get back to the primitive simplicity of the New Testament Church in spirit and methods, to be rid of the cumbrous machinery, the worldly methods of money getting, so much of form and ceremony, and to have in their place the Pentecostal baptism of the Holy Ghost and fire."[11] Phineas Bresee believed that this described original Methodism—indeed original Christianity—and it was his intention that the Church of the Nazarene be a faithful embodiment of both.[12]

---

10. Local Church Minutes, "Meeting of the Congregation," Los Angeles, CA (October 30, 1895) 3.

11. *The Church of the Nazarene* (pamphlet), Los Angeles, CA (November, 1895) 3.

12. For an analysis of Bresee's place among a variety of holiness "come-outers" at the end of the nineteenth century see Harold E. Raser, "'Christianizing Christianity:' The Holiness Movement as a Church, *the* Church, or No Church at All?," *Wesleyan Theological Journal* 41.1 (2006) 116–47.

BIBLIOGRAPHY

Bangs, Carl. *Phineas F. Bresee: His Life in Methodism, The Holiness Movement, and The Church of the Nazarene.* Kansas City, MO: Beacon Hill Press of Kansas City, 1995.

Girvin, E. A. *Phineas F. Bresee: A Prince In Israel.* Kansas City, MO: Nazarene Publishing House, 1916.

Raser, Harold E. "'Christianizing Christianity,' the Holiness Movement as a Church, THE Church, or No Church at All?" *Wesleyan Theological Journal* (Spring 2006) 116–47.

Schneider, Gregory A. *The Way Of The Cross Leads Home: The Domestication of American Methodism.* Bloomington: Indiana University Press, 1993.

16

John Alexander Dowie

Born to Command

D. William Faupel

JOHN ALEXANDER DOWIE WAS one of the most colorful figures to emerge on the North American scene at the close of the nineteenth century. Declaring himself to be Elijah, the Restorer, he announced pending judgment on the religious establishment and political order that would come about with Christ's imminent return. At the height of his influence in 1904 he claimed over 500,000 adherents world-wide.

Although he denounced Pentecostalism just before his death in 1907, thousands of his followers and hundreds in leadership roles would leave his organization to join this emerging movement. Today, many Pentecostal churches in North America, Europe, New Zealand, Australia and especially South Africa trace their origins to his ministry.[1]

DOWIE'S LIFE

Just who was John Alexander Dowie? Today he is almost unknown except to students of Pentecostal history. At the turn of the twentieth century however, he was as famous as Oral Roberts or a Pat Robertson. Dowie has been described as "a man born to command and incapable of following."[2] At the height of his power, his physical appearance was

1. E. L. Blumhofer, "A Pentecostal Branch Grows in Dowie's Zion," *Assemblies of God Heritage* (Fall, 1986) 3–5; W. J. Hollenweger, *The Pentecostals* (Minneapolis: Augsburg, 1972) 65, 120–21.

2. J. M. Buckley, "Dowie Analyzed and Classified," *The Century Magazine* 64 (October,

unimposing. At age fifty, he was a small, overweight, balding man with bowed legs and a flowing beard. But the force of his personality was such that few could escape the power in his presence. In private he was a perfect gentleman. He radiated confidence, sincerity, trust and understanding. Seeker and skeptic alike were captivated by his warm smile, penetrating gaze and listening ear. On the other hand, in the pulpit, dressed in long flowing liturgical robes, he would rail against the evils of his day and denounce a spineless Christianity for its failure to stand up to the forces of Satan. So compelling was his power, that his followers gladly sold their material possessions, joyously gave him their wealth, unquestioned loyalty, and total devotion.[3]

Dowie was born in Edinburgh, Scotland in 1847. He migrated with his parents to Australia at age fourteen. For seven years he worked as an apprentice for various firms. Feeling the call of God to the ministry, he went back to Edinburgh at age twenty-one, spending three years at New College. He returned to Australia in 1872 to become a Congregational minister. Holding a succession of pastorates, Dowie quickly climbed the ecclesiastical ladder. Within four years of his ordination, he was called to the prestigious Collegiate Church in Newton, a suburb of Sydney. With his future secure, Dowie abruptly resigned in 1878, announcing that he was leaving his denomination to devote himself to independent evangelistic work.[4]

The next few years were trying times for Dowie. Although he often preached to large crowds, finances were not sufficient to meet expenses. Gradually he had to sell off all of his assets to meet his bills. His former colleagues denounced him. His in-laws turned against him feeling that he was not taking adequate care of their daughter. The bitterest moment came in 1882 when his little daughter, Jeanie, died.[5]

Dowie's fortune turned in 1883. He determined to make Divine Healing the central focus of his ministry. The change resulted in instant success. Crowds came in droves to hear his new message. Testimonies of

---

1902) 928. Another investigative reporter concluded that Dowie could "no more follow than a fish can walk." J. Swain, "John Alexander Dowie: The Prophet and His Profits," *The Century Magazine* 64 (October, 1902) 936.

3. For an exhaustive analysis of Dowie's personality see R. Harlan, "Characterization," *John Alexander Dowie and the Christian Apostolic Church in Zion*, 40–69.

4. G. Lindsay, *The Life of John Alexander Dowie* (Shreveport, LA: Voice of Healing Publishing Company, 1951) 11–26; and Swain, "John Alexander Dowie," 934.

5. Ibid., 64–71.

miraculous healing were received daily. Finances to fund an expanding operation began to flow. He established the Free Christian Church in Melbourne. From this base, he conducted healing crusades throughout Australia and New Zealand. To sustain the fruit of these campaigns, he founded the Divine Healing Association.[6]

Flushed with newfound success, Dowie began to think in terms of worldwide ministry. He determined to visit England where he had many contacts. With London as a center, he reasoned that he would be able to develop a following throughout the British Empire.[7] To this end he set sail in March, 1888, determining to go by way of the United States.

Dowie received such a tremendous response to his ministry in North America that he never left. For two years he traveled up and down the Pacific Coast holding crusades before moving east across the continent. Wherever he went, he established branches of his Association, which had by this time been reorganized as the International Divine Healing Association. He continued his crusades until 1895, organizing branches in virtually every major American city.[8]

In 1890, Dowie decided to make Chicago, the second largest city in the United States, his headquarters. Centrally located, he was better able to keep a handle on his growing empire. The World's Fair, which opened in Chicago in 1893, provided Dowie with further opportunity. Always a strategic planner, he set up a tabernacle just outside the fairground's entrance, hoping to attract people from throughout the world. His strategy paid off handsomely. Ever increasing crowds attended, forcing him to locate in a succession of larger meeting places.[9]

The period following the World's Fair has been described by one biographer as his "Golden Years,"[10] They were filled with controversy, decisive action and huge success. Dowie's flamboyant style and pointed tongue soon alienated him from Chicago's power structure. The press, medical community, clergy and politicians sought to put him out of business. Dowie was able to turn this free publicity to his advantage.

6. Ibid., 72–75; and Swain, "John Alexander Dowie," 936.

7. Swain, "John Alexander Dowie," 936.

8. Ibid., 937; Harlan, *John Alexander Dowie,* 34; and Lindsay, *Life of John Alexander Dowie,* 90, 93–94.

9. Lindsay, *Life of John Alexander Dowie,* 104–5; Swain, "John Alexander Dowie," 937; and Harlan, *Life of John Alexander Dowie,* 34.

10. Lindsay, *Life of John Alexander Dowie,* 161.

The more headlines that denounced him, the larger his following grew. Though many would come out of curiosity or to heckle, they would often stay to pray. By this time Dowie had recognized that he had alienated the religious establishment. He therefore disbanded his interdenominational Divine Healing Association in November 1895, announcing that no longer would his followers be able to retain membership in their old denominations. Instead they must join the Christian Catholic Apostolic Church in Zion, which he formally established in February, 1896.[11]

Events moved with dizzying speed following the creation of his new denomination. On New Year's Eve 1899, Dowie announced plans to build Zion, a utopian community, forty miles north of Chicago. Zion soon became a bustling city of 8,000 residents with plans to grow to 200,000. Building was going on everywhere. Homes were erected. Stores for many businesses were constructed. A large hotel was built for persons coming from great distances to attend the healing meetings. An educational system from elementary school through college was established. A huge tabernacle holding 5,200 people was placed in the heart of Zion with plans to build a temple with a seating capacity of 25,000 on an adjacent block. Zion was the first and largest of several communities that he planned to establish around the world. A large farming development, planned for Mexico, was next on the agenda.[12]

In October 1903 Dowie launched a world tour beginning with a three-week crusade at Madison Square Garden in New York City. Three thousand of his "Restoration Host" came with him for this first meeting. During the day, they fanned out across the city passing out tracts, knocking on doors, inviting people to the evening meetings. Not surprisingly, the Garden was packed with over 5,000 people turned away nightly. From there, Mrs. Dowie with a smaller party went on to London, several cities on the European continent, South Africa, New Zealand and Australia. Dowie left for San Francisco, joining his wife in Australia and returning via India, Africa and Europe. Everywhere he went he held large rallies in the major cities, and then spoke privately to the community of followers he had in that part of the world. Returning to Chicago in September, 1904 he began plans to launch his Western campaign in 1905 when he

---

11. Harlan, *Life of John Alexander Dowie*, 34–37.

12. P. L. Cook, *Zion City, Illinois: Twentieth Century Utopia* (Syracuse, NY: Syracuse University Press, 1996) 31–32, 55, 61–67, 71–77, 169.

planned to "invade" St. Louis, Salt Lake City and San Francisco with 5,000 of his "Restoration Host."

Dowie's expanding empire was paralleled by the elevation of his status. He had named himself General Overseer of the Christian Catholic Apostolic Church upon its formation in 1896. In 1899, he proclaimed that he was the "Messenger of the Covenant" prophesied by the prophet Malachi. He declared himself to be Elijah, who was to be "The Restorer of All Things" in June, 1901. In September, 1904, he consecrated himself First Apostle of a new apostolic order. His psychological development caused at least one writer to speculate that had Dowie lived, he would have claimed to be the reincarnation of the Messiah.[13]

DOWIE'S SIGNIFICANCE

It would be easy to dismiss Dowie as a "nutcase" and his thousands of followers as mere "dupes." However, if one measures the value of a ministry by its lasting fruit, Dowie emerges as a person to be taken seriously. Like John Wesley, whom he deeply admired, Dowie's genius is best seen through the prism of "Practical Theologian," which I shall seek to illustrate under three subcategories: theology, praxis; and strategic thinking.

Theology

Dowie stood squarely in the Keswick tradition of the Holiness movement. He summed up his message by stating: "Zion stands for Salvation, Healing and Holy Living," which he referred to as the "Full Gospel."[14] Historian David Harrell calls Dowie the "father of healing revivalism in America" in that he was the "first man to bring national attention to divine healing.[15] Although others such as Charles Cullis, A. J. Gordon, and A. B. Simpson had taught and practiced the identical doctrine a few years before him, Dowie was the first to seize upon its captivating potential to attract converts to his movement.

Despite the fact that Dowie is most well known for his healing ministry, his adherents claimed that his emphasis on Holy Living was the

13. Harlan, *Life of John Alexander Dowie*, 36–39.

14. E. L. Blumhofer, "The Christian Catholic Church and the Apostolic Faith: A Study in the 1906, Pentecostals Revival," in *Charismatic Experiences in History*, ed. C. M. Robeck, Jr (Peabody, MA: Hendrickson, 1985) 9.

15. David Edwin Harrell Jr. *All Things Are Possible: The Healing and Charismatic Revivals in Modern America* (Bloomington: Indiana University Press, 1975) 13.

most significant part of his message.[16] For him, holiness was not a goal to be achieved but a way of life to be lived. Dowie was convinced that salvation brought not only pardon for the guilt of sin, but deliverance from its power as well. Correct teaching on this biblical concept was essential to bring correct thinking to people who had been nurtured on a weakened half-truth gospel. Persuasive preaching was needed to bring conviction and encouragement. These two tools in the hands of the leadership were essential provisions that God had given to assist the pilgrim on this spiritual journey. Visitors to Zion would often remark with surprise on the practical nature of Dowie's messages to the community, which helped them to find ways to deal with problems arising within family and communal life.[17] Thus like his teaching of divine healing, it was the praxis dimension of "holiness" that attracted him.

Praxis

Dowie's concern for the praxis of Holiness included both personal and social dimensions. His lists of guidelines to regulate individual behavior were endless. But he recognized that such behavior modification could best take place in a social context. This was the major reason for establishing the city of Zion. All life within the city was structured in ways to encourage the desired behavior. Land, leased to family for 1,100 years, could be revoked if a member of the family was caught violating one of the more serious codes. The city was divided into small sections for the purpose of weekly cottage prayer meetings. These occasions included not only a time for exhortation and prayer, but also a time for sharing personal struggles and victories.[18]

Dowie's hope to lead his flock in the way of perfection was especially manifested in Zion's educational system. Adherents recognized that their own spiritual progress had been hindered by worldly influences and association with apostate denominationalism. In their children, they saw the possibility for greater advancement in the way of holiness. Everything possible was provided to insure their prodigy would be a royal generation.[19]

16. Cook, *Zion City*, 116.

17. W. M. Hundley, "The Flag of the Salvation Army Eclipsed by the Standard of Zion City," *Physical Culture* (January, 1901) 276.

18. Cook, *Zion City*, 55, 115–25.

19. Ibid., 128; citing *The Coming City* (September 19, 1900).

Dowie's concern for Holy Living took on a social dimension as well. He tried to instill in every convert the conviction that God is the Father of all and that all humankind are our brothers and sisters. Mutual respect for all was taught. Policies were formed to discourage a multi-class society. Concern for Jews and for Blacks was stressed. One Negro visitor observing the conditions of his fellow Blacks stated that Dr. Dowie must be the most courageous man in the nation. Miscegenation was defended as a means to regain the purity and strength of the human race. Respect for fellow men brought Dowie to advocate a pacifist position. Because nation states created jealousy, he defended the concept of world government. A welfare system was devised to provide for the needs of the less fortunate. A home for orphans, a hospice for fallen women, and a retirement home were all centerpieces of the city.[20] Thus, the implications of Dowie's doctrine of Holy Living reached far beyond his sub-culture and became part of his evangelistic thrust. Zion was to become a model community to whom others could look, finding there a higher, better way for living. Such communities were to be established throughout the world. In a cooperative rather than coercive way, Dowie believed that his movement would eventually transform society. It would ultimately prepare the way for the return of Christ to rule as head of theocratic government. For him, the way of holiness was truly through the gates of Zion.

Strategic Thinking

From the beginning of his ministry, Dowie thought globally. Every initiative he undertook had long term developmental significance. In establishing the Christian Catholic Apostolic Church of Zion he realized that if his vision was to succeed, his work must be multiplied. Thus, he established his college, primarily for the task of training ministers. Among his converts were many ministers and Christian workers from other traditions, who after they were sufficiently schooled in his teaching, were either sent back to their former congregations or to new fields of harvest. But mission was not just the work of the trained clergy; the laity must be mobilized and equipped as well. Thus he established the Company of the Seventies. He based his new initiative on the 10th chapter of Luke where Jesus sent forth the seventy "two by two" into every city and place where He was about to come." Upon commissioning the first

20. Ibid., 91–97, 126–30.

"seventy" on September 18, 1898, Dowie stated: "For years it has been our great desire to see this moment when having trained some hundreds of God's own children, we should have the joy of sending them forth two by two into every street of this city of Chicago, knowing that the Lord wants to come into every street, and enter into every house in the city. We have not been idle as individuals, but we have been looking forward to the time when the church should organize its bands, and send them forth to do this work."[21]

This idea was not original with Dowie. He observed this plan at work when he visited the Mormons in Salt Lake City enroute to Chicago in 1890. Commenting on that visit, he noted, "I studied the Mormon Church. I watched that Seventy Movement of theirs and saw that they were able to send out common, apparently illiterate men into the world, who were devoted to their church, and were willing to die for it."[22]

Dowie began with an army of six "Seventies," organized to be sent forth to every home in the city of Chicago. The city was organized into districts, which could be visited by two people during the course of one week. The number of his "army" increased to 3,000 in Chicago alone, who devoted a part of their time each week going from house to house distributing materials, including copies of the *Leaves of Healing*. Soon bands of Seventies were operating in other major U.S. cites such as Cincinnati, Cleveland, Philadelphia, New York, St. Louis, San Francisco and a host of smaller towns. The pattern was extended to Dowie's work in England, Scotland, Ireland, Germany, Switzerland, France, South Africa, India, China, Australia, and New Zealand. Ultimately, Dowie envisioned a Zion City established outside every major city in the world that would at once supply the bands of seventy to evangelize those cities, while modeling within their own community "the way of holiness" to world.[23]

Dowie's life ended in personal tragedy and his movement splintered. But his vision did not die with him. Adherents in the Keswick Holiness tradition from which he sprung and those from the Pentecostal tradition which inadvertently helped birth are deeply in his debt. Much still can be learned from the study of the life and ministry of this enigmatic man.

---

21. "Sending of the Seventies," *Leaves of Healing* (October 22, 1898) 999.
22. "Opening of Zion's Hall of Seventies," *Leaves of Healing* (January 28, 1899) 255.
23. Lindsey, *Life of John Alexander Dowie*, 160.

17

Maria B. Woodworth-Etter

Bridging the Wesleyan-Pentecostal Divide

JOSHUA J. MCMULLEN

W HEN A STAFF WRITER for the *St. Louis Post-Dispatch* entered
Maria B. Woodworth's revival tent on August 21, 1890, he was
treated to "some of the most weird and entirely inexplicable scenes ever
witnessed."[1] The tent, which could accommodate between eight and nine
thousand people, held a large crowd seated on benches arranged upon
the saw-dust strewn floor. Maria Woodworth, the female evangelist who
had been holding revival services in St. Louis since April, stood upon
the platform preaching to the attentive audience. Shouts of "Amen" and
"God Help Us" could be heard throughout the crowd. Even more surprising than the vocal responses to the female preacher were the bodily
reactions to some unseen force within the tent. Those kneeling near the
altar began to drop over upon the floor. A corps of assistants numbering
around twenty-five carried the fallen individuals to nearby benches until
the "vicinity of the throne [was] covered with unconscious people."

Individuals lay all over the tent in a variety of cataleptic states.
Others shook or trembled. Scattered throughout the makeshift sanctuary were people experiencing visions as well. A young woman, about
eighteen years old, with a look of "extreme delight" upon her face called
out, "I see Him, I see Him." Such manifestations continued long after
Woodworth's closing prayer, and while many attendees made their way

---

1. "'Strange Scenes': The Remarkable Manifestations at the Woodworth Revival
Tent," *St. Louis Post-Dispatch* (August 21, 1890).

to the exit, others waited on friends and family to awake from their trance-like states. With only a few participants and observers remaining in the tent, the reporter also made his way towards the exit and "started away, thoroughly mystified."

The *Post-Dispatch* journalist was not the only one mystified by Woodworth's revival meetings. From mid-summer of 1890 through September of the same year, the gospel tent was filled with thousands of individuals, and on several occasions the multitudes were larger than the tent's capacity. Throughout Woodworth's stay in St. Louis the press was captivated by the meetings. The *St. Louis Post-Dispatch* headlined "Strange Scenes: The Remarkable Manifestations at the Woodworth Revival Tent," the *St. Louis Globe Democrat* ran "Want to See Wonders: An Enormous Crowd at the Woodworth Tent," while other reporters described Woodworth's "Power" and the "Miraculous Cures" taking place on a nightly basis. Maria Woodworth consistently maintained that the manifestations in her gospel tent were "simply the power of God exercised on the converts"; however, the evangelist's critics disagreed.[2] Medical and religious opponents alike claimed that Woodworth was engaging in hypnotism, a technique by which she coaxed her listeners into comatose states as well as enacted her healing cures.[3] Maintaining that Maria Woodworth was a detriment to the public health of St. Louis, two area doctors accused the evangelist of insanity in court, a charge that was eventually dismissed for lack of evidence.[4]

PHYSICAL MANIFESTATIONS OF THE SPIRIT

The debate concerning the Woodworth meetings in St. Louis is emblematic of the tensions and questions surrounding the female evangelist's whole career. Woodworth viewed her ministry as a renewal of earlier evangelical enthusiasm in a period that she believed had grown spiritually cold and formal. This enthusiasm, according to Woodworth, meant less

2. "She Has No Fears," *St. Louis Post-Dispatch* (September 2, 1890).

3. For the most part, doctors in St. Louis did not deny that cures were taking place at Woodworth's revivals but attributed them to hypnotism.

4. "Strange Scenes: The Remarkable Manifestations at the Woodworth Revival Tent" *St. Louis Post Dispatch* (August 21, 1890); "Want to See Wonders: An Enormous Crowd at the Woodworth Tent," *St. Louis Globe-Democrat* (August 22, 1890); "Claim to be Cured," *St. Louis Post-Dispatch* (September 4, 1890); "Miraculous Cures," *St. Louis Globe-Democrat* (August 26, 1890).

reliance on clerical education and administration and more openness to direct guidance by the Holy Spirit. With many individuals lamenting the supposed decline of evangelical zeal, Woodworth's distinctiveness does not lie in her emphasis on enthusiasm but rather her focus on physical manifestations—trances, visions, dreams and healings—as the most accurate markers of renewal.[5] Whereas earlier preachers may have seen religious manifestations as signs of God's presence, Woodworth viewed these phenomena as essential aspects of her revivals. By drawing on her Wesleyan theological heritage and the revival tradition of early evangelicalism, Maria Woodworth contended that her ministry was part of the larger stream of Protestant revivalism; nevertheless, she clearly reshaped both the theology and praxis of this tradition, making it look more akin to the later Pentecostal movement.

Neither the physical manifestations of the St. Louis revivals nor the popularity and criticism surrounding them were new to Maria B. Woodworth. According to the evangelist, the religious manifestations had begun in 1883 while she was conducting revival meetings at a Methodist Episcopal Church in Wilshire, Ohio.[6] Frightened that people would hold her responsible for the strange phenomena, Woodworth claims God took her back to a vision she had had before entering the ministry. She stood in a field of wheat and there were sheaves falling all around. God assured Woodworth that "the falling sheaves is what you see here tonight, the slaying power of God. This is My power . . ."[7] From this point onward, trances became a common feature at Woodworth revivals, earning her the epithet, "Trance Evangelist."

From the outset, Maria Woodworth received criticism concerning the physical manifestations in her services. Despite continual criticism by opponents and even reluctance on the part of some of her supporters,

5. For a fuller discussion of early evangelicalism, see: Cynthia Lynn Lyerly, *Methodism and the Southern Mind, 1770–1810* (New York: Oxford University Press, 1998); John H. Wigger, *Taking Heaven By Storm: Methodism and the Rise of Popular Christianity in America* (Urbana: University of Illinois Press, 1998); Nathan Hatch, *The Democratization of American Christianity* (New Haven: Yale University Press, 1989).

6. This account does not appear in Woodworth's earliest memoirs. It may have been included in later autobiographies because Woodworth sustained so much criticism for the trance experiences later in her ministry and was hoping to defend the religious manifestations by showing their divine sanction and mandate.

7. Maria Woodworth-Etter, *Signs and Wonders* (New Kensington, PA: Whitaker, 1997) 51.

Woodworth continued to make outward signs central aspects of her revival meetings. The evangelist saw the religious phenomena as validating signs of God's presence. Whereas critics viewed trances and healing as detractions from genuine religion, Woodworth saw them as legitimizing factors of her calling and ministry.

CALLED TO HEALING EVANGELISM

The evangelist was born Maria Beulah Underwood on July 22, 1844 in Lisbon, Ohio to ordinary and hard-working farmers. Despite joining the Disciples of Christ church when Maria was ten years old, the family was never particularly religious. The death of Maria's father from sunstroke when she was twelve years old was, as she described it, the "first great sorrow of my life."[8] Her father's death forced Maria and her siblings to seek work off the family farm, so that she would never have a formal education of any kind. When the future evangelist was in her late teens, she married Philo Woodworth, a returned Civil War veteran and local farmer, and it seemed that Maria would live out her life as a housewife in the Ohio countryside.

Like many who would become healing evangelists, Maria Woodworth experienced a series of illnesses throughout her adult life; however, perhaps even more significant was the fact that five out of her six children died at a young age. Though Woodworth had a conversion experience at the age of thirteen (only one year after her father's death), she also claims to have had a conversion experience in 1879 at the age of thirty-five. This latter experience was especially significant because it was only a year later, after the death of her fifth child, that Woodworth decided to engage in a preaching ministry. She had no theological training; she had no experience in active ministry or preaching; she was a thirty-six year old woman; and she had a husband who did not share her desire for a traveling ministry. Nonetheless, within five years, Woodworth would gain national attention and draw immense crowds until her death at the age of eighty in 1924.

Despite early ministerial success, the evangelist's own memoirs show a preoccupation with proper qualification for ministry, centered especially on the fact that Woodworth lacked a formal education and

---

8. Maria B. Woodworth, *Life and Experience of Maria B. Woodworth* (Dayton, OH: United Brethren, 1885) 17.

was a woman.[9] She wrote, "I wanted to go to school where I could learn, I longed for an education; and I often cried myself to sleep over this matter."[10] As she began to believe she was called to active ministry she was "more anxious now than ever for education." [11] Not only did Woodworth lack a formal education but she believed her sex presented an even more formidable obstacle. As a woman, she feared preaching "would subject [her] to ridicule and contempt among [her] friends and kindred, and bring reproach upon [their] glorious cause."[12]

Like female preachers in the early part of the nineteenth century, Woodworth would rely on enthusiastic religion to confirm her calling.[13] Indeed, her dilemma over education and gender was solved by a divine vision where God imbued her with scriptural wisdom.[14] The future evangelist claims, "I saw more in that vision than I could have learned in years of hard study." With this newfound scriptural insight, Woodworth saw that "in all ages of the world the Lord raised up of his own choosing, men, women, and children . . ."[15] Even more telling then Woodworth's use of scripture were her additional arguments for female preaching. She questioned her critics, "Who will arrogate to himself the power to

9. In addition to *Life and Experience* and *Signs and Wonders*, see Maria Woodworth-Etter, *Marvels and Miracles God Wrought in the Ministry of Mrs. M.B. Woodworth-Etter For Forty-Five Years* (Indianapolis: self-published, 1922). For additional work on Maria Woodworth-Etter, see: Wayne Warner, *The Woman Evangelist: The Life and Times of Charismatic Evangelist Maria B. Woodworth-Etter* (Metuchen, NJ: Scarecrow, 1986); Wayne Warner, "Maria Woodworth-Etter: A Powerful Voice in the Pentecostal Vanguard," *Enrichment Journal*. Assemblies of God Publishing, online: http://enrichmentjournal.ag.org/199901/086_woodsworth_etter.cfm; Robert Lairdon, *Woodworth-Etter: The Complete Collection of He Life Teachings* (Tulsa, OK: Albury, 2000).

10. Woodworth, *Life and Experience*, 16–17.

11. Ibid.

12. Ibid., 18.

13. For further discussion on female preaching see: Charles Edwin Jones, *A Guide to the Study of the Holiness Movement* (Metuchen, NJ: Scarecrow, 1974); Catherine Brekus, *Strangers and Pilgrims: Female Preaching in America, 1740–1845* (Chapel Hill, NC: University of North Carolina Press, 1999); Susie C. Stanley, *Holy Boldness: Women Preachers' Autobiographies and the Sanctified Self* (Knoxville: University of Tennessee Press, 2002); Nancy A. Hardesty, *Women Called to Witness: Evangelical Feminism in the Nineteenth Century* (Knoxville: University of Tennessee Press, 1999); Martin Marty, ed., *Modern American Protestantism and Its World: Number 12: Women and Women's Issues* (Munich: Saur, 1993).

14. Woodworth, *Life and Experience*, 37.

15. Ibid., 39.

determine the calling, seeing that more are invested with miraculous power?"[16] Furthermore, she asked her opponents why they did not offer the most encouragement to those who labored most successfully. The implication from these queries is clear—miraculous signs and large numbers of participants were indicators of divine sanction, and both would become central aspects of Woodworth's ministry.

Although Woodworth's initial meetings took place in her own home town, she soon expanded her preaching circuit to incorporate other villages in the region. In this early period, the budding evangelist functioned simultaneously as a female preacher and farmer/housewife; however, her reputation soon garnered her ministry offers from several denominations. Although Woodworth accepted an offer from the United Brethren, she was willing to preach and conduct revivals in almost any denomination that would open their doors to her. After parting with the United Brethren on good terms in 1885 to join the Church of God Winebrennerian, a holiness denomination, Woodworth continued to exhibit openness to a variety of churches. Despite the diversity of her ministerial activities, Maria Woodworth revealed a clear preoccupation with the Wesleyan/Methodist family, whose churches she ministered in more than any other sect or denomination.

Like many other holiness advocates, Maria Woodworth believed that the mainstream Methodist church, for the most part, had become formal and spiritually dead. Despite considerable similarities between Woodworth and holiness proponents, the female evangelist's emphasis on physical manifestations as the sign of God's activity created a significant rift. Although the language employed by Woodworth and holiness advocates was often the same, there was considerable difference in meaning. Both argued that God's power was the solution to cold and formal religion. Holiness camp meetings also exhibited many of the dramatic manifestations of Woodworth's revivals. In contrast to Woodworth, however, the Holiness movement more consistently connected God's "power" with moral living; in fact, Phoebe Palmer, one of the earliest leaders of the Holiness movement, argued "Purity and Power are identical."[17] The Holiness movement was open to religious enthusiasm but stress still lay on the doctrine of Christian Perfection. Although Woodworth did not

16. Ibid., 41–42.

17. Phoebe Palmer, *Pioneer Experiences, or The Gift of Power Received By Faith* (New York: Palmer, 1868) vi.

disregard the need for holiness in the Christian life, she stressed the need for spiritual phenomena as signs of God's presence.

Many individuals agreed with Woodworth and poured into the revival tent for the chance to witness displays of God's power. For two years, Woodworth saturated the state of Indiana, where she held an eldership with the Church of God, with her revival services. By 1887, the female evangelist had expanded her ministry to incorporate other regional states and was setting her sights on locations further west, including Oakland, California where she would hold controversial meetings in 1889. Maria Woodworth's single-minded focus on ministerial concerns makes it difficult to understand the evangelist's personality. This resolute vision both ostracized and endeared her to many throughout her career. With a tendency to view her own ministry as part of a larger cosmic drama, she frequently had little patience for her critics. On the other hand, testimonials from participants at Woodworth's revivals consistently noted the compassion with which the female evangelist ministered. By the time Maria Woodworth reached St. Louis in 1890, she was famous for her revival's dramatic effects, as well as infamous for the controversy surrounding them.

POWER, SIGNS, AND WONDERS

The intermediary role that Maria Woodworth played between the Wesleyan/Methodist tradition and Pentecostalism was central to the St. Louis debates. In defending herself against attacks by local ministers, Woodworth consistently connected her ministry to the earlier Methodist tradition. Woodworth asserted that the "power" present in her revivals was the same that was displayed when "Wesley, Whitfield and Cartwright [all related to Methodism] preached."[18] Many St. Louis residents drew the same connections. One editorialist claimed religious manifestations were common wherever "old-fashioned revivals" and "genuine camp meetings" were held.[19] Another writer claimed that "Similar scenes were enacted years ago by Peter Cartwright," who "gave meetings at which the same strange manifestations occurred."[20] Indeed, others argued that

18. "She Has No Fears," *St. Louis Post Dispatch* (September 2, 1890).

19. "Quackery and Emotional Religion," *St. Louis Republic* (September 3, 1890).

20. "The Woodworth Wonders," *St. Louis Post Dispatch* (August 24, 1890).

"it was common among early Methodists to hear such testimony of re-markable experiences in the trance state."[21]

Woodworth's critics disagreed. Reverend B. M. Messick, pastor of St. John's Methodist Church, dismissed Woodworth's connection to the ear-ly evangelical tradition, while Dr. Boswell of the First Methodist Church considered the movement as "exceedingly dangerous to the Church and to religion."[22] Dr. Matthews of Centenary Methodist Church, one of the largest and most prestigious churches in St. Louis, also bemoaned the Woodworth meetings. According to Dr. Matthews, the female evangelist had misconstrued the word "power" from its original evangelical mean-ing. The St. Louis pastor contended that the word "power" had been "sac-rilegiously used" by the female evangelist in order to designate "mere physical manifestations and dreams."[23] Dr. Matthews had pointed to the real interpretative issue at hand, and the St. Louis debates in general il-lustrate the varied and shifting understandings of Wesleyan thought in this era.

Maria Woodworth was a transitional figure representing the transitional nature of the Wesleyan/Methodist family as a whole in the late nineteenth and early twentieth centuries. While drawing from her Wesleyan/Holiness heritage, the female evangelist was also fashioning a new religious ethos. Emphasis on miraculous signs was both the boon and bane of Maria Woodworth's evangelistic career, and while never free of controversy, the evangelist experienced tremendous numerical success wherever she went. By 1893, Woodworth had conducted large revivals in New York, Florida, Kansas, Iowa, Oregon, and Southern California. By 1900, Woodworth had crossed the United States at least five times in her evangelistic efforts. In 1902, the female evangelist married Samuel Etter (having divorced Philo Woodworth on grounds of infidelity in 1891) at which point her career entered a relatively quiet period only to remerge forcefully in the Pentecostal movement.

The similarities between Maria Woodworth-Etter and her Pentecostal brethren were evident from the start. More than mere theological affin-ity, however, Woodworth-Etter, and others like her, had laid the theologi-cal and practical groundwork for the advent of Pentecostalism. Admired and emulated by scores of Pentecostal evangelists, Woodworth-Etter was

21. "A Pastor on the Power," *St. Louis Post Dispatch* (8 September, 1890).

22. "Claimed to Be Cured," *St. Louis Post Dispatch* (4 September 1890).

23. "A Pastor on the Power," *St. Louis Post Dispatch* (8 September, 1890).

a highly sought-after revivalist, participating in major Pentecostal meetings in Los Angeles and Chicago in 1913. Her books *Signs and Wonders* and *Marvels and Miracles*, whose titles reflect the evangelist's emphasis on physical signs, were incredibly popular and influential. From the time she settled down in 1918 at the age of seventy-three to establish "The Tabernacle" church in Indianapolis until her death in 1924, the female evangelist continued to be sought out for counsel and healing.

Maria Woodworth-Etter has been referred to by many as the "Grandmother of the Pentecostal Movement," a title rightly signifying that the female evangelist had provided part of Pentecostalism's identity—a portion of its DNA, so to speak. Just as important, however, is to recognize that Woodworth's own spiritual DNA was composed largely of Wesleyan/Methodist thought, a movement she consciously identified with. Always wary of many Pentecostal's strict connection between the Holy Spirit's work and speaking in tongues, she never seems to have fully embraced the movement. Similarly, her emphasis on physical manifestations as the truest signs of God's presence seems to have always kept her slightly alienated from the mainstream Holiness and Wesleyan movements. In large part, this is because Maria B. Woodworth-Etter acted as a link between these two worlds, embodying in her own life and ministry the religious transformations of her time.

BIBLIOGRAPHY

Warner, Wayne. *The Woman Evangelist: The Life and Times of Charismatic Evangelist Maria B. Woodworth-Etter.* Metuchen, NJ: Scarecrow, 1986.

Woodworth-Etter, Maria. *Signs and Wonders.* New Kensington, PA: Whitaker, 1997.

PART THREE

Pastoral Response

David Aaron JOHNSON

A PIONEER IS ONE who is first or among the earliest in any field of inquiry or enterprise. A pioneer is one who ventures into unknown or unclaimed territory for the sake of needed change. A pioneer also is one who gives birth to ideas that will progress a needed movement. These historical figures expand the definition of pioneer in a profound way: to include those who *encounter* God for the sake of creating ministries that begin to address the unmet needs of those in the world. For me, a pastor of an African American Church in Seattle, Washington, they are significant because they model how to discover new ways to make known and further God's desired purpose for the world. They possess a pioneering spirit for a more modern age that mirrors the Apostolic spirit that was so necessary to the initial growth and spread of the Church.

It was this God-engendered pioneering spirit that brought forth fruits of racial equality, women's liberation, reconciliation and spiritual renewal. Their words and life witness continue to challenge all of those in local ministries to seek the same encounter and resulting vision that will move those who lead and those who follow to move beyond the norm of our own day in order to seek God's desire for the church and for those who call upon the name of Jesus.

A pioneering spirit—a pioneer's perspective—begins with an encounter with God. Certainly John Wesley encountered God and then by leading others to better experience the "means of grace" redefined and forever expanded on a believer's everyday experience with God. While he built on the firm foundation of church and Christ Jesus' foundation, he reached beyond. He demonstrated a better way. We must have the same willingness to experience God in ways that will reveal new perspective— God's perspective for the world. This is what these later day pioneers were able to do. Through encounters with God they were able to build and expand upon what had previously been founded. They inspire us to have encounters with God, which causes us to engage issues in the world with the courage to see through God's eyes.

Encounters with God bring forth a spiritual renewal in the church that gives us empathy for what is urgent in the world. These pioneering figures warn us that when there ceases to be encounters with God, there tends to be a lack of "pioneering perspective"—a lack of God's perspective. When there ceases to be "pioneering perspective" like the failed court prophets of Israel, God's mission languishes unrecognized and not engaged.

Church movements need encounters with God that yield fresh insights into the needs of the world. When a movement is content to operate out of stale insights, it risks becoming irrelevant. Thus history speaks to us in ministry today that whenever there is stagnation, God calls us to encounters with God to pioneer what is needed for not only the moment but for the future.

We in ministry should not only imitate what these historical figures have pioneered but we should model the "pioneering perspective" of these historical figures by praying for and being open to our own "fresh encounters" with God. For if we only imitate what they did in ministry, we miss the process by which they grew in insight and in their ability to witness to God and minister to God's people. If we do not model, we risk missing the next call of ministry to a world that is in need of better ways to know and grow in God's purposes.

By embracing and practicing the principle of pioneering; by opening ourselves to fresh encounters with God, the church's ministry will always be alive, effective and relevant; meeting the needs of those in the world and fulfilling God's purposes. Guided by the pioneering spirit of these witnesses in faith, and opened to ever new challenges and encounters with God, the church today will continue to be the place of hope not only for the faithful community but for the whole world.

The Twentieth Century:
The Emergence of Pentecostalism

PART FOUR

Introduction[1]

THE FIRE BAPTISM

B Y THE END OF the nineteenth century terms such as "Pentecostal" and "baptism of the Holy Spirit" were used interchangeably with "Christian perfection" and "entire sanctification." The focus on the account of Pentecost this encouraged necessarily raised the issue of the relation of the "power" mentioned in the Book of Acts with "holiness." Some like Phoebe Palmer virtually equated the two terms—after all, women in particular had often found themselves empowered to speak publically for the first time either as a condition of receiving entire sanctification or as the result of having a sanctifying experience. Others believed holiness and power were distinct, but both were received when one received the baptism of the Holy Spirit. Some evangelists associated with the Keswick movement began emphasizing the reception of power to evangelize, making the holiness element secondary.

But there was another answer to the question. There were those who spoke of receiving *two* blessings following that of conversion. The first was entire sanctification which conveyed holiness, and following that was the baptism of the Holy Spirit, or the "fire-baptism," which was an enduement with power. The fire-baptized movement became a distinct and growing form of holiness radicalism. Although he was not the first to propose the doctrine, Benjamin H. Irwin, who was himself influenced

---

1. The best account of the history of Pentecostalism is Vinson Synan, *The Holiness-Pentecostal Tradition*, rev. ed. (Grand Rapids: Eerdmans, 1997). The best account of the development of Pentecostal theology is D. William Faupel, *The Everlasting Gospel* (New York: Sheffield Academic, 1996). An excellent cultural historical analysis is Grant Wacker, *Heaven Below: Early Pentecostalism and American Culture* (Cambridge: Harvard University Press, 1999).

by the theology of John Fletcher, institutionalized it in 1875 as the Fire Baptized Holiness Church. Irwin ultimately developed a theology of six distinct blessings, but it was the three-blessing theology that began to spread through parts of the holiness movement.

THE BEGINNINGS OF PENTECOSTALISM

One person who adopted the three-blessing teaching was former Methodist and healing evangelist Charles Parham. Convinced that the second coming of Christ would be preceded by a world-wide revival, Parham believed that revival would be inaugurated by an outpouring of power which would duplicate Pentecost. The reception of this baptism of the Holy Spirit would be evidenced by speaking in other tongues, which Parham understood to be foreign languages. In this way the gospel could then be proclaimed to all the nations, as prescribed in Matt 24:14.

There had been previous occasions of speaking in tongues (*glossolalia*) throughout the nineteenth century. In 1831 Edward Irving (1792–1834), a Presbyterian whose ministry in London anticipated Pentecostalism, had many congregants who spoke in tongues when they received the baptism of the Spirit. Irving later formed his own movement, the Catholic Apostolic Church.[2] In 1875, there is an account of some speaking in tongues at a D. L. Moody revival in London. Near the end of the century, at the Shearer Schoolhouse Revival in North Carolina in 1896, tongues speaking occurred along with divine healing, fainting, and other phenomena reminiscent of the early camp meetings. Those involved in this revival, who eventually became the Church of God (Cleveland, TN), interpreted speaking in tongues as a sign of a Pentecost-like outpouring of the Spirit.[3] While important, these outbreaks of speaking in tongues were not given the theological significance they would have with Parham, who understood *glossolalia* to be both the necessary initial evidence one had received the baptism of the Spirit and

2. On Edward Irving, see Gordon Stracham, *The Pentecostal Theology of Edward Irving* (Peabody, MA: Hendrickson, 1993).

3. This revival was held by the Christian Union, led by R. G. Spurling. In 1902 he joined with William F. Bryant, a Baptist layperson who taught entire sanctification, to form the Holiness Church at Camp Creek. Joined by A. J. Tomlinson, this movement of Holiness Churches began to be established throughout the region, taking the name Church of God in 1907.

the central element required to complete the mission to the nations prior to Christ's return.

Parham opened Bethel Gospel School in Topeka, Kansas in 1900. It was there that a Methodist student, Agnes Ozman (1870–1937) began to speak in an unknown tongue after Parham had laid hands on her and prayed for the baptism of the Spirit. A few days later, they all experienced Spirit baptism and began speaking in tongues.

Although the school in Topeka closed, Parham opened another in Houston, Texas in 1905, where he sought to begin a missionary movement. There an African-American pastor of a holiness church, Lucy Farrow (1851–1911) met Parham at an evangelistic meeting, and accepted a position as governess and cook for the Bible school. When Parham returned to Topeka, Farrow went with him, leaving her church in the hands of another African-American preacher, William J. Seymour. Seymour was himself a holiness preacher who had been a Methodist and was ordained by D. S. Warner's interracial Evening Light Saints.

Convinced of Parham's teaching, after returning to Houston Farrow urged Seymour to attend Parham's school. Although Seymour had to sit outside the door of the classroom due to segregation, he also was persuaded by Parham's teaching and Farrow's testimony.

In 1906 Pastor Julia Hutchins, who was seeking a replacement so she could go into the mission field, invited Seymour to preach at her holiness church in Los Angeles. When Seymour preached the new message, he was barred from the holiness churches in the city. However, he was invited to begin a prayer meeting in a parishioner's home. Joined by Lucy Farrow after a few weeks the interracial (though largely African, American) group experienced baptism in the Spirit evidenced by speaking in tongues.

Moving to a deserted AME church at 312 Azusa Street, the numbers of participants began to grow, eventually into the thousands. Seymour formed an interracial Board of Twelve men and women to oversee the work, and urged Parham to come and take charge. Parham, who had been bringing the new message to the disheartened residents of Alexander Dowie's Zion City in Illinois[4], finally came to Los Angeles. But he was shocked at the meetings, and this led to a break between him and Seymour.

4. Dowie's arbitrary leadership and financial mismanagement had led Zion City to depose him in 1905.

Part of Parham's disapproval, and the source of much ridicule and disgust by the secular press, was the interracial nature of the revival. But Seymour saw the revival as the beginning of a new day when distinctions of race, nationality, and gender would no longer divide the church. Frank Bartleman (1871–1936), a white preacher who wrote one of the earliest accounts of the revival,[5] declared "the color line was washed away in the blood."

The Azusa Street Revival lasted three years,[6] and caught the attention of holiness leaders throughout America. Its teaching of the baptism of the Holy Spirit as a third distinct work of grace subsequent to entire sanctification and evidenced by speaking in tongues was denounced by many, and embraced by many others. Those who were convinced that this was a "latter rain" paralleling the first Pentecost left Azusa Street to carry the message across America and throughout the world, sometimes sparking Azusa-type revivals and sometimes making connections with indigenous revivals already underway.[7]

Of course, the initial interpretation of *glossolalia* as foreign languages was soon seen as exceptional; in most cases it was understood to be a heavenly rather than an earthly language. A further distinction concerned the purpose of *glossolalia*. As an initial evidence, it was an assurance that one had been baptized in the Spirit; as a gift of the Spirit, it was a divinely-inspired word spoken to a congregation, requiring a divinely-given interpretation; as a devotional or prayer language, it was used for personal devotions or in the context of group prayer (and did not require an interpretation).

THE NATURE OF PENTECOSTALISM

Critics often focused on speaking in tongues as the central distinctive of Pentecostalism. While Pentecostals would rightly resist reducing the movement to an emphasis on *glossolalia*, one possible interpretation is to see Pentecostalism as a radical holiness movement in which Spirit-baptism is evidenced by speaking in tongues. Azusa Street proclaimed a five-fold "full gospel" in which Christ is savior, sanctifier, Spirit-baptizer,

5. Frank Bartleman, *Azusa Street* (published in many editions).

6. The best account of the Azusa Street Revival is Cecil M. Robeck, *The Azusa Street Mission and Revival* (Nashville: Nelson, 2006).

7. On the world-wide spread of Pentecostalism see Allan Anderson, *Spreading Fires: The Missionary Nature of Early Pentecostalism* (Maryknoll, NY: Orbis, 2007).

healer, and coming King. It was with the restored teaching of the baptism of the Spirit, building on what had already been restored by the Protestant reformation, Wesley, and the Holiness movement, that the "Apostolic Faith" had now been fully recovered. Initially known as the Apostolic Faith movement, it was soon called Pentecostalism because it saw itself as the result of a latter day Pentecost and insisted each Christian also needs to have a personal Pentecostal experience. It also continued and developed the emphasis on divine healing inherited from the holiness movement[8], and some would argue this was as central to the practice of early Pentecostalism as prayer for Spirit-baptism.

William Faupel suggests that the focus of early Pentecostalism was not on personal experience but salvation history. He argues the central theme of Pentecostalism is eschatology: a charismatic empowerment for mission in the latter days.[9] Just as the original disciples left Pentecost to preach the gospel throughout the Roman Empire, accompanied by acts of power, so missionaries left Azusa Street and other centers of Pentecostal awakening to carry the gospel across the globe.

In contrast, Walter Hollenweger describes Pentecostalism as an experience of God expressed in oral/narrative forms and manifested in prayer, dreams, visions, healing, and embodied worship.[10] Seeing Pentecostalism as the merger of Wesleyan Holiness and African-American spirituality, Hollenweger believes the doctrinal concepts are secondary to the spirituality itself. Whatever Christian movement manifests that spirituality he would therefore designate as "Pentecostal."

Steven J. Land presents a third perspective. He describes Pentecostalism as a longing for the coming kingdom of God, which is already experienced as an in-breaking into the present by the Holy Spirit. The result is a distinctive Pentecostal spirituality that integrates its beliefs and practices. This is constituted by the holy affections of gratitude for God's forgiveness and the gift of new birth, love as a result of God's gift of sanctification, and courage and hope as the result of God's gift of Spirit-baptism. Thus Pentecostal worship and mission is motivated by

8. For a thorough and insightful overview of the understanding and role of healing in the early movement, see Kimberly Ervin Alexander, *Pentecostal Healing: Models in Theology and Practice* (Blandford Forum, UK: Deo, 2007).

9. See Faupel, *The Everlasting Gospel.*

10. See Walter Hollenweger, *Pentecostalism: Origin and Developments Worldwide* (Peabody, MA: Hendrickson, 1997).

thanksgiving and praise, characterized by compassion, and empowered with the courage and boldness to witness.[11]

THE SPREAD AND THEOLOGICAL DIVERSIFICATION OF PENTECOSTALISM

Whatever the common doctrinal, missional, and experiential elements, Pentecostalism is a highly diverse movement. As we shall see, the movement itself fragments into three distinct theological branches. In addition, the initial interracial character is largely lost as the movement eventually begins to mirror the segregation of American society. Finally, early Pentecostal theologians each had distinctive emphases, teachings, and approaches—some were strongly polemical, other more irenic.[12]

We can begin by examining the impact of three of the most significant figures in early Pentecostalism. G. B. Cashwell (1861–1916)[13] was known as the "apostle of Pentecost" in the South. A Methodist, in 1903 Cashwell joined the Pentecostal Holiness Church, a fire-baptized denomination led by A. B. Crumpler. After traveling to Azusa Street in 1906, Cashwell wanted the baptism of the Holy Spirit but, as a white, resisted being prayed for by African-Americans. In his hotel room he said many things, including his racial prejudice, was crucified by God. Returning to the meeting, Seymour and other African-Americans prayed over him and he spoke in tongues.

Returning home to Dunn, North Carolina, Cashwell led an east coast version of the Azusa Street Revival, and subsequently toured throughout the South. Holiness people and even entire denominations were swept into the Pentecostal movement.[14] In Cleveland, Tennessee, A. J. Tomlinson (1865–1943)[15] and other leaders of the Church of God fell

11. See Steven J. Land, *Pentecostal Spirituality: A Passion for the Kingdom* (Sheffield: Sheffield Academic, 1993).

12. On the distinctive theologies of early Pentecostals, see Douglas Jacobsen, *Thinking in the Spirit: Theologies of the Early Pentecostal Movement* (Bloomington: Indiana University Press, 2003).

13. On Cashwell, see Doug Beacham, *Azusa East: The Life and Times of G. B. Cashwell* (Tampa: LSR, 2006).

14. Among the holiness denominations that became Pentecostal through Cashwell's ministry were the Fire-Baptized Holiness Church, the Pentecostal-Holiness Church, the Church of God (Cleveland, Tennessee), the Holiness Church (later United Holy Church of America), and the Pentecostal Free-Will Baptist Church.

15. On Tomlinson, see R. G. Robins, *A. J. Tomlinson: Plainfolk Modernist* (New York: Oxford University Press, 2004). Tomlinson was later removed as leader of the Church

to the ground and spoke in tongues as Cashwell preached. In his own denomination, A. B. Crumpler opposed the new Pentecostal teaching, but the majority in the Pentecostal Holiness Church sided with Cashwell.[16]

C. H. Mason, an African-American Baptist preacher, read the autobiography of Amanda Berry Smith in 1893 and became convinced of holiness teaching. When their preaching entire sanctification led to their expulsion from the National Baptist Convention, Mason and C. P. Jones founded the Church of God in Christ in 1897. When Mason went to Azusa Street in 1906 and received the baptism of the Holy Spirit with speaking in tongues, his advocacy of the Pentecostal teaching led to a split with Jones, who then founded the Church of Christ (Holiness). Because Mason's Church of God in Christ was the only incorporated denomination that could ordain ministers in the early days of Pentecostalism, it was a biracial organization until 1914. When white ministers from COGIC and other denominations formed the predominantly white Assemblies of God, and COGIC then became predominantly African-American.

Cashwell and Mason followed the three blessing teaching of Parham and Seymour, but the Assemblies of God would not. Their theology was influenced by William H. Durham, whose teaching would sharply divide the new movement. Durham was a holiness preacher in Chicago who received the baptism of the Holy Spirit at Azusa Street in 1907. Now as the leader of the Pentecostal movement in Chicago, Durham began to question the three blessing theology. Preaching "The finished work of Calvary," Durham argued that identification with Jesus Christ on the cross both saves and sanctifies, so a second work of grace (entire sanctification) is unnecessary. Durham thus taught two blessings, corresponding to Calvary and Pentecost. Believing that God is using Pentecostalism to separate truth from error, Durham aggressively promoted his new message; the erroneous three blessing teaching was, he argued, preventing Pentecostalism from fulfilling its divine mandate to be a witness for the truth.

Parham and Seymour, among many others, vigorously opposed Durham's finished work theology. But it became the position of the Assemblies of God and the majority of Pentecostals outside the South.

---

of God (Cleveland) due to a conflict over his financial management, and then founded the Church of God Prophecy.

16. The Fire-Baptized Holiness Church later merged with the Pentecostal Holiness Church to form what is now the International Pentecostal Holiness Church.

The four-fold full gospel it implies—Christ as Savior, Spirit-baptizer, Healer, and Coming King—was explicitly referenced in the name of another new denomination, the International Church of the Foursquare Gospel, founded by Aimee Semple McPherson.

McPherson's was one of a number of Pentecostal denominations founded by women. Florence L. Crawford (1872–1836) left Azusa Street in 1908 to begin her own Apostolic Faith Church in Portland, Oregon. Ida Robinson left the United Holy Church of America,[17] an African-American Pentecostal denomination, to form the Mt. Sinai Holy Church of America, a denomination committed to women's equality. Crawford and Robinson continued in the theological tradition of Seymour, while McPherson had adopted Durham's perspective.[18]

NEW ISSUES

Pentecostalism was born in the midst of the expectancy of many in the holiness movement that God would do a new thing—a fresh outpouring of the Spirit or a restoration of missing elements from the faith and practice of the apostles. Most believed the Azusa Street revival and the world-wide movement it sparked, along with the five-fold or four-fold "full gospel," was that outpouring and restoration. But what if God was not finished and had not yet revealed the full apostolic faith?

It was in that context of expecting yet another new thing from God that in 1913 R. E. McAlister noted in a sermon that in the Book of Acts, baptism was not in the name of the Trinity, as Jesus commanded at the end of Matthew, but in the name of Jesus Christ. Frank Ewart (1876–1947), who was Durham's successor in Chicago, questioned McAlister, who said the Lord Jesus Christ must be another name for the Trinity.

From this, Ewart drew several conclusions. First, Jesus is the divine Name for God, and it is vitally important to be identified with the Name. Therefore, those baptized in the name of the Father, Son, and Holy Spirit need to be re-baptized in the name of Jesus. Second, the doctrine of the Trinity is itself heretical. God is not three persons, which he believed was tri-theism, but God's glory dwells fully in Jesus. There is instead a three-

17. See William C. Turner, *The United Holy Church of America* (Piscataway, NJ: Gorgias, 2006).

18. On women in early Pentecostalism, see Estrelda Alexander, *The Women of Azusa Street* (Cleveland, OH: Pilgrim, 2005); and Estrelda Alexander, *Limited Liberty: The Legacy of Four Pentecostal Women Pioneers* (Cleveland, OH: Pilgrim, 2007).

fold revelation of the one God.[19] Third, at the end of the apostolic age, the Name was missing, and therefore miracles once performed in that Name no longer occurred. Once the Name is restored, apostolic miracles will return as well. In addition to these conclusions, there was the tendency to reduce the two or three blessings to one. Believers were to repent, be baptized in the Name of the Lord Jesus, and receive the baptism of the Holy Spirit evidenced by speaking in tongues. This in effect linked Spirit-baptism with the evidence of tongues with conversion.

What motivated Ewart and his colleagues was a deep concern to be truly apostolic by adhering strictly to New Testament beliefs and practices, especially as found in the book of Acts. From this perspective, they viewed the traditional doctrine of the Trinity as a post-apostolic imposition on the church.

Adherents of the new movement called themselves "Oneness" or "Jesus Name," while opponents labeled them the "New Issue" or "Jesus Only" movement. By 1915 the oneness teaching had spread through the finished work wing of Pentecostalism, and was adopted by about a quarter of the clergy in the Assemblies of God. G. T. Haywood, closely associated with the AG, became the leading African-American proponent of oneness teaching and one of its most articulate defenders. Opposition by AG leaders like J. Roswell Flower (1888–1970), formerly a member of the Christian and Missionary Alliance, kept the majority of the AG faithful to traditional trinitarianism. Oneness Pentecostals led by Haywood and others restructured the interracial Pentecostal Assemblies of the World into a oneness body; in 1924 many whites left to form the United Pentecostal Church.[20]

With the emergence of a strong Oneness tradition, Pentecostalism was now divided into three distinct theological branches: the "Wesleyan" three blessing strand reflecting the teaching of Parham and Seymour, the

19. The practice of baptism in the name of Jesus was used by some evangelical/holiness individuals and groups in the nineteenth century, as well as by some early Pentecostals. See the study by Doug Hogsten, "The Monadic Formula of Water Baptism: A Quest for Primitivism via a Christocentric and Restorationist Impulse," *Journal of Pentecostal Theology* 17.1 (2008) 70–95. However, for the most part these earlier antecedents were Trinitarian in their doctrine of God. On this see both Hogsten and Kimberly Ervin Alexander, "Matters of Conscience, Matters of Unity, Matters of Orthodoxy: Trinity and Water Baptism in Early Pentecostal Theology and Practice," *Journal of Pentecostal Theology* 17.1 (2008) 48–69.

20. See David Reed, *In Jesus Name: The History and Beliefs of Oneness Pentecostals* (Blandford Forum, UK: Deo, 2007).

"Baptistic" or "Keswick" strand reflecting the teaching of Durham, and the Oneness strand.

A fourth theological strand is represented by the very small but well-known group of serpent handling churches. Taking their inspiration from Mark 16:18, which they understood to contain a command to handle serpents, the group emerged from the Church of God (Cleveland, TN) in 1910 and spread across Appalachia. The original leader, George Hensley, formed the Church of God with Signs Following; now they can be found in a number of small denominations or independent churches, some Trinitarian and others Oneness.[21]

Not every new issue faced by Pentecostalism was doctrinal. For a missional movement, issues of contextualization of the gospel in different cultures and the development of indigenous leadership became important. While this was a world-wide challenge, there were ample illustrations of these issues in America itself. In the borderlands mission in the southwestern United States, AG missionaries Henry C. Ball and Alice E. Luce had distinctive approaches to Mexican-American evangelism, training, and leadership. Moreover, Latino Pentecostals like Francisco Olazábal had their own approach, one that challenged the culture of dependency on Anglo leadership. Lessons from these early years can provide direction for present-day reforms and more faithful missionary practices.

Pentecostalism, along with its Holiness parent, had a global missional vision. Whatever the limits of the cultural assumptions of its early missionaries, Pentecostalism has easily been adopted and adapted by a wide variety of cultures throughout the world. The spread of Pentecostalism from its emergence at the beginning of the twentieth century to representing (with its charismatic offspring) roughly one-fourth of Christians world-wide at the end makes it perhaps the most dynamic Christian movement in history.

---

21. See David L. Kimbrough, *Taking Up Serpents* (Macon, GA: Mercer University Press, 2002); Thomas Burton, *Serpent-Handling Believers* (Knoxville: University of Tennessee Press, 1993).

THE PENTECOSTAL MOVEMENT

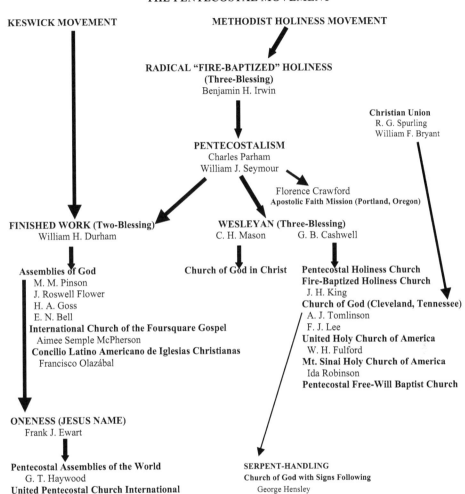

KESWICK MOVEMENT

METHODIST HOLINESS MOVEMENT

RADICAL "FIRE-BAPTIZED" HOLINESS
(Three-Blessing)
Benjamin H. Irwin

Christian Union
R. G. Spurling
William F. Bryant

PENTECOSTALISM
Charles Parham
William J. Seymour

Florence Crawford
Apostolic Faith Mission (Portland, Oregon)

FINISHED WORK (Two-Blessing)
William H. Durham

WESLEYAN (Three-Blessing)
C. H. Mason   G. B. Cashwell

Assemblies of God
M. M. Pinson
J. Roswell Flower
H. A. Goss
E. N. Bell
International Church of the Foursquare Gospel
Aimee Semple McPherson
Concilio Latino Americano de Iglesias Christianas
Francisco Olazábal

Church of God in Christ

Pentecostal Holiness Church
Fire-Baptized Holiness Church
J. H. King
Church of God (Cleveland, Tennessee)
A. J. Tomlinson
F. J. Lee
United Holy Church of America
W. H. Fulford
Mt. Sinai Holy Church of America
Ida Robinson
Pentecostal Free-Will Baptist Church

ONENESS (JESUS NAME)
Frank J. Ewart

Pentecostal Assemblies of the World
G. T. Haywood
United Pentecostal Church International

SERPENT-HANDLING
Church of God with Signs Following
George Hensley

Hal Knight, 2008

18

Charles Parham

Progenitor of Pentecostalism

LESLIE D. CALLAHAN

CHARLES FOX PARHAM WAS born in Muscatine, Iowa, on 4 June 1873, the third son of farming parents. Parham grew up on the Kansas frontier, following the migration of his parents from the East as they pursued the promise of economic opportunity in the West.[1] Unquestionably, the most formative aspect of Parham's early life was the challenge of physical infirmity, which first emerged when Parham was six months old and manifested periodically throughout his life.[2] In addition to serious illnesses such as a fever in infancy that rendered him an invalid and "inflammatory rheumatism" at age nine, Parham suffered a host of maladies and complications.[3] Converted during a revival meeting at age thirteen, Parham led his first revival meetings at age fifteen and later matriculated at Southwestern Kansas College in Winfield, where he briefly considered a respectable career as a physician.[4] Following a nearly fatal illness, Parham withdrew from college and began to hold

---

1. James R. Goff, *Fields White Unto Harvest: Charles F. Parham and the Missionary Origins of Pentecostalism* (Fayetteville: University of Arkansas Press, 1988) 17–18; Sarah E. Parham, *The Life of Charles F. Parham, Founder of the Apostolic Faith Movement*, The Higher Christian Life (New York: Garland, 1985) 1.

2. S. E. Parham, *Life*, 2.

3. Ibid.

4. Ibid., 5–6.

meetings in Tonganoxie, Kansas, where he met the Quaker family of his future wife Sarah Thistlethwaite.

Inasmuch as Parham had any denominational roots or ecclesiastical recognition, they were in the Methodist Episcopal Church, but his ties with Methodism were neither strong nor long-lasting. He had a two-year assignment, between 1893 and 1895, at the English Methodist Episcopal parish in Eudora, Kansas, and founded another smaller congregation at Linwood. The conference leaders had appointed Parham to the church in June 1893 to complete the pastoral term of the Reverend W. R. Davis, the founder of Baker University, whose illness had caused him to vacate the pulpit.[5] Parham's pastoral style emphasized his evangelical impulses such that his ongoing "protracted meetings" elicited remark in the local newspaper.[6] As was the case among many of his holiness counterparts, Parham's theological commitment to sanctification, along with his understanding of its practical implications, led him out of the Methodist connection and into independent itinerant ministry after just two years in the pastorate. He likewise shared the widespread holiness critique of ministers and established churches that embraced cultural respectability at the expense of ignoring the needs of common people and the evangelistic mandate of the gospel.

Beginning in 1898, following a miraculous healing during a recurrence of his rheumatic fever, healing ministry took center stage for Parham. He founded the Beth-El healing home in Topeka, Kansas, and it provided a site for the convergence of Parham's theological emphases, including salvation, healing, sanctification, the Second Coming of Christ, the baptism of the Holy Spirit, and water baptism by immersion.[7] After two successful years of ministry at Beth-El, though, usurpers deposed Parham from its leadership while he traveled East to study at Frank W. Sandford's Holy Ghost and Us Bible School in Maine.

5. *Eudora News* 8.3 (June 8, 1893), 3; Goff, *Fields White Unto Harvest*, 32; S. E. Parham, *Life*, 20.

6. See *Eudora News* 8.26 (November 16, 1893) 3; *Eudora News* 8.27 (November 23, 1893) 3; and *Eudora News* 8.33 (January 11, 1894) 3.

7. S. E. Parham, *Life*, 39. For a discussion of Parham's views on baptism, see ibid., 27.

PROJECTOR OF THE APOSTOLIC FAITH MOVEMENT

At the turn of the century, Parham tried his hand in the field of education, following the pattern he had learned during his Eastern tour. In October 1900, Bethel Bible College officially opened its doors in Topeka, Kansas.[8] Parham's travels the previous summer to visit the missions of John Alexander Dowie, A. B. Simpson, and Frank Sandford, all of whom were known throughout the holiness movement for their healing ministries, armed him with useful models for the college's design. Although the school lasted only from October 1900 to July 1901, in January 1901, it attracted widespread attention when the students there proclaimed the restoration of Pentecost through the supernatural ability to speak foreign languages "as the Spirit gave utterance." Parham identified this experience as the biblical evidence of the baptism of the Holy Spirit and a harbinger of the great revival that God was sending to begin the twentieth century. After the initial experiences among the students of tongues speech, Parham expected to launch an international ministry with Bethel as his base. The miraculous ability to speak foreign languages through the baptism of the Spirit would enable missionaries to proclaim the gospel to all the nations, inaugurating the world-wide revival that would precede the second coming of Christ. The sudden death of his infant son in March 1901, however, undermined the morale of his followers. The subsequent sale of the building he was renting ended Parham's work in Topeka and returned him to itinerant ministry around the state of Kansas. In 1902, he published his first book *Kol Kare Bomidbar: A Voice Crying in the Wilderness*, while living in Kansas City.[9] Although the book had a Hebrew title, there is no evidence that Parham ever had any formal training in Hebrew, and it is probable that the title was intended to reflect his interest in the relationship between Israel and the apocalypse.

After several unremarkable revival campaigns, Parham went back to his central emphasis on healing. This led Parham to move to Texas. In December 1905, Parham relocated his ministry headquarters to Houston and opened another Bible school. Perhaps owing to his recent success and with the obvious purpose of cementing his authority over

---

8. Ibid., 51; Charles Parham, *Voice Crying in the Wilderness*, 32.
9. Goff, *Fields White Unto Harvest*, 86; S. E. Parham, *Life*, 81.

the growing work, he began at this time to refer to himself as "Projector of the Apostolic Faith Movement."[10]

The designation "Projector" was important for Parham, although he never fully explicated its meanings in his writings. The Oxford English Dictionary defines a "projector," in the first instance, as "one who forms a project, who plans or designs some undertaking; a founder."[11] Parham's use of the term probably indicates that he saw himself as founder. Whatever subtlety Parham intended, the title Projector and the organizational structure that Parham instituted in the spring of 1906, in order to grant ministerial credentials and establish regional officers, signified Parham's understanding of himself as God's mouthpiece.[12] In connection with this identity, Parham acted as the director of the movement and the arbiter of its theological disputes.

The most famous and controversial of Parham's students in the Houston school was William J. Seymour, who had recently come to Houston from Cincinnati at the end of his search for relatives lost during slavery.[13] Seymour met Parham upon the recommendation of Lucy Farrow, the pastor of an African-American holiness assembly, who left her pastorate in Seymour's hands when she accompanied the Parham family to Kansas as a domestic worker.[14] When Seymour expressed his desire to study at Parham's school, a concession to state segregation laws forced Seymour to sit outside the classroom with the door ajar during classes.[15] Parham's intention was for Seymour to oversee the program of

---

10. Goff, *Fields White Unto Harvest*, 106. Goff identifies Parham's first use of the title Projector in December 1905 when he opens the Bible school. However, Charles Parham cited its emergence in the summer of 1905. Charles F. Parham, "Leadership," *Apostolic Faith* (Baxter Springs), June 1912, 7. Sarah Parham supports the earlier date in her citation of an article from the summer 1905 which identified Parham as "Projector." See S. Parham, *Life*, 121.

11. James Augustus Henry Murray et al., *A New English Dictionary on Historical Principles; Founded Mainly on the Materials Collected by the Philological Society* (Oxford: Clarendon, 1909).

12. Goff, *Fields White Unto Harvest*, 115–18. For information on the Apostolic Faith movement's organization see, *Apostolic Faith* (Houston) March 1906.

13. Douglas J. Nelson, "For Such a Time as This: The Story of Bishop William J. Seymour and the Azusa Street Revival: A Search for Pentecostal/Charismatic Roots" (PhD diss., University of Birmingham, 1981) 35.

14. Ibid., 167.

15. Goff, *Fields White Unto Harvest*, 107; Nelson, 157; S. E. Parham, *Life*, 142.

evangelism to the African American residents of Houston.[16] After about six weeks with Parham, however, Seymour received a call to a pastorate in Los Angeles, California, an invitation he determined to accept.[17] Parham sent Seymour forth and completed his own work in Houston. Seymour's move from Houston to Los Angeles and the Azusa Street revival that began in California during the spring of 1906 extended the message about the baptism of the Holy Spirit throughout the country, portending a wider reach for Parham's influence. Yet Parham's negative reaction to the character of the meetings at the Azusa Mission not only undermined his leadership in the nascent movement, but also tore asunder his relationship with Seymour.

The public relations fallout from Azusa was nothing when compared with the rumors of Parham's sexual immorality that began circulating early in 1907.[18] The rumors became concrete in July when officials arrested Parham in San Antonio and charged him with an "unnatural offense," along with a co-defendant, J. J. Jourdan.[19] Asserting that the arrest originated in a scheme by his enemies—"spite work," in the words of Sarah Parham—Parham denied the offense and vowed to fight the allegations.[20] His wife at his side on the date set for his indictment, Parham prepared himself for the fight. Yet the authorities dismissed the charges.[21] In the absence of any corroborating evidence and given the silence of Parham's co-defendant, all of the details were a matter of hearsay.

As is often the case with rumors, the accusation's validity was not nearly as important as its impact, and for Parham the charge of homosexual acts resulted in his loss of status as leader of the Apostolic Faith movement and created a climate of suspicion and scandal that followed him throughout the rest of his life.[22] Rejected as leader of the movement and prevented even from holding credentials therein, Parham spent his later years focused on itinerant ministry and asserted even more radical theological positions. From that time on, he turned his attention more specifically to eschatological issues and expanded his interest in Israel

16. S. E. Parham, *Life*, 142.

17. Nelson, "For Such a Time as This," 168.

18. Goff, *Fields White Unto Harvest*, 136.

19. Ibid.

20. Ibid., 137; S. E. Parham, *Life*, 198.

21. Goff, *Fields White Unto Harvest*, 137; S. E. Parham, *Life*, 198.

22. Goff, *Fields White Unto Harvest*, 141.

and Zionism.[23] Like many of his holiness and conservative evangelical counterparts, Parham associated the fate of the Jewish people with the ending of time and therefore advocated the Zionist goal of a Jewish state in Palestine. Parham, however, had deeper and more personal interest in the state of Israel because he believed that Anglo-Saxons were the racial descendants of the Ten Lost Tribes of Israel, who had been dispersed following the Assyrian invasion of 722 BCE. Parham had been introduced to this teaching, known as Anglo- or British-Israelism, early in his ministry, and had propounded its theological and social implications from the time, especially as it related to the end of time and the nature of human bodily destiny. In 1927, he realized his life-long dream of travel to Palestine and Egypt.

On January 29, 1929, he died at his home in Baxter Springs, Kansas, still holding faithfully to his resolve neither to be attended by physician nor to take medication.[24]

CONTINUITY AND DISCONTINUITY WITH EMERGING PENTECOSTAL THEOLOGY

In Parham's thought, the means by which the spiritual life affected the physical life occurred in sanctification. Parham's teachings on sanctification were not entirely consistent. At times, he seemed to consider it an instantaneous occurrence, and at other times a continuing process. It is likely that his wife Sarah expressed his perspective when she wrote, "Sanctification destroys the sinful desires of the flesh, but the natural, human desires of the flesh we must die daily to."[25] What was consistent, however, was the conviction that the sanctifying process had a singularly physical component. For Parham, sanctification addressed sin in a concrete and corporeal way by bringing the body into order and balance. He engaged the theology of his holiness and Pentecostal context, as well as assumptions and tensions of discourses around gender, race, and sexuality, well within fin-de-siecle American culture. Sanctification not only purified the soul; it cleansed the body from disease, authorized women's speech and men's discernment, policed racial boundaries, and solidified family ties. The alternative to the activity of the sanctified body Parham

---

23. Ibid., 159.

24. Ibid.; S. E. Parham, *Life*, 413.

25. S. E. Parham, *Life*, 22.

identified as "fleshly manifestations." Fleshly manifestations referred to bodily activity that expressed the depravity of human nature, rather than spiritual regeneration. Thus, Parham rejected "fleshly manifestations"—whether they be premarital sex, free love, racial integration, or fanatical worship—as the devilish tendency of unregenerate humanity to express disordered desire through excessive and inappropriate physical behaviors.

Pentecostals have tended to embrace Parham because of his significant role in developing the linchpin Pentecostal distinctive, the theology of tongues as initial evidence. Parham believed and taught from 1900 to the end of his life that the baptism of the Holy Spirit was accompanied by the miraculous ability to speak human languages, not only to signify that one had received the baptism of the Holy Spirit, but also to enable the believer to advance the gospel through foreign missions. He spread this view to Seymour who, at least for a time, propounded it in the Azusa mission.[26] Azusa adherents embraced this teaching and carried it with them as they evangelized and founded Pentecostal assemblies and denominations. Thus, Parham is a theological progenitor of the Pentecostal movement at large, a position he ambivalently continued to claim despite his criticisms of the theological and liturgical turns the movement had taken.

But Parham's religious imagination was not limited to a discussion of that linchpin teaching about ecstatic utterance. Parham's thought melded religious commitments with a restrictive understanding of the human body and its proper social relations. From the commonly held view that entire sanctification produced physical wellness to the unorthodox doctrine that unredeemed human bodies faced annihilation at the end of the age, rather than eternal torment in hell, Parham weaved a religious perspective that extended from birth to death and beyond. And his teachings regulated interactions between persons in the meantime. During his life journey, from his own conversion until his death, Parham evinced unremitting concern for the evidence of the Christian life in the physical person. This resulted in discussions about the proper interactions of men and women, socially, religiously, and sexually. It also had implications for racial understanding. And he was as committed to these propositions as he was to the teaching that tongues evidenced the

26. Some scholars assert that tongues as initial evidence receded from Seymour's theology and that rather than tongues love came to be viewed as the primary evidence of Spirit baptism.

baptism of the Holy Spirit. But his advocacy of theological and social positions that Pentecostals generally repudiated made Parham's views marginal to Pentecostalism in his lifetime and even more marginal to the movement as the generations went on.

Both in and out of Pentecostalism, Parham's life and religious teachings reveal a great deal about American religion and culture during the late nineteenth and early twentieth centuries. Parham participated in the larger discussions of health and perfection, manhood and womanhood, Anglo-Saxon identity and racial hierarchies, and marriage and divorce that occupied Americans at the turn of the twentieth century and continue to do so in the beginning of the twenty-first.

BIBLIOGRAPHY

Goff, James R. *Fields White Unto Harvest; Charles F. Parham and the Missionary Origins of Pentecostalism.* Fayetteville: University of Arkansas Press, 1988.
Jacobsen, Douglas. *Thinking in the Spirit: Theologies of Early Pentecostalism.* Bloomington: Indiana University Press, 2003.

19

William J. Seymour

The Father of the Holiness-Pentecostal Movement

STEVEN J. LAND

I N JOHN WESLEY ANCIENT spiritualities from the Eastern and Western branches of Christianity were joined with elements from Pietism and Puritanism to produce a revolutionary doctrine of entire sanctification and social holiness. This theology, marked by a pervasive tension between a "pessimism of nature" (original sin as total corruption) and an "optimism of grace" (Christian perfection), was introduced into America, where it thrived and was further shaped by 19th century holiness-revivalism and African-American spirituality. It was out of this rich heritage that Pentecostalism was born. Had there been no eighteenth-century Wesleyan and nineteenth-century holiness movements there would have been no twentieth-century Pentecostalism.

The marks of that heritage were evident from the beginning. Up until 1910, most Pentecostals would attest verbally, in prayers and gospel songs, that an experience of Christian perfection should precede Spirit baptism.[1] Indeed, almost all of nineteenth-century North American Protestantism, to some extent, was "Wesleyanized" and thus

---

1. Edith Blumhofer, "Purity and Preparation," in S. M. Burgess (ed.) *Reaching Beyond: Chapters in the History of Perfectionism* (Peabody, MA: Hendrickson, 1986) 275. See Also P. R. Wheelock, "Spirit Baptism in American Pentecostal Thought" (PhD dissertation, Emory University, 1983) 210.

"Arminianized." It was Wesleyanism, then, through the Holiness movement, that was the cradle of Pentecostalism.[2]

This is not to deny the early and continuing conflicts between Holiness and Pentecostal churches. But, as Melvin Dieter has observed, these conflicts have been a kind of family dispute between fraternal, if not identical, twins. As Dieter notes, even the more "baptistic" Pentecostal body, the Assemblies of God, has a spiritual dynamic that is

> at least equally or even more strongly derived from the historical camp meeting perfectionism as it is from any classical Reformed categories. The theological and experiential wineskins of the Keswick low-church Anglicans and others through whom the higher life message came back to its American home ... have been hard put to contain the holiness wine. To use another metaphor, the dominant genes of the vigorous Christocentric pneumatology residing in our common parents, the holiness revival, have left on all the progeny such a unified imprint of spirituality and experience, that each of us will be the loser, if we fail to recognize ... the ultimate charge that Warfield and his friends leveled against the movement [New School revivalism of Finney, Mahan, et al] was that, it was really "Methodist." The holiness connection is important for Pentecostals because it carries with it the 19th century concern for abolition, prohibition, women's rights, and the reform of society according to the righteous standards of God.[3]

SEYMOUR AND THE AZUSA STREET REVIVAL

In a wonderfully ironic providence there is a confluence of the above streams of Christianity into and out from the life of William Joseph Seymour. The son of former slaves, Seymour was born in Centerville, Louisiana on May 2, 1870. He was converted in a Methodist church and grew up believing in visions, dreams, and the premillinial soon-coming

2. W. M. Menzies, "The Non-Wesleyan Origins of the Pentecostal Movement," in Vinson Synan (ed.) *Aspects of Pentecostal-Charismatic Origins* (Plainfield, NJ: Logos, 1975) 97.

3. Melvin E. Dieter, "The Wesleyan Holiness and Pentecostal Movements: Commonality, Confrontation, and Dialogue" (unpublished paper, Society of Pentecostal Studies, Asbury Theological Seminary, Wilmore, KY, 1988); see also Melvin E. Dieter, "The Development of Nineteenth Century Holiness Theology," *Wesleyan Theological Journal* 20.1 (Spring, 1988) 61–77.

of the Lord.[4] In 1895, Seymour moved to Indianapolis where he worked as a waiter in various hotels and attended the Methodist Episcopal Church. During this time he contracted smallpox and lost the use of one of his eyes. He had further exposure to the radical holiness movement through Martin Wells Knapp, the founder of God's Bible School. It was during this time (1900–1902) that he joined the Church of God Reformation founded by Daniel Warner in 1880, which was then known as the Evening Light Saints. There he was taught that the outpouring of the Spirit in these last days was to precede the rapture, experienced entire sanctification, and was ordained to preach.

In 1903 he moved to Houston, Texas where he began an evangelistic ministry. A year or two later, obeying a revelation from God, Seymour traveled to Mississippi to receive mentoring from C. P. Jones and/or C. H. Mason, the leaders of the Church of God in Christ, then a Holiness (and later a Pentecostal) denomination.

In 1905 Charles Parham, who had been teaching baptism in the Spirit with the Bible evidence (speaking in tongues) since the turn of the century, moved his bible school from Topeka, Kansas to Houston. Seymour was then attending a holiness church pastored by Lucy Farrow. When Farrow accepted a position as a governess and began to travel with the Parham family, she asked Seymour to pastor the church in her absence.

Returning to Houston and having herself experienced the baptism in the Spirit, Farrow urged Seymour to attend Parham's school. Parham would allow Seymour to attend if he would sit in the hall outside the classroom door, in keeping with the racist protocol of the Jim Crow era. It was here that Seymour became convinced that baptism in the Spirit

---

4. The chronology of places and events that follows can be found in two articles H. V. Synan, "Seymour, William Joseph," in S. M. Burgess and G. B. McGee, eds., *Dictionary of Pentecostal and Charismatic Movements* (Grand Rapids: Zondervan, 1988) 778–81; and C.M. Robeck Jr., "Seymour, William Joseph," in S. M. Burgess, ed., *The New International Dictionary of Pentecostal and Charismatic Movements*, rev. ed. (Grand Rapids: Zondervan, 2002) 1053–58. For the most extensive, accurate and thoroughly readable account of Seymour, his times and thought see C. M. Robeck Jr., *The Azusa Street Mission and Revival: The Birth of the Global Pentecostal Movement* (Nashville: Nelson, 2006). See also R. G. W. Sanders, *William Seymour: Black Father of the 20th Century Pentecostal/Charismatic Movement* (Sandusky, OH: Alexandria, 2001); L. Martin, *The Life and Ministry of William J. Seymour* (Joplin, MO: Christian Life, 1999); and W. J. Seymour, *The Doctrines and Disciplines of the Azusa Street Apostolic Faith Mission* (1915; reprinted, Joplin, MO: Christian Life, 2000).

was distinct from entire sanctification and evidenced by speaking in tongues.

Answering a pastoral call to a holiness church in Los Angeles, Seymour boldly proclaimed the Pentecostal message, taking Acts 2:4 as a text, even though he himself had not received "the blessing." The local pastor, Julia Hutchins, promptly locked him out, and he moved to the home of Richard Asberry on Bonnie Brae Street. Here the participants, including eventually Seymour himself, were baptized in the Holy Spirit with the evidence of speaking in tongues. The prayer meeting grew, spilled out onto the front porch and street and then moved to a building at 312 Azusa Street that had once been an African Methodist Episcopal church, but more recently a stable and warehouse.

The revival began on April 14, 1906, just four days before the great San Francisco earthquake, and it continued through 1909—three years, three times a day, seven days a week. Thousands of persons came to Azusa Street seeking their baptism in the Spirit and then went forth to all parts of the country and around the world. Frank Bartleman, a participant observer, announced that the "color line had been washed away in the blood" of Jesus. One seeker from the southern United States testified that he had to wade through a seeming sea of black brothers and sisters as God broke him over the wheel of his prejudice, sanctified and filled him with the Holy Spirit. The *Los Angeles Times* heralded the, "wild scenes," "weird babble of tongues," and scandalous, "racial mixing." But to Seymour the interracial and egalitarian nature of the revival testified to its being a latter day Pentecost.

This was not true for Parham. Arriving at Azusa Street in October, 1906, Parham was alarmed at the intense exuberance of the worship and the mingling of the races. Parham's attempt to take over the revival was resisted by Seymour and the interracial board of elders of the Azusa Street Mission. Seymour now became the central leader of the young movement. Soon after the revival began Seymour incorporated the mission as the Pacific Apostolic Faith Movement and began a periodical, *The Apostolic Faith* (hereafter referred to as *AF*), which soon had garnered 50,000 plus subscribers nationally and internationally.

In 1910 William Durham rejected the Wesleyan-holiness teaching of entire sanctification and put forward his more Reformed doctrine of the finished work of Calvary. Seymour saw this as a fatal mistake, since power was to be upon the sanctified life, which excluded racial prejudice among other things. Indeed, most of the subsequent defections and splits were to come at the hands of white people, to most of whom Seymour continued to reach out and counseled his church to love. No wonder, when he revised the Doctrines and Disciplines and Constitution of the church, he included a statement making him its bishop and calling for his successor to be "a man of color."

By 1914 the Azusa Street Church had become yet another small black congregation in Los Angeles. After Seymour died on September 28, 1922, his wife, Jenny Moore Seymour, became the pastor; she died in 1936. They could not have realized the widespread global, and transdenominational impact they would have.

BELIEFS AND PRACTICES AT AZUSA STREET

Brief attention must now be given to the core beliefs and practices of the revival which were to leave a lasting imprint on this global movement of revival and mission. The editor of the *Apostolic Faith* placed "contend for the faith" on the masthead of each issue. In response to questions related to maintaining the anointing after the initial reception of the Holy Spirit, Seymour exhorted to keep on living in the word of God with a perfect heart of obedience. No antinomianism here! And what of the place of Bible study after receiving the Holy Ghost blessing? The editor responded, "Yes (we need to study); if not one becomes fanatical or many times will be led by deceptive spirits and begin to have revelations and dreams contrary to the word, and begin to prophesy and think ourselves some great one, bigger than some other Christians. But by reading the Bible prayerfully, waiting before God, we become just little children, and we never feel that we have got more than the least of God's children." [5]

The ongoing corporate reflection upon the living reality of God in their midst was the method of theological work at Azusa. Scripture reading, preaching, teaching, testimonies prayers, silent meditation, dancing, prayer vigils, songs, witness, poetry, dreams, visions— all these means of grace tended to form persons who shared a common story, who had become actors in a cosmic drama at a crucial point in salvation history. But in all of this the stated pre-eminent authority was Holy Scripture.[6] The Holy Spirit was the teacher who unfolded the drama of redemp-

5. *AF* 1.10 (September, 1907) 23.
6. Ibid., 2.

tion from Genesis to Revelation, and all they had to do was "to follow on." Free-lovism (contemporary expressions of sexual impropriety) was condemned as from the "pit of hell ... a dragon devouring those who get out of the Word ... but he has given His children to know these Spirits." Writing in unknown languages under spiritual inspiration was also condemned because it did not occur in Scripture[7]

An early statement of belief in the *Apostolic Faith* consisted of brief phrases, scriptural quotations, affirmations of restoration of apostolic gifts, signs and wonders, and the "old time religion" practices of camp meetings, revivals, missions, street and prison work, and Christian unity everywhere.[8] All of these practices and beliefs were drawn from the revivals of the eighteenth century Methodist and nineteenth century holiness adherents. "The difference was the gestalt, the particular mix of eschatological intensification evidenced in the urgency, expectancy, and manifestations of the Spirit which gave rise to a missionary fellowships whose "This is that" (Acts 2:16) affirmation of the Latter Rain (of God's Spirit) turned members of the Holiness movement into members of a global Pentecostal missionary force[9] now numbering well over 600 million and continuing to grow, especially in the new majority Christian locations of Africa, Asia, and Latin America.

The indeterminate but imminent second coming of Christ energized the ethical and missionary concerns of the revival participants. They were commissioned to warn the church to get ready, to consecrate and to witness. As was commonly reported,

> "Jesus is coming soon" is the message that the Holy Ghost is speaking today through nearly everyone that receives the baptism with the Holy Ghost. Many times they get the interpretation of the message spoken in an unknown language and many times others have understood the language spoken. Many receive visions of Jesus, and he says, "I am coming soon." Two saints recently in Minneapolis, fell under the power, were caught up to heaven, and they saw the New Jerusalem, the table spread and many of the saints there, both seeing the same visions at the same

---

7. Ibid.

8. *AF* 1.1 (1906) 2.

9. Steven J. Land, *Pentecostal Spirituality: A Passion for the Kingdom* (Sheffield: Sheffield Academic, 1993) 94.

time. They said Jesus was coming soon and for us to work as we
had little time.[10]

Central to the understanding, experience, and testimony of the
saints at Azusa was the reality of Christ. In their testimony to Him in His
fullness, they focused on his being their Savior, sanctifier, healer, Spirit
Baptizer and coming King. This functional Christology was also a short-
hand way of describing the full gospel. God had restored to the church's
life and doctrine, justification by faith through Martin Luther, sanctification by faith through John Wesley, and Spirit Baptism through the
Pentecostal latter rain outpouring. New emphasis on healing emerged
throughout the 19th century Holiness movement, accompanied by a
shift from post to premillenial expectancy regarding Christ's second
coming. Jesus Christ was "the same yesterday, today and forever."

This apostolic reality of the first century church was being restored
with accompanying experience, testimony and doctrine. Although regeneration (simultaneous with justification) sanctification and Spirit
Baptism might occur simultaneously, more often than not they were
separable experientially. They were crises within and with a view toward
a spiritual developmental journey which would turn believers into a
missionary force. "Salvation history was not primarily a matter of ideas,
illumination and belief. It was fundamentally deliverance, turning, listening, watching, walking, waiting on the Lord who had acted, was acting and would act.[11] Full salvation was verbal!

Seymour, reminiscent of John Wesley, answered a range of pastoral
questions in the *Apostolic Faith*. As might be expected, many of them
had to do with sanctification, Spirit baptism, and the Pentecostal believers' relationship to other Christians. When asked if a person should seek
sanctification before Spirit Baptism, he answered yes, because sanctification destroys the old adamic body of sin but the baptism in the Spirit
empowers for service and seals the believer for the day of redemption.
To the question concerning the real evidence of baptism in the Spirit,
Seymour replies that it is divine love and fruits of the Spirit (Gal 5.22).
So, is it necessary to have hands laid on in order to receive the Holy
Ghost? No, one can receive it right now by faith in the word of God and
in any location ("your closet"). But you should be sanctified, because
Spirit baptism is a "gift of power on the sanctified life, and when people

---

10. *AF* 1.11 (October-January, 1908) 2.

11. Land, *Pentecostal Spirituality*, 117.

receive it, sooner or later they will speak in tongues as the Spirit gives utterance . . . tongues are not salvation and not in the standard of fellowship with other Christians;" that comes "through the blood by the Spirit of Christ."[12]

To Pentecostals tempted to pride Seymour exhorted,

> When people run out of the love of God, they get to preaching something else; preaching dress, and meats, and doctrines of men, and preaching against churches. All these denominations are our brethren. The Spirit is not going to drive them out and send them to hell. We are to recognize every man that honors the Blood. So let us seek peace and not confusion. We that have the truth should handle it very carefully. The moment we feel we have all the truth or more than anyone else, we will drop.[13]

William Seymour believed sanctification in the perfect love of God was necessary for Spirit baptism, essential to racial reconciliation and unity, and preparation for the return of Christ for a Bride without "spot or wrinkle." He was a humble leader who empowered others, recognized multiple leadership (including women), did not hold grudges, exercised judicious pastoral discernment and prayed continually. All of this and more qualifies him to be designated the spiritual father of the modern global holiness-pentecostal movement and a key figure who represents some of the best of the traditions fleshed out in this book. Power upon the sanctified life for righteous witness and mission is still a worthy if not essential concern for responsible Christians today.

The heart of Seymour's spirituality and the unofficial theme song of the Azusa Street revival is found in the gospel song, "The Comforter Has Come."

> Verse 1: O spread the tidings round, wherever man is found,
> wherever human hearts and human woes abound;
> Let every Christian tongue proclaim the joyful sound:
> The comforter has come!

> Verse 2: The long, long night is past, the morning breaks at last,
> And hushed the dreadful wail and fury of the blast;
> As over the golden hills the day advances fast!
> The Comforter has come!

---

12. *AF* (October-January, 1908) 2.

13. "The Church Question," *AF* 1.5 (1907) 2.

Verse 3: Lo, the great King of kings with healing in His wing, to every captive soul a full deliverance brings;
And through the vacant cells the song of triumph rings:
The Comforter has come!

Verse 4: O boundless love divine, how shall this tongue of mine, to wondering mortals tell the matchless grace divine,
That I, a child of hell, should in His image shine!
The Comforter has come!

Verse 5: Sing till the echoes fly above the vaulted sky, and all the saints above to all below reply,
In strains of endless love, the song will never die:
The Comforter has come!

Chorus: The Comforter has come, the Comforter has come!
The Holy Ghost from Heaven, The Father's promise given;
O spread the tidings round, Wherever man is found,
The Comforter has come.[14]

BIBLIOGRAPHY

Jacobson, Douglas. *Thinking in the Spirit: Theologies of Early Pentecostalism*. Bloomington: Indiana University Press, 2003.
Robeck, Cecil M., Jr. *The Azusa Street Mission and Revival*. Nashville: Nelson, 2006.
Sanders, Rufus G. W. *William Seymour*. Sandusky, OH: Alexandria, 2002.

14. By Rev. F. Bottome.

20

C. H. Mason

Sanctified Reformer

L. F. THUSTON

CHARLES H. MASON IS the father of the largest holiness-pentecostal communion in America. It is difficult to find one word to classify him. Was he an evangelist, prophet, crusader, healer, mediator, innovator, mystic, mentor, or apostle? Early on Mason's Church of God in Christ constituency named him "chief apostle." Perhaps *Reformer* is the term that includes the sum of the dimensions of Mason's distinctive ministry. Mason embodied a concept of multi-dimensional holiness-pentecostalism that brought needed definition to the sanctified movement. The personal spirituality of C. H. Mason was lived out as the consummate *sanctified reformer*.

CONTEXTUALIZATION: MASON'S SPIRITUAL QUEST

The son of slaves, Mason was born in 1860–66 near Memphis, Tennessee, in a plantation environment. His mother Eliza's oppressed life was undergirded by intense and disciplined prayer. At the age of eight Charlie would lose his hard working father, a Civil War veteran (family legend suggests he was shot before Charlie's eyes during a common rural vindictive raid of former Confederate soldiers).[1] In the aftermath of his father's

---

1. Lelia Mason Byars, "Highlights of My Father's Life—Charles Harrison Mason," COGIC Historical Museum & Fine Arts Program (audio recording), (Memphis: November, 1988); James B. Boyer, "Preserving the Legacy of Bishop C. H. Mason," *The Whole Truth* (July, 2004).

untimely death, Charlie found it unbearable to see his mother labor under such austere circumstances and the child took his mother's place in the plantation fields. After the family moved to Plummersville, Arkansas during a yellow fever epidemic Mason, now almost fourteen, contracted the disease.[2] Physicians offered little hope for his survival. Mason recounts on the morning of the first Sunday of September, 1878, a physical healing occurred and he instantly recovered and began to skip, cry and shout "Praise His holy name . . . it appeared the very heaven had opened to him and he was numbered among the holy ones on high."[3] Mason's experiential spirituality had now become compounded by healing, his mother's prayers, and continuous dreams and visions. Young Mason is later baptized and answers the call to lay evangelistic ministry.

As a young adult he decided to temporarily set aside his ministry to acquire three things: a college education, a house, and marriage. His attempt to resume his ministry introduced major conflicts into the new marriage. Despite several attempts to salvage it, the marriage traumatically ended two years later when his wife initiated divorce. Mason not only lost his wife but plunged into such deep depression that suicide became a lingering demonic consideration.[4] After weeks of despair Mason returned to his home church, confessed he had lost all spiritual health, declared he is now "on my way to hell," and wished to be restored spiritually and to the congregation. Admitting his current state of spiritual lostness to a Baptist congregation that embraced "irreversisble conversion" placed the church at an impasse.[5] Several days later the congregation elected to allow his testimony and confirmed his restoration.

Mason's quest for truth was triggered by a sequence of dramatic episodes. The prayer life of his mother, the spiritual survival mechanisms of the Christian slave tradition, the tragic loss of his father, a failed marriage, along with his personal healing testimony drove him to explore scripture to address these ambivalences in his personal and social context. He struggled to grasp the jagged ambiguity between the spiritual

2. I. C. Clemmons, "Mason, Charles Harrison," in Stanley M. Burgess, ed., *The New International Dictionary of Pentecostal Charismatic Movements* (Grand Rapids: Zondervan, 2002) 865.

3. James Courts, ed., *The History and Life of Elder C. H. Mason and His Co-laborers* (n. p., 1920) 12.

4. Ithiel C. Clemmons, *Bishop C. H. Mason and the Roots of the Church of God in Christ* (Lanham, MD: Pneuma Life, 1996) 5.

5. Courts, ed., *History*, 14.

hollowness of his southern black Baptist denomination, the racism of white America, the abrupt backlash of post-reconstruction race reversals, and the unbridled passion he had for living victoriously the will of God. He resolved to dedicate the rest of his earthly life in pursuit of "seeking to know the God of the Holy Bible." Subsequently in 1893 he resolved to pursue college and in preparation was influenced by the recently published *An Autobiography: The Story of the Lord's Dealing with The Colored Evangelist, Mrs. Amanda Smith.* Her life story swept many blacks into the Holiness movement and certainly impacted Mason.[6] His affiliation with the emerging Holiness movement seemed to address the ambiguity of his context.

MASON AS HOLINESS REFORMER

In 1895 Mason and C. P. Jones joined with other holiness Baptist preachers in promulgating a second work of grace identified as "sanctification." As their message spread, holiness conventions, revivals, and periodicals precipitated the emergence of a reformation movement within the black Baptist and Methodist churches. The result was ejection from their pastorates, the Mississippi Baptist State Association and the National Baptist Convention. After fighting to remain in their native denomination, Mason and his comrades were forced to forge ahead with a new organization structure.

After much deliberation over a suitable name for this new communion it was concluded that "Church of Christ" and "Church of God" were already in use and a more distinctive biblical name was needed. While walking along a certain street in Little Rock, Mason received the revelation of the name "Church of God in Christ"(1 Thess 2:14; 2 Thess 1:1.)[7] Jones was designated General Overseer by this small fellowship of pastors and the revelation Mason received became the name of this growing movement. Mason and Jones led a reformation unprecedented in America and western culture. From the seventeenth through the nineteenth centuries, most blacks encountered Christianity under the aegis of forcibly segregated Baptist or Methodist churches. Mason and Jones birthed a unique Christian tradition that was theologically and racially

6. Clemmons, *Bishop*, 5.

7. Charles H. Pleas, *Fifty Years of Achievement from 1906–1956: A Period in the History of the Church of God in Christ* (Memphis: Church of God in Christ Publications, 1956; reprinted 1991) 6.

indigenous, and organizationally and doctrinally unconnected to any existing mainline Anglo denomination. There were other small minority denominations forming during this era (Fire Baptized, Church of the Living God, United Holy Church of America, Mt. Calvary Holy Church, etc.), but structural and national fluidity of COGIC was enhanced by the charismatic leadership synergy of Jones and Mason. The prolific writings and hymnology of Jones coupled by the popular dynamic preaching of Mason drove the Holiness movement throughout the South and southwest like an unstoppable force within the sustaining structure of COGIC.[8]

Although this new church was primarily located in the black community, it was never exclusively African-American. Though black holiness leaders spoke at white holiness conferences and occasionally a white holiness speaker would appear at a black conference, due to social convention "White clergy and congregations refrained from joining black Holiness fellowships."[9] The Mason-Jones brand of holiness never excluded whites, and other ethnicities and interracial configurations were always welcomed and anticipated.[10] Thus by the time the news reached Mason and the COGIC leadership of the 1906 Azusa Street Revival in Los Angeles, its multicultural flavor was a familiar concept.

William Seymour, its leader, had met Jones and Mason prior to the revival. Seymour was influenced by the Mason-Jones multi-racial inclusivity of the sanctified beloved community. Mason embraced the Wesleyan motif of Christian perfection. In the beloved community perfection in love and appetite for the witness of Christ's Spirit was antithetical to social fragmentation and oppression, and, eradication of racist disposition and behavior was evidence of the work of the Holy Spirit. Though it would be inaccurate to assert that Mason introduced Seymour to interracial holiness, clearly this was a tenet and practice they shared. From the genesis of the nation through the post-civil war years, race, class and culture had been glaring swords of division in church and community. The Mason-Jones-Seymour reformation message of

8. Clemmons in Burgess, *Dictionary*, 866.

9. David D. Daniels, "Charles Harrison Mason: The Interracial Impulse of Early Pentecostalism," in James R. Goff and Grant Wacker, eds., *Portraits of a Generation: Early Pentecostal Leaders* (Fayetteville: University of Arkansas Press, 2002) 262.

10. Ortho B. Cobbins, *History of the Church of Christ (Holiness), USA, 1895–1965* (New York: Vantage, 1966) 428.

sanctfication mandated the replacing of such barriers with bonds of non-segregated unity. This embrace of Wesleyan spiritual-social perfectionism proved definitive for Mason's reformation affiliation. It was this same quest that drew him to attend the Azusa Street Revival.

Mason's testimony of the Azusa experience was not well received by Overseer Jones in the COGIC convention of August 1907. Although these two holiness stalwarts had much in common, and their relationship was described as close, collaborative, and fruitful, Mason's third blessing report eventually terminated their partnership. Mason and colleague D. J. Young were unrelenting in their testimony as well as their doctrinal application (Mark 16:17; Acts 8:15–16; 19:1–6; 1 Cor 14:14, 28; Jude 20). Jones did not accept the Mason-Seymour hermeneutic and denounced the known tongues utterance of the Pentecostals. But Mason's Virginia July revival had confirmed the consistency of the third work of grace doctrine experienced at Azusa only weeks prior. Of the 6000 converted, at least half claimed the Spirit-baptismal sign of glossolalia.[11] Thus, Mason concurred with Young in the Azusa-Seymour position that not only was Spirit baptism a third work of grace, but speaking in tongues under Spirit control was the sign of Spirit baptism. The debate reached an impasse, and Jones and the majority withdrew and disfellowshipped Mason and Young.[12] Mason immediately called for a General Assembly of Pentecostal Church of God in Christ believers to meet him in Memphis the following month (September 1907). After three days of fasting and praying, D. J. Young stood before the small group of pastors with an interpretation of his glossolalic utterance, "God has given us Brother Mason to be our leader."[13] After two years of legal wrangling with Jones over local church property rights and the COGIC corporate name, Mason prevailed.

DENOMINATIONAL REFORMER: MASON AND THE CHURCH OF GOD IN CHRIST

Mason's own words were reformational: "The fight has been great. I was put out, because I believed that God did baptize me with the Holy Ghost

11. Vinson Synan, *The Holiness Pentecostal Tradition* (Grand Rapids: Eerdmans, 1997) 125–27.

12. Cobbins, *History*, 434, 120.

13. Samuel Mason Young. *A Brief Historical Sketch of our Founder D. J. Young* (Kansas City, Kansas, 1993) 5.

among you all. Well, He did it and it just suits me . . . His banner over me is love."[14] The Church of God in Christ would become a fresh force in America and in twentieth-century Christendom. Here the vestiges of slave religion were uniquely retained in the Mason context. Worship was holistic and often physically animated. Spontaneous dancing, enthusiastic singing and shouting, drums, visions and dreams, call and response preaching, epiphanies from nature's enigmas in roots and branches, and divine healing were among the features of the slave religious practice.[15] This type of cultural venue had proven immensely useful during the struggles for individual and communal survival throughout the toxic centuries of slavery and racism. While Baptist and Methodist traditions sought to replace such *africanisms* with more culturally accepted euro-liturgical components, Mason saw no conflict between experiential religion, communal worship and spontaneous spiritual expressions. Mason intuitively connected these ancient modalities as legitimate vehicles of the authentic and normative Christian expressions for individual devotional or corporate worship settings.

Retaining these cultural vestiges of sanctified spirituality was one side of this reformer's equation; the other was the Wesleyan understanding of sanctification. Mason had embraced the Wesleyan doctrine of perfected love as evidence of the grace of experiential sanctification.[16] Mason's brand of sanctified spirituality did not allow for unchecked racism in the beloved community. There was already occasional integrated leadership and worship among the believers in the holiness movement However not until Seymour at Azusa did it become official policy and not until Mason-COGIC did racial inclusivity become normative for Christian worship. Regression to the racist patterns of the majority culture became the greatest challenge to Azusa and the Pentecostal movement. Mason was unique in embracing a racially sanctified standard prior to Azusa and maintaining it for nearly 30 years after.

Mason's COGIC manual boldly claimed the unique reformation role of racial equality in 1917: "Many denominations have made distinctions between their colored and white members. . . . The Church of God

14. Leonard Lovett, "Black Holiness Pentecostalism: Implications for Ethics and Social Transformation" (PhD diss., Emory University, 1978) 423.

15. Clemmons, *Roots*, 31.

16. J. W. Macklin and Leonard Lovett, eds. *An Enduring Legacy: Building on Our Pentecostal Heritage* (Hayward, CA, 2001) 1.

in Christ recognizes the fact that all believers are one in Christ Jesus and all its members have equal rights. Its Overseers, both colored and white, have equal power and authority in the church"[17] Such reformation *koinonia* became a common practice in worship as well. Mason was audacious enough to implement the ideal into the current social-spiritual context of segregated Christendom. Even after 350 white clergy left COGIC to form the Assemblies of God in 1914, COGIC continued to be largely white until the early 1930s.[18] COGIC's structure attracted white clergy and congregations that joined a religious group with predominately black leadership in an era when segregation defined American Christianity and society.[19]

Mason devised a three dimensional construct to sustain this marvelous "holiness" ideal, what Daniels calls "the COGIC experiment". He allowed *compartmentalization,* white ministers credentialed in COGIC who wished to function in white compartmental segregated sub-fellowships. Secondly, Mason permitted *affiliation,* white regional dioceses with white overseers fully functioning within the general COGIC organizational mainstream. Thirdly, Mason preferred full *integration.* He encouraged and welcomed whites to serve in equal status and authority at all levels and in all departments. Under Mason's reformation leadership overseers, national officers, and thousands of white saints were seamlessly integrated into the life and structure of the church. This integrated leadership experiment validated the Seymour/Mason ideal of sanctified ecclesiastical witness and is indicative of Mason's optimism for restoring the consistency of primitive church's perfectionist social practice with its liturgical charismata.

However, by 1933 institutional tensions ended this idyllic leadership phase and Mason shifted to a decidedly urban episcopal leadership model. Between 1910 and 1970, 6.5 million African-Americans moved from the South to the North and Midwest and they brought their religion with them. In 1933 he conceded the end of the era of bi-racial leadership and, while retaining the virtue and practice of multi-cultural fellowship among the laity, now shifted to a new configuration of the COGIC bishopric. He consecrated five state overseers as prelates with regional geographical responsibilities. This shift set the landscape for

17. Daniels, in Goff, *Portraits,* 255.

18. Grant Wacker, *Heaven Below: Early Pentecostals and American Culture* (Cambridge: Harvard University Press, 2001) 231.

19. Daniels, in Goff, *Portraits,* 256

maximizing a fresh urban strategy to accommodate a rapidly changing demographic. This reformation technique is reminiscent of the New Testament urban leadership strategy, in which first-century charismatic apostles prioritized the key urban centers of the Roman Empire's for maximum evangelistic efficacy in reaching their world.

GLOBALIZATION: MASON'S PROPHETIC WORLDVIEW

Mason believed holiness could change the world. With his assault upon the widespread moral grossness of the times he also offered a sanctified community as the dynamic alternative. An alternative educational institution, alternative publishing house, alternative outreach departments, alternative response to world wars, alternative model for empowerment of women and alternative to Black Nationalism and white racism were components to his global vision of holiness. Many millennialist holiness leaders embraced a restorationist piety and personal evangelistic passion. However, Mason was concerned with more than simply equipping converts for the *eschaton*. His movement sought to create an alternative institutional system as a vehicle for holiness-pentecostal witness for empowered earthly living during the present.

Mason provided a resilient challenge to the hypocrisy of social and national policy. Mason denounced the arrogance of a nation that persisted in blood spilling to rescue people abroad as a despicable cover for oppression of Americans at home. "The rich man's war and a poor man's fight...." is descriptive not only of his critique of WW I, but also his prophetic assessment of the deplorable state of affairs in his own homeland. When Mason telegraphed President Wilson in 1914 to request conscientious objector status for COGIC soldiers, he also agreed to selling war bonds to demonstrate the support saints should exemplify towards the office of the Presidency.[20] Mason personally raised $3,000 in bond sales to bolster the nation economically during wartime.

No doubt much of his conflict that followed with local and federal government was also a disguise for bigoted rage against Mason's interracial policy and practice. Mason was arrested in Paris, Texas, Lexington, Mississippi, and San Francisco on charges of conspiracy to obstruct the

---

20 Theodore Kornweibel, "Bishop C. H. Mason and the Church of God in Christ During World War I: The Perils of Conscientious Objection," *Southern Studies: An Interdisciplinary Journal of the South* 26 (Winter, 1987) 277.

draft, impersonating government officials, and swindling.[21] When his brief case was searched for treasonous literature, only a bottle of anointing oil and a handkerchief in a Bible were discovered. Subsequent white grand juries refused to buckle under federal government pressure to indict the pacifist minister and all charges against Mason were dropped.

This was also an era of unbridled social optimism among minorities following centuries of suffocating oppression. The Black Nationalism movement associated with Marcus Garvey, DuBois, Noble Drew Ali, Father Divine and others had a swelling appeal. However, Mason's global prophetic voice was a stark contrast to a social and political construct void of true spiritual essence and power. Mason understood social liberation of oppressed people to be inherent in genuine spiritual Pentecost. He cautioned against a Christless spiritual trap as lethal to black America as it was in prosperous years of spiritually backslidden Israel of the prophetic Old Testament.

The Annual National Holy Convocation was another feature of Mason's global vision. Originally the constituency was largely southern agricultural laborers and by November farmers had harvested their crops. The pilgrimage to Memphis was logistically and financially feasible for the gathering of a powerful but dispossessed people. The COGIC convocation was a worship festival containing features of fellowship, networking, renewal, reporting, strategizing and gathering of denomination funds. After 21 days of convocation, laity and clergy would return to their agrarian jobs and homes renewed for another sanctified year. Perhaps nothing enhanced the annual convocation's appeal more than the display of Mason's healing ministry and spiritual gifts. The sick were brought from across the nation with scores of dramatic healing testimonies following anointing services.

Mason's globalization is also evidenced by establishing a publishing arm as early as 1907 and assigning D. J. Young, former AMEZ denominational publisher, over it. By 1919 Mason sanctioned the flow of the educational artery, and appointed a young academician and concert pianist, Arenia C. Mallory, to lead it. His appointment of a young female to such a prominent post was exceptionally bold in those days.

Mason's first departmental priority was women's ministries (1911). His sensitivity to the needs of women and desire to provide maximum ministry opportunities was consistent with Mason's global understand-

---

21. Ibid., 276–78.

ing of perfection and sanctification. Though his biblical hermeneutic that led him to oppose ordination of women has been often critiqued, Mason developed a unique structure that included women overseers, state mothers, church mothers, and female counterparts for every department at every level in the hierarchy. Sanders notes the "autonomous, parallel structure" of the Women's' Department "more closely resembled the dual sex political systems characteristic of some West African societies than the patriarchal polities of European origin."[22]

Mason passed from this world on November 17, 1961. He not only left a personal holiness-Pentecostal legacy; in COGIC he designed a structure that continues to proclaim the power of sanctification as a systemic global influence.

BIBLIOGRAPHY

Clemmons, Ithiel C. *Bishop C. H. Mason and the Roots of the Church of God in Christ.* Lanham, MD: Pneuma Life, 1996.

Daniels, David D. "The Interracial Impulse of Early Pentecostalism." In James R. Goff Jr. and Grant Wacker, eds., *Portraits of a Generation: Early Pentecostal Leaders.* Fayetteville: University of Arkansas Press, 2002.

22 Cheryl Sanders, "History of Women in the Pentecostal Movement," *Cyberjournal for Pentecostal/charismatic Research* 2 (July 1967) online: http://www.pctii.org/cybert-ab1.html.

21

William H. Durham and the Finished Work of Calvary

D. WILLIAM FAUPEL

DURING THE INITIAL PENTECOSTAL revival (1906–1910) persons coming into the movement embraced a Five-fold Gospel. This included justification by faith, entire sanctification as a second definite work, Spirit-baptism evidenced by speaking in tongues, divine healing as part of the atoning work of Christ, and His premillennial return. These doctrines were seen as "first principles" by which the Church had initially been established. These truths had been lost during the dark ages. Since the time of the Reformation, however, God had been restoring them to the Church.

It never occurred to the early Pentecostal leaders that any of these tenets would be challenged from within. However, in 1910, William H. Durham, a pastor from Chicago, did just that. He declared that the second tenet, the doctrine of entire sanctification, was not of Apostolic origin. The biblical understanding of sanctification, he argued, was part of Christ's "Finished Work of Calvary."

Within five years, his message rent the Pentecostalism from top to bottom. By the time the controversy subsided, sixty per cent of the Movement had adopted his "Finished Work" message. Only in Southeastern United States did a significant number (seventy-five per-cent) retain the original doctrine. In the rest of North America a full eighty per cent had embraced Durham's teaching.[1]

---

1. Robert Mapes Anderson, *Vision of the Disinherited: The Making of American Pentecostalism* (New York: Oxford University Press, 1979) 169.

DURHAM'S MINISTRY

Durham was born in Kentucky in 1873. He joined the Baptist church at 17 but was not converted until 1898. He accepted the Wesleyan doctrine of entire sanctification, receiving this experience in 1901. The following year, he responded to a call to ministry, accepting the pastorate of the Gospel Mission Church, a holiness mission, located at 943 North Avenue in Chicago in 1903.[2]

Durham learned about the Azusa Revival in 1906. Like many holiness adherents he expected that the gifts of the spirit would be restored to the church. The word that the gift of tongues was in operation brought joy to his heart. That fall he welcomed Mabel and Jessie Smith to give eye witness testimony of the revival. Several members of his congregation experienced Spirit-baptism. His moment would come a few weeks later when Louis Osterberg, a former parishioner, sent him train fare along with an invitation to attend the Azusa meetings.[3]

Arriving in February, 1907, he sensed the meetings were controlled by the Spirit. Five days later "tongues" began to flow. William Seymour, seeing Durham "slain in the spirit," prophesied that wherever Durham preached "the Holy Spirit would fall upon the people."[4] Durham returned to Chicago transformed. People started coming to his mission in such numbers that the building could not hold them.[5] Hundreds and then thousands came to hear him, and many left with the conviction that he was a new pulpit prodigy. Chicago began to rival Los Angeles as the movement's center.[6]

Among the hundreds who experienced "Pentecost" under Durham's ministry were several destined to become major leaders. These included: E. N. Bell, the first general superintendent of the Assemblies of God; A. H. Argue, who became a leader in the Pentecostal Assemblies of

2 *Pentecostal Testimony* 2 (July, 1912) 2–3; and W. H. Durham, "A Chicago Evangelist's Pentecost," *The Apostolic Faith* 1 (February-March, 1907) 4.

3. Ibid.; Stanley H. Frodsham, "*With Signs Following*": *The Story of the Latter Day Pentecostal Revival* (Springfield, MO: Gospel, 1926), 36; and H. D. Knight, *Ministry Aflame* (Carlinville, IL: Illinois District Council of the Assemblies of God, 1972) 36.

4. *Pentecostal Testimony* 1 (July, 1912) 3–4.

5. Carl Brumback, *Suddenly . . . From Heaven: A History of the Assemblies of God* (Springfield, MO: Gospel, 1961) 69.

6. Frank Ewart, *Phenomenon of Pentecost* (Houston: Herald, 1947), 73; and J. Roswell Flower, "History of the Assemblies of God," unpublished manuscript (Springfield, MO, 1949) 17.

Canada; Andrew Urshan, an eventual leader in the United Pentecostal Church; Louis Francisconi Giacomo Lombardi and Peter Ottolini founders of the Christian Church of North America; F. A. Sandgren, a Norwegian who established Pentecostal churches among Scandinavians throughout the mid-west; Daniel Berg and Gunnar Vingren, Swedes who took the message to Brazil; William H. Piper, pastor of the Stone Church in Chicago; and T. K. Leonard, a Christian and Missionary Alliance pastor who brought 26 CMA colleagues with him. In addition, Howard A Goss, who upon breaking with Charles Parham, brought with him a number of churches in the Southwest and Robert and Aimee Semple were deeply influenced by his teaching. By the time 1910 came to a close, Durham was recognized as the leader of the movement by those groups coming into Pentecostalism via Parham in the Southwest, Dowie in the Midwest; ethnic communities of the upper Midwest and the Pentecostal contingency within the Christian and Missionary Alliance.[7]

DURHAM'S MESSAGE

In May 1910, Durham addressed the annual Pentecostal Convention at the Stone Church with a sermon entitled "The Finished Work of Calvary."[8] The message was simple: "Identification with Jesus Christ saves and sanctifies, no second work of grace [is] taught [by Scripture] or necessary."[9] Perfection is maintained by accepting the historical reality of the cross. Inbred sin is crucified with Christ; imputed righteousness bears fruit in the believer's life. If sin appears it is a sign that the relation-

---

7. Stanley H. Frodsham, "A Brief Word of Biography," in E. N. Bell, *Questions and Answers* (Springfield, MO: Gospel, 1923) viii–x; Zelma Argue, *A Vision and a Vow: The Story of My Mother's Life* (Springfield, MO: Gospel, n.d.) 38; Andrew Urshan, *The Life Store of Andrew Bar David Urshan* (Stockton, CA: Apostolic Press, 1967) 109; S. Galvano, ed., *Fiftieth Anniversary, Christian Church of North America* (Sharon, PA: The General Council, Christian Church of North America, 1977) 27–28; Walter Hollenweger, *The Pentecostals: The Charismatic Movement in the Churches* (Minneapolis: Augsburg Press, 1972) 75, 251; William W. Menzies, *Anointed to Serve: The Story of the Assemblies of God* (Springfield, MO: Gospel, 1971) 64–67; Amiee Semple McPherson (Los Angeles: Echo Park Evangelistic Association, 1923) 56–59; and Ethel E. Goss, *The Winds of God: The Story of the Early Pentecostal Days (1901–14) in the Life of Howard A. Goss* (New York: Comet, 1958) 122–23.

8. Allen Clayton, "The Significance of William H. Durham for Pentecostal Historiography," *Pneuma: The Journal of the Society for Pentecostal Studies* 1 (Fall, 1979) 2.

9. Durham, "The Finished Work of Calvary," *Pentecostal Testimony* 2 (January, 1912) 1.

ship with Christ has been severed. Perfection is restored by placing faith once again in the power of the cross.[10]

He set his view over against the prevailing second work theory. He concurred with Wesleyans in that he acknowledged entire sanctification meant a crucifixion of the sinful nature. "We believed then, as now, that when God saves a man, He cleanses him from all sin."[11] But he argued that since Christ's atonement on the cross was complete, the Christian experienced this "finished work" by identifying with Christ in His death. Using Paul's analogy of baptism, he asserted that "by faith" we are crucified with Christ, buried with him and raised to resurrection life. Just as Christ's death was one act, so too, both justification (pardon from acts of sinfulness) and sanctification (cleansing from sin) are applied to the believer through one act of faith.[12]

This act did not change one's nature. He noted that throughout Scripture the normal meaning of sanctification is consecration, or the setting apart for service to God. Thus in the Old Testament the temple vessels, priestly garments, temple food were dedicated for holy service. Their nature did not change. They were made sacred by virtue of their relationship to God.[13]

This, he reasoned, is what happens at conversion. "God in conversion brings a man into Christ and makes him holy by washing away all his sins, inward and outward, and giving him a new clean heart, thus making a new creature of him." If later the Christian becomes defiled by wrongdoing, he/she must be cleansed in the same manner as the Old Testament priest before entering into the Holy of Holies.[14]

In response to the Holiness movement's contention that unless the sinful nature is eradicated or transformed, it is impossible for an individual to live a holy life, Durham argued from Romans that they were to be a "living sacrifice unto God . . . reckoning themselves to be dead to sin, and alive unto God in Jesus Christ."[15] This was accomplished by yielding

---

10. Ibid.

11. Durham, "Some Other Phases of Sanctification," *Pentecostal Testimony* 2 (July, 1912) 10.

12. Ibid., 3.

13. Ibid., 10.

14. Ibid., 10.

15. Durham, "The Finished Work of Calvary," *Pentecostal Testimony* 2 (January, 1912) 3, citing Rom 6:4–65, 11; and 12:1.

to the power of Christ. Like an alcoholic, forever addicted, the Christian could live an overcoming life by surrendering to the higher power now dwelling within. This need not be a "life-long struggle. By trusting in Christ, the Christian would be filled with the Spirit. Besides, experience had shown those who claimed a second work, found themselves just as subject to sin as those who rejected the view.[16]

WAS "FINISHED WORK" KESWICK?

Robert Anderson reflects the conviction of many historians of Pentecostalism when he wrote:

> Pentecostals from Calvinist and Keswick backgrounds, then, found the Finished Work doctrine more congenial because it resolved doubts raised by their earlier religious convictions, and because it fit better into the theological framework they had brought with them into the Pentecostal movement . . .With the elimination of sanctification as a second act of grace, the main body of the Pentecostal movement adopted a theological position that differed hardly at all from that preached by Torrey, Chapman, Simpson, and other Keswick-Fundamentalists.[17]

Initially, I found his analysis convincing. However, in rereading the contemporary response, I am stuck by the almost violent reaction Durham's message encountered everywhere he went. It was only after he engaged them and as "they searched the Word to prove him wrong," was his doctrine embraced. Furthermore, I find no evidence in the literature that Durham was charged with preaching "Keswick Holiness". Rather the charges that were made was that he taught a form of Lutheran pietism like that of Count Zinzendorf and the Moravian Brethren in the eighteenth century. J. H. King, leader of the Pentecostal Holiness Church stated in 1914: "We hear the cry of the 'finished work' throughout the world, heralded most ardently by many with an earnestness surpassing that of the first proclamation of Pentecost by the same individuals. It is Antinomianism, Darbyism dressed up in a Zinzindorfian garb and going through the land . . . doing its old destructive work among believers."[18]

---

16. Durham, "Some Other Phases of Sanctification," *Pentecostal Testimony* 2 (July, 1912) 10.

17. Ibid., 172–73.

18. J. H. King, *From Passover to Pentecost* (Memphis: Dixon, 1914) 106.

Thomas Farkas analyzed the doctrine in the context of four historic views of sanctification: Lutheran, Reformed, Keswick and Wesleyan. He concludes that the "Finished Work" is a radicalized Wesleyanism. "The theological label then which best represents the theological dynamic of the Finished Work doctrine is 'single work perfectionism,' granted the same qualifications Wesley insisted on for the term 'perfection' are applied. The status of the believer after conversion is for Durham identical to the condition Wesley saw the believer in after the second crisis of entire sanctification: cleansed of all sin, 'inward' and 'outward,' 'inherited' and 'actual,' free of any natural proclivity to sin and thus 'able not to sin.'"[19]

I have come to believe that Farkas is right. Durham never ceased to be Wesleyan though he broke with the nineteenth-century Holiness movement at two significant points: denying that sanctification was a separate experience and rejecting the theory of eradication.[20] It is therefore understandable why Durham's contemporaries would initially resist his message, while at the same time many long-time Holiness movement advocates would ultimately embrace it. It fit squarely[21] within the Luke–Acts hermeneutical lens that led them to embrace the Pentecostal message. At the same time it allowed them to believe that entire sanctification imparts Christ's nature. Thus, when the Statement of Fundamental Truths of the Assemblies of God was written in 1916, the doctrine of "entire sanctification" deleted the terms "second definite work" and "eradication" but the Wesleyan language was preserved.[22]

It is equally clear that Durham's Finished Work doctrine has not prevailed. To the extent that sanctification is taught at all in Pentecostal

19. Thomas George Farkas, "William H. Durham and the Sanctification Controversy in Early American Pentecostalism: 1906–16" (PhD diss., Southern Baptist Theological Seminary, 1993) 262.

20. Durham, "The Finished Work of Calvary," 3.

21. See my book *The Everlasting Gospel: The Significance of Eschatology in the Development of Pentecostal Thought* (Sheffield: Sheffield Academic, 1996) 257–60 where my analysis shows that theological commitments prior to becoming Pentecostal did not necessarily determine whether early adherents accepted or rejected the "Finished Work" theory of sanctification.

22. Brumback, *Suddenly . . . From Heaven,* 357–60. The statement reads: "Fundamental Truth Nine 'Entire Sanctification.' The scriptures teach a life of holiness without which no man shall see the Lord. By the power of the Holy Ghost we are able to obey the command 'Be ye holy, for I am holy.' Entire sanctification is the will of God for all believers, and should be earnestly pursued by walking in obedience to God's Word."

circles, it is a modified version of the Keswick understanding. There are two historical reasons for this.

First, on the heels of Durham's death, the Oneness controversy emerged. For the "Second Work" advocates who had not embraced "Finished Work," this move was the "logical and inevitable consequence of departing from the 'true' doctrine of entire sanctification.[23] Having rejected the logic of the first theological shift brought about by the Luke-Acts lens, they were totally unaffected by the second shift that followed. Such was not the case for the Finished Work advocates. The logic of Durham's message made the oneness message compelling. Two months after his famous declaration at the Stone Church in Chicago, Durham he wrote: "The Acts of the Apostles supplies us with a narrative of what took place on the Day of Pentecost, and, what is of equal importance, of what led up to it and followed from it."[24] What was important for him, it turned out, was that the narrative in Acts provided the hermeneutical key to understanding the whole plan of redemption. He continued: "The all-sufficient Atonement of Christ, justification by faith, the gift of the Spirit with His inward witness and inspired freedom, are shown to constitute a vital unity which determines the whole nature of the Christian religion."[25] This for Durham, was what constituted the Full Gospel. Entire sanctification as a separate crisis experience could not be accepted because it was not modeled in the book of Acts.

Beyond this, however, the Acts narrative focused Durham's attention on the work of Christ on the cross and the believer's *identification* with that work. "The doctrine of the Finished Work brings us back to the simple plan of salvation. Christ died for us. He became a substitute for every one of us . . . We are not saved simply because we are forgiven for our sins. We are saved through identification with our Savior Substitute, Jesus Christ. We are given life because He died and rose again."[26] Although he articulated this identification with Christ as coming in two stages, the logic of the message, even from his own lips was that it was really one ex-

23. For second work advocates initial response to the Oneness doctrine see such examples as: *The Pentecostal Holiness Advocate* (September 6, 1917) 10; *The Faithful Standard* (November 1922); and Charles Parham, *The Everlasting Gospel* (Baxter Springs, KS: The Apostolic Faith Church, 1942 reprint ed.) 118–20.

24. Durham, "The Experience is Standardized," *Word and Work* (July, 1910) 202.

25. Ibid.

26. Durham, "The Finished Work of Calvary—It Makes Plain the Great Work of Redemption," *Pentecostal Testimony* (July 1912) 5.

perience. "The Gospel is the power of God unto salvation. Gospel means glad tidings. It is the glad tidings concerning Jesus Christ, and His glorious and perfect work of redemption on the Cross of Calvary. This the Apostles were commanded to preach, and this is what they did preach. As they preached it the Holy Spirit fell upon their receptive hearers and filled and possessed them and spoke through them in other tongues."[27]

Durham understood identification with Christ to be "by faith alone" but his friend A. S. Copley quickly recognized that this identification also implied water baptism. Writing on the new doctrine of the Finished Work two months after Durham's Chicago declaration, Copley noted: "'Jewish' sanctification sees only that Christ died for us in our stead; but 'Christian' sanctification sees our identification with Christ. That is, it sees that we died with Christ and were buried with Him, and that we arise with Him, and are seated with Him in the heavenlies."[28] Those who had followed Durham's lead in jettisoning their old understanding of entire sanctification in order to seek complete identification with the person of Jesus in His finished work of Calvary were now being asked to identify with His name in baptism and reflect upon a whole range of theological implications of that identification. Perhaps it is not surprising that it was J. Roswell Flower, a person who embraced "Second Work" sanctification all of his life that ultimately persuaded the majority to reject the Oneness position. In so doing, it is not surprising the much of the power and significance of the "Finished Work" doctrine was lost to the movement as well.

This was coupled with a second historical reason. Durham had planned to articulate his doctrine in book form. He took sick and died, however, before the book could be written.[29] Diverted by the Oneness controversy that followed, few of his successors would go on to systematically develop his ideas. One of the few who did was Franklin Small of Winnipeg, Canada. He was aware of both the demise and misunderstanding of the Finished Work doctrine following the aftermath of the Oneness controversy. In an illuminating essay entitled "The Finished Work of Calvary Versus Modern Interpretations—Their Origin Exposed," Small lists six misconceptions regarding the doctrine. Virtually all were Keswick in origin. He writes: "These foregoing interpretations were for-

27. Durham, "The Gospel of Christ," *Pentecostal Testimony* (January 1912) 8.

28. A. S. Copley, "Sanctification—'Jewish' and 'Christian,'" 169.

29. *Pentecostal Testimony* (July 1912) 16.

eign teachings to the original Latter Rain movement, so called, from its first inception and during a number of subsequent years." Noting that little had been written on the issue by Durham's successors, he went on to explain how these "foreign" perceptions crept into the Movement.

> As the young movement commenced to grow, aspirations for schools of learning developed. Naturally teachers by appointment went in search of ready matter to give to student bodies, which material was found on book shelves from the hand of so-called fundamentalists. In these books there was found the subject of the Adamic sin in believers. These books have some good things admittedly, never-the-less, we know they are wrong on number of very vital points of doctrine associated with the experimental aspect of the Gospel.[30]

As a result of all these factors one of the lasting effects of Durham's teaching was not simply to reduce the "Full Gospel" from "five fold" to "four fold." Over time, entire sanctification as an existential reality of the believer identifying with Christ in His finished work on the cross gradually disappeared from the movement, often with tragic consequences.

---

30. Franklin Small, *Living Waters: A Sure Guide to Your Faith* (Winnipeg, Manitoba: Columbia, n.d.) 25–26.

22

Restoration, Accommodation, and Innovation

The Contributions of Aimee Semple McPherson

Kimberly Ervin Alexander

After her sudden death, her most vehement critic among the Los
Angeles clergy, Robert Shuler, wrote admiringly in *The Methodist
Challenge* of her appeal to "the people—the hungry-hearted peo-
ple" and, while he admitted that he could "never understand why
God used Aimee," also admitted that the army of preachers and
workers she left behind was "nearer akin to the army with which
Wesley started than we Methodists would rejoice to concede."[1]

IN MANY WAYS AIMEE Semple McPherson embodies the Pentecostal
movement: her preaching centered around salvation, healing, spirit
baptism and the second coming of Jesus; she was given to visionary experiences; she itinerated as an evangelist; her followers were among the
marginalized; her meetings were interracial; miracles accompanied her
ministry; and she was a charismatic speaker with a flair for the dramatic.
Yet "Sister" also was a departure from the "mainstream" of Pentecostalism:
she was the pastor a "megachurch"; wore Paris fashions and "bobbed"
hair; was widowed, divorced and remarried. While McPherson foreshadowed the stereotypical American Pentecostal superstar—her ministry
was marred by broken relationships, scandal, and disrepute—even her
detractors admitted, "God used Aimee."

1. John Updike, "Famous Aimee: The Life of Aimee Semple McPherson," *The New
Yorker* (April 30, 2007) 2.

FROM A MILK PAIL TO THE PULPIT

Born on October 9, 1890 Aimee Kennedy was raised on a small farm in Ontario, Canada. She was socially active in her teens, attending dances and playing roles in dramatic productions. Attending a revival conducted by Pentecostal evangelist Robert Semple, she experienced baptism in the Holy Spirit. Soon thereafter she married Semple. Within two years they left for China as missionaries. Upon arrival, Robert contracted malaria and died; a month later their daughter Roberta was born. Aimee had little choice but to return home, where she joined her mother, Minnie Kennedy, then working with the Salvation Army in New York.

With her second husband, Harold S. McPherson (m. 1912), Aimee began an evangelistic ministry. In 1915, she traveled along the East Coast, accompanied by her mother and children (her son by McPherson was born in 1913). In 1917 she began publishing *The Bridal Call* and in 1919 was ordained an evangelist by the Assemblies of God. Her meetings moved from tents pitched in vacant lots to city auditoriums.

Aimee and McPherson separated in 1918 and divorced in 1921. At the age of 31, Aimee traveled across the country in a "Gospel Car" with her mother and children, likely the first woman to drive across the United States. Realizing her children's need for a stable home, Aimee settled in Los Angeles, using it as a base for her evangelistic ministry. Eventually she started a church that evolved into a denomination, the Church of the Four Square Gospel. Aimee built Angelus Temple, where she staged musical and dramatic evangelistic presentations, attended by more than 5000, including Hollywood actors.

Fame turned to notoriety in 1926. She disappeared on May 18 while swimming off the coast of California. That night, at Angelus Temple, Minnie Kennedy announced, "Sister is with Jesus." In the midst of grief and media frenzy that followed it was discovered that Kenneth Ormiston, an engineer at her radio station had also gone missing. Thirty-five days after the incident, McPherson reappeared in the Mexican desert, claiming that she had been abducted. McPherson and her mother were indicted for obstruction of justice but the case was dropped.

McPherson always maintained her innocence but was no longer the "darling of the press." Her ministry waned. This era was marked by power struggles with her mother and daughter, a nervous breakdown, and another short-lived and scandal-ridden marriage.[2] The Great Depression provided McPherson with an opportunity to re-focus her ministry. After preaching in Oakland, California, Aimee was found dead in her hotel room on September 27, 1944, from an overdose of prescription drugs.

RESTORATION

The early climate of Pentecostalism, in keeping with that of the Holiness tradition, was fraught with the urgency to restore New Testament Christianity, what Wesley called the Primitive Church. Into this ethos Aimee Semple was immersed under the tutelage Robert Semple and their pastor William Durham. Shortly thereafter, Aimee received a vision of the restoration of the church. Her vision, later titled "Lost and Restored," illustrated a prophecy of Joel. She "saw a vision of a great circle, composed of ten smaller circles . . . This big circle seemed so big that its top reached the sky; it was the dispensation of the Holy Spirit, from its opening on the day of Pentecost, to its closing at the coming of the Lord Jesus."[3] McPherson held that the church had "fallen away" from its original vitality. Using Joel 1:4 as a lens through which to interpret this vision, she equated this "falling away" with the destruction of the palmerworm, locust, cankerworm and caterpillar. This loss culminated in the "dark ages." Joel 2:25 promised a restoration. McPherson saw this beginning with Luther's Reformation, continuing through the Wesleyan revival and Pentecostal revival. Restoration was complete when the fruit again appeared on the tree. McPherson saw her Foursquare Gospel as this finale.[4]

In keeping with the Wesleyan, Holiness and Pentecostal traditions, McPherson correlates her "Lost and Restored" vision with a three dispensations view of history: those of the Father, Son and Holy Spirit. The dispensation of the Father, coincides with the Old Testament; the age of the Son coincides with the time Jesus was on earth; the age of the Spirit

2. McPherson married opera singer David Hutton in 1931, which ended in 1934. Following the wedding, Hutton was sued by a woman for "breach of promise." In addition, Harold McPherson was still living, making the marriage a direct violation of teachings regarding marriage and divorce among most Pentecostal adherents.

3. Aimee Semple McPherson, *Centennial Edition, In Commemoration of the 100th Anniversary of the Birth of Aimee Semple McPherson 1890–1990: Sermons and Personal Testimony of Aimee Semple McPherson* (Los Angeles: Foursquare, 1990), 9.

4. See the cover art and 7–28 of *Centennial Edition* for an illustration and explication of this vision.

began on the day of Pentecost continuing to the present. This age is correlated with the first circle and tree: "rooted and grounded in the faith of Jesus, every limb, branch, leaf and fruit in perfect power and strength."[5]

In her restorationist vision, McPherson is consistent with early Pentecostal theology. She is also consistent in seeing her role in the restoration as significant. Earlier leaders beginning with proto-Pentecostals such as John Alexander Dowie, Frank Sandford and Pentecostal Charles Parham understood their place in the process of restoration.[6] Seymour and the leaders of the Azusa Street revival saw themselves in the Last Days Restoration movement. R. G. Spurling and A. J. Tomlinson of the Church of God (Cleveland, Tennessee) developed an ecclesiology that evolved from their restorationist worldview.[7]

In keeping with William Durham's "Finished Work" stream was McPherson's adherence to four doctrinal tenets: salvation, healing, spirit baptism, and the second coming of Jesus. This fourfold rubric, a deviation of A. B. Simpson's Fourfold Gospel (Jesus is Savior, Sanctifier, Healer, Coming King) and of Wesleyan-Pentecostalism's fivefold gospel (Jesus is Savior, Sanctifier, Spirit Baptizer, Healing and Coming King) was re-packaged as the Foursquare Gospel. She explained the doctrine in a narrative by a visionary experience she had while preaching on Ezekiel's vision of the being with four faces: "A complete Gospel for body, for soul, for spirit, and for eternity. A Gospel that faces squarely in every direction . . ."[8] She reflected, "The term 'Foursquare Gospel' which the Lord gave to me that day as vividly and fittingly distinguishing the message which He had given me to preach has become a household word throughout the Church."[9]

ACCOMMODATION

The complexity of McPherson can be seen in the fact that although she maintained a *restorationist* impulse, she *accommodated* to prevailing

5. McPherson, *Centennial Edition*, 15.

6. D. William Faupel, *The Everlasting Gospel*, JPTS 10 (Sheffield: Sheffield Academic, 1996).

7. See David Roebuck, "Restorationism and a Vision for World Harvest: A Brief History of the Church of God (Cleveland, Tennessee)," online: http://web2010.com/pctii/cyber/roebuck.html.

8. McPherson, *Centennial Edition*, 29.

9. Ibid., 30.

culture. Grant Wacker recognized this tendency in early Pentecostals labeling it "primitivism and pragmatism."[10] This seemingly contrary set of motives was a Wesleyan inheritance. Pentecostals, like their Wesleyan-Holiness foreparents, were adept promulgating "Scriptural Holiness" while practically working out a *method* that served the needs of the mission. Like those before her, Sister Aimee preached in tents and then auditoriums, utilized the most modern transportation available, and manipulated press to her benefit.

But McPherson took this accommodation a step further. As a person in the footlights, Aimee addressed theological and social issues in the public arena.[11] Thus, the debate over teaching Bible in public schools, the rise of atheism and the debate sparked by the Scopes Monkey Trial became part and parcel of her message.[12] Though it has been argued that Pentecostalism is an expression of Fundamentalism,[13] utilizing a Fundamentalist-Literalist hermeneutic,[14] before McPherson's rise to prominence Pentecostals did not identify with the Fundamentalist

---

10. Grant Wacker, *Heaven Below: Early Pentecostals and American Culture* (Cambridge: Harvard University Press, 2001).

11. McPherson had struggled over reconciling the biblical account of creation and Darwinian evolution when she had first encountered it in her high school science classes in Ingersoll, Canada. McPherson describes this struggle in her autobiography, *In the Service of the King: The Story of My Life* (New York: Boni and Liveright, 1927; reprinted, Foursquare Publications, 1988) 70–76. Blumhofer verifies this struggle in her work and includes a description of a letter to the editor of the Montreal *Family Herald and Weekly* written by McPherson in 1906. Edith L. Blumhofer, *Aimee Semple McPherson: Everybody's Sister* (Grand Rapids: Eerdmans, 1993) 56–57.

12. Matthew A. Sutton, "'Between the Refrigerator and the Wildfire': Aimee Semple McPherson, Pentecostalism, and the Fundamentalist-Modernist Controversy," *Church History* 72 (2003) 181.

13. See Donald N. Bowdle, "Holiness in the Highlands," in *Christianity in Appalachia: Profiles in Regional Pluralism*, ed. Bill Leonard (Knoxville: University of Tennessee Press, 1999). Bowdle argues that early Pentecostals of Appalachia would have resonated with the five points of fundamentalism. While they may have agreed with the statements if asked, it is noteworthy that these points are not the subject of either their preaching or writing. The "five points" stressed by early Pentecostals were what Steven J. Land has identified as the "Fivefold Gospel." See Steven J. Land, *Pentecostal Spirituality*, JPTS 1 (Sheffield: Sheffield Academic, 1993) 18.

14. See George Marsden, *Fundamentalism and American Culture—The Shaping of Twentieth Century Evangelicalism 1870–1925* (New York: Oxford University Press, 1980) 14–15. For an examination of the hermeneutical method of early Pentecostals see Kenneth C. Archer, *A Pentecostal Hermeneutic for the 21st Century: Spirit, Scripture, and Community*, JPTS 28 (London: T. & T. Clark, 2004).

movement and Fundamentalism did not include Pentecostals in their family tree!

With McPherson there was a shift in direction. She seized upon these public debates and identified herself in the literalist camp. With her characteristic dramatics and humor, "Sister" caricatured the evolutionists and played to the Fundamentalist audience.[15] Like Wesleyans and Pentecostals before her, she was practical in taking advantage of a prominent venue; unlike them she accommodated theologically, identifying with a particular group and becoming a spokesperson for their cause. Matthew A. Sutton speaks of "McPherson's participation in the fundamentalist-modernist debates," contending, "She created an open, ecumenical Pentecostalism that resonated with many fundamentalists, who in turn, allied with the evangelist, creating opportunities for her to contribute to the fundamentalist movement in important and previously unacknowledged ways."[16] More recently, Sutton described McPherson as a "strident nationalist" who identified America as a Christian nation encouraging the support of candidates holding similar views.[17] Ironically, McPherson understood her perspective as running counter to culture. Sutton writes, "Hence, McPherson and her followers saw themselves as dwindling remnant of the righteous, never truly accepted by the broader culture, living in the shadows of the oncoming apocalypse."[18]

This accommodation to culture led her to downplay charismatic gifts and Pentecostal themes. Daniel Epstein summarizes, "At first the climax of her services had been the altar call or, in smaller spaces, the baptism of the Holy Spirit. Then, from 1919 to 1922, her meetings culminated in prayers for the sick. But as of 1923 Aimee had so reduced her healing ministry, it could not attract the crowds she needed to sustain

15. This emphasis by McPherson has been documented in the "American Experience" documentary for PBS "Sister Aimee," online: http://www.pbs.org/wgbh/amex/sister.

16. Sutton, "'Between the Refrigerator and the Wildfire,'" 164.

17. Matthew Avery Sutton, "Uncovering Aimee Semple McPherson's Demons in 21st Century Evangelicalism," *George Mason University's History News Network*, online: http://hnn.us/articles/38391.html.

18. Sutton, "Uncovering." Karen Mundy and David Roebuck have observed this phenomenon in their study of the changing views of the role of women as evidenced in Pentecostal publications. (David G. Roebuck and Karen Carroll Mundy, "Women, Culture, and Post-World War Two Pentecostalism" in *The Spirit and the Mind: Essays in Informed Pentecostalism* [Lanham, MD: University Press of America, 2000]).

her."[19] Epstein concludes that McPherson drew the line at "unseemly manifestation" that might offend. At the height of her popularity she distanced herself from the designation "Pentecostal" finding it "more politic to avoid the term."[20] Manifestations of the Spirit were not totally absent at Angelus Temple; they were relegated to the "'500' room . . . next to the main sanctuary, where emotional outbursts would not disturb the devotions of the general public."[21] McPherson's distancing took even more tangible forms: in 1920 she received an exhorter's license in the Methodist Episcopal Church and in 1922 she was ordained by First Baptist Church of San Jose California.[22]

INNOVATION

Women ministers were not unusual in Holiness and Pentecostal circles. Even Wesley himself allowed women to lead class meetings and preach.[23] It was not McPherson's gender that set her apart from other Pentecostals, though it is likely that gender played a significant role in her rise to prominence as a pop icon. Aimee's innovations are the source of her prominence. A great observer of trends, she saw California, particularly Hollywood, as a new center of influence.[24] McPherson foreshadowed what many expressions of Pentecostalism and Evangelicalism would become, on the popular level. She embodied the quintessential flamboyant, mega-church pastor.

When Angelus Temple was dedicated on January 1, 1923, heralded by a float made of pink and white flowers in that day's Tournament of Roses parade in Pasadena, McPherson foresaw the rise of Pentecostalism's growth. Less than twenty years after Pentecostalism's humble beginnings

19. Daniel Epstein, *Sister Aimee: The Life of Aimee Semple McPherson* (NY: Harcourt Brace Jovanovich, 1993) 252.

20. Ibid., 265, 66.

21. Ibid., 266.

22. Sutton, "Uncovering," 171–73

23. See Charles Yrigoyen Jr., *John Wesley: Holiness of Heart and Life* (Nashville: Abingdon, 1999), 9. Yrigoyen writes, "In 1787, despite the objections of some of the male preachers, he officially authorized Sarah Mallet to preach, as long as she proclaimed the doctrines and adhered to the disciplines that all Methodist preachers were expected to accept."

24. The McPherson entourage arrived in 1918. To put their arrival in perspective the first studio was built by the Selig Film Manufacturing Company in 1908. The Hollywood sign was erected in 1923; online: http://www.legendsofamerica.com/CA-Hollywood.html.

in a converted horse stable across town, Angelus Temple was built to seat 5300 but often exceeded that number by more than two thousand. Services were conducted three times a day, every day.[25] Though not the largest in Los Angeles, it was the largest Pentecostal church in North America and by far the largest with a woman pastor.[26]

McPherson utilized the arts and theatre to present the gospel. With costumes, props, animals and scenery, she staged magnificent productions that attracted both saints and sinners.[27] Pentecostal preaching, long noted for its narrative and dramatic style, was taken to a new level in McPherson's "illustrated sermons."

She quickly took advantage of the trend toward utilizing new technologies to communicate the gospel. In April 1922, she became the first woman to preach a sermon on radio and by 1924 began broadcasting from her own radio station, KFSG, with towers mounted on top of Angelus Temple.[28] The station reached the Eastern and Southern states and occasionally New Zealand.[29] In addition, she procured a license for "an experimental television station" and incorporated a film company.[30]

McPherson's innovation in media went further than simply broadcasting her own sermons or worship services. The broadcast day was filled with choir, orchestra and organ recitals, children's' stories and dramatic serials. In this, McPherson anticipated the work of later twentieth-century televangelists Pat Robertson, Jim Bakker and Paul and Jan Crouch who pioneered television networks which provided not only Gospel presentation but Christian entertainment.

25. Online: http://www.angelustemple.org/angelus_temple.html.

26. Blumhofer describes the religious options available in Los Angeles. Temple Baptist had a membership of 10,000 (*Aimee Semple McPherson*, 240–41).

27. Charlie Chaplin is said to have admitted to attending pageants at Angelus Temple and later assisted in new stage renovations. See ibid., 318 and 351.

28. See Blumhofer, *Aimee Semple McPherson*, 183 and 268. It has been popularly reported that McPherson was the first woman to hold a radio license. This fact is disputed by Jim Hilliker, Los Angeles radio historian, though he surmises that it is likely that for many she years she was probably the only woman to do so and was probably the first woman to own and operate a Christian radio station. Jim Hilliker, "History of KFSG," online: http://members.aol.com/jeff560/kfsg.html.

29. Hillaker, "History."

30. Sutton, "Uncovering." See also Jim Hillaker, "Pioneer Christian Station Stops Broadcasting after 79 Years," online: http://www.radioheritage.net/Story61.asp); and Jeffrey K. Hadden and Charles E. Swann, *Prime Time Preachers: The Rising Power of Televangelism* (Boston: Addison-Wesley, 1981) 75–76.

ON THE MARGINS OF FAME

The Great Depression brought the marginalized into the forefront. Perhaps Sister Aimee, whose ministry, now marred by scandal, saw herself in those who were now desperately in need, either by circumstance or poor choices. According to her biographer Epstein, "Ask anyone who remembers the Depression in Los Angeles about Aimee Semple Mcpherson . . . everyone recalls that she kept tens of thousands of people from starving to death."[31] The extensive operation in which the Temple was engaged is detailed by Gregg Townsend: quilting bees produced thousands of quilts; the Free Dining Hall provided meals; the Foursquare Automobile Club provided emergency transportation; the "'Lonely' department" provided ministry to shut-ins, prisoners and the sick; the "'Probation Girls' department" worked with the police; the "'City Sisters'" cared for orphans; a "'Salvage' Department" recycled and repaired scrap metal, furniture and appliances.[32] McPherson's work in Los Angeles had always operated benevolence ministries. But the Depression era prompted a "regrouping" according to Blumhofer.[33] McPherson contended the new focus on assistance to the poor, regardless or creed or race, "deepened . . . the spirituality of the whole church."[34]

RE-VISIONING PENTECOSTALISM

If Aimee Semple McPherson is a picture of what Pentecostalism has become in public perception, then a positive light can be seen at the end of a dark tunnel. Angelus Temple, built as a gospel version of the Hollywood Dream, became a real "house of prayer for all people." Blumhofer writes, "Certainly during the Depression, Sister was a star to many Los Angeles Mexicans and others in desperate need. Illegal immigrants dreaded appealing to government agencies for relief, but they knew that Sister's people would help them, no questions asked. In fact, the extent of the relief offered the city through the Angelus Temple Commissary became legendary and won Sister the respect of some erstwhile critics at sophisticated magazines such as *The New Yorker*."[35]

31. Epstein, *Sister Aimee*, 369.

32. Gregg D. Townsend, "The Material Dream of Aimee Semple McPherson: A Lesson in Pentecostal Spirituality," *Pneuma* 14.2 (1992) 179–81.

33. Blumhofer, *Aimee Semple McPherson*, 324–58.

34. Ibid., 349.

35. Ibid., 344.

In an age, when the Pentecostal church in America is in danger of being subsumed into American culture, perhaps the cry of the alien and stranger and the oppressed will drown out the competing voices of social acceptance, nationalism and consumerism. "Sister" warned her church in words hauntingly appropriate for the twenty-first century:

> Watch that we do not fall into the same snare which other people formerly used of God have fallen into: snares of formality, of coldness and organization, building walls about ourselves and failing to recognize the other members of our body (for by one Spirit are we all baptized into ONE BODY). If ever we put up walls and fall into these snares of formality, God will step over our walls, and choose another people as surely as He did in days of yore. He will not give His glory to another but will take the foolish to confound the mighty, the weak to confound the strong.[36]

BIBLIOGRAPHY

Blumhofer, Edith L. *Aimee Semple McPherson: Everybody's Sister.* Grand Rapids: Eerdmans, 1993.

Epstein, Daniel. *Sister Aimee: The Life of Aimee Semple McPherson.* New York: Harcourt Brace Jovanovich, 1993.

Sutton, Matthew Avery. *Aimee Semple McPherson and the Resurrection of Christian America.* Cambridge: Harvard University Press, 2007.

36. McPherson, "The Three Dispensations," *Centennial Edition,* 27–28.

23

Ida Robinson

Loosing Women to Lead

Estrelda Alexander

IDA ROBINSON, VISIONARY LEADER of Mt. Sinai Holy Church of America, Inc, founded the largest African-American Pentecostal denomination established by a woman. Since its inception, the organized fellowship of churches has occupied a place of distinction by being the largest denomination of any Christian tradition headed by an African American woman that is continually headed by women.[1] Born in 1891 in Hazelhurst, Georgia, and reared in Pensacola, Florida, Ida was converted in her teens at a Church of God (Cleveland, Tennessee) street meeting. Almost immediately, her vocation began unfolding in home prayer meetings and on street corners where she preached to crowds who listened intently. Even as a young woman, Ida exemplified gifts that would repeatedly bring people to belief in Christ and Holy Spirit baptism, and later, draw them to her organization.

PASTOR AND REVIVALIST

Robinson's official ministry began in a Church of God congregation in Philadelphia in 1917 where she moved with her husband Oliver to es-

---

1. "Ida Robinson," in Dorothy Salem, ed., *African American Women: A Biographical Dictionary* (New York: Garland, 1993). Following the death of Bishop Amy Stevens in 2000, for the first time, the leadership of Mt. Sinai Holy Church of America was assumed by a man—Bishop Joseph Bell.

cape Southern racism and seek stable employment.[2] Two years later, she moved to a congregation which became a founding congregation of the Northern District of the United Holy Church of America,[3] and eventually was appointed its pastor.[4]

A gifted preacher and singer, people filled her church to hear her. Many became members, fueling rapid growth that forced the congregation to move to larger facilities three times within five years.[5] Robinson's reputation as a revivalist spread along the African American Pentecostal circuit from New York to North Carolina.[6] Her position with the UHC was assured, but her reputation posed a problem. Though in the 1920's UHC women outnumbered men two to one, women preachers were rare. Inspired by her success, women began to pursue more active roles in ministry and denominational leadership.[7] Their pursuit prodded UHC leaders to announce they would no longer "publicly" ordain women[8] and restrict already ordained women to lower levels of ministry.

COMING OUT TO "LOOSE THE WOMEN"

During a ten-day fast, Robinson dreamed God told her to leave UHC and create an environment in which women could be used at every level of the church.[9] From the beginning, she intended to start a denomination— not just a congregation—in which each woman had freedom to gain full clergy rights—including the right to ordination as bishop. When UHC

2. Rosalie Owens, "Bishop Ida Bell Robinson—'Woman Thou Art Loosed,'" *Yes Lord, Now!* 2.1 (2002) 50 [50–55].

3. The United Holy Church is currently the second largest African American Pentecostal body in the United States.

4. Minerva Bell and Joseph Bell, Sixty Fifth Commemorative Journal of the Mt. Sinai Holy Church of America, Inc. (September, 1989) 10.

5. Mt. Sinai United Holy Church of America, Inc. *Celebrating our Legacy*—Mt. Sinai Holy Church of America, Inc., vol. 1 (Philadelphia: Mt. Sinai Holy Church of America, 1999) 110.

6. According to the *Manual of the Mount Sinai Holy Church of America, Inc.*, rev. ed. (Philadelphia: Mt Sinai Holy Church of America, Inc., 1984) 11, she was especially noted for two songs, "What a Beautiful City" and "O I Want to See Him."

7. Felton Best, "Loosing the Women," paper presented to the Society for Pentecostal Studies, 24th Annual Meeting, Wheaton, Illinois (November 1994).

8. Whether the word "publicly" has any special import is uncertain, for it is not known whether they continued to ordain women privately or what such "private" ordination would have meant.

9. Bell and Bell, *Commemorative Journal*, 10.

denominational leaders' attempted to dissuade her, Robinson responded that God had instructed her to, "Come out on Mt. Sinai and loose the women."[10] Within three months, the Mt. Sinai organization was chartered in Pennsylvania and Robinson was organizing churches and ordaining ministers to lead them.[11] Moses' Mt. Sinai encounter with God, in which he received the Ten Commandments and was called to lead the Israelites out of Egyptian bondage, was foundational for Robinson's felt commission to lead women from bondage to freedom in ministry. Robinson saw Mary's mission as bearer of the incarnate Word of God as a compelling model for Pentecostal women's mission to carry the spoken word. For her, God's ironic choice of this lowly woman for this important mission dispelled any critiques of God's choice of women as carriers of the Gospel.

The break from the UHC was not over doctrinal issues; Robinson remained friendly with denominational leaders and patterned her polity and doctrine on theirs and elements from the Church of God. Several within UHC, including members of her congregation, women earlier rejected for ordination, and sympathetic male and female pastors followed Robinson.[12] A number of congregations from the parent body realigned themselves with Mt. Sinai. At its first convocation in September 1924, one-year after its founding, of the seventeen congregations represented, several had come from the United Holy Church.[13]

Robinson eventually moved the mother church to New York.[14] From then on, she pastored both congregations while serving as president of the organization.[15] Until 1936, she was personally involved in

10. Ibid.

11. One of her first acts was to seek legal counsel to set up a charter to create the Mt. Sinai Holy Church of America, Inc. See Rosalie Owens, "Out on Mt. Sinai: How Bishop Ida Bell Robinson Loosed the Women—An Examination of her Leadership Style" (Doctor of Strategic Leadership diss., Regent University, Center for Strategic Leadership, 2001) 36; or Minerva Bell, "Significant Female Leaders and Factors Leading to their Success" (MA thesis, Farleigh Dickerson University, 1974) 50.

12. Owens, "Out on Mt. Sinai," 36.

13. It is not known whether these congregations had formally joined the Mt. Sinai organization at that time, subsequently joined or were in fellowship with a sister organization, as is a custom among many Pentecostal bodies.

14. The headquarters of the denomination has subsequently been relocated back to Philadelphia and Mt. Olive again serves as the mother church.

15. Along with Bishop James Bell, who served as her first assistant pastor with the New York congregation, Robinson enlisted.

planting almost every new congregation. Concentrating her ministry in small towns and larger cities on the East coast, she conducted revivals, gleaned new converts and established congregations over which she placed pastors—many of these were women.[16] When she didn't personally establish a church, she sent others specifically for that purpose, but remained involved in its ongoing nurture, regularly traveling to check their health and encourage their pastors, often staying to preach a revival to help build up the congregation and its finances.

SHAPING MT. SINAI'S MINISTRY

While financial security eluded many blacks, Robinson's astute administration and business acuity made her financially successful. Yet Robinson eschewed a lavish lifestyle and used her financial resources to care for her people and congregations. She purchased several properties, in addition to church buildings, and ran several non-profit organizations, including a 140-acre farm.[17] Robinson Farm in Bridgeville, New Jersey provided housing and gainful employment for Mt. Sinai members and served as the "saints" gathering place for special events such as the annual mass baptism services.[18] In 1944–1945, the Federal government confiscated it as a German POW camp.[19] Congregants visiting the farm during those years talked to the prisoners between eating picnic lunches and playing games.[20] Throughout the 1930's, a boarding school serving elementary through high school was located next to Mt. Olive. Its curriculum included math, science, art, home economics, and, of course, religious studies, and employed only certified teachers.

Several members found a home in her residences for various lengths of time as their need required. After her death, the Mt. Sinai organization established a nursing home to take care of the elderly or ailing indigent members.[21] During the depression, Mt. Sinai attempted to minister to

16. For a region by region and church by church historical accounting of pastoral deployment see *Celebrating Our Legacy*, 24–135.

17. *Manual of the Mt. Sinai Holy Church*, 12.

18. Owens, "Out on Mt. Sinai," 69.

19. E. L. McCormick, "Without Honor: War on the Home Front: the Untold Story of German P.O.W.'s in Bridgeton and Fairton during World War II," *South Jersey Magazine* 19.1 (1990) 14–17.

20. Interview with Minerva Bell, September 23, 2001.

21. Larry Williams, "The Way God Led Them: A Historical Study of the Mt. Sinai

the temporal needs of the surrounding communities through setting up a soup kitchen and other outreach programs at Mt. Olive. R o b i n s o n also provided seed money for planting new churches, establishing a revolving fund for financing them. On some occasions, she took substantial offerings to fledgling congregations as grants or loans from the mother church.[22] Mt. Sinai also supported missionary work in South America.[23] The first mission church was organized in Cuba. Later a congregation was organized in British Guyana.[24] Currently, there are also seven house churches in India.

Mt. Sinai's rigorous moral code forbade members from attending secular entertainment and required abstinence from alcoholic beverages and tobacco products. Restrictions on dress, primarily for women, came in part from Robinson's early Church of God exposure. Impressed by "uniforms" the saints wore, she adopted the "Black dresses" with starched white cuffs and collars, which became the outfit identifying early Mt. Sinai women.[25] Men were restricted from wearing neckties or anything but white shirts with their dark suits.[26] Rigid sanctions against divorce precluded divorced persons with living ex-spouses from remarrying. Previously divorced and remarried persons were required to terminate their second marriage before joining Mt. Sinai—especially if they were involved in any form of ministry.

In many ways, however, Robinson was socially progressive and took unpopular stands on controversial issues that did not leave her without detractors. The FBI kept Robinson under surveillance in the 1930s and 40s for several reasons. First, during the height of segregation, even in the North, her congregation was racially mixed. Among the whites in her congregation was her secretary, a German woman, who was married to an Italian man. During the World War II, they were suspected of

---

Holy Church of America" (DMin thesis, Howard University School of Divinity, 1998) 94.

22. See, for example, *Celebrating our Legacy*, 24; and Owens, *Out on Mt. Sinai*, 62.

23. *Celebrating our Legacy*, 140.

24. *Manual of the Mt. Sinai Holy Church*, 12.

25. *Commemorative Journal*, 139.

26. Arthur H. Fauset, *Black Gods of the Metropolis* (Philadelphia: University of Pennsylvania Press, 1944) 20.

sympathizing with the enemy—bringing Mt. Sinai under suspicion of harboring enemy sympathizers.[27]

Because Robinson was an outspoken pacifist, like many early African American Pentecostals, Mt. Sinai members served in the armed forces only as conscientious objectors. On her radio broadcast, she took stands on her moral convictions, including against the war effort. Twice, in 1942, she was on the FBI list of suspected agitators for remarks disparaging the war against the Japanese.[28] This allegation was contested and her name was later dropped.

Before her time in many ways, Robinson used the power of the media for evangelistic outreach. Throughout the 1930s and 40s, an hour-long radio broadcast on New York's WNEW emanated from the Sunday worship services of the headquarters, Bethel Holy Church. Her messages reached as far as North Carolina. Many who heard her on the radio often made pilgrimages to see the dynamic preacher in action. Several stayed to become members.

Despite its eschatological title, Robinson used another medium of mass communication, the organization's newsletter, *The Latter Day Messenger,* to post articles on a variety of social issues: discussions on racial and economic discrimination, and women's role in the church stood side by side with doctrinal discussions. In an unsigned article attributed to her in the May 23, 1935 issue, "The Economic Persecution,"[29] she attacked racial discrimination and compared lynching to the Christian persecution by early pagan emperors,[30] chiding the White Southern church's hypocrisy in not standing against racism.[31]

Though socially progressive, Robinson maintained classic Pentecostal theology. The major unique theological point related to her Chris-

27. Interview with Harold Trulear, June 20, 2001.

28. Federal Bureau of Investigation. Foreign Inspired Agitation among the American Negroes in Philadelphia Division. File No. 100-135-37-2, Section 39497 July, 1942; and File No. 100-135-37-9, September, 1942. This document is available under the Freedom of Information Act. Though significant information are blocked, a list of those under surveillance is attached; Robinson's name clearly identified.

29. Ida Robinson, "The Economic Persecution," *The Latter Day Messenger* (May 23,1935) 2. Bettye Collier-Thomas cites this work as a sermon of Robinson's in *Daughters of Thunder: Black Women and Their Sermons: 1850–1979* (San Francisco, Jossey-Bass, 1998) 203–5.

30. Ibid.

31. Ibid.

tian anthropology, in which she surmised that there were four types of people on the earth. The first were the elect or chosen of God. Second were the compelled—who could not help but be saved. Third were the "whosoever wills," who could be—but were not entirely destined—to be saved. And, last were the damned, who were ordained for hell.[32]

"Women Preacher's Night" provided a safe place for women to minister and sharpen their preaching skills. Robinson observed preachers' strengths and weaknesses, then critiqued and instructed them. Gifted women, as well as men, were identified as Sunday School teachers, ushers and deacons, all the while being trained for increasingly important leadership roles. She also enlisted women to assist with personal needs. More than a ploy to gain cheap labor from loyal members, as they cleaned her house, served as her nurse, drove her or read to her, she mentored and prepared them for key leadership roles. Those who served well in these initial assignments were elevated through the ranks to denominational leadership.

The majority of those ordained as elders and bishops in Robinson's first ordination service were women who were placed in pastorates and other positions of authority.[33] The first pastor appointed to the first church established under the newly signed charter in Burgaw, North Carolina, was a woman.[34] The first four officers of the organization were women—Robinson as president, Elmira Jeffries as Vice President, Mary Jackson as Secretary and Rosa Bell as Treasurer. Six of the nine members of the organization's first Board of Elders were female.[35]

Under Robinson's leadership, however, Mt Sinai was a female-led, rather than female-dominated, organization. Robinson enlisted and credentialed men as well for every area of ministry. In her local congregation, for example, along with the women's night, Robinson instituted men preacher's night, giving equal opportunity for young men to sharpen their preaching skills and receive her encouragement and nurture.

---

32. Fauset, *Black Gods*, 16.

33. Felton O. Best, "Breaking the Gender Barrier: African-American Women and Leadership in Black Holiness-Pentecostal Churches 1890-Present," in Felton O. Best, ed. *Black Religious Leadership from the Slave Community to the Million Man March* (Lewiston, NY: Mellen, 1998) 159. As with most Pentecostal bodies, often women were sent out to "preach out" or start new congregations. However, unlike many other bodies, Mt. Sinai women were not replaced with male pastors once congregations achieved any size and were up and running.

34. *The Way God Led Them*, 83.

35. Ibid.

Two years before the end of her life, Robinson had a "heavenly experience of death." Following that vision, she made plans to visit each Mt. Sinai congregation to encourage each pastor, check on the congregation's health, and correct whatever was out of place. While carrying out these visits, Ida Robinson died suddenly[36] in Winter Haven, Florida in 1946, at the age of fifty-four.

INSTITUTIONAL AND THEOLOGICAL LEGACY

Robinson had led Mt. Sinai for twenty-two years, building a denomination of eighty-four churches primarily in the East.[37] By the time she died, the pattern of women's leadership seemed set. The next three presiding bishops were women whom Robinson had prepared to move into the highest levels of leadership. Elmira Jeffries, a charter member of Mt. Sinai from the UHC, assumed leadership directly after her death and served until 1964.[38] Starting in ministry by leading the Tuesday noonday tarrying service[39] at Mt Olive, she subsequently pastored several congregations, holding increasingly important positions, including vice president under Robinson.[40] Eighty-eight year old Mary Jackson, another charter member, succeeded Jeffries, serving until her death at age 102.[41] At Mt Olive, she taught the preacher's class and assisted Robinson with finances. She later presided over the Southern District, pastored several congregations including Mt. Olive, and served as denominational secretary and vice president under Jeffries.[42] Amy Stevens, elected presiding bishop[43] at age seventy-one,[44] served until her death in 2000 at age eighty-eight. She

36. No specific caused is cited for her death in any of the available sources.

37. *Celebrating our Legacy*, 140.

38. The succeeding Presiding Bishop is elected by the Board of Bishops at the time of the death of the existing presiding bishop.

39. Tarrying service is a special service when people gather to pray to receive the baptism of the Holy Spirit. The concept of tarrying (or waiting) is derived from an analogy to the biblical story of the day of Pentecost when the disciples waited (or tarried) in anticipation of fulfillment of Jesus' promise of the sending of the Holy Spirit.

40. *Celebrating our Legacy*, 142–43.

41. Ibid., 148.

42. *Black Gods*, 14.

43. Ibid., 5–6.

44. According to Williams, in *The Way God Led Them*, 95, Stevens' husband Charles was first nominated as President at age of ninety-one, but declined due his age, in favor of his wife who was subsequently elected to the position.

entered ministry at twenty-three and like the others, previously served in a number of capacities including usher and Sunday School teacher, and pastoring.

While Robinson never codified her view on women's leadership, her few public statements regarding the issue went farther than most in her day. In them, we see a picture of a woman who believed in women's equality before God and need for women to take their rightful place beside men in church leadership.

Harold Trulear insists that Robinson's biblical "hermeneutic" defending women's leadership tackled seemingly prohibitive Scriptural passages on four pivotal premises: 1) the creation narrative in Genesis 1 and 2; 2) Mary's example as Jesus' mother; 3) the story of women who first told of Jesus' resurrection; and 4) equality of male and female in the body of Christ.[45] Robinson distinguished between creation and formation of humanity as showing God's intention of gender equality. For her, Genesis 1 and 2 are chronological history. First, God *created* Adam in his image, with male and female essence and dominion over all the earth, investing both male and female with dominion. God then *formed* already created Adam and Eve as separate, yet equal, gendered beings.[46] In Mary, Robinson saw the model of women's role in the salvation story. Her retort, "If Mary can carry the Word of God in her womb, why can't I carry the Word of God on my lips,"[47] speaks of the import of that model for any woman God chooses to use.

For Robinson, the women disciples' resurrection announcement made them the newly formed church's first preachers. Their importance for Pentecostal women was underscored every Easter Sunday when Robinson led her congregation in singing:

> Didn't those women run . . .
> They ran the good news to spread . . ."[48]

She insisted Paul's proclamation that "there is neither male nor female"[49] was foundational for women's leadership as well as relationship with Christ. For her, Christ's redemptive act reiterated and restored

45. Harold Dean Trulear, "Ida Robinson," in Stanley M. Burgess et al., eds., *Dictionary of Pentecostal and Charismatic Movements* (Grand Rapids: Zondervan, 1988) 762.

46. Trulear, "Reshaping Black Pastoral Theology," 30.

47. Ibid.

48. Ibid., 31.

49. Galatians 3:28.

the equality of men and women before it was lost in the fall so that it would reflect what God intended at creation, which[50] included working in quality relations.

After Robinson's death, women's leadership in Mt. Sinai slowly—yet steadily—declined. Fifty-four years after its founding, leadership passed to a man, Bishop Joseph Bell. Though many women remain in ministry, the decline of those with pastorates or governing responsibilities has accelerated over the years. While by 1980, already less than one-half of Mt. Sinai bishops were women; by 2000, only one-third were women. Importantly, current women bishops are older and rose through the ranks during, or shortly after, Robinson's lifetime. Revered for their early involvement, they no longer make substantial contributions to denominational governance. Younger, more recently elected male bishops are the decision makers—the real leadership of Mt. Sinai.

Yet in the beginning, a vision of liberating women from hierarchical strictures and making a place for them in African American Pentecostalism drove Robinson to create a denomination offering them freedom to use their God-given gifts. She sought to train, nurture and place women whose exemplary spiritual character suited them for leadership, while maintaining a standard of holiness. The name and organization, "Mt. Sinai," stand as prophetic witness to a visionary woman's desire to bring about deliverance—to bring women to a "land of freedom" where gender barriers had been destroyed—even if this vision was short-lived.

BIBLIOGRAPHY

Collier-Thomas, Bettye. "Ida Robinson," in Bettye Collier-Thomas, ed., *Daughters of Thunder: Black Women and Their Sermons, 1850–1979*. San Francisco: Jossey-Bass, 1998.

Trulear, Harold Dean. "The Reshaping of Black Pastoral Theology: The Vision of Bishop Ida B. Robinson." *Journal of American Religious Thought* 46 (1989) 17–31.

50. Trulear hints at this connection in "Reshaping Pastoral Theology." One unfortunate consequence of the lack of primary sources from Robinson is that there is no more lengthy explication of her theological views outlined here.

24

Henry C. Ball, Francisco Olazábal, Alice E. Luce, and the Assemblies of God Borderlands Mission

ARLENE SANCHEZ WALSH

THE BORDERLANDS AREA OF Texas, Arizona, and California became a paradoxical success story for the Assemblies of God. It was here that cultural, social, and theological encounter initiated missionaries into the everyday lives of Mexicans, and brought Mexicans face to face with a different kind of Protestantism. Pentecostalism, which offered direct access to God, healing, and a grassroots outreach, gained adherents amongst this harsh landscape described by missionaries as poverty-stricken, degraded, destitute, and "hostile to the Gospel." While motivated by end time urgency, the AG mission was also about changing perceived weaknesses of character, intellect, and culture among the Mexicans.

Against a backdrop of anti-Catholicism this essay reveals how racialization of Mexican converts contributed to the way missionaries characterized their mission, proceeded with their ministry, and developed a culture of dependency that in some ways continues in the present. The focus will be on three pivotal figures: Henry C. Ball, Francisco Olazábal, and Alice E. Luce.

HENRY C. BALL

Henry C. Ball was born in 1898 in Brooklyn, Iowa to Quaker parents who converted to Methodism and eventually Pentecostalism. Ball moved to Texas in 1915 to start Mexican churches in Kingsville and San Antonio. His letters to the *Weekly Evangel* (*WE*) [later *Pentecostal Evangel* (*PE*)], were missions reports designed to elicit funds, and reflected a fear that AG adherents thought Mexicans unworthy of support.[1] Realizing that many in his area didn't like Mexicans, he urged "American saints in the place where they live" to "keep a friendly eye on them, speak to them now and again, encourage them to keep close to Jesus."[2] Later, he offered his own assessment: "Until then, while I had seen thousands of Mexicans all around me, I felt no liking or love for these people. As a matter of fact I looked upon them as very poor and degraded, which they have been and the majority still are . . . For centuries the people of Mexico have been in the grasp of Romanism. They worship the Virgin Mary much more than the Lord Jesus Christ." In 1935, he noted that the ministers in training would be ready to go back to "Old Mexico," if only he could train them faster. Ball asserted that the "Mexican work" in America was as much a foreign mission as any other.[3]

Ball expressed shock there would be as much, if not more poverty in California than in Texas:

> Many of our Mexican women in San Antonio work all week long shelling pecan nuts, making only 70 cents a week. Also many of our Mexican women sew, making the garments that are sold so cheaply in the East and elsewhere . . . They can now shell pecan nuts and at the same time be singing "Glory Be His Name." They have something now that fills the vacancy in their homes, something that seems to drive out the extreme poverty. It doesn't always fill their stomachs; but at least it fills their hearts with joy.[4]

Ball concluded that Mexicans are in dire straits because of Catholicism and their lack of exposure to American culture. He urged readers not to "think only of these people of darker skins in other lands, but also remember the one's here at home."[5] Underlying his plea for money was a need to counter the common assumption that in America one would not need such missionary assistance.

---

1. Contributions to any mission work was tepid at best: in 1933 only 30 percent of AG members gave to missions, and half of AG churches gave nothing. Edith Blumhofer, *Restoring the Faith: the Assemblies of God, Pentecostalism, and American Culture* (Bloomington: University of Illinois Press, 1993) 157.

2. Henry C. Ball, "Mexican Work," *WE* (25 June 1927) 7.

3. Ball, "Mexican Work," *PE* (13 July 1935) 11.

4. Ball, 3.

5. Ibid.

In 1936 he again blames Mexican poverty on Catholicism, and calls Mexico a "pathetic nation." Toward the end, he wrote: "The American people hold them down as much as they possibly can. They will not give them a real chance to prosper. The Mexican people have to take the hard work, the poorly paid work."[6]

Still struggling two years later to provide enough funds for the fledgling Latin American Bible Institute (LABI), Ball again describes Mexicans as poor and degraded Catholics, lost in "idolatry." He depicts his converts, many now preachers, as coming from the fields, and having little or no education;[7] relating how they complain of poor treatment and adequate compensation.[8] His study of Mexican history enabled him to view them more positively, if stereotypically:

> From these two people, both proud and of great historical and cultural heritages,... artistic and ... possessed of a deeply religious nature come the Mexicans of today . . . employers of Mexican labor speak of them in the highest terms, preferring them to all other imported laborers. One of these employers, representing a large railroad . . . gave the following six virtues: love of family, cleanliness, religious nature, love of music, bravery, and sobriety. In addition to the laborers on the fruit ranches, on the railroads, in factories, and in canneries, we find Latin Americans working as doctors, mechanics, lawyers, tailors, theatrical managers, restaurant owners . . . indeed they find occupation in every brand of industry.[9]

Historian Gilbert G. Gonzalez, who traced the roots of the anti-Mexican sentiment in America from the 1890s to 1920s, helps us understand Ball's attitudes, arguing that the American view of Mexicans stems from their representations as child-like peons. Such images implied Mexicans were easily led, manageable, and easily converted.[10] His overview of dozens of writers, demonstrates how often immigrants were identified with the peon class. Gonzales concludes, "That Mexico's immigrants came from the peon classes of Mexico seemed to define with

6. Ball, "Mexican Work in Texas," *PE* (14 March 1936) 6.

7. Ball, Mexican Work" *PE* (30 April 1938) 10.

8. Ibid., 11.

9. Ball, and Alice E. Luce, *Glimpses of our Latin American Work in the U.S. and Latin America* (Springfield, MO: Department of Missions, Assemblies of God, 1940) 5–7.

10. Gilbert G. Gonzalez, *Culture of Empire: American Writers, Mexico, and Mexican Immigrants 1880–1930* (Austin: University of Texas Press, 2004) 85.

some precision just who these newcomers were and surfaced with every discussion of Mexican immigrants."[11]

Like Gonzalez's writers, Ball referred to Mexicans as living in a "degraded" state. Gonzalez calls them an "indigestible mass that posed dire social and cultural consequences for the U.S."[12] For Ball, the consequences of inadequate funds to continue his work meant that Mexicans would not be converted from "Romanism" and would not be trained to return to Mexico to "save" that country from "darkness." Gonzalez rightly notes: "[I]n cities across the Southwest, Protestant missionaries implemented their own version of Americanization, a process that had it its origins in Mexico. Protestant leaders defined the Mexican problem in religious terms, yet they critiqued the very same traits that secular Americanizers critiqued, such as immorality, deceit, imitation, indolence, fatalism, [and] thievery."[13]

Despite his patronizing attitude, Ball's mission appeared successful judging by its numerical growth and the installation of a Latino superintendent. Conversions among the Mexican population in Texas and the Southwest grew at a steady pace. By 1927 there were 100 AG churches and missions in Texas, New Mexico, Arizona, California, and seven states in Mexico. Ball's newsletter, *La Luz Apostólica* grew from 11 subscriptions in 1916 to 2000 in 1927.[14] In 1932, one of Ball's students, Demetrio Bazán, became the first Latino leader in the AG. Bazán's workers established churches throughout the Rocky Mountain states of Utah, Colorado, and New Mexico. Many other Latino leaders were trained at LABI. Throughout the 1930s, many Latinos joined the AG at conventions. In 1933, the Latin American Convention counted 17 ordained ministers, 32 licensed, and 10 "exhorters." The 1935 convention in Dallas reported 41 ordained ministers, 96 licensed ministers and 37 "exhorters."[15]

11. Ibid., 143.

12. Ibid.

13. Ibid., 169.

14. *PE* (25 June 1927) 7.

15. Arlene Sánchez Walsh, *Latino Pentecostal Identity: Evangelical Faith, Society and the Self* (New York: Columbia University Press, 2003), 44; Ball, *La Luz Apostolica* (September 1966) 1.

FRANCISCO OLAZÁBAL

Francisco Olazábal was born on October 12, 1886 in Sinaloa, Cohuila Mexico. At age 12 his mother became a Methodist in Mazatlan. His father left shortly thereafter. Olazábal attended the Colegio Wesleyano in San Luis Potosi, receiving a BA. Upon graduation, he took a job selling Bibles before attending Moody Bible Institute in 1911. Next he pastored Iglesia Metodista Episcopal in Los Angeles followed by other pastorates throughout California.[16] Olazábal accepted Pentecostalism through Carrie and George Montgomery in 1915. Joining the AG, he held revival services in Los Angeles with Alice Luce in April 1918[17] His reputation preceded him; many remembered him as a Methodist pastor who had criticized the growing Pentecostal movement.[18]

Olazábal articulated a need for a Latino Bible institute in 1919.[19] J. W. Welch, an AG General Presbyter concurred in 1920, adding: "Mexicans are an intelligent people, and Pentecost is not without competitors in the Mexican field." Noting that opening a school must be done with caution: "supervision by Americans will always be helpful" he concluded: "A movement is afoot in Texas to establish a Bible training school for the American work. It would be a splendid thing if it might include a Spanish department."[20]

During his first three years with the Assemblies, Olazábal received support and encouragement. As his growing ministry required more donations, the AG leadership became uncomfortable. In January 1923 J. R. Flower, the AG Secretary, stated Olazábal's attempts to begin a school in El Paso failed so badly that Flower, Ball, Olazábal, and Luce held an emergency meeting in December 1922. They concluded that El Paso school was too far away from most Mexicans to be effective, Olazábal "agreed that he would devote his time and energies to the ministry rather than ... attempt to build up a school ... which would take him from the field." Flower moved the efforts to build a school to San Antonio placing it under the A/G's Missionary Commission's supervision. Ball took charge of administration; Alice Luce took charge of the faculty.

16. Roberto Dominguez, *Pioneros de Pentecostes* vol. 1 Norteamérica y las Antillas (Barcelona: Clie, 1990) 31–32.

17. *WE* (20 April 1918) 11.

18. "Mexican Work Along the Border," *WE* 15 June 1918, 11.

19. "El Paso, Texas," *WE* (29 November 1919) 16.

20. *WE* (12 June 1920) 10–11.

Miguel Guillen, chronicler of Olazábal's story, provides an alternative account. He states that Olazábal was asked to leave the AG because of problems arising from fund raising. He contends the AG was intent on denying Olazábal any position of leadership and terminated his ministry in an effort to silence his powerful presence amid the growing Mexican Pentecostal community. In response the Mexican members of the Texas AG voted to start their own district council. Isabel Flores, a former AG minister, states the plan required Olazábal to run the council from his El Paso church and establish a bible institute and printing press. Opposition to Olazábal's promotion came from the white members of the AG, believed that "el pueblo Mexicano no estaba capacitado para dirigir el trabajo."[21]

Olazábal's ouster planted the roots of dependency among AG Latinos. The alternative was to leave and form independent churches. The Concilio Latino Americano de Iglesias Cristianas was founded in Houston Texas in 1923. Olazábal broadened his core constituency until his death in an auto accident in 1937. His New York revivals and trips to Puerto Rico were particularly successful. 20,000 heard Olazábal preach in New York, and 100,000 were touched by his healing ministry during his campaigns. By 1937, the Concilio was established in Texas, California, New Mexico, Arizona, Colorado, Missouri, Illinois, Indiana, Wisconsin, Ohio, New York, Mexico and Puerto Rico.[22]

Following Olazábal's death the Concilio split. At the 1938 Houston convention Roberto Dominguez reports that a resolution was made to elect the president, secretary, and treasurer for life. This offended many Puerto Rican pastors, who left the denomination rather than vote in the affirmative. Dominguez' quotes Olazábal protégé Carlos Sepúlveda as saying that if passed, it would ensure that the Concilio would be run by Olazábal confidant Miguel Guillen and his widow, Macrina.[23] Sepúlveda did not vote for the resolution. Concilio members, seeing this as a sign of division, replaced the dissenting pastors with those who were favorable.

The dissenting pastors founded the Asamblea de Iglesias Cristianas in Washington D.C. in 1939. Its strength is in the New York area and Puerto Rico. Iglesia Cristiana Damascus is its largest church and Leoncia "Mama Leo" Rosado its best-known minister.

21. "The Mexican people do not have the capacity to direct the work."

22. Dominguez, *Pioneros de Pentecostes*, 23.

23. Ibid., 278–82.

ALICE E. LUCE

The person charged with running the Assemblies bible school in California was Alice E. Luce. While Luce publicly supported Mexican autonomy, her actions did not always match her rhetoric. Luce began her "Mexican work" as a missionary to Mexico. Forced to leave on the eve of the Revolution, she ministered to Mexicans in California. She urged the AG to support the Mexican work in an open letter: "we are proving the good old gospel to be the power of God unto salvation for these poor, dark Mexicans, just as for the white people." Luce preached a modified autonomy, pressing for Mexican control as soon as churches were "ready."

Luce founded a Pentecostal mission in the Plaita in 1917. In 1922 she moved her fledging mission to the Belvedere section of Los Angeles. Relying heavily on Mexican workers run El Aposento Alto, she placed Francisco and Natividad Nevarez in charge. They pastored the church into the 1950s.

LABI was perpetually under funded, but stabilized enough to graduate ministers during the Dust Bowl era. In 1930, noting an influx of Mexicans who "could work on the fruit ranches and in the cotton fields." Luce requested funds to produce Spanish tracts and bibles to take to the migrant labor camps and fields surrounding LABI. Her promotion of Pentecostalism in Spanish-language tracts found resonance. Many migrant workers began attending LABI. G. H. Thomas, an instructor, requested PE readers to make donations to defray tuition costs. When school ended students spent the summer picking fruit, which also went toward tuition.[24]

Although Luce believed in autonomy, she practiced supervision when faced with the competitive market of religious ideas. Unlike Ball, she did not denigrate Mexicans, although her writing had a tone of maternalism. She believed Mexicans could run their own affairs, but feared erosion to Oneness Pentecostalism, Mormons, Christian Science, and Jehovah's Witnesses. Like Ball, Luce had little positive to say about Roman Catholics. However, she urged her students to be nice when seeking to convert them, and not obnoxious and brutish as some missionaries had.

---

24. Sánchez Walsh, *Latino Pentecostal Identity*, 47.

After years of wavering Luce finally came down on the side of full autonomy. In 1939, she equated her work in California to a biblical model. Jerusalem was one's hometown, then missionaries were to go to Judea, which was the USA, and Samaria was Latin America. Since the hometowns and large parts of the U.S. were already evangelized, Luce saw the last outpost to be Latin America.[25]

> It seems that we have a fundamental principle which we do well to observe, namely that of handing over the oversight of everything that concerns the local church to its own members . . . The native Christians would make mistakes but they would learn from their failures, as we all do; and if only we could keep humble enough to help and advise them when they ask us to do so…Even when there is no apparent discontent, it seems to me that we foreigners ought to urge the native converts to carry on the work themselves and to make them feel that theirs is the responsibility of evangelizing their own country.[26]

A PARADOXICAL LEGACY

Despite Luce's leanings, the reality was that the Latino-led districts in the AG did not gain full autonomy until the 1970's. The two bible institutes in Texas and California are still unaccredited and perpetually underfunded. There is talk of a merger of the LABI California campus with the more affluent and accredited liberal arts college, Vanguard University. The paradox is that as the financial inequality continues. Latinos are one of the main ethnic groups that contribute to the AG's numerical growth. It is ironic that this success continues to happen despite the paternalism of Henry Ball, the maternalism of Alice Luce, and the marginalization of Francisco Olazábal.

Ball represents much of evangelical/Pentecostal missions of the twentieth century that failed to recognize the need for power sharing. While most of the churches he started eventually had Mexican pastors, one wonders if this was his intention. Mexican autonomy was never a high priority in his articles or letters.

Alice E. Luce presents a complicated picture of a woman who simultaneously promoted Mexican autonomy, but failed to trust their theological choices. The school in Los Angeles that has trained pastors

25. Alice E. Luce, "Strangers at our Gates," *PE* (November 11, 1939) 11.

26. Ibid.

for eighty years has been her most successful legacy; but one wonders how much more could have been accomplished had it gained accreditation and given adequate funding.

The most conflicted legacy involves Francisco Olazábal. His restless itinerancy drove his ministry outside the Southwestern U.S., and his influence thrived when released from AG restrictions. The churches birthed from his New York and Puerto Rican campaigns are truly impressive. His own denomination, the Concilio, however, never recovered from his death in 1937. With the mismanaged convention in 1938, and subsequent splits thereafter, the Concilio remains small, focusing on generational growth in its geographic strongholds of Texas and the Southwest. Had Olazábal's pan-Latino emphasis been realized there might be an autonomous Latino/a Pentecostal movement in the U.S. today. Instead there are splintered autonomous Latino Pentecostal groups, and four generations of Latino Pentecostals that share the legacy of Henry Ball, Alice Luce, and Francisco Olazábal within the Assemblies of God. In time they will decide whether there has been enough progress made for power sharing and autonomy.

BIBLIOGRAPHY

Walsh, Arlene Sanchez. *Latino Pentecostal Identity: Evangelical Faith, Society and the Self.* New York: Columbia University Press, 2003.

25

G. T. Haywood and the Emergence
of Oneness Pentecostalism

ESTRELDA ALEXANDER

THE EARLY PENTECOSTAL MOVEMENT saw rapid expansion from Los Angeles, up the coast to the Northwest, then eastward to the Midwest, South, and Northeast. This dynamic push was led by a cadre of zealous, Spirit-enthused disciples passionate to see the message of Holy Spirit empowerment explode the life of the church into a new vibrancy. Most cities, and even many small hamlets, did not escape visitation by these "missionaries of the one-way ticket."[1] A major vehicle for fanning the Azusa Street revival flames was numerous camp meetings springing up along the Pentecostal religious landscape. One of these meetings, in 1913, at Arroyo Seco, California, not only pushed the movement into a new phase, but sparked the beginning of its second major schism. Already torn almost neatly in half two years earlier by the Wesleyan/ Finished Work controversy induced by William Durham,[2] this "new issue" was initially over the appropriate biblical formula for words of commitment in water baptism. Eventually, however, it encompassed differences in conceptions of the nature of the Godhead and requirements for salvation.

---

1. Vinson Synan, *The Spirit Said "Grow": The Astounding Worldwide Expansion of Pentecostal and Charismatic Churches* (Monrovia, CA: MARC, 1992) 39.

2. The issue at stake here was whether there were three distinctive, identifiable stages in the salvation process—regeneration, sanctification and baptism in the Holy Ghost—as Wesleyan proponents insisted, or two stages—regeneration and baptism of the Holy Spirit, with sanctification being a progressive process as Durham declared.

African American pastor Garfield Thomas Haywood (1880–1931) would become a major figure in this controversy. He would also be instrumental in building three formidable institutions: a prominent Indianapolis congregation, Christ Temple Apostolic Faith Church; a denomination, the Pentecostal Assemblies of the World; and a movement, African American Oneness Pentecostalism.

LIFE AND EARLY MINISTRY

Haywood was born in 1880 in rural Greencastle, Indiana, fifty miles southwest of Indianapolis. By the time he was three, his family had relocated to the Indianapolis area, settling in Haughville, on the city's western edge. Now the young boy was in the place he would finish his education, marry and live out his vocation as a pastor, denominational leader and champion of oneness Pentecostalism, racial pride, and racial unity. Haywood was one of ten siblings in a devout family. During his youth, the family was members of St. Paul Baptist Church in Haughville, but Garfield was active in a local Methodist congregation as well, serving as Sunday school superintendent in both congregations by the time he was a young man. He attended the prestigious Short Ridge School, one of the country's oldest free high schools, noted for both its openness to blacks and its academic excellence. However, after completing his sophomore year, Haywood dropped out, using his artistic ability to land positions as a cartoonist on two black weekly newspapers, *The Indianapolis Freedmen* and *The Indianapolis Reporter*, to help support the large family. Haywood's truncated education did not assuage his voracious love for learning; throughout his life he added to his knowledge by reading books, newspapers and periodicals, studying religion and a variety of subjects and traveling extensively. He also continued to hone his artistic skills and would later call on them, adding a talent for songwriting, to promote his religious passion.

After marrying Ida Howard in 1902, Haywood left the newspaper business and , like his father before him, went to work in an iron foundry to support his young family, which soon included a daughter. For the next several years, Haywood was a member of the lodge organization, Knights of Pythias, an involvement that would be providential. One of his recently converted lodge brothers, Oddus Barbour, had received the Pentecostal Spirit baptism. He began to witness to Haywood about this experience. This testimony deepened Haywood's faith, and he began to sense a call to preach. Finding little support from his wife, however, he initially backed off from pursuing the ministry.

The foundry was the site of another seemingly providential circumstance. While working there in 1907, Haywood sustained a serious injury that left him incapacitated for a period. During his recovery, he immersed himself in prayer, sensing an even stronger call to ministry. After recuperating, he accompanied Barbour to a meeting in little tin shop mission church pastored by Azusa Street veteran Henry Prentiss.[3] During that first visit, both Haywood and his wife received their Pentecostal Spirit baptism. He also received a definitive call to preach and determined from that moment to vigorously pursue the ministry— this time with his wife's full support.

The small storefront church would soon become Haywood's spiritual home. Prentiss had been a compassionate pastor, but lacked the gifting to build the fledgling congregation beyond a few members. Within the year, he turned the fellowship of thirteen members over to his young protégé and returned to his native New York City to evangelize there. Haywood, on the other hand, would used his preaching and teaching gifts, enthusiasm, innovation, and charismatic personality to spur growth so that within a short time the racially mixed congregation expanded to more than 400 members.

Five years after the beginning of the Azusa Street Revival, and three years after taking over Prentiss' pastorate, Haywood was ordained in the Pentecostal Assemblies of the World (PAW), one of several small bodies formed as an afterglow of the Revival, and brought his congregation into the denomination, which at the time, like other Wesleyan groups, held to a Trinitarian theology. The congregation was gaining prominence among local and Midwestern Pentecostals and was the largest, most racially integrated Pentecostal congregation in Indiana (and probably in the Midwest) during a period when the Ku Klux Klan held its greatest influence in that state.

BAPTISM "IN THE NAME OF JESUS"

At The Arroyo Seco camp meeting, Canadian evangelist Robert McAclister had preached that the Apostles never explicitly invoked

---

3. Larry Martin, *The Life and Ministry of William J. Seymour* (Hazelwood, MO: Christian Life, 1999) 252–54, 311.

Jesus' Great Commission formula, "in the name of the Father, and of the Son, and of the Holy Ghost." Rather, he insisted, they understood this as a command to baptize in the "the name of Jesus." He further implied that this more faithful formula should be used by Pentecostal congregations. Shortly, several prominent Pentecostal leaders, including Azusa Street veterans Frank Ewart and Glenn Cook, adopted the new teaching and began re-baptizing those who accepted their message. They worked vigorously through preaching and periodicals to convince others of the doctrine's truth. Opponents, such as Assemblies of God (AG) leader J. Roswell Flowers, worked equally hard through sermons, personal correspondence, and periodicals such as the AG's *Weekly Evangel*. They sought to head off what they saw as the unbiblical, destructive, heretical message causing "unstable souls, who know not the Word of God, [to be] swept off their feet."[4] When Cook initially approached him with the new doctrine, Haywood was skeptical. Flower made a personal attempt to deter his colleague, but his warning was too little, too late. After praying about it and becoming convinced of its validity, Haywood not only accepted the message and was re-baptized, but subsequently re-baptized most of the members of his sizeable entire congregation.

The ensuing controversy galvanized the AG's Third General Council, with both sides sending strong delegations to protect their interests. Many sources report that tension over the issue caused Haywood, who had been a founding member of the Assemblies of God and had risen to a position of some prominence, to break with that organization. However, though Haywood (like C. H. Mason) attended at least one session of the organizing meeting, and it would have been significant for a black leader to be part of the new denomination, he never actually held AG credentials.[5] He did, however, maintain close association with prominent AG leaders and frequently spoke at local AG congregations and larger meetings. This close relationship with several AG leaders afforded him the opportunity to be a part of their deliberations regarding the new issue.

4. J. Roswell Flower, "Editorial Comment on the Issue," *Weekly Evangel* 99 (July 17, 1915) 1.

5. [I] "have never been connected with the Assemblies of God as a movement since its organization . . . in 1914. I carried PAW credentials since 1911. It would be impossible to 'go back' to a place you have never been." From *The Voice in the* Wilderness, 1921, cited in Morris Golder, *History of the Pentecostal Assemblies of the World* (Indianapolis, IN: s. n., 1973) 36.

After considering the situation, the Council proposed a compromise—pastors and congregations could use either formula and continue teaching their respective beliefs without imposing them on others. But oneness proponents became more aggressive in attempting to convert those who remained skeptical, insuring that the next General Council would be more volatile. Prior to the meeting, both camps repeatedly accused each other of heresy through sermons and periodical articles, and worked behind the scenes to win allegiance of anyone who had not made up his mind. Haywood was invited to address the issue. Characterizations of the meetings highlight their contentiousness nature, and specifically the racial undertones that colored them. Reportedly, for example, AG leader T. K. Leonard singled out Haywood for attack, calling his new understanding "hay, wood, and stubble", and, alluding to Haywood's publication *The Voice in the Wilderness*, contended that those who followed Haywood were "all in the wilderness, and . . . hav[ing] a voice in the wilderness."[6]

At the end, more than one hundred ministers pulled out of the AG to form the General Assembly of the Apostolic Assemblies as a new oneness fellowship. When the short-lived organization dissipated a year later, Haywood was instrumental in helping restructure PAW to incorporate GAAA ministers into its ranks. With this move, the young body became the most integrated of the existing Pentecostal fellowships. It would remain so for several years, though maintaining this over time would not prove easy.

DENOMINATIONAL LEADER

Haywood's prominence and influence throughout the Midwest drew large numbers of both blacks and whites into the movement and denomination, and he joined Howard Goss, J. J. Frazee (the founder), D. C. O. Opperman, and Ewart in re-forming PAW as a oneness denomination. Since initially most constituents were white, the earliest leaders, except Haywood, were white. At the first general meeting of the new body, in 1913, three white men were elected as leaders: Frazee as General

6. Robert Mapes Anderson, *Vision of the Disinherited: The Making of American Pentecostalism* (New York: Oxford University Press, 1979) 189–90. Leonard was a former minister in the Christian and Missionary Alliance and founder of the Gospel School in Finley, Ohio, and worked with secretly Flower to draft the resolution that became the basis for organization of the Assemblies of God.

Superintendent and Chairman, and former AG leaders Opperman as Secretary and Goss as Treasurer. Haywood and Ewart were tapped to sign ministerial credentials. Additionally four blacks—Haywood, Robert Lawson, Alexander R. Schooler and F. I. Douglas—were elected to serve along with several white field superintendents.[7]

Haywood's newsletter, *The Voice in the Wilderness*, was published between 1910 and 1922, and served as vigorous advocate, first for Pentecostal, then for oneness doctrine. In it, he not only wrote articles, but used his talent as an artist to illustrate principle points. When PAW consolidated it with Ewart's *Meat in Due Season* and Opperman's *The Blessed Truth* to become *The Christian Outlook,* Haywood was tapped as editor. The oneness apologist used the new periodical, along with numerous tracts and pamphlets, to continue to promulgate oneness theology among the faithful and attempt to convince others of its truth. His writing helped spread oneness tenets throughout the African American community and helped formulate foundational theological conceptions still held by contemporary oneness churches. He was a prolific hymnist, and several of the dozens of his hymns penned in the early twentieth century continue to be sung, not only in oneness circles, but throughout the Holiness-Pentecostal community. One of the most recognizable, "I See a Crimson Stream of Blood," is regularly sung by Pentecostal and other Evangelical congregations. Others, such as "Jesus, the Son of God," "Do All in Jesus' Name," and "Baptized into the Body" with more clearly oneness themes are sung by oneness Pentecostals throughout the world.

When PAW was formally incorporated in 1919, after having been first based in Portland, Oregon and then St. Louis, Missouri, its headquarter was moved to Indianapolis and a board of elders was put in place to assist the general secretary with the growing denomination. By then, nearly three-fourth of its membership was white. During that general conference, Haywood was elected to a one year appointment as general secretary. For the next several years, as the denomination grew, Haywood held a number of positions of ever expanding authority and influence.

The headquarters' move, Haywood's popularity, and PAW's commitment to racial equality continued to attract blacks to PAW in such large numbers it changed "the complexion of the organization . . . from one that was predominantly white to one where blacks represented the

7. Golder, *History*, 48.

majority of its membership."[8] This change made some whites uncomfortable and racial tensions within the organization simmered beneath the surface of this seemingly successful experiment in racial unity. In 1924, the smoldering tension erupted into full flame. At first the white leaders proposed separating the denomination into an Eastern (black) branch and a Midwestern (white) branch, each with its own polity and leaders under the umbrella of a single denomination. When that motion failed, several whites broke away to form the Pentecostal Ministerial Alliance, leaving the parent denomination with a larger black majority, but still maintaining a commitment to racial equality. The remaining members reorganized what had been a loose fellowship with congregational polity into an episcopal structure, electing Haywood as presiding bishop. He served in that post for only five years, from 1925–1931. During that time, the denomination continued to grow through a series of amalgamations and mergers, and by still drawing both blacks and whites who were attracted to its commitment to racial unity. Haywood and other leaders fought to vigorously maintain that interracial character in the middle of an always tenuous situation. Further, he also introduced more structure into the organization, creating, for example, a missions department to organize the disparate missions operations into a cohesive unit, and tapping a woman, Hilda Reeder, as Secretary-Treasurer. During those years Haywood traveled extensively throughout the United States, Canada and the Caribbean encouraging pastors and congregations and continuing to promote the oneness message.

By most accounts, Haywood would prove to be a capable and compassionate leader. From the time he took the highest office, however, his leadership was not unchallenged, even with the majority of PAW constituency being black. The 1930 General Assembly proved to be particularly taxing on his spirit and health. Delegates from the powerful Eastern District questioned the denomination's financial structure and sought to impose more accountability for leaders by creating an associate board of bishops. Samuel Grimes was elected editor of *The Christian Outlook,* a move which decentralized some of the power which had previous been held solely in the hands of Haywood.[9]

Haywood was among those early Pentecostals who vehemently believed in divine healing and eschewed use of conventional medicine. He

8. Morris E. Golder, *The Life and Works of Bishop Garfield Thomas Haywood (1880–1931)* (Indianapolis, IN?: s.n., 1977) 64.

9. Golder, *History*, 94–95.

(and all of his brothers) was also heir to a hereditary condition to which each would eventually succumb—a condition that was, possibly, correctable by medical treatment and worsened by the heavy pace of seeing to the fledgling denomination and movement, and the tireless work of pastoring an ever-growing congregation.

Within the severe climate of early oneness Pentecostalism, Haywood's detractors considered many of his views liberal. He refused to take an otherworldly stance, but wanted the saints to enjoy the fruit of salvation in this present world. At a time when the Pentecostal movement had begun to back away from its commitment to radical gender equality, Haywood openly supported the ministry of women, allowing women to preach from the pulpit of his congregation and encouraging them to work alongside their brethren to plant and pastor churches. He aggressively defended oneness theology, drawing on his earlier training with the secular press to establish a printing press and used every form of written media— a newspaper, books, tracts, elaborate charts and numerous hymns—to elucidate and defend the oneness faith. Several full length works including "The Finest of the Wheat," and essays including, "The Birth of the Spirit and the Mystery of the Godhead," "Divine Names and Titles of Jehovah," "Victim of the Flaming Sword" appeared without a date. English and foreign language versions of many of these works were sent throughout the world, including several African nations, China, Japan and Russia.

His opponents considered him both a visionary and a maverick. He introduced such controversial innovations into his congregation as a choir, and using a movie camera to record his trip to the Holy Land for use in educating his congregation. At the time of his death at age 51, plans were underway to for a semi-monthly radio broadcast from the sanctuary of Christ Temple on the Columbia Broadcasting System (CBS). By then, Christ Temple Church was the largest congregation in Indianapolis with 1500 members. The racial balance he had been unable to maintain in the PAW was maintained within that local congregation, and nearly half its members were white. The church had become among the most prominent congregations in Indianapolis and Haywood's stature as a leader within the city religious and secular circles had been established.

BIBLIOGRAPHY

Dugas, Paul P., editor. *The Life and Writings of Elder G. T. Haywood.* Stockton, CA: Apostolic, 1968.

Garrett, Gary W. *A Man Ahead of His Time: The Life & Times of Bishop Garfield Thomas Haywood.* Springfield, MO: Apostolic Christian, 2002.

Golder, Morris E. *The History of the Pentecostal Assemblies of the World.* Indianapolis, IN: s.n., 1973.

———. *The Life and Works of Bishop Garfield Thomas Haywood (1880–1931).* Indianapolis, IN: s.n., 1977.

Pastoral Response

J. C. KELLEY

WHAT IS YOUR DEFINITION of the gospel? Does your understanding of the "good news" have any real power to bring about change? I find that one of the defining marks of the early Pentecostal movement was a gospel with the vision and power to affect change.

A RADICAL GOSPEL

When reflecting on the significance of the Pentecostal movement, one must notice its effect on society's former barriers of division. One's race, gender or bank account were no longer defining factors to his or her existence. *All* were truly made one in Christ and this was to be a reality in their churches. This was not always well received by the public or for that matter by some of the missionaries working on the American borderlands near Mexico. It was, however, an expectation of the gospel in which they tried to live.

In our post-modern world, where almost every barrier has been shattered, it would seem that the gospel we proclaim should lead the way. It is my observation the church follows society in implementing change instead of it being the other way around.

This current reality leads me to underscore and appreciate the radical nature of the early Pentecostal gospel. As the introduction to part 4 says, "Seymour saw the revival as the beginning of a new day when distinctions of race, nationality, and gender would no longer divide the church." The question this raises for us in the early twenty-first century is, "What walls standing today need to be shattered by the power of the Pentecostal movement?"

In light of all of this, maybe the questions we should continue to ask are, "Where does the gospel make us uncomfortable? Where does it cause us to squirm?" Those may be the entry points where the radical gospel of the early Pentecostal movement seeks to be unleashed.

A HOLISTIC GOSPEL

In my denomination, the United Methodist Church, there is a gulf between those who see the gospel as "social action" and those who see it as "personal salvation." Actually this is a reality for most mainline churches. The chapter on Aimee Semple McPherson was extremely instructive here. It explicated in vivid detail a holistic gospel that bridged the gulf between social and personal salvation. Not only did McPherson draw large crowds and use the available technology of her day to spread the gospel, but she also led a church in Los Angeles during the Great Depression that "kept tens of thousands of people from starving to death."

For churches like my own, it's not the latter half of this equation that needs attention. They have a passion for being in ministry in the community and the world. They feed the hungry and clothe the naked and always desire to do more. It is the first part of this equation that needs attention—lives changed through Jesus Christ. I find that mainline denominations are often timid about claiming too much when it comes to being made new in Christ or for that matter, the need for it. The early Pentecostal movement did not make this mistake. They preached a gospel that not only included lives changed through Jesus Christ but power from God through the Baptism in the Holy Spirit to live faithfully and be in ministry.

THEOLOGICAL REFLECTION ON THE GOSPEL

I was intrigued by how the understanding of the gospel worked itself out during early Pentecostalism. There was intense theological reflection on whether the Apostolic Faith consisted of a "Five-fold" or "Four-fold" gospel, and with that whether sanctification was a distinct blessing or should be collapsed into Durham's Finished Work of Calvary theology. The important point is that they continued to work on their theology.

The movement took seriously its theology as it tried to recapture the "Apostolic Faith."

Today, in mainline churches theological reflection flows like a garden hose that floods the yard because it is left running. Where we could profit is asking have we lost the "Apostolic Faith?" Is whatever theology that is in vogue at the moment a representation of the "Apostolic" gospel or a perversion of it? This may not be as true in evangelical denominations but it certainly is an issue in mainline denominations. Is our theology in line with the Apostolic faith or has it completely gone off course? It is a question that we would do well to ask ourselves.

THE VISION OF THE GOSPEL

Vision, the ability to see the not yet as though it is presently a reality, is what fueled the emergence of the Pentecostal movement. It was a sense of expectation that God was about to do something special. The ardent hope was that there would be a "latter rain" which would parallel the first Pentecost, which would be for the purpose of carrying the gospel message across the world.

One thing which is significantly missing from churches today is the expectation that God will do anything. In mainline churches like my own, which are saddled with a sense of decline and subtle depression that the best days are behind them, the reemergence of this type of hope on the part of our people could be the beginning of a significant turnaround. This, of course, could only come by prayer, but it is a prayer God could answer. The prayer that God would pour out His Spirit on the church again for the purpose of connecting people to Jesus Christ and changing not only lives but the world, is a prayer which could energize us to look at ministry with new eyes.

The Twentieth Century:
The Methodist and Holiness Search
for Identity

Introduction

T HE FIRST HALF OF the twentieth century was a time of massive change in America. The number of Americans living in cities now surpassed those in the countryside, and industrial capitalism overcame agriculture as the predominant force in the economy. The enormous concentrations of wealth among the captains of industry was in sharp contrast to the low wages and poor living and working conditions of much of the working class, leading to repeated episodes of labor unrest. Farmers found themselves at the mercy of those who provided their supplies and moved their goods to market. Lacking any social safety net, the ability of both workers and farmers to earn a living was vulnerable to sickness, injury, economic downturn, and (in the case of farmers) weather. The resulting protests found political embodiment in both Populist and Progressive movements. In the church it took the form of the Social Gospel.

Proponents of the Social Gospel argued that social reform would not occur simply through individual conversions but also required changing the institutions and structures of society. The Methodist Episcopal Church gave strong endorsement to this approach when the General Conference in 1908 adopted a Social Creed that called for improved working conditions, a living wage, recognition of labor unions, and greater protection for women and children who worked in the factories.

PERSONAL AND SOCIAL GOSPEL

A perceived conflict between the Social Gospel and the emphasis on personal salvation found in the revival tradition often led to conflict between their adherents. Yet many Methodists, in Wesleyan fashion, continued to embrace both. This is nowhere more evident than in the African American Methodist tradition, as exemplified by AME Bishop Archibald Carey Sr. and his pastor son, Archibald Carey Jr. Both were strong advocates of the Social Gospel and Civil Rights, while at the same time continuing to emphasize personal salvation in their Chicago ministries. These perspectives led both to pursue politics as intrinsic to their ministries. The results of their efforts for those they served were mixed. They nonetheless model an understanding of Wesleyan Christianity in which personal and social, and church and society, are intrinsically and inescapably related.

The linkage of personal salvation and social ministry was emphatically affirmed by some of the prominent leaders in missions within the Methodist Episcopal traditions. Lucy Rider Meyer (1849–1922) was a primary figure behind the deaconess movement in Methodism, founding the Chicago Training School in 1885. While she was focused on the plight of impoverished children in the cities, she called deaconesses to minister to both bodies and souls. "Our need is not evangelism or social service," she insisted, "but evangelism and social service, now and forever, one and inseparable."[1]

Meyer's views on the role of deaconesses was strongly contested by Jane Bancroft Robinson (1847–1932), who led the Deaconess Bureau of the Women's Home Missionary Society (WHMS) in the Methodist Episcopal Church. Both were tireless and effective promoters of the deaconess movement. But Meyer argued that deaconesses should not be marginalized but be considered an integral part of the general church, while Robinson, like many women reformers in the Progressive Era, insisted they should belong to more autonomous institutions under the control of women. Robinson also opposed Meyer's emphasis on evangelism, understanding the work of a deaconess to be more in the area of social service.

Iva Durham Vennard (1871–1945) provides a third model of a Methodist deaconess. A holiness evangelist, she understood the work of a deaconess much like Meyer, though even more toward evangelism. Resigning from her position with Robinson's bureau in the WHMS, in 1902 Vennard founded the Epworth Evangelistic Institute in a poor

---

1. Cited by Laceye Warner, "Methodist Episcopal Deaconesses and the Social Gospel: Social Service with Evangelistic Ministry," *Journal of the Academy for Evangelism in Theological Education* 16 (October, 2001) 36–49.

neighborhood in St. Louis in order to train deaconesses in evangelism and social service. In 1909 while she was away on maternity leave, male clergy and laity in the St. Louis Annual Conference of the MEC who strongly opposed women evangelists and preachers took over the school, removed the courses on evangelism from the curriculum, and replaced all women bible and theology teachers with men. Vennard then moved to Chicago in 1910, and there founded the Chicago Evangelistic Institute, which she led until her death.[2]

This same linkage of personal salvation and social ministry advocated by Meyer and Vennard is evident in the ministry of Methodism's most influential missionary, E. Stanley Jones (1884–1973). Himself mentored by leaders in the Holiness movement, who combined a commitment to entire sanctification with radical calls to remedy the economic distress of farmers and laborers, Jones preached and practiced a holistic gospel. As a missionary to India he not only was influenced by that culture, but came to see more clearly how American culture had compromised the gospel with its individualism, materialism, and racism. The authentic gospel, he believed, would dramatically change both persons and society. "The Gospel of the person of Jesus and the Gospel of the Kingdom viewed as one puts together the individual and the social," he argued "An individual gospel without a social gospel is a soul without a body, and a social gospel without an individual gospel is a body without a soul ... I want both."[3]

This combining of personal salvation and social reform is also found in the preeminent Methodist evangelist of this period, Harry Denman (1883–1976). As a lay evangelist Denman had by the 1930s moved to become the denominational leader in evangelism, first for the Methodist Episcopal Church, South, and then for the reunited Methodist Church. For Denman, social witness was inseparable from evangelism, and he believed materialism and racism were the two chief reasons the church's message was so often ineffective. His simple lifestyle rivaled that of John Wesley, and his opposition to anti-Semitism and racism was emphatic. Denman maintained membership in two Methodist Churches, one

2. For more on the relationship between Meyer, Robinson, and Vennard, and their impact on the deaconess movement, see Priscilla Pope-Levison, "A 'Thirty Year War' and More: Exposing Complexities in the Methodist Deaconess Movement," *Methodist History* 47.2 (2009) 101–16.

3. E. Stanley Jones, *The Reconstruction of the Church—On What Pattern?* (Nashville: Abingdon, 1970) 93.

white and one black, in the hope for a day when the church would be truly one.[4]

Of course, the exhortations of persons like Meyer, Vennard, Jones, and Denman to keep personal evangelism and social reform together were being made to a church increasingly inclined to ignore both. Nonetheless they motivated many, and communicated clearly their vision of a holistic gospel.

THE CHALLENGE OF THEOLOGICAL LIBERALISM

A second source of division would not be so easily reconciled. Theological liberalism began to take hold in the intellectual and educational centers of mainline Methodism, and within decades came to dominate. With their more immanent divinity, more human Jesus, and more critical stance toward scripture, liberals were able to re-envision Christianity in a way that was in greater continuity with contemporary intellectual currents, at the cost of increased tension with the older tradition. Their views were strongly contested by those who remained close to the Holiness movement.

This divergence in sensibility can be well illustrated by comparing the careers of Borden Parker Bowne and Henry Clay Morrison, both of whom had roots in the Holiness movement. Bowne found German personal idealism to be a highly persuasive and intellectually satisfying way of thinking about God and creation, and he sought to recast Wesleyanism in its terms. From his position at Boston University he led a philosophical and theological revolution with Methodism. Morrison was a faithful adherent of Wesleyan holiness theology, opposing the worldliness of the middle class and urging support for the poor, labor unions, and women's ordination. He founded Asbury Theological Seminary in 1923 as a center for ministerial education in the Wesleyan holiness tradition. But over time the confrontation with liberalism pushed Morrison to emphasize more his conservative views of Scripture and theology. With both sides claiming to be the true heirs of Wesley, the identity of Methodism became much more contested.

As the story of Morrison demonstrates, the Fundamentalist/ Modernist controversy in the early decades of the twentieth century had

---

4. A popular biography of Denman is Harold Rogers, *Harry Denman* (Nashville: Upper Room, 1977).

a gradual but significant impact on the Holiness movement. The late nineteenth century concern for the economic well-being of farmers and laborers, women's suffrage, prohibition of alcohol, and in some quarters, racial equality which characterized much of the movement was eclipsed by a new set of concerns. Of course, some of this was undoubtedly due to the success of some of the reform movements: women received the right to vote and alcohol was banned by Constitutional amendments in 1920 (though Prohibition proved unworkable and was later repealed), and Progressive legislation addressed many economic concerns. But it is nonetheless striking that in their conflict with liberal theology, both Holiness and Pentecostal writers began to focus on issues like the authority of scripture, the substitutionary atonement, eschatology, and evolution, and many came to adopt Fundamentalist positions.

It was in the 1920s that Fundamentalist language concerning scripture began to be common in the Church of the Nazarene. This understanding of the Bible as the inerrant word of God, verifiable by reason, gradually supplanted the older historic orthodoxy that held scripture to be the inspired word of God because it uniquely and authoritatively witnesses to Christ the Living Word, and is authenticated by the internal testimony of the Holy Spirit. Notably H. Orton Wiley (1877–1961), the most prominent Nazarene theologian of the first half of the twentieth century, resisted this Fundamentalist trend by offering a Wesleyan alternative to both Fundamentalism and liberal theology that was more in continuity with this earlier orthodoxy.[5]

THE NATURE OF HOLINESS

The identity of the Holiness movement was not only made more ambiguous by its being reshaped by the Fundamentalist/Modernist controversy, but by confusion over holiness itself. By the 1940s many members of Holiness denominations were reflecting the lifestyle of middle class America. Seeing this as an abandonment of holiness patterns of behavior and dress and a compromise with worldliness, Wesleyan Methodist H.

---

5. This is discussed in Paul H. Bassett, "The Fundamentalist Leavening of the Holiness Movement, 1914–1940," *Wesleyan Theological Journal* 13.1 (1978) 65–91. Although clearly an evangelical work, Wiley's *Christian Theology* (1941) critically draws upon a personalist anthropology associated with the more liberal theology of Bowne and his successors. Wiley was not alone in this, as many other conservative Wesleyans borrowed the relational concepts of personalism.

E. Schmul (1921–1998) formed the Inter-Church Holiness Convention in 1951 as an annual convention in support of Holiness conservatives. While the IHC was not itself a denomination, new denominations were formed by Holiness conservatives. Among them was the Bible Missionary Church formed in 1955 by Nazarene evangelist Glenn Griffith (1894–1976) and the Allegheny Wesleyan Methodist Connection and the Bible Methodist Connection of Churches, both of which broke away from the Wesleyan Methodist Church in the 1960s.[6]

The issue of identity raised by the Conservative Holiness movement is perennial and has taken many forms. The central question is how can holiness of life be contextualized in a manner that does not at the same time rob it of its power and integrity. In the antebellum nineteenth century, Charles Finney and Phoebe Palmer in different ways sought to promote holiness in a way that would enable it to move from the frontier camp meeting to middle class and urban America, but to do so in a way that would challenge as well as connect to middle class audiences. Yet others, like Orange Scott and B. T. Roberts, called for more radical versions of holiness that were in sharper tension with middle class respectability.

Not only holiness of life but holiness of heart could be the occasion for theological conflict. It had become common in Holiness theology to describe entire sanctification as the removal of sin, almost as if sin were a substance. When Nazarene theologian Mildred Bangs Wynkoop proposed a more relational and participatory understanding of sanctification, describing it as the presence of love, she faced strong criticism from those defending the more substantivist position. While they saw her as abandoning the Wesleyan insistence of a real transformation of the heart, Wynkoop argued that she was recovering the way Wesley actually understood that real transformation to occur. Wynkoop in turn became an inspiration and catalyst for a new generation of Holiness theologians.

By the end of the twentieth century, many American Pentecostals would join Methodist and Holiness traditions in their struggle over identity. Such a struggle is perhaps inevitable in the face of large scale cultural

---

6. The story of the Conservative Holiness movement is found in Wallace Thornton Jr., *Radical Righteousness: Personal Ethics and the Development of the Holiness Movement* (Salem, OH: Schmul, 1988); and Brian Black, *The Holiness Heritage: The Rise of the Conservative Holiness Movement* (Salem, OH: Allegheny, 2003).

and intellectual change. Those who seek renewal are sometimes drawn to the younger and more vibrant churches of the Southern hemisphere, where Wesleyan, Holiness, and Pentecostal theologies are embraced and lived out in new cultural contexts. But they are also drawn back to their historical roots, not to live in the past, but to find there insight for who they are and how they can faithfully live and minister in a new century.

26

Borden Parker Bowne and Henry Clay Morrison

Conflicting Conceptions of Twentieth-Century Methodism

DOUGLAS M. STRONG

ALTHOUGH BOTH BORDEN PARKER Bowne (1847–1910) and Henry Clay Morrison (1857–1942) had a similar ambition to determine the direction of twentieth century Methodism, the two leaders could not have been more different in personal temperament or religious persuasion. These two pivotal figures and their respective theological schools represent two distinct, competing movements within twentieth century Methodism—theologically liberal mainline Methodism and theologically conservative Holiness Methodism.

Bowne was the leading theological voice for the initial generation of faculty and students at Boston University School of Theology (B.U.), the best-known seminary of the Methodist Episcopal Church during the first two-thirds of the twentieth century. As exponents of "Boston Personalism"—a form of Protestant liberalism—Bowne and his successors at B.U. provided a new and highly influential theological orientation for a large portion of American Methodism, intentionally moving the Church away from what they perceived as its outdated beliefs and embarrassing nineteenth century cultural mores.

Bowne's contemporary, Henry Clay Morrison, was one of the most prominent Holiness preachers of the period. Unlike some Holiness evangelists in the late nineteenth and early twentieth century, who left Methodism in order to form separate sects such as the Church of the Nazarene, Morrison decided not to depart from his cherished denomination. Instead, Morrison sought to "ask for the old paths" of revivalistic Methodism.[1] This goal would be accomplished, he believed, by preaching about the experience of entire sanctification and (later in his life) by establishing Asbury Theological Seminary as a school for the training of sanctified Holiness pastors opposed to the theological "modernism" taught at Boston, Vanderbilt, and elsewhere.

BORDEN PARKER BOWNE

Borden Parker Bowne's story represents the ascendency of both theological liberalism and upper middle class mainline values in American Methodism, seemingly the very opposite of many of the emphases characteristic of the Wesleyan/Holiness/Pentecostal trajectory. It is nonetheless important to include Bowne and his liberal compatriots, not only because their religious roots came from the nineteenth century Holiness movement, but also because mainline Methodism was a significant movement within twentieth century religious history that serves as a kind of anti-type for the larger narrative described in this book.

Bowne was raised in a relatively affluent, deeply pious Methodist home in central New Jersey. His parents were abolitionists at a time when that position was unpopular. His father was a local preacher in the Methodist Episcopal Church and his mother was a devotee of Phoebe Palmer's parlor holiness. Bowne reported that Palmer's *Guide to Holiness* was read in his home as faithfully as the Bible.[2]

Two aspects of the early part of Bowne's life are relevant for our purposes. First, a significant childhood remembrance of Bowne's was the impact made by a number of Holiness evangelists who stayed at his home as they traveled through New Jersey. Bowne recalled that he was not impressed by the behavior or the personality of these preachers; they seemed to be sanctimonious, self-serving and hypocritical manipulators of the feelings of their auditors. Drawing from these recollections, Bowne labored for the rest of his life against what he considered to be excessive sentimentality within the Methodist Episcopal Church.

Bowne's biographer and former student, Francis McConnell (one of the leading liberal bishops of the twentieth century), stated that Bowne "recognized within himself the tendencies to mysticism which, if not

1. *The Old Methodist* 1:4 (March 1889) 1.
2. Francis J. McConnell, *Borden Parker Bowne* (New York: Abingdon, 1929) 13.

checked, could easily run into excess." Therefore, Bowne self-consciously developed a logical and predominantly rationalistic temperament. He was consistently described as very formal, businesslike and orderly—even with family members. He also spoke frequently of the need "to guard against emotional aspects of religion." The result, according to McConnell, was that Bowne's "service to Methodism [was] in correcting a tendency to overemotionalism."[3]

Secondly, Bowne's education shaped him profoundly. After attending Pennington Seminary, a Methodist prep school in New Jersey, Bowne went to New York University, where he was the valedictorian of his class. He then took a pastoral appointment for one year before becoming intellectually restless, and went off to Germany to study with Rudolf Lotze at Gottingen. Steeped in Hegelian Idealism and Ritschlian philosophy, Bowne developed his own philosophical theism, which he came to term Personalism.

Personalism highlights the concept of self-conscious individualism, the essential freedom of the human person and the importance of an individual's internal authority, reflective of the Enlightenment view of self-autonomy. Although the divine Spirit is manifestly immanent, each person is the "captain of his soul." Bowne stressed the capacity of the human will, which was both directive and determinative, and underplayed the experience of divine grace. He "insisted on a morality which, without emotion, touched all phases of conduct." He held a progressive view of human anthropology, and was open to evolutionary theory (though he chided atheistic evolutionists).[4] All of these emphases, of course, flew in the face of nineteenth century-style Methodism. "For evangelistic methods as ordinarily practiced, he had little sympathy, but for the bringing in of the Kingdom through persuading men to yield their wills to the divine will he had every regard." Bishop McConnell admitted that some traditionalists felt a "chilling influence of his teaching on the evangelical temper" in the Methodist Episcopal Church.[5]

Bowne's most controversial theological beliefs related to his views on miracles and the atonement. Given God's immanence, he held to the idea that God works through natural methods, which are an expression of the divine purpose. Oppositely, all that seems to us as natural is rooted

3. Ibid., 14.

4. Ibid., 14.

5. Ibid., 222.

in the supernatural Cause. Nature cannot run itself, but is dependent upon the continuous activity of the immanent Cause. Since all events proceed from the will of the Infinite Person, then everything is a miracle—or conversely, perhaps, nothing is a miracle.

Regarding the atonement, Bowne held to the moral influence theory. He adamantly rejected the notion of the imputation of Christ's merit and righteousness to sinners. Thus, he rejected John Wesley's more Protestant concept of justification and reformulated Wesley's concept of sanctification to be a kind of Pelagianized progression toward good works.[6]

In 1876, Bowne was invited to become the first professor of philosophy at the eight-year old Methodist attempt at a full-blown university—Boston University. Operating in the shadow of Harvard, B.U. was trying to make a name for itself as a reputable institution. Though often asked to join other faculties, Bowne stayed at B.U. for his entire career—until his death in 1910—becoming the dean of the graduate school and supervising many dissertations.[7] Under Bowne's direction, Boston University became the premier Methodist university, educating hundreds of Methodist ministers in Boston Personalism and creating the dominant theological school for Protestant liberalism in the twentieth century.

Bowne and his students were extremely self-assured regarding the correctness and the influence of their ideas, a disposition that historian Gary Dorrien describes as "confident liberal self-assertiveness." Buttressing this sense of certainty and aplomb was the fact that, by the early twentieth century, B.U. and other Methodist universities were becoming places of scholarly distinction and social respectability. Bowne's career path and cultural location illustrated this socio-economic progression, as evidenced by his regular attendance at Saint Mark's

---

6. Gary Dorrien, *The Making of American Liberal Theology: Imagining Progressive Religion 1805–1900* (Louisville: Westminster John Knox Press, 2001) 387.

7. Given Bowne's supervision of John Wesley Edward Bowen as the first African-American to receive a university doctorate, it is disturbing to discover that Bowne was silent in his writings on the race question, held insensitive and racially biased views, and seemed unaware of the plight of African Americans in society. Rufus Burrow Jr., "Borden Parker Bowne: The First Thoroughgoing Personalist," *Methodist History* 36:1 (October, 1997) 52–53.

Methodist Episcopal Church, a genteel, upwardly-mobile congregation in Brookline, Massachusetts, not far from the university. [8]

The tensions between B.U.'s refined, urban-oriented liberalism and the more traditional views and attitudes typically characteristic of populist Methodism came to a head when Bowne's friend and colleague, Hinckley G. Mitchell, was tried for heresy in 1900. Mitchell had been teaching students about the higher criticism of the Old Testament. Later, in 1904, Bowne himself was brought up on heresy charges, related to his teachings on the Trinity, miracles, the atonement, sin, salvation, and justification. At his church trial, Bowne was defended by Frank Mason North, a prominent pastor in New York City and the leading figure of the social gospel within Methodism, who helped Bowne to be exonerated of all charges. When Bowne was acquitted, his victory symbolized for many the triumph of theological liberalism in Methodism and also cemented in people's minds the connection between liberal thought and the social gospel. [9]

HENRY CLAY MORRISON[10]

Boston University was the prime example of the late nineteenth century trend among Methodists to place a high value on theological education obtained at professional divinity schools, particularly those established at large universities. Henry Clay Morrison became an embodiment of this phenomenon when he left his native Kentucky to attend Vanderbilt University. Even though Vanderbilt Divinity School was still awash in Southern evangelical piety in 1884 when Morrison matriculated, he was uncertain about the appropriateness of his attendance, and so he spent only one year there. Morrison appreciated the erudition of his professors, but his single-minded commitment to evangelism compelled him to withdraw from academic pursuits. The Lord's service, he believed, called him away from "scholarly culture." Morrison admired the value

---

8 Dorrien, *Making of American Liberal Theology*, 378, 383; Burrow, "Borden Parker Bowne," 47.

9. James M. Buckley, "The Acquittal of Professor Bowne," *Christian Advocate 79* (April 14, 1904) 571–73 (reprinted in *Zion's Herald* 16 (April 20, 1904) 489f.

10. Portions of this section draw upon Douglas M. Strong, "Henry Clay Morrison and the Transformation of the Holiness Movement" (*Wesleyan Theological Journal* 40:2, 2005).

and even the social status of education, but when he sensed that he was actually becoming part of that academic ethos, he drew away. [11]

A few years later, during Morrison's successful pastorate of a prosperous congregation, he experienced a dramatic infilling of the Holy Spirit in entire sanctification. Soon thereafter, he left his appointment as a local pastor, began an itinerant evangelistic ministry, and started his own newspaper, *The Old Methodist*, later renamed the *Pentecostal Herald*. In the paper, Morrison stressed the urgent need for revival and the importance of living a life of holiness. "Worldliness," Morrison was convinced, was the greatest enemy of holiness, and it assumed many guises. It could come, for example, in the form of the temptation to "preach 'growth' as a substitute for entire sanctification." Given his insistence on an experiential crisis associated with Christian holiness, Morrison was particularly disturbed by the tendency of ministers to de-emphasize the second (or even the first) definite work of God's grace in a person's life in favor of one's gradual spiritual nurture through Christian education. [12]

Morrison was convinced that urbane ministers had become worldly in the formalism of their worship, eschewing the affective spirituality and warmly emotional services of the early days of Methodism. "There is a stiffness and coldness in our city churches that freezes out the common people. The pastors of our city churches are not soul winners." Morrison critiqued the culture of commodity and acquisition, of intellectualism and sophistication. He was deeply concerned because the Christian values of the rural plain folk—a sense of community, self-denial, and moral fortitude—were being replaced by the values of the "rich and cultured mob." Universities had made theology inaccessible to the average layperson, and clergymen in the "fastidious city church[es]" had become "too scholarly in their culture."[13]

Among Holiness advocates in the late nineteenth and early twentieth century, living a holy life meant a reaction against the standards of the present world, a non-accommodation with the dominant culture. The opposite of worldliness was a lifestyle of Christian purity, indicated

---

11 C. F. Wimberly, *Henry Clay Morrison* (New York: Revell, 1922) 85–89.

12. *Pentecostal Herald* 10 (January 19, 1898) 1; Wimberly, *Henry Clay Morrison*, 93–106.

13. *Pentecostal Herald* 11 (January 25, 1899) 8; 35 (March 21, 1923) 1; (March 28, 1923) 8; (April 18, 1923) 8; Morrison, *The Christ of the Gospels* (New York: Revell, 1926) 76–79.

by following a code of moralistic behavior. The specific behaviors to be shunned or pursued, according to the Holiness people, were those that were consistent with the rejection of the commercialized culture of the day.[14] For Morrison, such holy living meant identification with the poor. "As for worldly possessions, very few deeply pious men have ever had them . . . God has chosen the poor of this world, rich in faith, to be heirs of His kingdom." He railed against status distinctions that came from paying too much attention to the fashions of dress or other "worldly pursuits."[15]

In the period following the First World War, Morrison also railed against another type of worldliness that he increasingly discovered among Methodist ministers and congregations: the "unbelief" that he felt characterized the "new theology" then circulating in the divinity schools. This "destructive criticism" was damaging true faith by subverting the biblical basis for Christian morality, producing a spirit of doubt in the minds of converts that "put out evangelistic fires." Morrison specified the doctrinal issues with which he was most concerned: the inspiration of the Scriptures; the "fact of sin"; the deity of Jesus; the importance of believing in the whole realm of the supernatural, including miracles; and the need for a vicarious blood atonement for sins. This last was seen as important for Morrison because without the "finished work of the atonement," there could be no cleansing blood for inward sin by the baptism of the Holy Spirit."[16]

Morrison connected these perceived doctrinal errors to a critique of the commercialized values intrinsic in the capitalism of industrial America. According to his reasoning, moral and religious skepticism simply reflected the mindset that developed when one became captive to the prevailing market mentality. He asserted that his contemporaries had "put Christ on the market." Many a Methodist minister, Morrison charged would "stand up before an unregenerated and wealthy congregation of people and sell Christ. He tells them that Jesus is not of Virgin Birth; . . . that He never performed any miracles; that He made no atonement for sin in His death. Isn't this selling Christ?" Morrison declared that the "false teachers" of the new theology were "slaves of their selfish

14. *Old Methodist* 1:12 (November 1889) 3.

15. *Old Methodist* 1:12 (November 1889) 1; *Pentecostal Herald* 9 (August 11, 1897): 2; Henry Clay Morrison, *Christ of the Gospels*, 77–79.

16. *Pentecostal Herald* 35 (March 21, 1923) 1, 8; (March 28, 1923) 1; (April 11, 1923) 1, 8; (April 18, 1923) 1, 8.

appetites, who love to worship at the shrine of their own culture and supposed superior intellectuality."[17]

By the 1920s, Morrison was convinced that the divinity programs at Boston and other universities—including at his beloved Vanderbilt—had been taken over by the forces of modernism, which caused him "to lose confidence in men and things." What was needed, Morrison determined, was an uncompromising Holiness school. In the midst of religious insecurity, when "large numbers of preachers . . . have ceased to believe the plain work of the Bible . . . [and] are preaching their unbelief," his new seminary—eventually founded on the campus of Asbury College in Wilmore, Kentucky—would "stand true to the Bible from first to last." As a Holiness Methodist who supported academic training but was also wary of it, Morrison intended that his school would fulfill America's need for a "well-educated, Spirit-filled, evangelistic ministry who are loyal to the Word of God and the Son of God."[18]

THE DIVIDED LEGACY OF TWENTIETH-CENTURY METHODISM

Henry Clay Morrison's career is illustrative of the character of Holiness people who remained within Methodism; they rejected a large portion of Gilded Age culture but they also accepted some aspects of that culture. Morrison frequently took the middle ground on issues. Regarding his attitude toward the institutional church, for instance, he remained loyal to the church of his youth, supporting its structure and its discipline at the same time that other Holiness leaders disowned denominational Methodism. Nonetheless, he frequently criticized the moral leniency and effete decorum of the mainline Methodist churches. Regarding the enthusiasm of religious experience, Morrison was proud that "none of the excesses bordering on fanaticism that marked the work of some holiness warriors" attended his ministry; his revival meetings were fervent without being uncontrolled. He harshly criticized, however, liberal Methodist ministers' disregard for conversion and sanctification experiences. Regarding higher education, Morrison envisioned a corps of revivalists who were well-educated but not wrapped up in the "scholarly culture" of

17. *Pentecostal Herald* 35 (March 21, 1923) 1; Morrison, *Christ of the Gospels*, 44–47.

18. *Pentecostal Herald* 35 (April 4, 1923) 8; (April 25, 1923) 1.

modernism. He saw an advantage to accreditation as a legitimation of the academic worth of Holiness schools, but he did not put much stock in the world's standards of academic excellence, especially as taught at university-based divinity schools.[19]

Meanwhile, the second and third generation of Boston Personalists, under the tutelage of Bowne's successors, Albert C. Knudsen and Edgar S. Brightman, became increasingly deprecating of convictional experiences of faith in favor of religious nurture based on the continual discipline of an individual's will. They encouraged people to model themselves after the supreme ethical perfection of Jesus. This understanding of the Christian life was manifest in much of the popular religion of early to mid twentieth century Methodism. Earl Marlatt, a B.U. graduate and, later, Professor of Religious Education, expressed this religious sentiment in his well-known popular 1926 hymn, "Are Ye Able":

> Are ye able, said the Master, to be crucified with me. Yea, the sturdy dreamers answer, to the death we follow thee. Lord, we are able. Our spirits are thine. Remold them, make us, like thee, divine. Thy guiding radiance above us shall be a beacon to God, to love, and loyalty.[20]

In Marlatt's hymn, there is no sin and therefore no need for grace or salvation. Rather, "sturdy dreamers" are challenged to follow Jesus' "guiding radiance" as a "beacon to God" through the exercise of their will, which they are perfectly able to do.

Bowne and his followers stressed the importance of religious education and the cultivation of virtue. Nothing should interfere with a child's growing independence and "the precious human possibilities" in each young person. Bowne "saw in Methodism . . . the potentialities of enormous conquests for the kingdom if zeal could be joined with disciplined knowledge." Bowne's theological stress on "disciplined knowledge" had a strong influence on people like John H. Vincent, the co-founder of Chautauqua Institution and a promoter of the Sunday School movement. Later, when Vincent was a bishop in California, he was the primary opponent of the enthusiastic holiness message (the "zeal") of Phineas Bresee, the leading early figure of the Church of the

---

19. *Pentecostal Herald* 9 (August 11, 1897) 4–5, 8; 10 (January 12, 1898) 8, 9.

20. H. Augustine Smith, ed., *American Student Hymnal* (New York: Century, 1928) 160, ("Preface" by Earl Marlatt); Robert Guy McCutchan, *Our Hymnody: A Manual of the Methodist Hymnal* (New York: Abingdon, 1937) 306–7.

Nazarene. Bowne also influenced other bishops, professors, scores of pastors and many influential laymen, including William Hocking, who was later the author of the famous 1932 report critical of evangelism efforts in foreign missions work.[21] More than perhaps anyone else, Bowne helped to clarify the thinking of Methodists as to the role of religious experience, altering it from the witness of the Spirit regarding Christ's saving work on the cross to an apprehension of God's divine will in one's life. Other Methodists, such as Morrison, hoped to retain the conventional Wesleyan understanding of Christian "affections" as an assurance of faith. These two belief systems, and their corresponding social locations, created a dual approach to Methodism that lasted for most of the twentieth century.

BIBLIOGRAPHY

McConnell, Francis J. *Borden Parker Bowne.* New York: Abingdon, 1929.

Dorrien, Gary. *The Making of American Liberal Theology.* Louisville: Westminster/Knox, 2001.

Wimberly, C. F. *Henry Clay Morrison.* New York: Revell, 1922.

21. McConnell, *Borden Parker Bowne*, 223, 234–35; William E. Hocking, "The Metaphysics of Borden P. Bowne," *Methodist Review* 105 (May 1922) 371–74; William E. Hocking, ed., *Re-Thinking Missions: A Laymen's Inquiry after One Hundred Years* (New York, Harper, 1932).

27

E. Stanley Jones

The Holiness Evangelist as Social Critic

WILLIAM C. KOSTLEVY

> "Some theological students asked a prominent Christian [Riehold
> Niebuhr I suspect] why he had abandoned his former position
> against war for one of moral approval. In reply he unfolded a map
> of Europe, pointed to it and said, 'that map is my reason.' He got
> his morals from a map . . . he looked to the Nazis instead of the
> Nazarene . . . The Christian begins with Christ and works from
> Him out to problems."[1]

FOR TWO DECADES BEGINNING in the 1930s, Reinhold Niebuhr and
Methodist evangelist E. Stanley Jones engaged in a spirited debate on
the nature of Christian social teaching and the relevance of the teachings
of Jesus for contemporary Christians. As Niebuhr made clear on several
occasions his feud with Jones was far more than a feud with Liberalism.
It was a contemporary expression of "responsible" Christianity's age old
internal struggle against "utopian" Christianity, also known as perfectionism. As Niebuhr wrote in *The Nature and Destiny of Man*, citing
George Fox as a prime example, "in more extreme sects . . . the legitimate
majesty of government is not apprehended." "Usually," Niebuhr continues, citing E. Stanley Jones as his prime example, "the failure to appreciate the necessity of government is derived from perfectionist illusions."
As Niebuhr elaborated, such "anarchistic social theories are explicitly
sanctificationist in their theories of redemption." Further (accurately I

---

1. E. Stanley Jones, *The Way* (New York: Abingdon, 1946) 323.

would contend) he places Jones in the company of such English Civil War "anticipators" of Marxism as the Levelers and Diggers. In this paper, I argue Jones is, in fact, best identified as a holiness radical, albeit perhaps a holiness radical of a higher order. In fairness to Niebuhr, Jones was reluctant to identify too closely with a tradition that was easily dismissed by the very American Brahmins that often sought spiritual solace at his, at least to the initiated, thinly disguised "holy roller" revivals.[2]

Before looking at the Niebuhr-Jones feud, it is important to understand the depth of the hostility to public expressions of holiness worship among intellectual and cultural elites during the 1930s and 1940s. John Steuart Curry, a struggling New York-based magazine illustrator, became an international sensation with his *Baptism in Kansas*, a depiction described by one critic "as a gorgeous piece of satire" of the "religious fanaticism of the hinterland." Meanwhile Sinclair Lewis had relocated to Kansas City, an ideal location, it seems, for research on his highly publicized novel exposing American religious fanaticism, *Elmer Gantry*.[3]

The popular attitudes of principal purveyors of American culture are nicely described again by Arthur Schlesinger Jr. in his autobiography. In 1940, the younger Schlesinger bravely ventured into the wilds east of the Hudson River. At Coeur d'Alene, Idaho, Schlesinger witnessed his first "evangelical camp meeting." As he wrote his parents, "he had rarely seen so disgusting a scene." Individuals were moaning, in trances, or "hysterically weeping, shouting 'Jesus, come to me.'" Lest we accuse Schlesinger of only a bias against American expressions of religious devotion, it should be noted that as a sixteen year old he had been equally offended by sights and ecstasies of Benares' pilgrims bathing in the Ganges. Schlesinger did report a real sense of shame for his prejudices concerning Hindu expressions of faith. As the narrative makes clear his

---

2 Reinhold Niebuhr, *The Nature and Destiny of Man*, vol. 1: *Human Destiny* (New York: Scribner, 1943) 279–80. Church of the Brethren scholar Dale W. Brown recalls his astonishment as a teenager when the respected Jones ended a meeting in Wichita, Kansas, by inviting all seeking the Baptism of the Holy Spirit to come forward. This was not exactly the introduction to Gandhi-style non-violence Brown was expecting.

3. H. Richard Niebuhr, *The Social Sources of Denominationalism* (New York: Holt, 1929) 75. On Curry and Lewis see Robert Smith Bader, *Hayseeds, Moralizers and Methodists: The Twentieth-Century Image of Kansas* (Lawrence: University Press of Kansas, 1988) 41–71.

feelings about the religious expressions of Idahoans evoked no similar sense of shame.[4]

Traveling with Schlesinger was his Harvard friend and mentor, the noted author of western historical narratives and founder of the History Book Club, Bernard DeVoto. Raised in Utah, the son of a marriage between a lapsed Catholic father and a lapsed Mormon mother, Devoto had fled his native state as a college sophomore, finding sanctuary in Cambridge, Massachusetts. In East St. Louis, Illinois, Devoto recalled being passed by a truck "advertising a Nazarene revival and telling us that we must repent for the day of God's vengeance was at hand."[5] In both narratives of the same trip, the traveling companions situate these stories in the context of the global struggle against Fascism. In both the camp meeting in Idaho and the Nazarene revival in East St. Louis holiness religion serves as an opiate for the social marginalized.

In fact, both Schlesinger and Devoto pointedly suggest that such expressions of faith are dangerous distractions from the sacred national mission of the United States, the defeat of Hitler (and for Schlesinger after 1945, the USSR). In this sacred battle Holiness people were a pathetic side show. The perfectionism of E. Stanley Jones, on the other hand, was not a side show. It was a utopian social vision with a clear strategy suggesting alternatives to both Fascism and Communism. It was not pie in the sky eschatological fantasy. It was far worse. It proposed actually living in history in light of the teachings and values of Jesus. For a generation committed to the rehabilitation of Augustine and the Puritan fathers, E. Stanley Jones poised a threat and an alternative. To understand the source and character of that threat requires an exploration into the lost

---

4. Arthur M. Schlesinger, *A Life in the Twentieth Century: Innocent Beginnings, 1917–1950* (Boston: Houghton Mifflin, 2000) 101, 235. In this book Schlesinger recounts Reinhold Niebuhr's fear that the popular Jones was undermining American resistance to Hitler. Schlesinger does not indicate the denominational affiliation of the camp meeting. Given its location, my sense is that it was likely a Church of the Nazarene meeting. Glenn Griffith, the Idaho-Oregon District Superintendent at the time, often told the story that he had never spent a night in jail until he was entirely sanctified. The charges were, of course, disturbing the peace. William McLoughlin in *Modern Revivalism: Charles Grandison Finney to Billy Graham* (New York: Ronald, 1959) 475, derisively refers to such holiness figures as Steven Paine, Paul Rees and Leslie Marston, as the "social and intellectual elite of the marginal middle class."

5. Bernard DeVoto, *The Western Paradox: A Conservation Reader*, edited by Douglas Brinkley and Patricia Limerick with a foreword by Arthur S. Schlesinger Jr. (New Haven: Yale University Press, 2000) 183.

social milieu of the turn of the century Holiness revival of his mentors, especially in this paper L. L. Pickett and Henry Clay Morrison.

E. STANLEY JONES: A BRIEF BIOGRAPHICAL SKETCH

A native of Maryland, Jones was converted in 1899, and mentored by a converted alcoholic and Methodist class leader Robert J. Batemen. Under Methodist auspicious he experienced entire sanctification in 1902. Desiring to preach like the famed holiness evangelist Henry Clay Morrison, he enrolled at Asbury College. Later in life Jones would express ambivalence about both the adequacy of his training at Asbury and implicitly the narrowness of the Southern white holiness world view. An academic career that begins with an entire course devoted to *Butler's Analogy* (It seems that even in 1902 Holiness folks found great solace in the thought of dead white male eighteenth century Anglicans) did not seem ideally suited for someone whose primary intent as a student was on mastering the oratorical techniques required of a first rate Holiness evangelist. Still Jones, as he insisted years later, believed that he had been "providentially" guided to Asbury. The two emphases of Asbury that would remain with him were passions for an authentic warm hearted Christian experience and trans-national evangelism. As Jones insightfully notes "Asbury was not held together by a cantankerous conservatism, witch-hunting for heresy . . . [but] a common experience of the fullness of the Holy Ghost." It was at Asbury among "those rougher and more emotional Kentuckians" that the future evangelist had the inner fetters of his sense of intellectual of superiority burned away in an intense spiritual experience that he likened to Pentecost. "I was free—free from the herd and its superiorities and inferiorities," he remembered.[6]

In brief, following graduation from Asbury, Jones served as a missionary pastor in Lucknow, India (1907–1911). In 1915 he experienced a physical and emotional breakdown. Convinced that he had not been called to defend the western evangelical faith he had inherited, Jones now merely introduced Indians to a Christ who both transcended national

---

6. On Jones see David Bundy, "The Kingdom of God in the Theology of E. Stanley Jones," *Wesleyan Theological Journal* 23 (1988) 58–80. See also Douglas M. Strong, *They Walked in the Spirit: Personal Faith and Social Action in America* (Louisville: Westminster John Knox) 77–89. The actual biographical material is drawn from my entry for Jones in the *Historical Dictionary of the Holiness Movement*, edited by William C. Kostlevy et al. (Lanham, MD: Scarecrow, 2001) 146–47. The quotations are from Jones, *A Song of Ascent: A Spiritual Autobiography* (Nashville: Abingdon, 1968) 67, 71.

and cultural boundaries yet paradoxically sought incarnation within these very cultures. His 1925 book, the *Christ of the Indian Road*, which became an international bestseller, expresses his mature Christological reflections.

Continuing his intentional effort to root Christianity in indigenous social institutions, Jones created the first Christian ashram, modeled after Hindu spiritual retreats in 1930. Fascinated by the popularity of Marxism among intellectuals and within the colonial independence movements, Jones visited Russia in 1934. Convinced that the West had much to learn from Marxism, Jones nevertheless believed that Christ's teachings, particularly in the Sermon on the Mount and in the biblical materials articulating the present and coming Kingdom, of God provided a superior model of social regeneration. In *Christ's Alternative to Communism* (1935), *The Choice before Us* (1937) and *Is the Kingdom of God Realism?* (1940), Jones outlined his vision for a non-capitalist egalitarian social order.

On furlough in the United States in the early 1940s, Jones directly confronted America's history of racial segregation. In his 1944 book, *The Christ of the American Road*, Jones urged African Americans to employ Gandhi style civil disobedience to achieve equality in American society. A friend of Gandhi, Jones wrote *Mahatma Gandhi: An Interpretation* following the Indian leader's assassination. An immensely popular author and perhaps the most popular evangelist of the late 1930s and 1940s, Jones never lacked high profile critics. These critics included a virtual popular front of such unlikely allies as principal neo-orthodox figures, evangelicals and some holiness evangelists such as John Paul whose own personal contribution to the inter-racial movement had been the attempted segregation of the Taylor University dining hall during the 1920s. Jones was, in fact, dismissed as a naïve liberal by writers as diverse as Walter Horton, Niebuhr, Keswick author Robert C. McQuilkin and Paul. Even my copy of *The Christ of the Indian Road*, which was once owned by the late great Mennonite theologian John C. Wenger (and Westminster Seminary graduate it should be noted), contains the disclaimer, "read with discrimination."

THE CHILIASM OF HOPE, OR WHY NIEBUHR
UNDERSTOOD JONES AND MOST WESLEYANS DO NOT

The Jones-Niebuhr feud, as close as I can tell, was initiated by Stanley Jones himself in his account of his 1934 trip to the USSR, *Christ's Alternative to Communism*. As Jones wrote, "When Dr. Reinhold Niebuhr says that the new day cannot be accomplished except by force—and by force he must mean military force—he definitely throws away the Christian weapons and the takes the Marxian . . . When the Crusaders waded through blood to capture the holy city of Jerusalem from the Moslems, they found that Christ was not there. He had been lost in the very weapons used."[7]

Niebuhr's response was both curt and direct. Writing several months later, he dismissed the book as "the most perfect swan song of liberal politics." The very suggestion that the "Lord's Year of Jubilee may be nearer than we suppose" was another example of the "sentimental hopes" of a perfectly irrelevant "liberal Christian." In 1937, Jones responded. "Niebuhr is right," Jones said, "when he says that "the conflict between Christianity and Communism is a contest between a religion with an inadequate political strategy, and a social idealism which falsely raises a political strategy to the heights of a religion. But we do not admit that no adequate political strategy is at hand . . . Give us the method of Democracy with no reservation as to its full application, and the Kingdom-of-God motive behind it and the program of the Kingdom of God on earth before it and we can remake the earth."[8]

As Niebuhr suggested Jones clearly believed that the Kingdom of God was intended to be a literal reality occurring on earth among those now living. As the writings of Jones' Asbury mentors make clear, chiliastic ruminations were the common currency of the early twentieth century movement. However the radicalism of early twentieth century holiness millennialism has far more in common with Medieval, Reformation era and English Civil War social radicals than mid- and late-twentieth-century popular apocalyptic writers. To understand that continuity one needs to return to the actual views of Henry Clay Morrison and L. L. Pickett (whose home Jones lived in while a student at Asbury College). Interestingly while both had embraced premillemialism, they remained deeply committed to key elements of the Populism of William Jennings

7. Jones, *Christ's Alternative to Communism* (New York: Abingdon, 1935) 177.

8. Reinhold Niebuhr, *An Interpretation of Christian Ethics* (New York: Harper, 1935) 162. Jones, *The Choice before Us* (New York: Abingdon, 1937) 134.

Bryan. In 1901 Pickett wrote, "He who denied Himself and became poor and homeless ... for the salvation of men will judge the covetousness and selfishness which hoards while others hunger, bloats while others beg, and fattens while others starve." As Southern Democrats inspired by the Populism commonly associated with Bryan, they were hardly given, in E. P. Thompson's telling phrase, to the "chiliasm of despair." In fact, during the first year that Jones lived in the Pickett house in Wilmore, L. L. Pickett was working on a manuscript published in 1903 as *The Renewed Earth or the Coming and Reign of Jesus Christ.* In it Pickett insists that during the coming millennial reign the "poor of the earth shall be the possessors of the kingdom, the glory, the honor and wealth of nations."[9]

A Kentucky native and a Bryan enthusiast, Henry Clay Morrison looked forward to the returning Messiah who would give the poor land, destroy concentrated wealth, and bring peace. "For a number of years," Morrison wrote, "the country has been largely dominated by and, many of its citizens of the poor laboring classes have been enslaved, by a heartless capitalism." As Morrison argued, the Old Testament prophesies of Micah and Isaiah suggested otherwise. God promised a literal liberation for the poor now living to be inaugurated in the near future by Jesus. True to this heritage of holiness radicalism that looked to Jesus for liberation, E. Stanley Jones found much that was familiar in the promises of Communism.[10]

Seventy years later, *Christ's Alternative to Communism* is a very interesting read. "We expect Christianity," Jones wrote, "to outlast Communism because it has a deeper and a more meaningful universe and a firmer ground for believing in man." As Jones insisted, "materialism in the end will lack dynamic." Christianity he believed offered humanity a goal, the Kingdom of God on earth—a Kingdom without poverty, classes and sickness inaugurated by the Lord's Jubilee and empowered not by human effort but the Spirit of God.[11]

As the noted evangelist makes clear in *The Choice before Us,* the choice among Fascism, Communism and Christianity presents Christianity with a real opportunity. As Jones' argued, Christianity actu-

9. On the radicalism of Bryan, see Michael Kazin, *A Godly Hero: The Life of William Jennings Bryan* (New York: Knopf, 2006). L. L. Pickett, *The Blessed Hope of His Glorious Appearing* (Louisville: Pickett, 1901) 37–38; and Pickett, *The Renewal of the Earth or the Coming Reign of Jesus Christ* (Louisville: Pickett, 1903) 30–31.

10. Morrison, *Will God Set Up a Visible Kingdom on Earth?* (Louisville: Pentecostal, 1934) 135–36.

11. Jones, *Christ's Alternative to Communism,* 194.

ally has elements of a real social program, a program announced at the beginning of Jesus' ministry in his "Nazareth Manifesto." It is a manifesto that includes "good news to the poor," release to the captives, freedom to the physically disinherited, setting at liberty the morally and spiritually disinherited, proclaiming the Lord's Year of Jubilee and all this empowered by the "Spirit of the Lord." Further (and of course this is Niebuhr's real objection to Jones' perfectionism) the methods to bring about the Kingdom must be consistent with the Spirit of Christ. In other words, Christians could not use force and war. The reconstruction of the economic, social, and political orders requires means consistent with the intended ends.[12]

How would the Kingdom come? It would come, the mature Jones argued, by "gradualism" and "apocalypticism." The coming of the Kingdom is both like the leaven that gradually works throughout the loaf and the thief who comes suddenly in the night. "While gradualism gives us our task," Jones insisted, "the apocalyptic gives us our hope." In *Is the Kingdom of God Realism?*, a direct response to the skepticism of Niebuhr and other so-called Christian realists, Jones admitted that "the idea of liberalism has been smashed on a million battlefields." There was a time" Jones admitted, "when I was afraid of the apocalyptic side of the coming kingdom. I now see my mistake." It had been the mistake of liberalism that it urged Christians to "build the kingdom." People are told "to see, to enter, to receive" the kingdom not to create it. It is merely accepting God's reign and God's values. As he argued "the Kingdom of God is our nature—our real nature, the way we are made to work."[13]

CONCLUSION

The new apocalyptic that emerges from the thought of the mature Jones has dropped certain elements from the older chiliasm of Pickett and Morrison. It eschews speculative eschatology and assumes a certain degree of human agency. Nevertheless Jones shares a common hope with the old premillennial optimism of his Asbury mentors. The promises of the Old Testament prophets and actual teachings of Jesus assume a rel-

---

12. Jones, *The Choice before Us*, 36–41. It should be noted that John Howard Yoder indicates that his famous contention in the influential *Politics of Jesus* that Jesus was proclaiming a year of Jubilee was proposed by Jones in *Christ's Alternative to Communism*. See John Howard, *The Politics of Jesus* (Grand Rapids: Eerdmans, 1972) 36.

13. Jones, *Is the Kingdom of God Realism?* (New York: Abingdon, 1940) 61–62.

evance usually reserved for Christian radicals such as Anthony, Francis, the Anabaptists, Quakers, and the Catholic Worker Movement. In this regard Jones was and remains a radical.

BIBLIOGRAPHY

Bundy, David. "The Kingdom of God in the Theology of E. Stanley Jones." *Wesleyan Theological Journal* 23 (1998) 58–80.

Graham, Stephan A. *Ordinary Man, Extraordinary Mission: The Life and Work of E. Stanley Jones.* Nashville: Abingdon, 2005.

———. *The Totalitarian Kingdom of God: The Political Philosophy of E. Stanley Jones.* Lanham, MD: University Press of America, 1998.

28

Archibald J. Carey Jr., African Methodism, and the Public Square

Dennis C. Dickerson

ARCHIBALD J. CAREY SR. (1868–1931), a bishop in the African Methodist Episcopal Church and a political broker, and his son and namesake, Archibald J. Carey Jr. (1908–1931), a pastor, attorney, and officeholder, played large roles in Chicago religious and civic affairs through most of the twentieth century. As grounded and self-conscious Wesleyan ministers, the Careys believed "the new creation" required them to work in private and public spheres to bring justice and equity for blacks and the disadvantaged in preparation for the perfecting parousia when Jesus Christ would establish of Kingdom of Grace. The senior Carey through an aggressive advocacy of the Social Gospel as a pastor and bishop and also as a member of the Chicago Civil Service Commission assumed the role as a black rights champion. The junior Carey, who earned the BD from Garrett Biblical Institute at Northwestern University and the LLB from the Kent College of Law, developed two Chicago churches into socially conscious congregations. Additionally, he won two elections as a Chicago alderman and served the Eisenhower Administration as chair of a federal fair employment agency. Through these religious and civic involvements they showed their serious embrace of the tradition of the A.M.E. Church founder, Bishop Richard Allen, who envisaged a Wesleyan denomination that affirmed Wesleyan spirituality, sanctification, and perfectionist practice and a "practical divinity" that stressed Christian formation and Christian witness in the private and public lives of believers. Both Careys integrated within their ministries religious and civic concerns and made each sphere intrinsic to the other as clergy in the pulpit and in the public square.[1]

A METHODIST LEGACY

In an address to the 1960 World Methodist Conference in Oslo, Norway, Archibald J. Carey Jr., as an A.M.E. representative, observed that African American Methodists had become pivotal to the burgeoning civil rights movement. Several A.M.E.s, he said, developed an especially poignant witness for human rights. For example, Rosa Parks, a stewardess at St. Paul A.M.E. Church in Montgomery, Alabama, and a local N.A.A.C.P. activist, helped to spearhead the now famous bus boycott that propelled Martin Luther King Jr. to national prominence. Oliver L. Brown, an A.M.E. pastor in Topeka, Kansas, sued in behalf of his daughter, Linda, because the school nearest to her denied her admission. This suit became the landmark *Brown Vs. The Board of Education* in which the Supreme Court in 1954 declared public school segregation unconstitutional. He also mentioned that James L. Farmer, a member of the Methodist Church's segregated Central Jurisdiction, had become the national head of the Congress of Racial Equality. Carey neglected to credit himself as a C.O.R.E. benefactor in its initial years as a fledgling student organization in Chicago in 1942 and 1943. The first C.O.R.E. members, including Farmer, established their headquarters and held their first national meeting in Carey's Woodlawn A.M.E. Church.[2]

Though he did not specifically use these terms, to be a Methodist for Carey meant the pursuit of "practical divinity" and embodying "the new creation." The legacy of Bishop Richard Allen, the A.M.E. Church founder and a quintessential Wesleyan, shaped Carey's understanding of ministry and its concomitant obligation to fight for the poor and disadvantaged in the public square. Carey called Allen "a fighter against segregation" and "a workman in the building of the Kingdom of God." Bishop Allen, he added, had been "dedicated not only to the calling of God but to service of man" and "in making a kingdom of men (into) a kingdom of heaven." Therefore, black Methodist ministers needed to be involved with the N.A.A.C.P., the National Urban League, and other civil

1. See Joseph Logsdon, "The Reverend A. J. Carey and the Negro in Chicago Politics" (MA Thesis, University of Chicago, 1961); *The Chicago Defender*, April 22, 1981.

2. Archibald J. Carey Jr., "Speech on Negro Methodists," Box 43, Folder 304, *Archibald J. Carey, Jr. Papers*, Chicago Historical Society, Chicago, IL.

rights organizations that aimed at destroying the second class citizen-
ship that had long oppressed African Americans. That was a Wesleyan
mandate and Carey patterned his ministerial career to conform to this
interpretation of Methodism.[3]

Whenever Carey had an opportunity, he reminded religious and political audiences that he was a fourth-generation minister in the African
Methodist Episcopal Church. In Georgia his great-grandfather and
grandfather, both former slaves, and both named Jefferson Carey, served
respectively as a local preacher and itinerant elder. Jefferson Carey Jr. led
congregations throughout the "Empire State of African Methodism" and
participated in politics. Hence, dual commitments to church and civic
affairs were already a family legacy when Archibald J. Carey Sr. was grad-
uated from Atlanta University and commenced as a pastor in Athens,
Georgia, in the 1890s. After a transfer to a large church in Jacksonville,
Florida, where he was involved in the presidential campaign of William
McKinley, Carey became pastor of the large and historic Quinn Chapel
Church in Chicago, Illinois. At this church and others that he served
in the Windy City Carey became a G.O.P. broker and political appoin-
tee whose influence in city politics was unprecedented for an African
American clergyman. Though elected a bishop in 1920 and assigned to
various districts beyond Chicago, he maintained his political profile in
the city until his denomination transferred him in 1928 to preside in
Illinois and its adjacent states. At the time of his father's death in 1931
Archibald J. Carey Jr. had been nurtured in both religious and public
affairs. Bishop Carey paid for the best seminary and legal education for
his son and ordained him to the same Methodist ministry as his three
male forebears.[4]

THE MINISTRY OF ARCHIBALD CAREY JR.

Bishop Carey assigned his son in 1930 to his first pastoral appointment, a
mission congregation of 49 members. Effective preaching and a socially

3. Archibald J. Carey Jr., "Address to the Connectional Council," February 25, 1953,
Box 14, Folder 95; Carey, "Because My Time in Office Expires," 1950?, Box 10, Folder 68,
AJC, JR. PAPERS, CHS.

4. Archibald J. Carey Jr., "Speech," Box 50, Folder 356; "Prominent Citizen File for
Park Name" attached to George S. Cooley to AJC, JR., April 29, 1958, *AJC, JR. PAPERS*;
CHS; *Chicago Daily Journal*, April 13, 1927; Logsdon, 6; 8; Richard R. Wright Jr., *The
Bishops of The African Methodist Episcopal Church* (Nashville: A.M.E. Sunday School
Union, 1963) 127–29.

conscious ministry expanded the church to 1,500 members a decade later. By 1938 the junior Carey raised a building fund of $40,000 and later purchased a large edifice and other properties. In 1949 Bishop George W. Baber re-assigned Carey to Quinn Chapel, the same church that the elder Carey had served. Similar membership increases and physical improvements occurred during a pastorate that lasted into the 1960s. At both churches Carey became known as a community activist. In the 1930s he pressed the school board to provide a new building for black residents. Some urged his appointment to the city school board. When A. Philip Randolph initiated the March on Washington Movement to agitate for federal guarantees against employment discrimination, Carey became an avid supporter. He was a supporter of the Scottsboro Defense Committee in 1937 and joined other Chicagoans in sponsoring a rally to free the unjustly incarcerated black Alabamians. He also backed efforts for a federal ban on lynching. In the late 1940s Carey became particularly active in the N.A.A.C.P. and joined its nationwide speaking circuit. He usually viewed the African American struggle for freedom in a global context. He often compared the condition of blacks with colonized peoples in the Third World and noted that politicians who ignored racism in America imperiled the nation's international credibility.[5]

Like his father, Carey, while retaining his pastorates, became politically involved. He was elected and reelected as a Republican as an alderman for Chicago's Third Ward. In 1949 he fought a long but unsuccessful battle to outlaw racial discrimination in publicly funded housing. The Carey Ordinance, though failing to pass, won nationwide notice and identified Carey as an emerging civil rights spokesman. That was his platform in an unsuccessful run for Congress in 1950 against the powerful Congressman William L. Dawson and his effective Democratic political machine. Though he lost his aldermanic position in 1955 against a Dawson backed opponent, Carey already had been rescued as a national G.O.P. officeholder. As an active campaigner for Dwight D. Eisenhower, Carey who had endorsed the General's 1952 presidential nomination, had become an attractive Republican speaker. At the convention Carey

5. Richard R. Wright Jr., *Encyclopedia of African Methodism* (Philadelphia: Book Concern of the A.M.E. Church, 1947) 62–63; *The Chicago Defender*, March 21, 1936; March 28, 1936; April 4, 1936, Box 1, 1909–April 1942 (1923–1936) 1-1 Folder; John Dale Russell to Mabel P. Simpson, October 5, 1939; Edward J. Kelly to John W. Banks, October 4, 1939; Archibald J. Carey Jr. to Madison Carey Jr., June 21, 1943, Box 2, Folder 8 (January–June 1943), *AJC, JR. PAPERS*, CHS.

said it had been "the Republican Party that freed America of the blot of slavery." Then he asked, "what does the Negro-American want?" The answer was "nothing special." He declared "all we want is the right to live and work and play, to vote and be promoted, to fight for our country and hope to be President, like everyone else." Carey added "We, Negro-Americans, sing with other Americans:[6]

> My country, 'tis of thee
> Sweet land of liberty
> Of thee I sing
> Land where my fathers died
> Land of the Pilgrim's pride
> From every mountain side
> Let freedom ring!"

Then in a rhythmic refrain he proclaimed:

> "From every mountain side, freedom ring.
> Not only from the Green Mountains and
> The White Mountains of Vermont and New Hampshire;
> Not only from the Catskills of New York, but from
> The Ozarks in Arkansas; from the Stone Mountain in
> Georgia, from the Great Smokies of Tennessee and
> From the Blue Ridge Mountains of Virginia
> Not only for the minorities of the United States, but for the
> Persecuted of Europe, for the rejected of Asia, for the
> Disfranchised of South Africa and for the disinherited of
> All earth-may the Republican Party, under God, from
> Every mountain side, LET FREEDOM RING."[7]

Martin Luther King Jr. in his famous "I Have a Dream" speech borrowed liberally from Carey's Republican rhetoric. But it was fine with the Chicago pastor and politician. He had become a confidante to King while the young minister was initiating nonviolent civil rights campaigns from his pastorate in Montgomery, Alabama. Carey became a background benefactor to the civil rights movement. Not only did he advise King, but he served as Eisenhower's Chairman of a federal commission against government employment discrimination. Both locally and nationally

---

6. Dennis C. Dickerson, *A Liberated Past: Explorations in A.M.E. Church History* (Nashville: A.M.E. Sunday School Union, 2003) 177.

7. Ibid., 178–79

Carey was living out a Wesleyan witness to bring his sermons in behalf of the disadvantaged into the public square.[8]

In the 1960s, after a few unsuccessful attempts, Carey won a judgeship in Chicago, but only after switching from the G.O.P. to the Democrats. Though a stroke compelled him to relinquish an active pastorate, Carey continued on the bench for several additional years and stayed as pastor-emeritus at Quinn Chapel. His death in 1981 occurred in the wake of a busy schedule of speaking, preaching, and advocating the Wesley/Allen legacy of church and civic involvement.

8. Ibid., 177; W. Arthur McCoy to Maxwell Raab, November 28, 1956, Box 29, Folder 198; "Dr. Carey's Opening Remarks," Box 33, Folder 28; *AJC, JR. PAPERS*, CHS; Memorandum: Max(well) Raab to Governor (Sherman) Adams, March 13, 1957, *Central Files*, Official File, Box 474, 103-U, President's Committee on Government Employment Policy (4), Dwight D. Eisenhower Library, Abilene, Kansas.

29

Mildred Bangs Wynkoop

Bridging the Credibility Gap

Diane K. Leclerc

Mildred Bangs Wynkoop emerged as a significant theologian in the Holiness movement in the late 1960s. Her denominational context was the Church of the Nazarene, but her influence has been broader. Interestingly, Wynkoop's scholarly contributions to the church started late in her life. She did not receive her doctorate until the age of 50. Subsequently, she spent many of her first years teaching in relative seclusion and anonymity, on assignment in Japan away from the "significant" theological chatter in the American context of Nazarene higher education. She could have remained that way, for she experienced difficulty finding employment inside the denomination upon her return from Asia. But she landed, very unexpectedly for this thoroughly Northwestern woman, in the deep South at Trevecca Nazarene College. Ironically perhaps, this was where she was embraced and given opportunities as (Religion) professor and scholar—unheard of for a Nazarene woman.[1] But she is not being chosen per se for this volume because of

1. The only other woman to teach religion classes in a Nazarene College in the United States prior to Mildred Bangs Wynkoop was Dr. Olive Winchester, who taught New Testament and Greek at Northwest Nazarene College in the 1920s. Besides short stints by women given teaching opportunities by various "Missionary in Residence" programs, I was the next woman to teach after Wynkoop, beginning my career at Northwest Nazarene University as Professor of Historical Theology in 1998. Simultaneous to my hiring, Lisa Bernal began teaching Ethics at Point Loma Nazarene University. Presently, the following women teach in Nazarene Universities: Jeanne Serrão, Professor of New

her gender. It is her theology that gave the movement new language, new metaphors, new theological paradigms for a new day.

The world obviously shifted in dramatic ways in the 1960s. As much as the Holiness movement might have wanted to isolate itself from the social upheaval around it,[2] and hold on to a pejorative view of any theological "correlationalism" with such radical cultural change, for an emerging generation with new eyes, theology as usual was inadequate. This new theological voice might itself be over sixty years old, but it had a tenor that offered hope. The Holiness movement was not dead (yet).[3] The question was, would it allow this voice and others like it to speak? Could it let go of its legalism, personified by a post-war American suburban "perfectionism," and all of its unnamed sins? Mildred Bangs Wynkoop represents one attempt to call the movement to higher ground.

HER LIFE AND MINISTRY

Mildred Bangs was born in Seattle in 1905. Her parents were immigrants, her mother from Switzerland, and her father from Norway. Mildred was the oldest of five—she had three sisters, and one younger brother, Carl (who also became a religious academic as Mildred would). Her parents attended the Salvation Army in Seattle, but heard of the beginnings of the Church of the Nazarene, and became extremely dedicated to their local congregation in Seattle as original members. Her father liked to believe that he was somehow related to the famous Methodist minister, Nathan Bangs, but it is unlikely.[4] Mildred was, however, influenced by

---

Testament at Mount Vernon Nazarene University; Heather Ross, Professor of Philosophy at Point Loma Nazarene University; Rhonda Carrim, Professor of Bible and Theology at Northwest Nazarene University; Lori Niles, Professor of Christian Education at Mid-America Nazarene University; and Mary Lou Shea, Professor of Church History and Missions at Eastern Nazarene College. Judy Schwantz, Professor of Pastoral Theology, and Vickie Copp, Professor of Supervised Ministry teach at Nazarene Theological Seminary. Just last year, Carol Rotz, Professor of New Testament retired from NNU, and Dr. Mary Paul, Professor at Olivet moved into a Vice President position at PLNU. The denomination has several women pursuing PhDs presently, including one at Princeton and one at SMU. It is obvious that Wykoop broke through an important glass ceiling.

2. See the "Introduction" to Donald Dayton, *Discovering An Evangelical Heritage* (Peabody, MA: Hendrickson, 1988), for an insightful commentary of just such an occurrence.

3. The idea that "the Holiness Movement is dead" was a hotly debated topic as the last century came to a close.

4. Her father most likely arrived in America with the name "Bang" rather than "Bangs."

some of the great early preachers of the Holiness Movement and the young Nazarene denomination, including Phineas Bresee.

Highly influential in Mildred's life was H. Orton Wiley, the first "real" theologian of the Church of the Nazarene.[5] He was president of Northwest Nazarene College when Mildred came as a freshman. She traveled with him in the college quartet as they ministered throughout the Northwest region. When Wiley decided to move to Pasadena Nazarene College as its president (which became Point Loma Nazarene College/ University years later), Mildred followed. She majored in sociology, but was highly active in the literary society and the ministerial fellowships, foreshadows of what was to come.

It was at Pasadena that Mildred met Ralph Wynkoop. They traveled together in the same singing group. After graduating with both an AB and ThB degree, Mildred married Ralph in 1928; they began their life together as evangelists.[6] They both preached, and were in high demand in California, Oregon, and Washington. They would also pastor together through the years. (Mildred was actually ordained before Ralph.) At times, she struggled with whether she was living in the holiness experience about which she preached, but finally settled the question regarding her own sanctification. This did not, however, prevent her from experiencing some very dark nights. There is a period in the late 30s when her journal reveals some "sickness" that made her feel weak, nauseous, faint for several weeks. She then abruptly stops her journal, not picking it up again for years. A possible miscarriage? She never had children, and seems to have had medical problems that prevented it.[7]

Mildred had, from an early age, been an insatiable learner. Within the decade of the mid 1940s to the mid 50s she accomplished something remarkable. She received a Master's degree from the University of Oregon, a Master of Divinity degree from Western Evangelical Seminary (W.E.S.), and a ThD, from Northern Baptist University in Chicago at the age of 50. During this time, she also commenced her teaching career at her seminary alma mater, W.E.S. Her associations there would take

5. Wiley had been influenced by Boston Personalism. In college, Mildred had the responsibility to type many of Wiley's handwritten notes and manuscripts, as well as sit under his teaching.

6. An interesting element of Mildred's itinerant ministry was that she used magic to interest her audiences, apparently not unheard of for evangelists of the 1930s and 40s.

7. Or the illness could have been related to a previous bout with tuberculosis.

her to various places in Asia, Taiwan being her favorite country because of its people's eager receptivity. After this short term missionary experience, she and her husband Ralph were asked to go to Japan, where she served as president and professor at Japan Christian Junior College and Japanese Nazarene Theological Seminary (from 1960–1966). She studied the culture intensely, attempting to understand not only how relationships worked, but also how she might best articulate holiness theology to the Asian mind. It is clear that this experience expanded her own "theological vocabulary" that later has had such a profound effect on those who read her "wholistic" understanding of holiness.

After returning from Japan, she searched for a job. For a time, it seemed that she had more respect from colleges outside than within her own denomination. But in the end, she joined the religion faculty at Trevecca Nazarene College under the leadership of Rev. Dr. William Greathouse, who was extremely interested in her scholarship ever since he read her *Foundations of Wesleyan-Arminian Theology*.[8] Her students loved her style of teaching, and her personal interest in their lives. She was voted "Professor of the Year" during her tenure there. When Dr. Greathouse, a highly recognized theologian in his own right, was elected president of Nazarene Theological Seminary, he very much wanted to take Mildred Bangs Wynkoop with him. He all but promised this would happen, but he did not have to power to enact it as quickly as he had anticipated. It took several years before Wynkoop joined the Seminary faculty as "theologian in residence" in 1976 (the first woman ever to be faculty there). The two colleagues were together again. But in a strange "providential" turn of events, Greathouse was elected General Superintendent soon after the Wynkoops went to Kansas City. At NTS, like everywhere else she taught, she was deeply loved by her students, and recognized as a remarkable scholar. And yet, at the seminary and in the denominational publishing house, she had her antagonists.

As a theologian, she was well-known and a much sought after speaker, both inside and outside the denomination; she traveled to many non-Nazarene Holiness colleges, Methodist gatherings, and even Notre Dame. In 1974 she was elected by her peers to be President of the Wesleyan Theological Society. But criticism of her work by persons within the denomination continued until long after her death. For her

---

8. Mildred Bangs Wynkoop, *Foundations of Wesleyan-Arminian Theology* (Kansas City, MO: Beacon Hill, 1967).

admirers, it was her remarkable book published in 1972, *A Theology of Love: the Dynamic of Wesleyanism*, that "revolutionized" the Church of the Nazarene in its articulation of holiness and "saved" the denomination from imploding on its own legalism. It was her interpretation of John Wesley's theology of Perfect Love that further fueled a movement toward "rediscovering Wesley" as a way of moving the Movement forward.

Like Wesley, Wynkoop was eclectic in her thought, creative, synthetic, and thus unique. What the book did was challenge models that had represented the "only" perspective of the denomination on entire sanctification. This created tension for those in leadership or otherwise (who mistakenly misunderstood the *language* that they used as equivalent to the *spiritual reality* of what they articulated); and for many (particularly theologian Richard S. Taylor),[9] Wynkoop was deemed too radical (even heretical) not to counter forcefully. Those who had been struggling with the rigidity of the denomination's articulation found in Wynkoop a kindred spirit. Countless have said it was Wynkoop's book that kept them in the denomination.[10] For many, it came "just in time." The book continues to be used in Nazarene higher education, and continues, over thirty years later, to speak deeply to its readers. It also still has its critics.

What made Wynkoop's theology so helpful to so many? The following will serve as the most basic introduction to her unique syntheses.

"PLAIN TRUTH FOR PLAIN PEOPLE"

Not unlike Phoebe Palmer a century before, a young pre-adolescent Mildred believed that "if she ever became a preacher, she would say things so that they could be understood." Wynkoop fulfilled her promise. During both her preaching and teaching careers, she seeks to follow John Wesley's desire to give "plain truth for plain people."[11] Wynkoop quotes Wesley at length on this point. "I labor to avoid all words," Wesley says, "which are not used in common life; and, in particular, those kinds of technical terms that so frequently occur in bodies of divinity."[12] She

9. Taylor was a professor of theology at Nazarene Theological Seminary, and editor at Nazarene Publishing House.

10. See a collection of letters to Wynkoop held at Nazarene Archives, Kansas City, Missouri.

11. From Wesley's preface to his *Standard Sermons*.

12. Ibid.

then says that Wesley's sentiment on this point "underlines [her] entire book."[13] In this vein, Wynkoop offers her readers a "glossary of words" at the very beginning of her treatise. Here she defines dozens of words of Holiness lingo. She does not sacrifice anything in her search for "plain truth." *A Theology of Love* does not lack, in any way, theological depth or sophistication. Indeed her "problem with words" goes deeper than the need to communicate effectively to everyone.

"THE PROBLEM WITH WORDS"

Wynkoop was keenly aware, in a way that some of her peers were not, that language is metaphorical. But rather than conclude "words don't matter," Wynkoop believed that words that paint metaphors participate in the very spiritual reality to which they point. She writes,

> Modern [persons] cannot 'hear' the disembodied word—mere sounds whose connotation has not been formed by contact with living examples of their true meaning. Holiness theology must become incarnate . . . The peculiarity of Wesleyan theology is its emphasis on holiness as personal experience . . . Scriptural holiness means much more than lacing theology together with proper words—even biblical words. It means to hold together in vital, everyday life such diverse matters as life and doctrine, crisis and process, the absolute and the relative, divine and human, spiritual and natural, the individual and society, separation from the world and full involvement in it, proclamation and reconciliation (to name a few), with losing the essential vitality of either.[14]

Implicit in her comments is her concern that her immediate predecessors and peers had begun to mistake certain privileged metaphors for holiness for holiness itself. Holiness language had become rigidified, reified, and antiquated. Her deeper concern was that this had brought a "credibility gap" between holiness doctrine and praxis in the Church of the Nazarene.

"THE CREDIBILITY GAP"

At the very heart of Wynkoop's theology is a loyalty to the Wesleyan-Holiness doctrines of holiness and sanctification. She states the

13. Mildred Bangs Wynkoop, *A Theology of Love: The Dynamic of Wesleyanism* (Kansas City, MO: Beacon Hill, 1972).

14. Ibid., 43–44.

Wesleyanism's "peculiar and identifying and absolutely essential character is God's grace actualized in life."[15] Out of her teaching experience with "young people" Wynkoop began to discern a "credibility gap" between what the students had been taught as denominational doctrine and how they watched people live their lives. She labels what they had been taught "perfectionism" as opposed to Wesley's understanding of Christian perfection. In sum, it contained expectations and idealisms regarding holiness that could never really be lived. "When this theology retreats from 'history'" she warns, "curling back in on itself in protective isolation, it becomes no more than an empty shell whose beauty condemns it."[16] The deep conviction that holiness must "live" in human life brought her to a theology which intriguingly synthesized an intense Wesleyan optimism about grace with the focus on human experience brought by the usually foreboding philosophy of existentialism.

FROM EXISTENTIALISM TO RELATIONALISM

In a very early attempt to articulate her emerging theology of holiness, Wynkoop penned an unpublished work entitled, "An Existential Interpretation of the Doctrine of Holiness."[17] What she finds in existentialism is a radical honesty about human life. This, combined with her reflection on Wesley's early Methodism and its extreme practicality, led her to what could be identified as a clear Wynkoopian mantra. Holiness must breathe, its heart must beat, its feet must walk in the footsteps of Christ. Holiness must live. But more so, holiness only exists in its expression, which is love. By taking existentialism's hyper-focused "humanism" and putting it in dialogue with the power of God's grace to make us truly loving persons and communities, "existentialism" becomes "relationalism." Love is expressed in relationships, namely our relationship with God and others. Indeed the purpose for which we are created is not to "glorify God and enjoy him forever," but to *love* God with our entire being and to *love* our neighbors as ourselves. In fact, this human potential for love is the *Imago Dei* for Wynkoop. In sum, love (and therefore holiness) lives only in the "dynamic" between God and humans. This re-

---

15. Ibid., 44.

16. Ibid.

17. I own one of the few typewritten manuscripts she copied. It is over 300 pages in length. It was written in the year 1958; some the material from this work makes it into *Theology of Love*, published in 1972.

lationalism, misunderstood, was one of the points that brought the most heat from her critics.

SIN AND SANCTIFICATION

If holiness is relational for Wynkoop, then so is her hamartiology. Unfortunately Wynkoop has been misinterpreted as only believing in "positional holiness" (a charge that invokes a simultaneous suspicion of a masked Calvinism—holiness being "imputed righteousness" alone). This is a clear misunderstanding of Wynkoop's theology. In reality, she is among the strongest supporters of Wesley's understanding of "imparted righteousness" and "real" sanctification. Part of the misunderstanding of her theology of holiness comes from the lack of tolerance of various metaphors elaborated above. But it goes even deeper. Wynkoop stands with traditional Christianity (Augustine in particular) in its view that (technically) sin does not "exist." Augustine, who follows Plato on this point, imagines sin without substance; sin is nothing other than the *absence* of Good. It had become commonplace in the language of holiness writers in the mid-twentieth century to explicate sin as if it were "substantival." This can be most clearly seen in the preferenced metaphor for sanctification during this era: one is sanctified when sin (or the sinful nature) is *eradicated*. Wynkoop rightly resists this tendency. Holiness would be best defined under this paradigm by the absence of sin. But Wynkoop, following Wesley, believes that defining holiness by an absence is nonsensical. Holiness is the *presence* of love. The "sinlessness" model led many to envision entire sanctification as a *state* of grace. This would never do for Wynkoop. Holiness, even entire sanctification is a *dynamic* that never "arrives" at a state, for every subsequent moment is a moment to actualize love. And again, this love is the purpose of our individual and collective humanity.

HUMANIZING GRACE

One of the most powerful insights of Mildred Bangs Wynkoop is her simple assertion that to become truly holy is to become truly human. Sin distorts true humanity, is alien to it, and destructive of it. Sin enslaves our true selves; sanctification frees us to become our true selves. Similarly, holiness can never be defined as something "superhuman" for which to strive. Rather, the sanctifying grace of God renews us in the image of God and restores to us our true experience of being fully human.

For those who remained a part of a denomination obviously suffering the effects of a period of perfectionistic legalism, Wynkoop's voice rang out as a call to freedom in Christ's grace—a message very present in the early years of the Holiness movement, but one that had been increasingly muffled over the century. In Wesley's day, this metaphor of freedom was expressed in the pursuit of "Christian Perfection." In America, the metaphor shifted to the Pentecostal power of the Holy Spirit to free us from the oppression of sin (and at times, from social oppression as well). Wynkoop was not afraid to offer new metaphors in order to bring doctrine and real life into alignment. Her example should spur us on to find ways to connect the reality of the holiness message with life, real life, in the twentieth century.

PART FIVE

Pastoral Response

LAURA GUY

How does one respond to God's call to take on a big problem? For Moses, the response he gives God in Exodus 3 is incredulity. If God wants to find someone to take on a problem as big as the enslavement of the Hebrews, then surely God could find someone more qualified than Moses. The one chosen for that job should be holy and righteous, a charismatic speaker and born leader. Moses was well aware of his own limitations, his own sinfulness. How could God use a flawed individual such as him to change the plight of a whole nation of enslaved people? Why would God choose him? Yet it was precisely the context of Moses's life and his relationship to this God who hears the cries of oppressed people that compelled Moses to do something. He, too, had heard the cries of the slaves and seen the brutality under which they lived. His reluctant obedience became the catalyst to liberate God's people and change the course of history.

I see that same contextualized call in the lives of these men and women of faith who lived in the early part of the twentieth century. They, too, saw the conditions around them that created suffering. Unlike Moses, however, they had access to newly created mass media that allowed them to see and hear more than just the suffering in their local communities. They saw injustice everywhere and heard the cries of the oppressed in cities all over the nation and even around the world. People of faith knew that the world was not the way God wanted it to be. And, like Moses, they also heard God's call to do something about it.

For Carey and Wynkoop, the barriers of gender and race in the U.S. became intolerable when placed on the world stage. They saw that foreign countries were making greater progress in civil rights than this "Christian nation." Carey chose to pursue racial equality through active means, whereas Wynkoop appeared to break glass ceilings using her intellect and personality. The twentieth century also brought news to the world stage of wars spanning continents and experiments with socialism—Christian and otherwise. Jones developed a theology that encompassed and addressed those fearful changes. Henry Clay Morrison and others felt compelled by God to define holiness concretely, in terms of what it was against rather than what it meant in strictly theoretical terms. In the quickly-changing world of the twentieth century, there were all kinds of societal ills for holiness to stand against.

Like Moses, each of these holy activists was aware of his or her limitations, and they must have had moments of incredulity, too. Before they became outspoken champions of the Gospel, they were just ordinary folks. God chose them for their tasks because they too lived in the right place at the right time to take on the big problems God wanted to challenge. Their reluctant obedience became the catalyst to liberate God's people and change the course of history.

It is so easy for the church to read stories of these heroes in the faith—biblical heroes and historic heroes—and think, "Wow, what faith they must have had!" We seem to overlook the truth that they were ordinary people who were called out by God to do extraordinary things because they lived in the right place at the right time and had the right gifts of the Spirit to change the status quo. More importantly, they said "yes" to God's call, moving forward in faith, trusting in God even when they couldn't see the next step. That's what it takes to become a person who changes the world.

To raise the next generation of men and women who will speak up and step out in faith, we must continue to tell the stories of these ordinary people empowered by an extraordinary God. We must recount the lives of those who saw that things needed to be changed, and who said "yes" when God called them to change the things they saw. The more we celebrate and remember what they accomplished in their contexts, the more opportunities we have to hear what God is calling us to do in the world in which we live.

What might change for us, as the church, if we began to see our-selves as ordinary folks who happen to live in the right context, the right place and time, to make a difference? After all, we, too, hear cries of injustice and suffering in our local communities and in the global com-munity. We see places where the Good News has yet to be proclaimed. We know that the world is not the way God intends it to be. What if we saw ourselves as the very ordinary, flawed people that God is calling to change the world? What if we began to see our context, the place and time in which we live, as a Spiritual gift, something God has given us for the purpose of mission and ministry? God intends for us to use *our* circumstances, however ordinary they may be, to impact the world with the Gospel message. The days of heroes are not over yet.

PART SIX

Interpretations

PART SIX

Introduction

INTERPRETING A TRADITION AS diverse as the Wesleyan, Holiness and Pentecostal family is not simple. It requires an attention to what they share in common that does not obscure distinctive differences of theology, historical context, ethnicity, gender and personality. But in addition, there is no one way to "sum up" this tradition. Dozens of insightful interpretations from multiple perspectives are possible. We have decided in this volume to include four interpretations, all of which emerged out of presentations and discussions at meetings of the Wesleyan/Pentecostal Consultation.

From an historical perspective, John H. Wigger identifies features of piety, cultural engagement, and organization as common to all of these movements and argues retaining or regaining them will be vital to their future flourishing. Stephen W. Rankin, taking a theological approach, shows how recent philosophical insights on the cognitive and evaluative role of emotions invites these movements to reclaim the Wesleyan theology of holy affections or tempers, and vigorously proclaim the promise of sanctification to the church and world today. Philip R. Hamner, from a pastor's perspective, encourages churches to listen afresh to the shared witness of these movements, and in the process recover a wider and deeper vision of the power of the gospel, the mission of God, and how to navigate the tension between cultural relevance and cultural accommodation. Finally, drawing on a discussion that occurred during a meeting of the Consultation, Henry H. Knight III develops the theme of a "new humanity" marked by holiness and power, showing how this vision was ecclesial as well as personal, and called for new or renewed churches marked especially by holiness and apostolicity.

30

A Historical Interpretation

John H. Wigger

Picture all of the people presented in this volume gathered together in one place to discuss the movements they helped to found and direct, a kind of time travelers' reunion for the leaders of the Wesleyan, Holiness, and Pentecostal movements. There would of course be much to divide them in terms of dress, manners, and sensibilities. Some would be surprised at how short John Wesley was or how little Francis Asbury ate. A few might give Lorenzo Dow a wide berth, wishing he had paid more attention to personal hygiene. There would also be differences over doctrine and belief, including healing, approaches to reforming society, women in ministry, race, speaking in tongues, the end times, and what exactly it means to be baptized in the Holy Spirit. But would these differences prove insurmountable, or would our time travelers recognize in one another a set of more basic connections? Would they see one another as brothers and sisters in the faith, or as distant and somewhat disagreeable cousins?

This volume is built on the premise that there is indeed a close family resemblance between the Wesleyan, Holiness, and Pentecostal movements across nearly four centuries. The individual chapters in this volume confirm this resemblance, reflecting again and again common traits across institutional affiliations, cultural contexts, and time. Though some of the subjects of this volume were more closely affiliated than others, I would like to suggest that three basic characteristics connect them all.

First, they valued piety and spiritual discipline, the persistent call to holiness, above nearly all else. If nothing else, the leaders of these movements would have been able to pray together, or at least would have respected one another for the time they spent in prayer and Bible reading. The pursuit of "holiness of heart and life" came before everything else for John Wesley. When Francis Asbury rose at 4 or 5 a.m. to pray in the stillness before dawn, as was his custom, he would not have been alone. Whenever this focus on piety waned in one channel of the Wesleyan tradition, it was picked up in another. Many of the groups discussed in this volume were started as a reaction against a perceived loss of discipline and real spiritual depth in the parent church. This was certainly the case with B. T. Roberts and the Free Methodist Church and Phineas Bresee and the Church of the Nazarene. But across the tradition as a whole, this emphasis on piety represents more of a continuity than a point of disagreement.

Implicit in this quest for holiness was the belief that God still speaks to believers and intervenes in their lives. The autobiography of Benjamin Abbott (1732–1796), who spent most of his career as an unpaid American Methodist local preacher, is filled with stories of visions, prophetic dreams and noisy meetings at which people fell, slain in the Spirit. The work of the Holy Spirit was anything but remote as Abbott experienced it. At least twenty-one editions of his memoir were published between 1813 and 1892. It is a testament to the force of this idea that Abbott's autobiography was widely read by holiness people and early Pentecostals, who saw Abbott as one of them. Frank Bartleman, chronicler of the early Pentecostal movement, recalled receiving "great help" from Abbott's autobiography about 1903.[1] Perhaps this focus on experience has at times "impoverished" the Wesleyan understanding of doctrine, as Steve Rankin suggests, but it has also freed and engaged countless believers who could lay little claim to a sophisticated theological education.

Along with a certain base-line piety, Wesleyan, Holiness, and Pentecostal people had an instinctive feel for cultural engagement. Here the list could include every person discussed in this volume, to one degree

---

1. Benjamin Abbott, *The Experience and Gospel Labors of the Rev. Benjamin Abbott* (New York: Daniel Hitt and Thomas Ware, 1813), and later editions; Frank Bartleman, *From Plow to Pulpit, From Maine to California* (Los Angeles: Bartleman, 1924; reprinted in *Witness to Pentecost: The Life of Frank Bartleman* (New York: Garland, 1985) 95–96.

or another. Phoebe Palmer shaped Wesleyan holiness to fit the parlors of New York City, Daniel Payne sought to transform the lives of former slaves by driving out "heathenish" worship from the A.M.E. Church and replacing it with a more refined and dignified version of Wesleyanism, Amanda Berry Smith used her ministry in part to bridge the divide between black Methodism and the white holiness movement, Maria Woodworth-Etter deliberately staged her big tent revivals to engage new audiences in cities like St. Louis, and Aimee Semple McPherson, perhaps more than anyone else, tried a number of new approaches, including radio and elaborately staged productions that blurred the line between preaching and Hollywood.

Yet the embrace of popular culture in general and consumerism in particular was never complete or without reservation. Ministry to the poor remained a significant focus for many of the people and groups covered in this volume, as did an admiration for voluntary poverty and a distrust of lavish consumption. John Wesley often preached against "the deceitfulness of riches." He urged his followers to "gain" all they could, "save" all they could, and then "give" all they could, though he often had cause to lament that they were better at the first two than the third.[2] Likewise Richard Allen focused much of his energy on support for the poor in Philadelphia, as did Phineas Bresee in Los Angeles. Much the same could be said of B. T. Roberts, Aimee Semple McPherson, and Ida Robinson.

Wesleyan, Holiness, and Pentecostal people also engaged culture on a number of other levels, whether it be opposition to slavery in antebellum America, women in ministry, or civil rights. Examples here include B. T. Roberts and the Free Methodists, who were forthrightly opposed to slavery; Aimee Semple McPherson and Ida Robinson, who set a pattern of women's leadership; and Archibald Carey, a powerful voice for black rights in the twentieth century.

Along with their piety and cultural engagement, Wesleyan, Holiness, and Pentecostal leaders built churches and ministries that were effectively organized. The administrative cohesion of early Methodism under John Wesley and Francis Asbury are well known. The Holiness and Pentecostal movements do not represent a single organizational structure, but within the scope of these movements ambitious leaders

---

2. *The Works of John Wesley*, ed. Albert C. Outler, vol. 2, *Sermons II, 34–70* (Nashville: Abingdon, 1985) 560–61.

constructed networks that reached around the world with astonishing speed. The numbers who visited the Azusa Street revival and then carried its message across the United States and to distant corners of the world is truly astonishing. Aimee Semple McPherson's ministry at Angelus Temple carried on a wide range of activities designed to contact people at many different points of need, everything from prison ministry, to meals, to emergency transportation. Schisms within the Wesleyan, Holiness, and Pentecostal tradition have not been infrequent, but often they have led to new and effective ways of doing things.

Key to this organizational success was the degree to which these groups allowed, even demanded, that ordinary believers take an active role in the daily life of their churches. Early American Methodists drew thousands of people into leadership roles as class leaders, exhorters, and local and itinerant preachers in a way that the churches of colonial America never allowed. The Methodists were able to do this in part because they created a culture of discipline among members, beginning with mandatory attendance at class meetings and love feasts limited to members only. Later Holiness and Pentecostal groups nurtured a similar culture of discipline through similar programs and structures. For all of his oddities, John Alexander Dowie followed this pattern by establishing his army of "Seventies," trained lay volunteers sent out two by two, first in Chicago and then to other U.S. cities and around the world.

What is the more recent legacy of these patterns? A great deal of continuity remains, but its distribution has become increasingly uneven. While many groups continue to grow, particularly outside the United States, some have seen membership in America decline. At the other end of the spectrum are ministries that have grown rapidly, at least in the short term, by selecting out certain elements of the Wesleyan, Holiness, and Pentecostal tradition. A good example is Jim Bakker and his PTL television network and Heritage USA theme park, complete with giant water slides and an upscale hotel. Ordained in the Assemblies of God, there was much about Bakker's early ministry that placed him well within the bounds of one of the leading Pentecostal denominations. Like many of the people discussed in this volume, Bakker had an instinctive feel for the subtle currents of popular culture, particularly the consumerism and emphases on self help and self fulfillment that became so much a part of American life after World War II. God loves you, you can make it, tomorrow will be a better day.[3]

Both his TV ministry and theme park allowed Bakker to market his ideas. Television provided a platform to reach a large audience who felt unfulfilled in their local church, who were looking for something more dynamic and seemingly relevant to the world around them. These were the same impulses that had drawn people to camp meetings in the early nineteenth century, big tent revivals in the late-nineteenth century, and radio broadcasts in the mid-twentieth century. Heritage USA allowed Bakker's followers to step outside their daily lives, if only for a time, and focus on things that seemed more important. Heritage included ample opportunity to pray, sing, and attend more traditional religious meetings, but it added a new dimension of fun and recreation, reflecting a growing preoccupation with the good life. At its height, Heritage USA attracted nearly six million visitors a year.

But Bakker was different from most of the leaders discussed in this volume in ways that ultimately brought him down. Television allowed for the appearance of transparency while at the same time allowing Bakker to shield much of his life from public view. In contrast, Francis Asbury spent his forty-five year career in America living as a houseguest among his people, literally rubbing shoulders with them every day. They saw him at unguarded moments, when he got up in the morning and when he went to bed at night. Bakker's followers saw him only for an hour or so a day, across the vast divide of the camera lens, on a set that he skillfully manipulated. While his piety in front of the camera seemed genuine and energetic, away from the camera he spent little time in prayer or study.

---

3. The literature on Bakker and PTL is fairly large. It includes James A. Albert, *Jim Bakker: Miscarriage of Justice?* (Chicago: Open Court, 1998); Jay Bakker, *Son of a Preacher Man: My Search for Grace in the Shadows* (New York: HarperCollins, 2001); Jim Bakker, *I Was Wrong* (Nashville: Nelson, 1996); Tammy Bakker, *I Gotta Be Me* (Harrison, AR: New Leaf, 1978); Joe E. Barnhart, *Jim and Tammy: Charismatic Intrigue Inside PTL* (Buffalo, NY: Prometheus, 1988); Jeffrey K. Hadden and Anson Shupe, *Televangelism: Power and Politics on God's Frontier* (New York: Holt, 1988); Hunter James, *Smile Pretty and Say Jesus: The Last Great Days of PTL* (Athens: University of Georgia Press, 1993); Larry Martz, *Ministry of Greed: The Inside Story of the Televangelists and Their Holy Wars* (New York: Weidenfeld & Nicolson, 1988); Michael Richardson, *The Edge of Disaster* (New York: St. Martin's, 1987); Charles E. Shepard, *Forgiven: The Rise and Fall of Jim Bakker and the PTL Ministry* (New York: Atlantic Monthly, 1989); John Stewart, *Holy War: An Inside Account of the Battle for PTL* (Enid, OK: Fireside, 1987); Gary L. Tidwell, *Anatomy of a Fraud: Inside the Finances of the PTL Ministries* (New York: Wiley, 1993).

Though many embraced the prosperity gospel that Bakker preached in the 1980s, few could imagine the extravagance of his lifestyle, and of course they knew nothing of Jessica Hahn until 1987, nearly seven years after the affair.

Bakker's organizational methods also pulled in elements of the Wesleyan, Holiness, and Pentecostal tradition. Like countless faith missions before him, Bakker would often launch new projects before the funds were in hand as an act of faith, trusting God to supply what was needed. By contributing to various missions campaigns and to the building of Heritage USA, Bakker's "partners" could feel that they were actively involved in winning the world for Christ. Most were less concerned with a scrupulous accounting of how their money was spent than with the number of sinners saved, marriages restored, addicts reclaimed, and so on. This was nothing new. In the eighteenth century the Methodist Book Concern operated at a significant deficit because the itinerant preachers were much more concerned with distributing books than with collecting payment for them. But the distance that TV created between Bakker and his followers allowed him to spend money in ways he never disclosed to his donors.

Most of the people presented in this volume have been included for their virtues, for the positive elements they contributed to the Wesleyan, Holiness, and Pentecostal tradition. Nearly everyone across this tradition could embrace John Wesley as one of them. Others, like Jim Bakker, have kept some of the tradition's core elements while slicing away others. What then is vital to remaining family? I would argue that the key features of this tradition from beginning to end have been its core piety and practice of spiritual discipline, its ability to connect with the surrounding culture, and its ability to organize broadly, particularly its ability to draw on the energy and resourcefulness of the laity. What remains to be seen is whether these traits will prevail, and in which wings of the movement.

31

A Theological Interpretation

Stephen W. Rankin

THE PRIMARY MOTIVATING PREMISE of the Wesleyan-Pentecostal Consultation (and the publication of these essays) is twofold. First, Christians in Wesleyan, Holiness, and Pentecostal churches and groups share certain theological convictions and experiences that distinguish them from other more well-known Protestant traditions. Although many persons within these streams might use the term "evangelical" to describe their beliefs (to set off their theology, for example, from Protestant liberal theology), they also realize that they stand apart from well-known and studied Reformed and Puritan traditions.

Second, participants in the Wesleyan-Pentecostal Consultation believe that this part of the story has been under-told. Fortunately, Nathan Hatch raised this concern a generation ago with the publication of his *Church History* article, "The Puzzle of Methodism,"[1] sparking a significant body of subsequent research. Unfortunately, this literature tends to stay within scholarly circles. The present volume seeks to make a contribution to the telling and interpreting of this under-represented story for the broader church, thereby aiming at doing its part to help strengthen and renew, where needed, the church's life.

Reading the stories in this work is, in itself, refreshing. If one is interested in engaging at a deeper level, however, one begins to notice certain consistent theological themes. Not surprisingly, one finds an

1. Nathan O. Hatch, "The Puzzle of Methodism," *Church History* 63 (1975) 175–89. This article was reprinted in Nathan O. Hatch and John Wigger, eds., *Methodism and the Shaping of American Culture* (Nashville: Kingswood, 1994).

emphasis on the continuous work of the Holy Spirit. Pentecostals and Charismatics, of course, are well-known for this emphasis, but more so-called mainline United Methodists might be surprised to discover that this robust pneumatology has played a major role in their own tradition. The Wesleyan-Holiness-Pentecostal stream offers an important corrective to the "practical binitarianism" of much of modern American Protestant Christianity. Like the disciples in Ephesus (Acts 19:1–2), it is as if some present-day Christians "have not even heard of the Holy Spirit." It cannot but help, therefore, to reflect on how the similarities of thought and experience across a sometimes divergent range of peoples point to the work of the Spirit, which invites consideration for the Spirit's work in our day.

In the next few pages, therefore, I wish to summarize recent scholarship, especially (and probably surprisingly) in philosophy that bears upon Wesleyan theology, particularly the two characteristic themes of the religious affections and sanctification. With regard to the affections, contemporary research on the contribution that emotions make to knowledge will come to our attention. I will conclude with the claim that Wesley's doctrine of Christian perfection, in light of contemporary research, deserves a fresh reading and application.

Before we get to our main task, some recounting of the context of western intellectual history is required. One of the main legacies from the Enlightenment has to do with how truth claims can be justified. Two criteria came to stand as requirements. (1) For a claim to count as real knowledge, it has to be empirical (public and available to more than one observer), testable and repeatable.[2] (2) Knowledge claims must be as empty of bias as is humanly possible. Emotions (according to the Enlightenment view) tip the balance in the wrong direction. They permit too much subjectivity and bias. Emotions, therefore, must have no part in knowledge claims.

One can see immediately the problems these criteria posed for religious (particularly theological) truth claims. More to the point, one can see how "knowledge" came to be viewed as a public project while "faith" came to be regarded (by the intellectual elites) as private, subjective, and emotional, therefore *not* knowledge. Faith and knowledge were divided. "Knowledge" according to this standard was viewed as rational, even-

---

2. One can see why in today's world any knowledge that is described as "scientific" seems to count over other forms of knowledge.

handed and public. "Faith" was seen as non-rational (even irrational), subjective and private (or limited to the group of people who think along the same religious terms). The most hostile Enlightenment responses to religion came in the forms of logical positivism, which considered any metaphorical statement as completely devoid of meaning, and the field of modern psychology while it was firmly under the sway of Sigmund Freud, who thought of religion as an illusion. Some experts in Freud's wake even thought that being religious should be considered a form of mental illness.

In the twentieth century, philosophers and social science researchers alike began to reconsider the aforementioned core Enlightenment concerns. Starting roughly in the 1950s, psychologists, for example, began to explore the positive role of emotions for a flourishing life.[3] Within a generation, philosophers began to soften and revise their pessimism toward emotions. This shift coincides with the work of other philosophers regarding knowledge (epistemology), such that religious truth claims began to be considered in a more favorable light. Today, we work in a decidedly different and friendlier environment than did our forbears of even two generations ago.

One major point of debate today among philosophers has to do with whether emotions[4] actually have cognitive content. This point may seem self-evident to us as we contemplate everyday life, but it is possible to regard the emotion as the feeling state itself, without regard to the mental content that may be associated with the feeling. Nevertheless, a growing body of philosophers is arguing that emotions have cognitive content.[5] That is, an emotion is "about" something. If, for example, you hear of or read about an earthquake and, imagining yourself facing one,

3. Gordon Allport, a humanistic psychologist, was one of the pioneers of this movement. For a brief but helpful summary of Allport's work, see Robert P. Cavalier, *Personal Motivation: A Model for Decision-Making* (Westport, CN: Praeger, 2000). See especially, chapter 1, "Thank You, Dr. Allport."

4. An emotion is defined by Robert Audi as ". . . any number of general types of mental states...such as fear, anger, and joy." See *The Cambridge Dictionary of Philosophy* (Cambridge: Cambridge University Press, 1995) 222–23.

5. See for example Robert C. Solomon, *The Passions: Emotions and the Meaning of Life* (Indianapolis: Hackett, 1993), a revision to the original 1976 edition, and *True to Our Feelings* (New York: Oxford University Press, 2007); Martha C. Nussbaum, *Upheavals of Thought: The Intelligence of Emotions* (Cambridge: Cambridge University Press, 2001); Robert C. Roberts, *Emotions: An Essay in Aid of Moral Psychology* (Cambridge: Cambridge University Press, 2003).

you feel fear, then the fear is "about" the earthquake. The emotion of fear is "content-specific."[6] If you feel angry toward someone because of some reprehensible action, then your anger is "about" the act. Admittedly, we can feel emotions without always being able to connect them to some mental content, but often we can and do make that connection. This is why some philosophers argue for the cognitive nature of emotions.

If emotions have cognitive content—if they are usually "about" something—then it is a short step to the conclusion that emotions are, in some sense, evaluative. That is, they assist us in making judgments about an object of attention. Furthermore, it is likely that the emotion-judgment corresponds to some quality or characteristic (the philosophical term is "property") in the object. If I am hiking in Alaska, for example, and I encounter a grizzly bear, I immediately feel fear.[7] Although the feeling happens so rapidly that I am unaware of what I am thinking, there still is cognitive content at play. The qualities of the bear: "big," "powerful," "wild," maybe "hungry," and "dangerous" all are content-specific. Therefore, the emotion of fear is in part a representation and a judgment of the situation of being encountered by an "other"—the grizzly bear. The point is that, often, emotions do come with cognitive content. They are not just cognitively empty feeling states.

In the view that I am describing, emotions are like perceptions. A "percept" is a datum, a "bit" of consciousness of some property in an object. A sense perception may be heat or cold or taste or smell. A mental percept is the awareness of the experience of an idea "just popping into" one's mind. In other words, one becomes aware of the idea just being in the mind, without any steps ("inferences") of thought preceding that thought. A percept could be an intuition, for example or a memory. All of us have had the experience of thinking about one thing and something completely different "just pops into" one's consciousness. There may be some underlying connection that, in retrospect, we can see, but in the experience, there were not mental steps in between one thought and the other.

---

6. Audi's term in the dictionary article cited in note 5 above.

7. I am aware that some people who have studied grizzly bears and understand their behaviors in a way that common lay people do not, may criticize the feeling of fear as unnecessary, therefore irrational, therefore as standing against my argument. Still, the combination of my being in a place not familiar to me and encountering a powerful wild animal not familiar to me makes the feeling of fear seem quite rational.

The interesting feature in thinking about emotion as a perception is what it suggests about certain objects of experience (that, by extension, we can easily spot in the Christian life). If my emotions are properly shaped, I will respond in emotionally appropriate ways to the objects of experience. To use a too-technical term, such objects have "response-dependent" properties,[8] that is, there is some feature in the object itself which "pulls out" of me, so to speak, the appropriate emotional response. When I feel love in this moment, I am also experiencing cognitive content, not a mere feeling. The content is connected to the loveable properties in the beloved. This point will show itself as especially relevant when we turn to the source for religious affections at the end of this essay, but we can anticipate briefly here. God is an object of our experience (of course, God is really the subject, but in terms of this discussion, to be consistent, I refer to God as object here). God has response-dependent properties. God is characterized by certain properties that pull out of believers certain kinds of emotion-based responses.

Christian history is replete with testimonies of great saints and regular Christians alike who have experienced and still do moments of insight, joy, release, forgiveness, peace and love, which they attribute to the work of God. According to philosophers like William Alston and William Abraham,[9] these experiences are perceptual. They are not mediated by other thoughts, but come immediately to one's consciousness. Stories of experiences of this perceptual quality are found in the pages of this volume and, given the emphasis on experience[10] that Wesleyan, Holiness and Pentecostal people uphold, it is no wonder. The new and interesting factor in today's intellectual climate is that a growing number of philosophers can agree with theologians that these experiences are more than mere subjective, private "faith" experiences. They have epistemological weight.[11]

Before looking at the implications for specific theological themes, let us re-state a crucial point: the features of Wesleyan, Holiness and

8. Catherine Z. Elgin, "Emotion and Understanding," in Georg Bruno, et. al. *Epistemology and Emotions*, 36ff.

9. See William P. Alston, *Perceiving God* (Ithaca, NY: Cornell University Press, 1993); William J. Abraham, *Crossing the Threshold of Divine Revelation* (Grand Rapids: Eerdmans, 2008).

10. Perception is a form of experience.

11. William Abraham states boldly that divine revelation constitutes knowledge (in an epistemological sense); see Abraham, *Crossing the Threshold of Divine Revelation*.

Pentecostal belief and practice that have been dismissed, derided, or, more subtly, simply ignored because of the power of specific Enlightenment assumptions and the understandable desire of Christians to be accepted in respectable society, turn out to have significant epistemological and theological importance. Assessments of the epistemological function of emotions by philosophers (to name only one category of scholar which could be named) call for new investigations of the theological significance of the religious affections, particularly with regard to the doctrine of sanctification. Of all people, then, Wesleyan, Holiness and Pentecostal people should re-engage (if they have stopped) their own tradition. In the final few paragraphs of this chapter, then, we will consider how the research just sketched provides a way of construing sanctification, even Christian perfection that permits re-appropriation. My observations are suggestive and still half-digested, but they are offered in the hopes of sparking useful conversation.

Very near the end of John Wesley's long life he wrote a letter that names the doctrine of Christian perfection as the "grand depositum" for which the Methodists were chiefly brought into existence.[12] Interspersed throughout his Journal, one finds references either to people experiencing "perfect love" or to Wesley's encouragement to his preachers (and demonstrated in his own preaching) to hold out for the people the anticipation of being made perfect in love "in this lifetime." This doctrine which he believed so crucial to Methodist faith and practice was also perhaps the most contentious of Wesley's teachings. "A Plain Account of Christian Perfection" is Wesley's mature summary of the doctrine that, according to his own testimony, he had preached since at least 1733.[13] A cascade of scripture references describes this core doctrine. It is having the mind of Christ and walking as Christ walked (Phil 2:5). It is love for God and neighbor (Matt 22:37–39). It is the love of God shed abroad in our hearts by the Holy Spirit (Rom 5:5). It is the love that casts out fear (1 John 4:18). It is the power that destroys sin and the work of the devil (1 John 3:5, 8). It is the fruit of the Spirit (Gal 5:22–23).

A survey of this treatise repeatedly demonstrates Wesley's central understanding of Christian perfection as affectional. Hence, the overriding characteristics of Wesley's description of Christian perfection is

---

12. Letter to Robert Carr Brackenbury

13. John Wesley, "The Circumcision of the Heart," in Albert C. Outler, ed., *The Works of John Wesley*, Sermons (Nashville: Abingdon, 1984) 1:398–414.

that one who is made perfect in love "feels" a certain set of affections or dispositions. He uses words like "tranquility," "serenity," "desire," "peace," and "joy."[14] Affections (or "tempers") are inclinations of the will or motives that are shaped by the Holy Spirit and love is the supreme affection: love for God, love for neighbor, even love for enemy. As Henry Knight points out, holy affections "are both capacities (enabling us to love) and dispositions (inclining us to love)."[15] In a real way, love (for God, neighbor and enemy) is definitive of the holy affections. "Love" is not merely, as it has often been taught, the self-sacrificial commitment toward the good of the other, independent of emotion.[16] On the contrary, love is inherently emotional.

I have just given a standard and quite spare description of Wesley's grand *depositum*. There is nothing new here. What *is* new is the possibility of taking recent research in the cognitive dimension of emotions and begin to consider implications. First is the suggestion that Wesleyan, Holiness and Pentecostal believers stand on good epistemological ground when they regard the holy affections as normative for the Christian life. Emotions that are shaped by Christian practices contribute more to the Christian life than just feeling the way Christians "are supposed to feel." They actually put us epistemologically closer in touch with the God who created us. Theologically speaking, emotions are more than merely anthropological. Rather than appearing to assert this claim on the basis of an alleged faulty reading of scripture regarding sanctification, Wesleyan, Holiness and Pentecostal Christians can bring to bear substantial research and philosophical argumentation in support of their claims. Rather than simply marking this tradition as one of several "choices" that people can make for guiding their faith (and not a very "intellectual choice" at that), it comes forward with strong support from recent scholarship. It therefore deserves serious consideration on its own theological merits.

14. John Wesley, "A Plain Account of Christian Perfection," in Thomas Jackson, ed., *The Works of John Wesley* (Grand Rapids: Baker, 1986; reprinted from the 1872 edition issued by the Wesleyan Book Room) 11:370–72. The whole treatise is laced with affection/emotion descriptions for Christian perfection.

15. Henry H. Knight III, *The Presence of God in the Christian Life: John Wesley and the Means of Grace*, Pietist and Wesleyan Studies 3 (Lanham, MD: Scarecrow, 1992) 19.

16. For a very helpful study of the emotional quality of love as depicted in the scriptures (including the emotional quality of God's love for people), see Matthew A. Elliot, *Faithful Feelings: Re-thinking Emotion in the New Testament* (Grand Rapids: Kregel, 2006).

More importantly, the line of argument in this chapter suggests the need to reconsider the doctrine of God, on two fronts. Parallel to the philosophical work on the cognitive content of emotions, a few scholars[17] in both biblical studies and theology are re-thinking the nature of God in terms of the possibility of God having an emotional life, as well as thoughts and intentions. I hasten to state clearly that I am not claiming that God has feelings just like humans have feelings. However, the claim that, for example, God's impassibility means that God *feels nothing* and that we only experience God *as if* God has real feelings, needs modification. Conversely, it is worth considering that human feelings, according to our being created in God's image, are or can be (under the work of the Spirit) roughly approximate of God's feelings. Our hearts can "break with the things that break God's heart."[18] Reflecting on the possibilities of developing this line of thought would give added weight, I would argue, to another of Wesley's emphases, that sanctification involves the renewal of the image of God in the believer.

The other front for consideration relative to the doctrine of God comes back to pneumatology. Because the Bible consistently upholds the work of the Spirit, all Christian traditions acknowledge that work, but, in truth, such acknowledgement is often little more than lip service. As I mentioned earlier, one of the major problems of contemporary Protestant American Christianity is that it functionally rather severely proscribes the Spirit's work. The focus always tends toward cognitive and moral or ethical concerns: the Spirit guides us into truth (sound doctrine) and the Spirit prompts us to do the good and avoid evil. Certainly these concerns are important, but if what this chapter has argued is true, then concentrating solely on doctrine and morality/ethics without due attention to the affectional life short-circuits the whole order of salvation. The very emphases found within the Wesleyan-Holiness-Pentecostal stream turn

---

17. Examples of scholars who are working on how best to understand scriptural claims about God's emotions are: John Sanders, *The God Who Risks: A Theology of Divine Providence*, 2nd ed. (Wheaton, IL: InterVarsity Academic, 2007); Matthew Elliott (see endnote #15), Terence E. Fretheim, *The Suffering of God: An Old Testament Perspective*, Overtures to Biblical Theology (Philadelphia: Fortress, 1984). Even scholars in the more "hardcore" Reformed tradition who uphold God's sovereignty in a particularly acute way see the value of according God a real emotional life. See D. A. Carson, *The Difficult Doctrine of the Love of God* (Wheaton, IL: Crossway, 2000).

18. This quote is attributed to Bob Pierce, founder of World Vision.

out to be more than the emotional window-dressing of a set of second-tier traditions. They lie at the very heart of the Christian faith.

32

A Pastoral Interpretation

PHILIP R. HAMNER

WHEN I WAS FIRST invited to join the Wesleyan/Pentecostal consultation, I wondered what I might have to offer to the conversation. I was a relative newcomer to the Holiness movement, and I was simply unsure about my own perspective on the relationship between the various groups represented. Furthermore, although I was trained in the Wesleyan theological tradition, I had virtually no experience with Wesleyan Pentecostals. In good Wesleyan fashion Scripture, tradition, reason, and experience were brought to bear on the conversations we shared. Now six years on I am delighted to call these Wesleyans—all of them—my friends and colleagues. They have infused in me a passion for renewal in all aspects of church life.

As a pastor for nearly eighteen years, the importance of the chapters in this current volume cannot be overstated. The reader is able to go directly to particular chapters and focus on specific figures, but if the reader were to read the book in its entirety, some very important lessons emerge. Wesleyan, Holiness, and Pentecostal churches (WPC) would do well to revisit their roots in order to discern a clearer picture of their future.

The temptation in recent decades has been to co-opt or borrow worship, evangelism and discipleship strategies from other wings of the Christian church. Nothing is inherently wrong with mining the depths of the full Christian tradition for practices faithful to Jesus Christ. Yet, what would happen if WPC churches were to rediscover their own proven and faithful practices in worship, evangelism and discipleship?

Those same churches just might find resources long since neglected, but desperately needed even now. Churches willing to rediscover their roots will surely reignite a passion for renewal in every aspect of ministry.

So what are those important lessons? First, the spiritual children of John Wesley affirm the power of a shared witness. Shared witness is the capacity of the tradition to speak about its relationship to God with similar words and ideas. That is, the people represented in this volume sense in their brothers and sisters a common identity and purpose. For example, Charles Wesley can write the hymn *And Can It Be* in response to his own experience with God, and an African American Methodist, Richard Allen, can speak of his own personal experience with similar words. This is not because no other words are possible, but these shared words reflect a shared sense of the fullness of the gospel to radically transform human existence.

Shared witness also reflects a shared expectation of the scope of the gospel. Christ's death and resurrection makes possible a radical deliverance from the ravages of sin. The coming of the Holy Spirit in power and purity offers the believer the possibility of becoming like Christ. WPC Christians have never been satisfied with a "getting by" religion. They have from the very beginning been convinced of the deep work of God to heal the human heart fully and bring the same powerful and full healing to all of creation. Thus, the gospel is the vehicle for making all things new. Ministry around the altar in worship services is about the business of bringing the new into the lives of individual believers. The new then drives the believer into places where the old has run rampant for too long. Homes for unwed mothers, rescue missions, and drug and alcohol rehabilitation centers are all part of the shared witness that speaks of new creation.

It is perhaps the greatest contribution of the WPC Christians that they have continually witnessed to the need to go to the margins of society. Shared witness involves bringing the kingdom of God to places of hopelessness. This emphasis drove John Wesley to preach in the open air and in English prisons. The same emphasis drove Phineas Bresee and the Church of the Nazarene into the margins of Los Angeles. The shared witness of new creation is at home where the need is so very great.

The shared witness of WPC Christians does not imply, however, a complete or total capitulation to one way of being church. It certainly does not imply a shared agreement about polity and practice. Thus, a second important lesson to arise from the experiences of WPC churches is the genius of the outsider living in tension with the institutional church. No doubt many in the institutional church would not appreciate such a quality, but those who have served Christ through the holiness ethic have found great comfort from this approach. Again, John Wesley and the early Methodists were instructive to the future of the various movements. Ever the faithful Anglican, Wesley pushed the edges of his church with preaching houses and accountability groups. He demanded the gospel be preached at great risk to his own safety. He called other believers to give account for their attitudes and actions.

Living in tension with the institutional church does not imply opposition for opposition's sake. Rather, this was creative tension coupled with an opposition toward a church that became comfortable with itself. It is out of necessity that this tension must continue to exist in WPC churches. The tension keeps the church's preaching honest and biblically alert. The tension requires the church to always justify its existence for the sake of the gospel. It never allows a church to rest on its own merits. Instead, a church is called to redemptive honesty in carrying out its mission.

The people represented in this volume have not always appreciated the tension within their own ranks. They have at times become what they originally protested against. The move to respectability and status had turned some in the WPC into the establishment. The temptation to upward mobility proved too enticing to overcome. In the end, new movements have created sufficient tension to call out the institution. The creative tension reminded the church that God was always about the business of making all things new. The new came in unexpected ways and places. Whether it was the Holy Club of Oxford, the Azusa Revival, or the explosive growth of missionary enterprises, God worked at the creative tension between what had been and what would be.

Another of the inherent qualities of the movements represented in this volume is the recognition that the gospel of Jesus Christ promises the power necessary for personal fulfillment. This is a tricky, double-edged sword of an issue though. On the one hand, WPC Christians firmly believe what many other evangelicals affirm. Namely, these Christians affirm the conviction that Jesus Christ is personal Savior. They believe his death and resurrection offer personal forgiveness, personal cleansing and personal healing. The personal nature of salvation means a very real answer to the specific needs of the individual. It is no wonder then that these holiness Christians have committed themselves to ministries that highlight personal fulfillment. What are those kinds of ministries? What are the foci of such a conviction? Revivalism certainly provided a meaningful answer to those questions. Tent revivals and annual revival gatherings in specific locations became a primary means of getting the message out that Jesus Christ was fully capable of solving what was wrong in one's life. People responded personally to the call of the gospel, though it needs to be mentioned that personal commitments were not necessarily individualistic claims about the gospel. Prayer at the altar during revival services is anything but an individualistic exercise.

The personal qualities of the gospel claims also came through in the goals of holiness ministries. Many of the specific ministries initiated by WPC churches were intended to effect personal transformation. So, compassionate ministries centers, rescue missions, pregnancy centers were intended to alleviate personal need. Their ministry plans were aimed at the dynamic reconstruction of one's life by investing in the whole person and the whole person's needs. While some may argue that this personal emphasis is simply reflective of a rugged individualism which values the self-made man or woman, the real impetus it seems has been to enable the believer to find Christ and offer their spiritual gifts to the edification of the Body of Christ.

On the other hand, WPC Christians have continuously wrestled with this principle of personal fulfillment. This has been the case because holiness people have struggled to understand how they are to live in relationship to the world. The various movements represented in this volume have experienced pendulum swings in its engagement with the world or withdrawal from it. Thus, at times personal fulfillment has meant a full retreat from the challenges of world engagement. The elements of this conviction can be found in the rejection of socially accepted practices of the use of tobacco and alcoholic drinks. It was believed by many of these holiness Christians that there was simply too much potential of personal abuse. Personal abuse of this kind would undoubtedly hinder a believer from reaching their potential in Jesus Christ.

If retreat from the world was a reality for WPC Christians, over-engagement with the world is also a distinct challenge, as well. Techniques of psychological manipulation have at times been identified in revivalism. Theatrical "enhancements" to worship or to revival meetings have often given participants the sense that everything was being orchestrated toward a particular end. This means the personal aspects of the gospel have given way to the institutional preoccupation with getting numbers to respond. So, the evaluation of gospel effectiveness has at times slipped into a manipulation of the outcome. Personal transformation could be too easily identified with a large response at the altar.

An even more dangerous implication of over-engagement with the world is apparent in too many of the churches represented in this volume today. It began as a subtle shift in logic, but has over time made the gospel a means to an end rather than the end itself. The concern here is that the gospel of Jesus Christ has been co-opted for one's personal gain in all areas of life. Unfortunately, the gospel has become a systematic blessing machine. This blessing machine is for the purpose of giving the person the blessings of life. Thus, too many preachers present a God whose sole purpose is to grant the wishes of humankind. This beautiful gospel principle of God meeting our needs has been turned on its head. The gospel now offers a short cut to personal wealth and financial success. This must come as a great surprise to Christians in the Horn of Africa who live daily in abject poverty and under intense persecution. This must come as a startling surprise to the victims of the Haiti earthquake who were already brothers and sisters living in the most intense poverty of the western hemisphere. Are they to imagine that they have not received the blessings of God and, thus, do not have the power of God at work in their lives?

The real failure of this perversion of the gospel of Jesus Christ appears to be in the actual conception of the purpose of the gospel itself. The gospel operates from a very different priority than our personal fulfillment of *our* perceived wants and needs. It is as N.T. Wright so convincingly states, ". . . we are not the center of the universe. God is not circling around us. We are circling around him."[1] Furthermore, the gospel of Jesus Christ has another very important priority. Namely, it is the priority of mission to the world. Salvation has a purpose to it, but it is God's purpose. Again N.T. Wright makes a most astute observation about this purpose:

> God made humans for a purpose: not simply for themselves,
> not simply so they could be in a relationship with him, but so

1. N. T. Wright, *Justification: God's Plan & Paul's Vision* (Downers Grove, IL: InterVarsity, 2009) 23.

> that *through* them, as his image-bearers, he could bring his wise,
> glad, fruitful order to the world . . . The intimate relationship with
> God which is indeed promised and celebrated in that great scene
> of the New Jerusalem issues at once in an out flowing, a further
> healing creativity, the river of the water of life flowing out from
> the city and the tree of life springing up, with leaves that are for
> the healing of the nations.[2]

A more positive way to affirm this concern is to again re-emphasize an important conviction in the holiness ethic. This important ethic is the power of the gospel of Jesus Christ for personal involvement in the work of the kingdom. WPC Christians have believed consistently throughout their history that the encounter with Jesus Christ in personal conversion would always lead to a strong desire to take the news of this encounter and its subsequent transformation to a broken and hurting world.

So where does all of this lead us? How do we navigate the way forward into the days of ministry to come? As has been argued earlier in this essay, Christians of the Wesleyan, Holiness and Pentecostal churches will find valuable tools for this future engagement from within their common tradition. Instead of imaging that the church began just a few days ago the task will be to listen again to the shared witness of the tradition. The Spirit has spoken forcefully to WPC churches in the past. Lessons were learned and they will no doubt prove fruitful lessons for believers today.

Several years ago my family was engaged in a conversation with other families with whom we were ministering in a local church. Our son became quite disturbed by the conversation as several people shared what they knew about their family histories and genealogies. After our friends had left my wife and I inquired why our son seemed so unsettled. This was a difficult question for him to answer. He was simply too young to put into words what he was feeling.

Yet, as the evening went on and it was approaching bedtime, he became virtually inconsolable. As we attempted to bring comfort, we began to get a picture of what was wrong. Our boy was adopted from Guatemala when he was just a few months old. His entire life of memory had been with us. We very enthusiastically had told him about his adoption, about his country of birth. Still, when others began to talk about their family histories he became anxious. He did not know in that mo-

---

2. Ibid., 23–24.

ment what he would say if he were asked about his family story. We assured him he had a story with us. We recounted that story. It wasn't until we got out the laptop computer and began to search the web for pictures of Guatemalans did he begin to feel at ease.

Last year when he was old enough to offer the words of his feelings did we begin to understand fully the anxiety of that moment. He assured us he knew we were his family, but he just didn't know what to say about his birth country and family of origin. He wanted to be able to tell his whole story from beginning to end like our friends and guests that night long ago. He wanted to live out of the fullness of his story.

Christians in the Wesleyan, Holiness and Pentecostal churches would do well to learn this important lesson. We will be incomplete in our testimony and anemic in witness unless we live out of the heart of our identity. It's a lesson I have learned in the midst of pastoral ministry. It is a lesson worth repeating over and over again.

33

Visions of a New Humanity

Henry H. Knight III

Just as we have borne the image of the man of dust,
we will also bear the image of the man of heaven.

(1 Corinthians 15:49, NRSV)

A CONSISTENT CHARACTERISTIC OF Wesleyan, Holiness, and Pentecostal movements is just how seriously they took the scriptural
promise of a new humanity in Christ. They were dissatisfied with a gospel that promised forgiveness and a happy afterlife while leaving lives
in this age essentially unchanged. Wesley had insisted that salvation is a
present thing, and his followers and successors took this to heart, seeking to proclaim and experience that salvation in all its sanctifying and
empowering fullness.

What is often missed is the ecclesial nature of this vision. They were
not only seeking personal transformation but the creation of new communities characterized by love and committed to mission. While they
could affirm all four classic marks of the church—oneness, catholicity,
holiness, and apostolicity—it was the latter two that garnered their sustained attention.

Holiness could be seen as a matter of recovering what has been lost
by the fall of humanity into sin, the restoration of the *imago Dei*. But it
was always more than this. Ultimately, whether in personal sanctification
or in the life of the church, holiness was an eschatological inbreaking, a
manifestation of the life of the coming kingdom in the present through
the power of the Holy Spirit.

361

Whenever this holiness was seriously sought and lived out, communities were formed that were in some ways at odds with the dominant culture. To truly be "in Christ" had concrete implications for what was valued and how persons related with others both within and outside the church. For John Wesley, love for God and neighbor meant a turning away from acquisition and consumption to lives oriented by mutual sharing, generosity, and compassion for others. For Richard Allen it meant communities of racial equality. For Phoebe Palmer it meant both sons and daughters would prophecy. For B. T. Roberts it meant churches that refused to distinguish persons by class or wealth, except to manifest God's special care for the poor. For William Seymour, it meant a oneness in Christ that would put an end to barriers between race, class, and nationality.

Apostolicity involved recovering the teaching, practices, experience, and mission of the early church. It was not about tracing a succession of ordinations back to the apostles or (for most) recovering a distinctive New Testament polity. It had everything to do with the presence and power of God, such that the church today could confidently expect God to work in the same manner as God did in the days of the apostles. For most the actual structure of the church was evaluated as a means to an end: whether it could effectively accomplish mission in the world and promote the spiritual growth of Christians. Even those who did seek to recover a New Testament polity, such as some Pentecostals who sought to structure churches on the basis of the five offices listed in Ephesians 4:11, did so because they believed that structure was essential for faithfulness to God's mission in the world.

Apostolic churches, then, were both motivated and empowered by the Holy Spirit to engage in mission. Methodism early on developed a vision for mission that not only spanned a continent but the globe. The Holiness movement, with its empowering experience of entire sanctification, produced thousands of missionaries at home and abroad, including Amanda Berry Smith and E. Stanley Jones, as well as proponents of mission like A. B. Simpson. Impelled by the conviction that they were in the latter days, the Pentecostal followers of Parham, Seymour, and Durham sought to build a global missionary movement. Pentecostals from Azusa Street took the message out, some to the end of the streetcar lines in Los Angeles, others to the ends of the earth.

Proponents of a renewed holy and apostolic church were divided on how to bring it about. Many took a more "Puritan" approach. By "Puritan" I am not specifically referring to the historic Puritan movement of the seventeenth century but their approach of "coming out" of unfaithful denominations in order to start afresh. Many in Methodist, Holiness, or Pentecostal traditions adopted a similar strategy of "coming out."

Some of these left their home denomination with reluctance, only after experiencing insurmountable barriers to their vision of a new humanity. Richard Allen left to create a racially egalitarian church, and B. T. Roberts, who was forced out, left to create an egalitarian church especially in terms of social class. Phineas Bresee left in order to be free to minister to the urban poor. C. H. Mason was forced to leave his Baptist denomination in order to proclaim the promise of entire sanctification. Ida Robinson left her denomination to create a church in which women as well as men could aspire to leadership in ministry.

Others who left with reluctance adopted more radical ecclesial structures. Wesleyan Methodists not only promoted equality in terms of race and gender, but sought to replace episcopal hierarchy with a more democratic polity. In contrast, William and Catherine Booth's egalitarian vision was manifested in a military style of polity designed to mobilize Christians for urban mission.

Then there those who believed their vision compelled them to come out. Some, like Martin Wells Knapp, advocated holiness associations that brought together those within many different denominations who held to a New Testament vision of holiness. Others, like D. S. Warner, sought to replace denominationalism with one egalitarian, interracial holiness Church of God. A nondenominational apostolic vision also lay behind R. G. Spurling's Christian Union, which eventually became the Church of God (Cleveland).

The major alternative to the "Puritan" approach was the "Pietist" strategy of renewal from within. Again, I am not so much referring specifically to the seventeenth-century Pietist movement but to their strategy for renewal. John Wesley's movement is the prime example. By creating a network of lay preachers and small groups, and holding his Methodists accountable to spiritual discipline, Wesley sought to renew the Church of England in holiness. Phoebe Palmer's Tuesday Meetings, and John Inskip's holiness camp meetings continued this strategy of renewing existing denominations. While Pentecostalism spawned a diverse array of new denominations, the original intent was to be both a warning and a promise to existing churches and denominations, leading to their renewal. Later, in the 1950s and 1960s, the charismatic offspring of Pentecostalism would intentionally pursue the renewal of their respective denominations in apostolic faith and power

These two strategies, the "Puritan" and "Pietist," continue to be utilized as means to manifest the new humanity in the life of the church. The "Puritan" has been a necessity for thwarted reformers and a preference for those impatient with slow and gradual change. It has historically had some notable success, especially in creating a more egalitarian structure and ethos. Yet it has had difficulty maintaining the initial infusion of holy love and apostolic power over time.

"Pietist" renewal movements at their best contribute to an already/not yet eschatological tension within the churches they seek to renew. They do this through holding out before the entire church a vision of a new humanity renewed in holiness and empowered by the Spirit. Maintaining that tension while remaining faithful to that witness has proven difficult; many like the early Methodists end up "coming out" and making a fresh start. But there is value in maintaining that tension, not the least of which is holding together the riches of tradition in the church with the life and power of God to which the movement testifies.

But whatever the strategy, all of these traditions share a fundamental commitment: holiness and empowerment are not gifts for a select few, but are given by God to ordinary people, to be manifested in everyday life. Just as in the New Testament, God is present and active among the people. What sustains the life of the church through times of rapid cultural change and in new missional contexts is not new programs or efficiently run polities but the promise and reality of a new humanity, renewed in love and open to the power and guidance of the Spirit.

Appendix

American Denominational Families

THE FOLLOWING ARE LISTS of denominations in America that are part of the Wesleyan/Pentecostal tradition. Predecessor bodies that later merged to form a present denomination are listed in *italics* under that denomination's name. Bodies that split from denominations have their name followed by brackets that include the initials of the denomination from which they emerged and the date of the split.

The Wesleyans have as major categories the United Methodist, African Methodist, and Holiness traditions. United Methodism contains both the Methodist Episcopal and Evangelical United Brethren traditions; those who split from those traditions are also listed in separate categories. The chart also indicates which denominations belong to the World Methodist Council and the Commission on Pan-Methodist Cooperation and Union.

Not included on this chart are denominations that emerged out of the Keswick wing of the Holiness movement. The most significant of these is the Christian and Missionary Alliance.

The Pentecostals have as major categories the Wesleyan, Finished Work, and Oneness traditions, with distinctive strands such as the Church of God and Pentecostal Holiness traditions listed under the major categories. The chart also indicates which denominations belong to the Pentecostal-Charismatic Churches of North America.

The Church of the Living God, The Pillar and Ground of the Truth, Inc., founded by Mary Magdelena Tate, is a Wesleyan Pentecostal body with an unusually complex history not shown on the chart. Upon her death in 1930, the denomination split into three separate bodies: Church of the Living God, the Pillar and Ground of the Truth Which He Purchased with His Own Blood, Inc. [McLeod Dominion]; The Church of the Living God, the Pillar and Ground of Truth, Inc. [Lewis

Dominion]; and The House of the Lord Which is the Church of the Living God, the Pillar and Ground of the Truth Without Controversy [Keith Dominion]. Prior to this there were three schisms from the church: First Born Church of the Living God (1910), House of God, Holy Church of God, the Pillar and Ground of Truth House of Prayer for All People (1914), and The House of God, the Church of the Living God, Pillar and Ground of Truth, Inc. [White Dominion] (1916). The complicated story of this distinctive tradition is found in Estrelda Alexander, *Limited Liberty: The Legacy of Four Women Pentecostal Pioneers* (Cleveland, OH: Pilgrim Press, 2007).

WESLEYAN DENOMINATIONAL FAMILIES IN AMERICA

UNITED METHODISM

United Methodist Church (1968)+*
Evangelical United Brethren Church(1948)
  United Brethren Church
  Evangelical Association
The Methodist Church (1939)
  Methodist Episcopal Church
  Methodist Episcopal Church, South
  Methodist Protestant Church

FROM METHODIST EPISCOPAL TRADITION

Congregational Methodist Church [from ME,S, 1852]
Southern Methodist Church [from ME, S, 1939]#
Fundamental Methodist Church [from MP/MC, 1942]
Evangelical Methodist Church [from MC, 1946]
  Evangelical Methodist Church
  Evangel Church (1960)
  People's Methodist Church (1962)
Association of Independent Methodists [from MC, 1965]

FROM EUB TRADITION

Church of the United Brethren in Christ [from UB, 1889]#
Evangelical Church of North America [from EUB, 1968]**
Evangelical Congregational Church [from United
  Evangelical Church, 1922]#

AFRICAN METHODISM

African Methodist Episcopal Church+*
African Methodist Episcopal Zion Church+*
Christian Methodist Episcopal Church+*
Union American Methodist Episcopal Church*
African Union Methodist Protestant Church*
Reformed Zion Union Apostolic Church
  [from AMEZ, 1869]
Reformed Methodist Union Episcopal
  Church [from AME, 1885]

BRETHREN CHURCH

Brethren in Christ Church

FROM ENGLISH METHODISM

Primitive Methodist Church#

HOLINESS CHURCHES

Church of the Nazarene+
Wesleyan Church (1968)+
  Wesleyan Methodist Church
  Pilgrim Holiness Church
Free Methodist Church+
Church of Christ (Holiness)
Church of Christ in Christian Union
Church of God (Holiness)
Allegheny Wesleyan Methodist Church
  [from WM, 1968]
Wesleyan Holiness Association of Churches
Evangelical Christian Church
Bible Holiness Church (Wesleyan)
Pillar of Fire, International
Churches of God (Independent Holiness
  People) [from CoG (H), 1897]

Church of God (D. S. Warner) Holiness Tradition

Church of God (Anderson, IN)
Church of God (Guthrie, OK) [from CoG(A), 1910]
Church of God (Sumas, WA) [from CoG (G), 1980s]

Salvation Army Holiness Tradition

Salvation Army
American Rescue Workers
Volunteers of America, Inc

+Members of World Methodist Council
*Members of the Commission on Pan-Methodist Cooperation and Union

#These are associated with one another.
** Includes Methodist and Holiness churches

Hal Knight, 2008

PENTECOSTAL DENOMINATIONS IN AMERICA

TRINITARIAN DENOMINATIONS

WESLEYAN ("Three-Blessing")

Church of God in Christ*
Church of God in Christ, International [from COGIC, 1969]
United Holy Church of America*
Mt. Sinai Holy Church of America* [from UHCoA, 1924]
The Pentecostal Free Will Baptist Church*
Elim Fellowship*
Church of God of the Apostolic Faith*
The International Pentecostal Church of Christ (1976)*
  International Pentecostal Assemblies
  Pentecostal Church of Christ
Apostolic Faith Mission of Portland, Oregon

Church of God Tradition

Church of God (Cleveland, TN)*
Church of God of Prophecy [from COG, 1923]*
The (Original) Church of God Inc. [from COG, 1909]
Church of God (Huntsville, AL) [from COGOP, 1943]
The Church of God of the Mountain Assembly
Churches of God of the Original Mountain Assembly
  [from COGOTMA,1946]

Pentecostal Holiness Tradition

International Pentecostal Holiness Church (1911, 1915)*
  Fire-Baptized Holiness Church
  Pentecostal Holiness Church
  Tabernacle Pentecostal Church
Congregational Holiness Church [from IPHC, 1920]*
Pentecostal Fire-Baptized Holiness Church (1919)
  Pentecostal Fire-Baptized Holiness Church
  [from IPHC, 1918]
  Pentecostal Free-Will Baptist Church
Fire-Baptized Holiness Church of God of the
  Americas

Churches of the Living God

Church of the Living God, Christian Workers for Fellowship
Church of the Living God, the Pillar and Ground of Truth

FINISHED WORK ("Two-Blessing")

Assemblies of God*
International Church of the Foursquare Gospel*
Pentecostal Church of God*
Christian Church of North America, General Council
Independent Assemblies of God International
  Fellowship (Independent/ Not Affiliated)*
Full Gospel Assemblies, International [from AOG,1962]
Latin American Council of Christian Churches
Assembly of Christian Churches
Spanish Christian Church

OTHER PENTECOSTAL CHURCHES

Open Bible Standard Churches (1935)*
  Bible Standard Churches,
  [from AFM, Portland, 1919]
  Open Bible Evangelistic Association
  [from ICOTFG,1932]
Full Gospel Fellowship of Churches and
  Ministers, International
The Bible Church of Christ

ONENESS DENOMINATIONS

Pentecostal Assemblies of the World
United Pentecostal Church, Internat. (1945)
  Pentecostal Assemblies of Jesus Christ
  Pentecostal Church
Apostolic Assembly of Faith in Jesus Christ
Church of Our Lord Jesus Christ of the
  Apostolic Faith
Church of the Lord Jesus Christ of the
  Apostolic Faith
  [from COOLJC, 1930]
Bible Way Church of Our Lord Jesus Christ
  Worldwide
  [from COOLJC, 1957]
Apostolic Faith Mission Church of God
Church of Jesus Christ
Assemblies of the Lord Jesus Christ (1952)
  Assemblies of the Church of Jesus
  Christ [from COJC, 1934]
  Jesus Only Apostolic Church of God
  Church of the Lord Jesus Christ

Wesleyan Oneness

Apostolic Overcoming Holy Church of God

* member of Pentecostal-Charismatic Churches of North America

368

Contributors

CORKY ALEXANDER is Director of Instruction, Bradley Cleveland Services, Cleveland, Tennessee, and Adjunct Instructor at Patten University, Oakland, California, and Pentecostal Theological Seminary, Cleveland, Tennessee.

ESTRELDA ALEXANDER is Professor of Theology, Regent University Divinity School, Virginia Beach, Virginia.

KIMBERLY ERVIN ALEXANDER is Associate Professor of Historical Theology, Pentecostal Theological Seminary, Cleveland, Tennessee.

LESLIE D. CALLAHAN is Assistant Professor of Modern Church History and African American Religion at New York Theological Seminary and Pastor of St. Paul's Baptist Church, Philadelphia, Pennsylvania.

BARRY L. CALLEN is University Professor and Dean Emeritus, Anderson University, Anderson, Indiana.

DOUGLAS R. CULLUM is Academic Dean and Professor of Historical and Pastoral Theology, Northeastern Seminary at Roberts Wesleyan College, Rochester, New York.

DENNIS C. DICKERSON is James M. Lawson, Jr. Professor of History, Vanderbilt University, Nashville, Tennessee.

D. WILLIAM FAUPEL is Director of Library Services and Professor of History of Christianity, Wesley Theological Seminary, Washington, DC.

LAURA GUY is Pastor of Living Water Christian Church, Parkville, MO and Executive Assistant for the Wesleyan/Pentecostal Consultation.

PHILIP HAMNER is Pastor of the Overland Park Church of the Nazarene, Overland Park, Kansas.

DAVID AARON JOHNSON is Pastor of Walker Chapel African Methodist Episcopal Church, Seattle, Washington.

J. C. KELLEY is Pastor of East Heights United Methodist Church, Wichita, Kansas.

HENRY H. KNIGHT III is Donald and Pearl Wright Professor of Wesleyan Studies, Saint Paul School of Theology, Kansas City, Missouri.

WILLIAM C. KOSTLEVY is Associate Professor of History and Political Science, Tabor College, Hillsboro, Kansas.

STEVEN J. LAND is President and Professor of Pentecostal Theology, Pentecostal Theological Seminary, Cleveland, Tennessee.

DIANE K. LECLERC is Professor of Historical Theology and Homiletics, Northwest Nazarene University. Nampa, Idaho.

JOSHUA J. MCMULLEN is a PhD student at the University of Missouri, Columbia.

RODNEY MCNEALL is Pastor of the Carrollton United Methodist Church, Carrollton, Missouri.

STEPHEN W. RANKIN is University Chaplain at Southern Methodist University, Dallas, Texas; he was formerly Professor of Religion, Southwestern College, Winfield, Kansas.

HAROLD E. RASER is Professor of the History of Christianity and Director of the MA (Theological Studies) Degree, Nazarene Theological Seminary, Kansas City, Missouri.

DOUGLAS M. STRONG is Dean of the School of Theology, Seattle Pacific University, Seattle, Washington; he was formerly Professor of the History of Christianity, Wesley Theological Seminary, Washington, DC.

MATTHEW K. THOMPSON is Assistant Professor of Religious Studies, Southwestern College, Winfield, Kansas.

WALLACE THORNTON JR. is Pastor of the Moberly Church of the Nazarene, Moberly, MO and Adjunct Professor, Allegheny Wesleyan College, Salem, Ohio.

L. F. THUSTON is Bishop of the Kansas East Jurisdiction and Pastor of the Boone Tabernacle Church of God in Christ, Kansas City, Missouri.

ARLENE SANCHEZ WALSH is Associate Professor of Church History and Latino/a Studies, Haggard School of Theology, Azusa Pacific University, Azusa, California.

JOHN H. WIGGER is Professor of History, University of Missouri, Columbia.

Made in the USA
Lexington, KY
10 January 2017